Praise for *Kierkegaard: Exposition & Critique*

'Placed in his Lutheran context (instead of air-lifted up into 'philosophy') the Dane is beguiling once more.'   *Oxford Today*

'We owe Professor Hampson a genuine debt of gratitude for a most thorough exposition of a key Christian thinker.'   John Turnbull, *New Directions*

'With her very engaging style, and commitment to honest and open dialogue with subject and reader alike, Hampson is never dull.'
John Saxbee, *The Church Times*

'Known for her polished style and ability to simplify complex ideas, Hampson offers a highly readable introduction to Kierkegaard.'
Mark Mattes, *Lutheran Quarterly*

'This book is not only a fitting tribute to Kierkegaard and an absorbing and stimulating introduction to his work, but, in its breadth of learning and wisdom, reflects the spirit of the man himself.'
Susan Halstead, *LMH Brown Book*

'Hampson wonderfully orchestrates a critical dialogue with Kierkegaard in a way that provides ample demonstration of the importance of his thought today. This highly readable work represents a valuable contribution to Kierkegaard studies.'   Jon Stewart, Associate Research Professor,
Søren Kierkegaard Research Centre, Copenhagen

'A marvel of scholarship. Hampson is one of the few interpreters of Kierkegaard able to take account of both the philosophical and theological backdrop of Kierkegaard's thought. Clear, comprehensive, and elegantly written.'
Gordon Marino, Professor of Philosophy;
Director, Hong Kierkegaard Library, St Olaf's College

'A delightful and powerful new book on Kierkegaard....Combining a forthright accessible style with real scholarship and familiarity with Kierkegaard's personal, intellectual, and spiritual struggles, she brings him vividly to life for our time.'   David Wood, Professor of Philosophy, Vanderbilt University

'Hampson has inspired many students to engage with this most demanding of writers. Setting Kierkegaard in his intellectual context, this book guides readers through the key texts, identifying and debating the questions they provoke.'   George Pattison, Professor of Divinity, University of Glasgow

D1596794

R.

Kierkegaard

Exposition and Critique

Daphne Hampson

OXFORD
UNIVERSITY PRESS

OXFORD
UNIVERSITY PRESS

Great Clarendon Street, Oxford, OX2 6DP,
United Kingdom

Oxford University Press is a department of the University of Oxford.
It furthers the University's objective of excellence in research, scholarship,
and education by publishing worldwide. Oxford is a registered trade mark of
Oxford University Press in the UK and in certain other countries

© Daphne Hampson 2013

The moral rights of the author have been asserted

First Edition published in 2013
First published in paperback 2014

All rights reserved. No part of this publication may be reproduced, stored in
a retrieval system, or transmitted, in any form or by any means, without the
prior permission in writing of Oxford University Press, or as expressly permitted
by law, by licence or under terms agreed with the appropriate reprographics
rights organization. Enquiries concerning reproduction outside the scope of the
above should be sent to the Rights Department, Oxford University Press, at the
address above

You must not circulate this work in any other form
and you must impose this same condition on any acquirer

Published in the United States of America by Oxford University Press
198 Madison Avenue, New York, NY 10016, United States of America

British Library Cataloguing in Publication Data
Data available

ISBN 978-0-19-967323-0 (Hbk)
ISBN 978-0-19-872321-9 (Pbk)

B
4377
.H346
2014

Preface

Kierkegaard has been with me for many years and I have numerous debts of gratitude. Turning to theology in my mid-twenties I knew I had to study Kierkegaard. Professor Dick Niebuhr at Harvard was generous enough with his time as to give me an individual reading course. So it was that I first tackled the texts of which I write today. From 1974 onwards I have myself taught Kierkegaard to innumerable students at the Universities of Stirling, St Andrews, and most recently in my retirement in Oxford. It is in large part to this experience that the genesis of the book owes. Fascinating he may be, but Kierkegaard is no easy read. I lacked a book that devoted chapters in turn to Kierkegaard's major texts, giving background information, expounding and finally commenting on the text. Eventually one writes it oneself! Further research and the task of composition have thus been a deeply satisfying culmination to what has been a life-long involvement with these texts.

Of author-related societies, the world-wide community of Kierkegaard scholars must be one of the best connected. I have over the years benefited from national and international conferences, in the UK, Copenhagen, and the States. I am grateful to have been able to work in the Kierkegaard libraries and research centres at St Olaf College in Northfield, Minnesota, and in Copenhagen. Initial work on the book was undertaken at Clare Hall, Cambridge, where as a Visiting Scholar I was part of a quite exceptional international community. Particular thanks are due to Simon Podmore, who, originally studying his Kierkegaard with me and now a fine Kierkegaard scholar, has helped with questions relating to referencing and Kierkegaard research websites: it is good when things come full circle. Gillian Northcott Liles and Kathie Gill have been a meticulous copy editors. Finally, a big thank you to staff at Oxford University Press, particularly to Tom Perridge, Lizzie Robottom and Jenny Lunsford; I have found it the best press to work with that I have yet encountered.

A word on translations. Given that they have become standard, I have by default given references to the series of translations *Kierkegaard's Writings* by Howard and Edna Hong and in one case Reidar Thomte.

However, the earlier translations of David Swenson and Walter Lowrie still ring through my ears with what strikes me as their greater subtlety and poetic quality suited to 19th-century texts, and not infrequently greater clarity. On occasion, particularly in the final chapter, I have in preference given quotations from these texts. Unfortunately I do not have Danish. Thanks are due to Arne Grøn and George Pattison for elucidation as to the connotations of various words. Not infrequently if giving a Danish word I have also given the equivalent German thinking this useful to the many more readers who will know that language. Unless otherwise stated translations from German are my own.

A word too on the puzzling question of the use of gendered versus gender-inclusive language. I choose to continue to use gendered language when discussing texts from a former age; this alone can reflect the sensibilities of that world, in which male was axiomatically normative and employed without question for generic humanity. When speaking of persons today I of course use gender-inclusive language.

I do not know whether it is permitted in a preface to acknowledge a debt of gratitude to the author of whom one writes? My life would have been subtly different had I not encountered Kierkegaard. He has been a source of delight and edification with his insights and perspicacity. I am moved by his love of God, his sensitivity to others, and his sparkling wit. But furthermore he set before me the implications of Christian claims and, not having been brought up in orthodox Christian belief (though awareness of God), enabled me to understand with greater clarity why I should not wish to be Christian. He has thus been a significant dialogue partner. I fundamentally agree with him as to the importance of truth and integrity: that theology cannot simply be an academic discipline but that the theologian–philosopher must be existentially engaged as a person. The time gap that separates us culturally is significant, yet he also lives in the same universe as do I, reading many of the same texts—and it is that that makes the dialogue with him so worthwhile. Would that he could but know that he was indeed discovered (as in darker moments he feared he might not be) by future generations. I can only hope that in my work he would find his thought faithfully portrayed.

Acknowledgements

The following are acknowledged with thanks: Princeton University Press, for permission to cite quotations from Howard V. Hong & Edna H. Hong, eds and trans. *The Collected Writings of Søren Kierkegaard*, vol. 1– (series); Indiana University Press, for permission to cite quotations from Howard V. Hong & Edna H. Hong, eds and trans. *Søren Kierkegaard's Journals and Papers*, vols 1–6; the Royal Library, Copenhagen, Department of Maps, Prints, and Photographs for permission to use the cover illustrations.

Contents

List of Abbreviations

Kierkegaard's Texts Sigla

CA   Reidar Thomte, ed. & trans., *The Concept of Anxiety* (previously translated as *The Concept of Dread* and in this book known as *The Concept Angst*) (Princeton NJ, 1980).

CD   Howard V. Hong & Edna H. Hong, eds & trans., *Christian Discourses* (Princeton, NJ, 1997).

COR   Howard V. Hong & Edna H. Hong, eds & trans., *The Corsair Affair* (Princeton, NJ, 1982).

CUP   Howard V. Hong & Edna H. Hong, eds & trans., *Concluding Unscientific Postscript to 'Philosophical Fragments'*, vol. I (Princeton, NJ, 1992).

EO, I;   Howard V. Hong & Edna H. Hong, eds & trans., *Either/Or,*
EO, II   vols I/II (Princeton, NJ, 1987).

FT   Howard V. Hong & Edna H. Hong, eds & trans., *Fear and Trembling* and *Repetition* (Princeton, NJ, 1983).

JC   *Johannes Climacus*: see *PF.*

LD   Howard V. Hong & Edna H. Hong, eds & trans., *Works of Love* (in this book known as *Love's Deeds*) (Princeton, NJ, 1995).

PF   Howard V. Hong & Edna H. Hong, eds & trans., *Philosophical Fragments* and *Johannes Climacus* (Princeton, NJ, 1985).

PC   Howard V. Hong & Edna H. Hong, eds & trans., *Practice in Christianity* (previously translated as *Training in Christianity*) (Princeton, NJ, 1991).

PV   Howard V. Hong & Edna H. Hong, eds & trans., *The Point of View etc.* (Princeton, NJ, 1998).

SuD   Howard V. Hong & Edna H. Hong, eds & trans., *The Sickness Unto Death* (Princeton, NJ, 1980).

TM   Howard V. Hong & Edna H. Hong, eds & trans., *The Moment and Late Writings* (Princeton, NJ, 1998).

In the chapter on a certain book, page references to that book are given in brackets; if a reference is given to a book other than that under consideration the *siglum* for that book is also given.

On occasion a quotation has been given from an earlier translation, in which case that translator is given before the page number; thus (Lowrie, 109) and the book footnoted.

Kierkegaard's Journals and Papers

Various English translations of Kierkegaard's journals and papers have been used. In the case of the Hongs' selection the volume number followed by the citation number is given; in the case of Dru's and Rosenmeier's selections the citation number; in the case of Hannay's the page number. The reference to the Danish *papirer* is placed in brackets afterwards (or occasionally, when quoting from an author writing in English who has translated the Danish, given as the main reference). The sources and abbreviations used are as follows:

Dru   Alexander Dru, ed. & trans., *The Journals of Søren Kierkegaard: a selection* (Oxford, 1938).

Hannay   Alastair Hannay, ed. & trans., *Søren Kierkegaard: Papers and Journals, A Selection* (London, 1996).

JP   Howard V. Hong & Edna H. Hong, eds & trans., *Søren Kierkegaard's Journals and Papers* (Bloomington, IN & London, 1967–78).

Pap.   Niels Thulstrup, ed., *Søren Kierkegaards Papirer* (Gyldendal, 1968–)

Rosenmeier   Henrik Rosenmeier, ed. & trans., *Kierkegaard: Letters and Documents* [vol. xxv, *Kierkegaard's Writings*] (Princeton, NJ, 2009).

Thus: *JP* 5:6083 (*Pap.* VIII¹ A 447), n.d., 1847. The translation cited is in Hong & Hong, *Journals and Papers*, vol. 5, number 6083; the Danish original in *Søren Kierkegaards Papirer* with the reference given; it is not dated other than 1847.

Other

IKC: International Kierkegaard Commentary. (A series of commentaries edited by Robert L. Perkins, Macon, GA.) Abbreviated thus: IKC PF.

WA: D. *Martin Luthers Werke: kritische Gesamtausgabe* (Weimar, 1883–).

Time Chart

(continued)

DATE (AGE)	PUBLICATION	EVENTS IN SK's LIFE	WIDER EVENTS
1813–42 (to 29)		1813, May 5: born 1828, April 29: confirmed by Mynster 1830, Oct 30: student, Univ. Copenhagen 1833–4 attends Clausen's lectures 1834, July 31: mother dies 1837, May: meets Regine Olsen 1838, Aug 9: father dies 1840, July: finishes theological exam, journey to Jutland; Sept: engaged to Regine 1841, Oct: breaks engagement; goes to Berlin 1842, March: returns	1831 d. Hegel 1833 Schleiermacher visits Copenhagen 1834 d. Schleiermacher 1834–6 Martensen travels 1835/6 Strauss *The Life of Jesus Critically Examined* 1837 Martensen appointed faculty Copenhagen 1840 Strauss *On Christian Doctrine* 1841 Feuerbach *The Essence of Christianity*
	1841, Sept: *Concept of Irony*		
1843 (29–30)	Feb 20: *Either-Or* Oct 16: **Fear and Trembling**; Repetition	May: Berlin July: learns of Regine's engagement	
1844 (30–31)	June 13: **Philosophical Fragments** June 17: **The Concept Angst**	Moves to family home	Chambers *Vestiges of Creation* Darwin's first article on natural selection
1845 (31–32)	April 30: *Stages on Life's Way* Dec 30: mss *Postscript* to printer	May 13–24: Berlin	
1846 (32–33)	Feb 27: **Concluding Unscientific Postscript**	Jan: *Corsair* affair	

Continued

Date (Age)	Publication	Events in SK's Life	Wider Events
1846 cont.	March 30: *A Literary Review*, containing *The Present Age*	May 2–16: Berlin Oct 2: Goldschmidt gives up editorship *Corsair*	
1847 (33–34)	Sept 29: *Love's Deeds*	Nov 3: Regine marries Dec 24: sells family home	
1848 (34–35)	Dec 1: *The Book on Adler* completed April 26: *Christian Discourses* Nov: *The Point of View for my Work as an Author* 'as good as finished'	April 19: Easter religious experience. Easter: moves out of family home	Jan 20: death Christian VIII 'February Revolution' Paris March 23: Rising in Holstein European Revolutions
1849 (35–36)	July 30: *The Sickness Unto Death*		Martensen *Christian Dogmatics*
1850 (36–37)	Sept 27: *Practice in Christianity*		
1851 (37–38)	Sept 10: *For Self-Examination* *Judge for Yourself*		
1852–5 (38–42)	1854, Feb: 'Was Bishop Mynster a witness to the truth?' written; pubd Dec 1855, Jan–May: *Fatherland* articles 1855, May: *PC* 2nd edn. 1855, May–Sept: *The Moment*	1854, Jan 30: death Mynster April 15: Martensen succeeds 1855, Oct 2: taken to hospital Nov 11: dies	
1859	*The Point of View for My Work as an Author*		

Introduction: Why Read Kierkegaard?

and what of this present book?

Reading Kierkegaard opens out a world. An eclectic and versatile
author, he has much of interest to say on a range of subjects: theology,
the nature of philosophical writing, ethics, the concept of the individual, politics, and human relations. Employing a variety of genres,
philosophical, pastoral, and lyrical, he can write didactically, movingly, and not least be hilariously funny. Kierkegaard plumbs the
depths of what it is to be a human being; one who lives with anxiety
and aspiration, and who trusts and rejoices in God, finding in that
relationship the resources that make for wholeness. Often extolled as
the ur-existentialist, possessed of an observant eye for human foibles
and the pathos of existence Kierkegaard delves into the minutiae of
human lives. He will elaborate an intricate understanding of what it is
to be a self that, willing to be itself and grounded in God, comes
into its own; an understanding to which one can well hold in the wider
way in which he first depicts this without necessarily going along with
his specifically Christian twist. His edifying writings extol us to be
strict if also gentle with ourselves while compassionately observant
and thus merciful in our dealings with others; his political judgements
if conservative are strikingly apposite; his prayers sheer poetry.
Returning once and again to these texts one never fails to be struck

exhort
?

by new insights. Thinkers with whom it is this worthwhile to engage are few indeed.

But—surmounting these many merits of the authorship—there is a profounder reason to grapple with Kierkegaard. To a greater degree than any other of whom I am aware, Kierkegaard grasped the challenge that modernity represents to Christian claims, recasting how Christianity must present itself in the light of it. For, as he well understood, Christian contentions are compatible neither with the epistemology (the understanding as to what is knowledge) nor the moral axioms of a post-Enlightenment age. However, having acknowledged the depth of his probing and the imaginative nature of his response, as one delves deeper one comes to recognize that his response is undergirded by a whole epistemology which is quite foreign to how (one must surmise) most of us think today. Kierkegaard is surprisingly all of a piece: he holds suppositions that allow him to think as he does (albeit that he knows Christian claims paradoxical to reason). It is when one has uncovered this that a debate can take place with him at the much deeper level of epistemological presuppositions. We are into fascinating territory; that one who lived so recently could think so differently. It was largely his Lutheran context that allowed Kierkegaard in developing Lutheran thought to make the response that he did to modernity; and that that is the case will be a major theme of this book. There are other ways too, as for example his ideas about the origin of humankind or his social and political presuppositions, in which Kierkegaard's position is at odds with what we now know or hold. Exploring these sheds a shaft of light on the extraordinary transitions which humanity has negotiated in the past 170 or so years.

What, we may well ask, is it to consider questions of truth and ethics in relation to the thought of a past yet relatively recent author? There is a sense in which one must necessarily deliberate in relation to the thinking of those who have preceded us: one cannot progress in a vacuum. Quoting the person whose insights were perhaps more seminal than those of any other for his own work, allowing him to take up the position that he did, Kierkegaard muses:

'Write. For whom? Write for the dead, for those in the past whom you love. Will they read me? Yes, for they come back as posterity.' (Johann Georg Hamann).

Write. For whom? Write for the dead, for those in the past whom you love. Will they read me? No![1]

Meanwhile the past thinker, even if read, is always engaged in a one-sided dialogue! No more could Hamann read Kierkegaard than can Kierkegaard respond to me. But do the dead come back as posterity? It is conceivable that in considering my critique of Kierkegaard there will be those inclined to side with him against me. That would be a debate that I would that I could enter into. My sense, however, is that change is fundamental and that such a person would not express what he or she had to say quite as did Kierkegaard. There are a range of matters such a discussion would need to take into account which were not fully on the scene at the time that Kierkegaard wrote (or it must be said, in as much as they were present, Kierkegaard was not always minded to face). What is so interesting is that although the past world may be intelligible one can never simply stand in its shoes.

Recognition of such change has inclined some in Arts subjects (particularly it would seem in North America) to conclude that one cannot adjudicate on truth, that there are but fashions and opinions. Now the present author is far from unsympathetic to Continental philosophy, if indeed such thinking has been a correct interpretation of the thought of one like Jacques Derrida, which I doubt. What strikes me, however, is that on the contrary in a discipline like theology we cannot evade questions of truth. That discipline is historical and relative in as much as those statements that (until very recently) have been held absolute, the great Christological statements of the 4th and 5th centuries, were worked out within a particular philosophical climate (and, not least, judged politically apposite). But otherwise it must be said that it is both that we now think within a different philosophical milieu and that, in an objective sense, we have knowledge which undermines or casts in doubt what was earlier deemed truth. It was after all because with part of himself Kierkegaard was a modern man that he saw so clearly the challenges that Christianity was up against. Meanwhile in the field of ethics not only is it that we have broken through to biological knowledge (such that notably it is no longer possible to hold the male of the species

---

[1] *Søren Kierkegaard's Journals and Papers*, eds and trans. Howard V. Hong & Edna H. Hong (Bloomington, IN and London, 1967–78) [henceforth *JP*], vol. 2, no. 1550 (*Pap.* X² A 15), n.d., 1843.

normative for humanity), but furthermore we have thought through the implications of a priori principles first enunciated in the Enlightenment as to the humanity and equality of all persons. But none of this means that, in the field of ethics, Kierkegaard has not much to teach us; he is astute in his thinking about how one shall treat others.

Of Kierkegaard one might say something similar, though in his case he chooses to revivify the past in light of present. In many respects as I have already indicated (and this could hardly not be the case of a thinker writing in the 1840s) Kierkegaard was a child of modernity. Living this side of Hegel, he has a sense of the human being as social, knows that the self is formed relationally, though he ostentatiously amends this in contending (together with his Lutheran tradition) that such a self is formed in the first instance in relation to God. Furthermore, living post-Kant he has a strong sense of the autonomy and hence also the responsibility and integrity of human beings. The question becomes how he shall bring together a sense of self with the foundational nature of the relationship to God. Kierkegaard cannot simply go back to Luther; though surprisingly modern, Luther did not have a post-Enlightenment sense of the individual. He cannot even go back to the time of Lessing, in many ways his hero. A whole revolution in human self-understanding has intervened with the Enlightenment and Romanticism. Furthermore, after Kant in particular, there was no way in which human beings could reason to God, no natural theology possible. Deeply apprised of these developments, Kierkegaard thinks humanity to have taken a wrong turning. But Kierkegaard did not write as though these developments had never taken place: he was profoundly indebted to them. What he must do, drawing on his native Lutheranism, was to take up a novel stance in relation to them.

Where there is a real gap between Kierkegaard's ways of thinking and how I surmise most modern Europeans and many North Americans think today is in the realm of what one might name the epistemology of history. Kierkegaard seems to have almost no sense of what I shall call the fact that there is a causal nexus; that is to say that events are repeatable, that they are one of a type, that there are no interventions. To employ 19th-century terms, Kierkegaard is a 'supernaturalist' not a 'naturalist'. As we shall see, he seems to have held to a notion somewhat akin to what in the patristic period is known as 'recapitulation', namely 'figuralism', such that God is held to intervene once and again, but in a cyclical pattern, bringing his purposes to fulfilment. This Kierkegaard combines with a Lutheran structure of thought whereby God (or the 'future') is actively present in the moment (to employ Kierkegaard's vocabulary). Could I but debate with Kierkegaard it would be this whole different sense of things that would perforce be the subject-matter of our initial conversation! For (much as I believe in the effectiveness of prayer or quiet loving thought for another) I take for granted that there can in this sense be no interventions. That we become ourselves by holding together our future and our present in the moment is another matter and may well be the case; here it may be said that (coming out of his Lutheran context) Kierkegaard was the first modern existentialist. The wholly other sense present in Kierkegaard of the future's relation to the individual, let alone of God, as compared with Hegel's social and collective thinking whereby *Geist* (rather than God) becomes one with the unfolding of history, is momentous.

But why choose Kierkegaard as the one in the presence of whom to think through such fundamental matters? Precisely perhaps because he was in so many ways conservative, if radically conservative. He wishes to re-situate Christianity in the midst of modernity and also in the face of modernity. His was a conservative (or traditional) form of Christianity: not for Kierkegaard the attempt that notably Schleier-macher had made to accommodate it to the post-Enlightenment world. It is significant that Kierkegaard did not really want to know about critical historical analysis of the bible, willing simply to circumvent its results as not relevant to the issue of faith. The benchmark as to what is Christianity which underlies his early *Philosophical Fragments* and with which he persists throughout the authorship is that of the Formula of Chalcedon of 451; that the second *persona* of a triune God was in two natures, fully divine and fully human. That, for Kierkegaard, is Christianity. Yet it is a radical conservatism as, drawing on the intrinsic existentialism of his Lutheran heritage, he seeks to find a way to relate to such a 'truth' in the modern age. Thus for him faith will stand over against reason. His stance may indeed be how Christianity must necessarily commend itself today, but if that is the case it follows that there are profound questions, not only epistemological but also ethical, that must confront Christian belief and to which Kierkegaard may well have no answer.

While I of course consider these issues, in the first instance this book is intended to enable those who have not as yet read Kierkegaard to do so with intelligence. Hence my subtitle 'Exposition and

Critique'. On the one hand I expound Kierkegaard, setting him in his intellectual context and historical setting; on the other pursue a far-flung consideration of the issues that his authorship raises. Of course there will also be much to appreciate about these texts. Kierkegaard felt he lacked dialogue partners, writing:

I am neither proud nor self-important nor vainglorious—I am a thinker, an immensely passionate thinker. And what irritates me is just this, that some would like to abuse and insult me, others to plague me with distinctions and honours—but, help me if possible to go further, be of assistance in understanding more than I have understood, none, none, not a single mother's soul will do that. . . . And it is an agony to have to live in such a way that, in effect, I have to let them think me mad just to be allowed to think—otherwise a great fuss may be made about me, I will have to tap my wine-glass and make speeches at gatherings, loved and honoured by all those who do not think.[2]

Even in its 'golden age', to which Kierkegaard belonged, Copenhagen, that 'market town' as he was wont to call it (Copenhagen = merchants' harbour), could not provide the intellectual interchange that he desired. What I am noting, however, is that today the dialogue takes place over a time gap.

Should one not, however, take on the dead? I am reminded here of Karl Barth's listing of Schleiermacher among those with whom upon reaching the kingdom of heaven (after paying his respects to Mozart—in this Kierkegaard would not have dissented) he will wish to converse. That is to say he who Barth's life work had been intent on overthrowing. That fine Schleiermacher scholar Richard R. Niebuhr once told me that having completed his decidedly non-Barthian book on Schleiermacher he went with some trepidation to visit Barth. Now the Barth family lived in one of those Swiss houses designed in former days to house cattle on the ground floor, such that a staircase rose to the living quarters on the first. Beside each step of the staircase there hung a picture of one of the greats of theology, from Kant and Schleiermacher forwards (a veritable Protestant theology in the 19th century). Upon Niebuhr's enquiring whether the order be 'ascending' or 'descending', Barth proclaimed it to be 'descending', that is to say Kant and Schleiermacher were the greatest and things had steadily

---

[2] *Søren Kierkegaard: Papers and Journals, A Selection*, ed. and trans. Alastair Hannay (Harmondsworth, 1996) [henceforth Hannay], 316–17 (*Pap.* IX A 161).

got worse. And who is it with whom Kierkegaard sought to dialogue; whom he elevated as worth his attention? Those whose thought stood in many ways diametrically opposed to his own; Socrates the pagan and Lessing the sceptic. But they had integrity. It is this thought that should surely give us licence not simply to report on Kierkegaard but to think that we may and should take issue with him. It is, after all, to take him seriously.

Through the manner of his writing Kierkegaard precisely invites such dialogue. Perhaps it was his love of Socrates that taught him to engage his reader in this way. Maybe he was also in this respect attentive to Schleiermacher, whose *Vertraute Briefe über Friedrich Schlegels Lucinde* he much admired. But then Schleiermacher, the great translator of Plato into German, had himself presumably absorbed engaged thinking from the ancient world. As did Plato in his dialogues, Kierkegaard will develop different intellectual (and existential) positions through depicting different characters. He may himself take up no one position, though one may well know what he thinks. Kierkegaard's writing is often in tantalizing fashion open ended. This enables the reader to enter into the writing, developing his or her own thinking in terms of his categories (though one may also want to mould a position otherwise than occurred to Kierkegaard). The use of pseudonyms, moreover, allowed Kierke- gaard to take some useful distance from his text, giving the reader space.[3]

---

[3] I do not believe that one needs to go overboard on the issue of the pseudo- nymity of Kierkegaard's authorship. Undoubtedly, as I have suggested, it served a purpose. There is some tension within the opus as a whole as between different pseudonymous positions, but this tension would seem to reflect a tension intrin- sic to Lutheran thought. It was scarcely that Kierkegaard was trying to hide his authorship, frequently giving his name as 'editor'—and everyone knew who had penned the works. One should remark that it was a common device in his society to employ a pseudonym; the Danish primus J. P. Mynster did likewise, equally allowing his authorship to be instantly recognized. Some commentators make much of the fact that, at the conclusion of the *Postscript*, Kierkegaard comments that in the pseudonymous authorship there is not a single word from him. But I do not think that one's judgement on the pseudonymity should be distorted by a single, possibly flippant remark made at the time that Kierkegaard was thinking of taking up a pastorate and it could have been awkward directly to own the work. It has to be said that the published work in its development has an inner consistency and that it is deeply commensurate with the thoughts that Kierkegaard committed to the privacy of his *Journal*. Furthermore, it has come to light that on not a few occasions he only decided at the last moment to publish under a pseudonym.

The Kierkegaardian texts that I grapple with in this book are those central to the theological and philosophical themes of the authorship. (Thus I must notably omit *Either/Or* and there are other texts to which I make the odd reference without having the space to consider them.) My thinking is that, having tackled these texts, the novice reader can surely make his or her own way. It is difficult to know in what detail to expound Kierkegaard's writing. There may well be Kierkegaard scholars who on other counts (notably my drawing attention to the Lutheran context of Kierkegaard's work) find it profitable to read my book for whom such exposition is unnecessary. (Though it is in the context of expounding the text that I often draw attention to other matters and not least the Lutheran presuppositions present.) For the novice reader, however, it is all-important to be able to comprehend the texts, invariably either unwieldly on the one hand or dense on the other. One may initially lack a compass as to what they actually concern, which is frequently none too obvious. (If any reader thinks I am mistaken in my interpretation I shall be glad to know.) What has interested me, moreover, is to find that the material I give in the Introductions to chapters is often not easily available. Readers desiring to know more of Kierkegaard as a person may wish to turn to the final chapter at an early stage. The introductory chapter, 'Kierkegaard's Intellectual Context', is designed to enable those less informed about modern Continental philosophy or ignorant of Lutheran thought to get on board.

Behind this authorship lay a human life lived, one may say, 'ecstatically'. Kierkegaard sensed time was short; he had long nursed a premonition that he would die young and was frequently none too well. Spending ten years as a student, reading everything except the theology he was supposed to be studying, he had had a superb education, in literature, philosophy, and the thought of the ancient world. That he crammed what must be one of the major authorships of modern times into little more than a decade was an extraordinary achievement. Meanwhile he did not fail to live life to the full. As a young man he had enjoyed an exuberant existence—which he was later to regret as he became more religious. He entertained friendships and clearly delighted in children. Nor did he spurn the poor. Kierkegaard was known for the way in which, on his walks around Copenhagen, he would converse with all and sundry. He comments on the fact that people would pass by horses that had their nose bags tangled such that they could not feed, so one must surmise that he helped. Highly observant, all he encountered was potentially raw material for the authorship. It is this that makes his writing so engaging. Born into advantaged circumstances, for much of his life he was well-off, feasting on fine food and having a penchant for fashionable clothes. But he also knew what it was to fear poverty, leaving at his death almost nothing. This was a very human life, running the gamut of human emotions. He worked to ward off depression.

From such a life an authorship emerged that is literature. Kierkegaard said of himself that he was the greatest prose writer that the Danish language had known and his fellow countrymen have not dissented. It was his fate to write in a minor European language—or should we say his fortune given that he writes 'I am proud of my mother tongue whose secrets I know, the language I treat more lovingly than a flautist his instrument'.[4] In this regard I have a striking memory of sitting in the theatre in Copenhagen at the time of that city's celebration of its status as that year's 'European City of Culture', a single actor on the stage under a spotlight reading Kierkegaard. The audience was spellbound, alternately so silent you could have heard a pin drop and falling about in laughter. It was an indication of something often not realized about one who has been given the epithet the 'gloomy' Dane. Indeed Kierkegaard takes 'sin' seriously and is no optimist about humankind. He will never let human beings be self-satisfiedly comfortable, failing to confront ultimate issues. But a great love of life emerges from his writings. Of course much is inevitably lost in translation: the alliteration, the play on words. But it is still the case that more particularly in his 'edifying' or spiritual discourses the cadences of his prose in some way comes through in translation. What is striking is Kierkegaard's ability to find the right tone, style, and structure to suit each of his books, so various in their subject-matter. The authorship is extraordinarily eclectic. Of his time, Kierkegaard was also in his writing style before his time; this, too, contributing to the time lag in his discovery.

We possess few images of Kierkegaard who, decidedly shy about having his portrait drawn, would fail to turn up for sittings. Nor did

[4] *JP* 6:6259 (*Pap.* IX A 298).

he deign to have a photograph (or daguerreotype as this new technique was known) taken, an unfortunate oversight on the part of one who aspired to be discovered by 'posterity'. In his day an Italian had already set up his stall in Copenhagen. Fascinated by steam engines (American, locomotives) and hot-air balloons Kierkegaard was not entirely averse to modernity, so he had better have availed himself of this opportunity. The well-known sketch on the front cover of this book owes to his second cousin, Christian Kierkegaard, by profession a drawing master. If it was executed in 1840, Kierkegaard was 27. We have furthermore an interesting sketch from his later years by one H. P. Hansen, reproduced on the back cover. It appears to have been drawn from a first-floor window as, with flamboyant hat and spectacles perched on his nose, Kierkegaard marched by. Walking the streets of Copenhagen today one can still piece together something of the sights and the world that was his. Would that that city's most famous son could hear of the waves he has caused (as he half expected he would) and know of the affection in which today he is held by so many.

1

Kierkegaard's Intellectual Context

The aim of this chapter is to sketch in the necessary background that will enable comprehension of Kierkegaard's authorship. I commence with a brief consideration of his philosophical and intellectual context, continue by expounding the structure of Lutheran thought (so crucial but rarely known or alluded to by Kierkegaard scholars), and conclude by exploring in greater detail the question of what I have called the epistemology of history.

It strikes me that a good way to 'read' Kierkegaard is to say that, translating the structure of Lutheran thought into an epistemological key more thoroughly than it had occurred to the Reformers to do, he attempts to counter the import of the Enlightenment for Christian belief and so find a way forward for Christianity. Early Christians, if proclaiming a startling revelation, had found it possible to express their claims in terms of the philosophical thought forms that had grown up in the pagan world. In medieval times there existed a 'Christian civilization' that had engaged the best philosophical minds of the age. It was a synthesis broken asunder in the Reformation, though the classical Christian statements of faith, concerning trinity and incarnation, were recast rather than denied. With the loss in the Enlightenment of the credibility of past ways of thinking, classical Christian belief was placed in a radically new situation. Kierkegaard must open up another front which would allow it to be secured. He will ratchet up what is at stake, proclaiming faith in the face of Enlightenment reason. A question that could thus well be asked of him is whether he did not build a castle in the air (something incidentally of which he accused Hegel), in Kierkegaard's case lacking any foundation in the thought of modernity.

A good a point at which to dive into this maelstrom is with a consideration of the thought of Immanuel Kant (1724–1804). Kant's thought was critical in every respect: in his 'pure' philosophy (epistemology), his moral philosophy, and his 'reading' of Christian scripture and doctrine. In regard to the first of these, Kant contended in his 'First' *Critique* (1781) that there could be no *knowledge* of God; since for knowledge to arise there is need of sense perceptions and, in the case of God, there are none. Thus Kant showed to be false, as making a category mistake, traditional arguments for the existence of God that sought, by extrapolation from this world, to reach to that which lay 'beyond'. He placed a 'ceiling' on human knowledge. In a famous metaphor Kant compares the domain of that of which we can know to an island. Though we may think to discern forms in the fog beyond they are but an illusion.[1] Subsequent to Newton's discovery of the basis of order in the world and with the demise in the 18th century of belief in miracles, a new argument for God's existence from the very design of the world had been advanced. Dented by the Lisbon earthquake of 1755, the viability of any such argument was laid to rest by the Scottish philosopher David Hume's posthumously published *Dialogues on Religion*.[2] Kierkegaard never suggests that there is anything about the world that should allow us to reason to God.

Turning to Kant's moral philosophy, what is decisive is his Enlightenment sense that a mature human being exercises autonomy. In his seminal essay 'What is Enlightenment?' (1784), submitted for a prize, Kant responds in characteristic form that Enlightenment is humanity's exodus from its self-incurred minority (the German word employed is that for one not yet come of age). Kant avers: *sapere aude*, dare to know, 'that is the motto of the Enlightenment'.[3] In relation to our present concern it is significant that two of the three

---

[1] Norman Kemp Smith, trans., *Immanuel Kant's Critique of Pure Reason* (London, 1929), ch. III, B295/A236.
[2] David Hume, *Dialogues Concerning Natural Religion*, ed. Henry D. Aiken (New York, 1948).
[3] Immanuel Kant, 'What is Enlightenment?' in Lewis White Beck, ed. & trans., *Kant: On History* (Indianapolis, IN, 1963), 3.

examples of human immaturity he adduces are ecclesiastical: a book (the bible) which, and a pastor who, I allow to think for me. Kantian ethics rests on the presupposition of responsibility on the part of an individual who, considering what he should do, universalizes, asking whether what he intends conforms to what he could envisage should be a universal maxim for humanity. In such a world there can be no private interest nor selfish advantage. By extrapolation from this state of affairs, Kant argues in his 'Second' *Critique* (1788) that, if faith in the efficacy of our good will is not to be undermined, we must postulate an ideal set of circumstances, a *summum bonum*, in which (unlike what pertains in this world) virtue is rewarded with happiness, and consequently that there must be an 'eternal life' in which the present disparity is righted; furthermore that we must also conjecture that there is that exterior to the nexus in which we are caught up which will bring about this coincidence (the concept of God). This was not to postulate the *existence* of 'eternal life' and of 'God' (the proof for the belief in which Kant had just removed), but is rather an imaginative conception of the presumptions needed to secure our moral action. At a later date Kant was to regret these postulations.[4]

The norms of Kantian ethics went deep in the next generation; indeed Kant could well be said to have laid the foundations for ethics in the modern world. When Kierkegaard speaks of 'ethics' he presumes his reader will think in terms of the universal. Kierkegaard's own attitude towards what we might in a broad sense call ethics is perhaps more complex as we shall see. But whatever ambivalence he may have had, he is certainly much happier in the company of Kant than he is with the Hegelian overlay and adaptation of Kantian ethics. Troubled at the schizophrenic nature of Kant's ethics (which Kierkegaard well expresses when he says that, in attempting to conform to the ideal of the universal which one has placed before one's eyes, one has one's self outside one's self and within),[5] G. W. F. Hegel suggested

---

[4] Cf. Theodore Greene, 'Kant's *Religion*', I. Kant, *Religion within the Limits of Reason Alone*, eds and trans. T. M. Green and H. H. Hudson (New York, 1960), pp. lxv–lxvii.
[5] Cf. Howard V. Hong & Edna H. Hong, eds & trans., *Either/Or*, II (Princeton, NJ, 1987) [henceforth *E/O* II], 263.

that to behave ethically was to conform to the ethical norms (*Sittlichkeiten*, ethical conventions) of one's society. But this could induce a worrisome conformity, causing many, Kierkegaard included, unease. In common with others in the early 19th century (Schleiermacher also gave great weight to the family and to the people, *Volk*, as ethical associations), Hegel desired to make ethics societal and historical. However, he too saw that this could potentially lead to a clash between conformity to a traditional ethical stance (as in the case of Antigone who, in adherence to the norms of her society, insists that she should bury her dead brother) and the more abstract law of the state (represented by Creon, who has it in his power to lay down the law that she shall not do this or face death). There was a problem here about individual conscience.

But thirdly, to return again to Kant, what was perhaps the most problematic for the future of theology was the stance taken in his *Religion within the Limits of Reason Alone* (1793). In the first fully coherent 'reading' of biblical myth and Christian doctrine, Kant expounded this what he calls 'historical' or 'positive' religion as being but an exteriorization (in mythical form) of truths that humankind recognize about themselves. With consummate skill Kant shows Christian 'truths' to fit hand in glove with the diagnosis of ethical failings and of human 'redemption' given in his ethical philosophy. Ethics, thus, has priority, the myth simply a 'vehicle' (to employ Kant's vocabulary) through which these understandings are communicated, and ultimately dispensable.

Kant's book had an extraordinary impact on the young Hegel, as indeed on a generation (and we know Kierkegaard to have read it). It is an open question whether the mature Hegel came to change his mind about Christianity or, as seems more likely, simply recognized that were he to foster his career it would be prudent to keep quiet as to his true beliefs, his early writings lying unpublished. Distinguishing between concepts (*Begriffe*) and their representation (*Vorstellungen*), as had Kant in saying that the myth is but a representation of an abstract truth, Hegel considers that he can absorb Christian truths in the form of concepts into his system of thought. Thus, discussing the relationship of religion to philosophy in the 'Introduction' to his *Encyclopaedia* (1830), Hegel writes: 'The true content of our consciousness is preserved in its translation into the form of thought and concept, and indeed only then placed in its proper light'.[6] In the process, however, having no independent existence Christianity becomes but a stage in human development, to be surpassed by philosophy. It was this that enraged Kierkegaard. He thought Hegel, more particularly 'Hegelian' theologians, disingenuous.

We should retrace our steps. In the early 18th century Gottfried Leibniz in his *Monadology* (1714) had reinvigorated the distinction, derived from the ancient world, between the eternal, the ultimately real, and what is in flux and thereby imperfect, the flow of history. As he writes: 'There are two kinds of truths: those of reasoning and those of fact. The truths of reasoning are necessary, and their opposite is impossible. Those of fact are contingent, and their opposite is possible.'[7] There opens up an unbridgeable gulf between the historical contingency of the man Jesus Christ and the idea of God who, changeless and perfect, is cast on the side of those things that are non-contingent. In a famous tract 'On the Proof of the Spirit and of Power' (published 1777), Gotthold Lessing argued that it was not possible to move from contingent facts of history to truths which had the absolute status of those that reason could uncover: 'That, then, is the ugly great ditch which I cannot cross, however often and however earnestly I have tried to make that leap.'[8] Kierkegaard was heir to this distinction. Consonantly with Leibniz, Lessing, and the thought of the ancient world, he took for granted that 'God' connotes that which is eternal, absolute, perfect, and changeless. The fact that (according to the Chalcedonian Formula of 451) Christ is both fully divine and fully human in one *persona*, or entity, led straight to what, given the respective natures of divinity and of humanity, was a Christological paradox (which I shall henceforth connote the Paradox).[9] In Lessing Kierkegaard believed he had found an ally against

---

[6] Klaus Brinkmann & Daniel Dahlstrom, eds & trans., *Encyclopaedia of the Philosophical Sciences in Basic Outline*, i: *Logic* (Leiden, 2010), §5, 32.

[7] Nicholas Rescher, ed., *G. W. Leibniz's Monadology: an edition for students* (London, 1991), §33, 120.

[8] Gotthold Lessing, 'On the Proof of the Spirit and of Power' in Henry Chadwick, ed., *Lessing's Theological Writings: Selections* (London, 1956), 51–6.

[9] This practice was adopted by David Swenson, the original translator of *Philosophical Fragments* into English, but has not been maintained by Howard and Edna Hong. It is difficult to know what to do: in the 19th-century Danish nouns had capitals so the question did not arise. I have in this book adopted this capitalization for clarity.

the Hegelian attempt to make all truth historical. In dissolving the Christological paradox Hegel, so thought Kierkegaard, had lost what is of the essence of Christian belief: that the eternal entered time in the particular.

We should say something more of the great liberal theologian of the generation immediately preceding Kierkegaard, of whose work he had as a student made an intensive study, Friedrich Schleiermacher. Responding to the Kantian interdiction on arguments for the existence of God, Schleiermacher thought he found a novel starting point for theology. Questioning neither Kant's epistemology nor his ethics (other than that he finds the postulation of God and of eternal life superfluous to the latter), in a manner not dissimilar to Kant's consideration in his 'third' Critique, the *Critique of Judgement* (1790), Schleiermacher draws attention to the fact that not only are we knowers and ethical agents but moreover endowed with a third basic capacity, that of feeling, sensibility, or awareness. It is in this sphere of immediate awareness that Schleiermacher, the theologian of Romanticism, will ground religion. Spelling this out systematically in his mature work *The Christian Faith* (1821/22, second edition 1830/31), Schleiermacher contends that, in addition to the reciprocal relationship we enjoy with the world, we sense ourselves as having a *schlechthinniges Abhängigkeitsgefühl*, a sense of utter dependence, of *woher* or 'whenceness', which is our awareness of God. Kierkegaard was in agreement with Hegel in being critical of such immediacy as a foundation for theology. This notwithstanding, he held Schleiermacher in considerable regard.[10]

The exploration of the inner nature of human beings in their moods and sensibilities, coming to the fore in the Romanticism of the early 19th century, together with the suggestion stemming largely from Kant (though present earlier in Lessing) that the myths of religion are but vehicles of our self-knowledge, proved fertile ground in which another significant trend of thought could arise. In his great *Phenomenology of Mind/Spirit* of 1807, Hegel advances the thought

---

[10] In *The Concept Angst* Kierkegaard credits Schleiermacher with being 'a thinker in the beautiful Greek sense, a thinker who spoke only of what he knew' (*CA*, 20), high praise coming from one who was wont to speak thus of Socrates. Nevertheless of Schleiermacher's 'God-consciousness' he remarks: 'That is supposed to be Christianity–no thanks' (*JP* 3:2822. *Pap.* X^2 A 232).

that man projects an idea of perfection, casting himself by comparison as lacking; possessed thus of an 'unhappy consciousness' (*unglückliches Bewusstsein*). It was a short step for the materialist Ludwig Feuerbach in his book of 1841, *Das Wesen des Christentums* (translated by the atheist George Eliot as *The Essence of Christianity*), to suggest that, through reappropriating what he had projected, man might come into his own.[11] Set in the midst of a world from which he was alienated, the myths of religion were but a reflection of his dreams and desires. The message was not lost on the young Marx, exactly of Kierkegaard's generation. For Kierkegaard, Feuerbach's projection-thesis represented the ultimate threat to Christianity, undermining belief in its objective veracity. It must, he thought, be countered through finding a way to speak of relating to Christian claims understood as possessed of objectivity.

It will be good to make brief mention also of some other movements and trains of thought which formed the intellectual horizon as Kierkegaard gained maturity. There was the beginnings of a textual criticism of the biblical literature, placing it in historical context; which could appear yet another form of reductionism. During Kierkegaard's years as a student, David Friedrich Strauss's *Das Leben Jesu, kritisch bearbeitet*, 1835–6 (translated into English, also by George Eliot, as *The Life of Jesus, Critically Examined*), burst onto the Copenhagen scene causing a sensation. Christian claims were shown to have undergone a process of development, finding expression in the outlook of the time; with the clear implication that given the cultural context of their genesis they were essentially explicable. Curiously (and we may think significantly) we have no evidence that Kierkegaard ever possessed or read the book. It was as though he was unable to come to terms with this threat, which potentially undermined the very basis of the Christological contention that encapsulated Christian belief. Kierkegaard does not address the questions that were raised, but rather attempts to hermetically seal Christianity against their relevance. But, as we may think, his inability to face the historicity of Christian claims was to give his project feet of clay. It is a matter that we shall need to consider.

---

[11] Ludwig Feuerbach, *The Essence of Christianity*, trans. G. Eliot (New York, 1957).

We should furthermore take cognizance of the fact that, by the 1840s, largely through Dutch and French work, there was dawning recognition of the kinship of humanity to the rest of the animal kingdom—and thus also of human evolution. The publication in 1859 of Darwin's *The Origin of Species*, which in advancing natural selection as the mechanism that propelled evolution provided the lynchpin, still lay in the future. But speculation among European intelligentsia was rife. On the Continent (in this ahead of British thought) already in the work of Kant, followed in this by both Hegel and Schleiermacher, 'Adam' has become a symbolic individual pertaining to each man rather than an original ancestor. These developments had far-reaching implications for Christian dogmatics (which, lacking in this respect the mindset of our quite recent ancestors, it may be difficult for us to get our mind around). If man was related to the brute creation, in what sense could he be said to possess a spirit or soul? What were the implications for the doctrine of original sin; held since Augustine (354–430) to have been handed down by procreation through the generations from a historic Fall? Were there no such Fall, what then of the work of Christ; and what of the nature of his Person, who as the 'Second Adam' had effected man's redemption? Furthermore, the fundamental question as to the reliability of biblical witness, and so also the inspiration of Scripture, was called in question. Kierkegaard was immune from none of this.

What will be clear is that Kierkegaard came to maturity at a time of extraordinary intellectual ferment in which Christianity was challenged as perhaps never before. Raised in a strictly pietistic and orthodox Christian home, though one to which debate (in which he delighted) was not foreign, one can only imagine the impact upon him of his university studies. It owes to the fact that he drank deeply from the wells of philosophy and modern thought, rarely dismissing the pertinence of the questions raised, that Kierkegaard's writing possesses the dynamic power that it does. For a time his adherence to Christian faith was placed in doubt. How it was that he came to think it viable to hold to Christian truth we shall immediately consider below. What alarmed Kierkegaard was not simply that Christianity might be lost, but that it could be distorted beyond recognition and thus essentially erased while the world stood by. A Christianized culture, fed by Hegelian ideology, might swallow or absorb Christianity without trace. In consequence the project must be, as Kierkegaard put it, to 'reintroduce' Christianity into Christendom: to make evident what it was that Christianity claimed. Only thus could his contemporaries be presented with the momentous choice that it was theirs to make—as to whether to acknowledge Christ.

What seems to have been the turning point for Kierkegaard in regard to his own adherence to Christianity—and this will be of the greatest significance for his future authorship—was his encounter with the thought of the maverick 18th-century thinker Georg Hamann (1730–88), who left but cryptic sayings. There is a *Journal* entry for 1835 (Kierkegaard was 22) in which he makes reference to the Lutheran 'Formula of Concord' (1577), which declares that the natural man before Christ is not simply passive, like a block of wood, but actively rages against him. Kierkegaard concludes that philosophy and Christianity allow of no reconciliation. As he writes: 'Christianity is a radical cure which one shrinks from', which he opines no doubt explains why many early Christians postponed until the last moment making 'the despairing leap'.[12] In 1849, retrospectively to the bulk of his authorship, Kierkegaard expressed in a nutshell what he owed to Hamann.

Hamann rightly declares: Just as 'law' abrogates 'grace', so 'to comprehend' abrogates 'to have faith'. It is, in fact, my thesis. But in Hamann it is merely an aphorism; whereas I have fought it through or have fought it out of a whole given philosophy and culture and into the thesis: to comprehend that faith cannot be comprehended or (the more ethical and God-fearing side) to comprehend that faith must not be comprehended.[13]

I believe this exactly pertinent and it will be important to explore Kierkegaard's remark and its Lutheran context. No one better states what is at stake (though without making reference in this context to Kierkegaard) than does Karl Barth with his profound knowledge of Reformation theology. Barth remarked that it was the lack of

[12] Hannay, 43–4 (*Pap.* I A 99).
[13] *JP* 2:1559 (*Pap.* X² A 225, n.d., 1849). Cf. a letter of Hamann's to Kant: 'Reason is not given to you in order that you may become wise, but that you may know your folly and ignorance; as the Mosaic law was not given to the Jews to make them righteous, but to make their sins more sinful to them.' (Quoted by Ronald Gregor Smith, *J. G. Hamann*, London, 1960, 50.) Cf. also a letter to J. G. Lindner: 'Our reason is therefore just what Paul calls the law.' (Gregor Smith, *Hamann*, 58).

acquaintance with Thomas Aquinas in the 16th century which had
the effect that the Reformers:

> ...could not clearly perceive...the decisive connection which exists in the
> Roman Catholic system between the problem of justification and the prob-
> lem of knowledge of God, between reconciliation and revelation.... Hence
> they did not feel themselves called upon to clarify the problem of the *formal*
> relation between reason...and the absolute claim of revelation in the same
> way in which they treated...the relation between the will and work of man
> and the reconciliation once and for all effected in Christ.... They saw and
> attacked the possibility of an intellectual work-righteousness in the basis of
> theological thought. But they did not do so as widely, as clearly and as
> fundamentally as they did with respect to the possibility of a moral work-
> righteousness in the basis of knowledge.[14]

That is to say that, while grasping the contradiction between on the
one hand work-righteousness (the attempt of humankind through
their own works to secure themselves in relation to God) and on the
other what it is to be 'in Christ', seeing this contradiction in moral or
ethical terms (in terms of the will), the 16th-century Reformers failed
with the same clarity to align human reason (intellectual work-
righteousness) over against revelation. It is of course the case that
within Lutheran theology the attempt, setting 'the law' before oneself
to fulfil its demands, is viewed negatively; it is an attempt to justify
oneself, i.e. works-righteousness. What Hamann enabled Kierkegaard
to grasp was that just as in the moral sphere 'the law' abrogated grace,
so also human reason (the human will to comprehend and so control) stood over against faith. In other words, nudged by Hamann,
Kierkegaard took the Lutheran dichotomy between faith and works,
translating it from an ethical sphere into an epistemological sphere to
an extent that although present in the Reformation had not been
followed through.

We are thus brought to say something of the structure of Lutheran
thought, fundamental to comprehending Kierkegaard.[15] What I

---

[14] Peter Fraenkel, trans., *Natural Theology: comprising 'Nature and Grace'
by Professor Emil Brunner and the reply 'No!' by Karl Barth* (London, 1946),
101–2 [1934].

[15] Readers who would like a fuller discussion may wish to turn to my fifty-page
summary, ch. I, 'Luther's Revolution', *Christian Contradictions: The Structures of
Lutheran and Catholic Thought* (Cambridge, 2001).

believe crucial to grasp, absorbing its ramifications, is that the pattern of Lutheran thought is other than that of the western Catholic tradition. Of Catholicism, whether Augustinian or Thomistic, one may say that, in accord with the thought patterns of the ancient world (or indeed any kind of humanism), it is 'linear'. Catholicism is concerned for our change, as nature (that which is given in creation) is perfected through grace.[16] Again, revelation is understood to advance upon, but to be cognate with, reason. Predicated on revelation, Lutheran thought, by contrast, revolves around a 'dialectic', an either/or, as the implications of the unexpected nature of the gospel play out. Human ratiocination is cast into a place of untruth; as also 'good works' (the human attempt to be good enough for God) are accounted a false wager at independence, whereas the creature is rightly dependent on the Creator. Furthermore, operating with Aristotelian presuppositions, Catholicism conceives of a person in 'substantial' terms, possessed of 'being' and bearing an analogy of being (an *analogia entis*) to God, who is Being itself. Within such a context Catholicism can speak of a person as in a 'state' of sin or grace. Again by contrast, breaking with an Aristotelian world of thought, Luther and following him the Lutheran tradition conceive of the person in what we may call (modern) existential and personal terms, as the person, grounded in God, relates to self and to others. The importance of this different mind-set, other philosophical presuppositions, and concomitant structures of thought would be difficult to over-emphasize.

Thus for Lutheran thought there are two opposing stances that the human can take up in relation to God. To look to God in trust, consenting to a relation of dependence (relating as creature to Creator) is what is meant by faith. The failure to do this, the wager that we can ground ourselves, existing in independence of God, is what is understood by sin; it is if you will hubris, pride. (Cf. Rom. 14.23: 'Everything which is not of faith is of sin.') We may neatly express the difference in structure from Catholicism by remarking that, for the Neoplatonist Augustine, sin is to be 'bent down' to the ground, such that conversion

---

[16] Cf. 'Decree Concerning Justification', 'The Canons and Decrees of the Council of Trent', in J. Leith, ed., *Creeds of the Churches* (Richmond, VA, 1973), 408–24.

consists in a reorientation of the appetites so that our desire is directed to God who alone is our true good. As Augustine says in the opening lines of his *Confessions*, 'Thou has made us for thyself and our hearts are restless until they find their rest in thee'.[17] By contrast, for Luther sin is to be bent into oneself (*incurvatus in se*)[18]; as also his companion Philipp Melanchthon in his *Apology* speaks of the heart as turned in upon itself, a *cor incurvatum in seipsum*.[19] Sin is the staking out of a self-enclosed independence. As we shall see this comes through in Kierkegaard in the contention that the 'ethical' man, the one who believes himself adequate of himself, able of his own volition to do the good, stands at the furthest remove from Christian faith.

A different way of putting the Lutheran dichotomy (as we have already seen) is to say that revelation stands over against reason. For the natural man conforms to a humanistic system, assuming that God accepts the good while punishing sinners. Luther will lump together human religions (the papist, Turk, and Jew) in this respect. By contrast the Christian gospel proclaims the unimaginable: that God accepts sinners. Luther's breakthrough came when he read Paul in Romans 1.17, 'For... the righteousness of God is revealed through faith for faith; as it is written, "He who through faith is righteous shall live"', as intending that it is by Christ's and not our own righteousness that we live. Hence Lutherans speak of 'extrinsic' righteousness, as opposed to the Catholic conception of our having an 'intrinsic' righteousness, acquired through our co-operation with God's infused grace. Faith is that movement whereby we 'transfer our centre of gravity' (to employ an apt phrase of the British Luther scholar Philip Watson)[20] to Christ in God. As Paul (or his follower) expressed it, 'our lives are hid with Christ in God' (Col. 3.3). At the turning point of his seminal essay of 1520 'The Freedom of a Christian', in which he broke through to a full Reformation understanding, Luther remarks: 'A Christian lives not in himself but in Christ... By faith he is caught

[17] Augustine, *Confessions*, trans. R. S. Pine-Coffin (Harmondsworth, 1961), book I.1, 21.
[18] *D. Martin Luthers Werke: kritische Gesamtausgabe* (Weimar, 1883–) [henceforth *WA*], 56.356.4–6.
[19] Philip Melanchthon, *Apology* of the Augsburg Confession, 1530, 2.7, 14, 24, in Theodore G. Tappert, trans. & ed., *The Book of Concord: The Confessions of the Evangelical Lutheran Church* (Philadelphia, PA, 1959), 101–2.
[20] Philip Watson, *Let God be God* (London, 1947), 34, 52.

up beyond himself into God', adding 'otherwise he is not a Christian'.[21] To be Christian is to entertain this changed self-understanding.

Thus the epithet that came to encapsulate Lutheran faith is that we are *simul justus et peccator* (at once sinner and justified). By this is not intended as—in a profound misunderstanding, translating the phrase into what it would have to mean within a Catholic framework—it has often been read by Catholics, that in part transformed through God's grace we are in part still sinner. Lutheranism does not focus on the 'internal' situation of the person, nor does it operate with Aristotelian presuppositions that allow talk of a change of 'state' through the infusion of God's grace. We may say that is not for Luther that God 'transfers' anything to us. What the phrase is intended to convey is that the Christian possesses a double sense of self; at once grounded in God *extra se* (outside ourselves) and thus living 'from' God, but also meanwhile simply human (and humans, situated in the world, are sinners). Of course it is the case that in a 'second righteousness' we must become what we truly are; in Luther's delightful metaphor we must pull our feet up under the garment of God's grace (his dispositional attitude) with which he covers us.[22] But what it is crucial to note is that the fact that we are human (sinners), does not keep us apart from God. Within Catholicism with its Aristotelian basis it is impossible to say straightforwardly that 'God accepts sinners'. Rather is it that God accepts us in so far as we are not sinners but transformed by God's grace, for it is understood that it is on account of our analogous being to God that we stand in relation to God (and on an Aristotelian understanding being and goodness are interchangeable).[23]

To Lutheran ways of thinking the self-satisfaction and general contentment to which our works are liable to incline us hides from us our need for God. Even our conception of God will, in our quest for independence, be used to serve our own ends. Reason is but another form of pride; it blinds us to the God revealed in Christ. It is alone the recognition of our neediness that opens us up to hearing the gospel. The gospel speaks to whom? To the self-assured? No: to the one who is

---

[21] WA 7.32.14–15 (German), 7.61.34–5 (Latin); English trans. Martin Luther, 'The Freedom of a Christian', in John Dillenberger, ed., *Martin Luther: Selections from his Writings* (Garden City, NY, 1961), 80.

[22] WA 39, 1.521.5–522.3.

[23] Cf. Thomas Aquinas *Summa Theologica* I, qu. 20, art. 2, body and reply 4.

heavy-laden. The attempt to be good of our own account must always fail. In Kierkegaardian language, it is only as the 'ethical' person falls down before his or her own eyes that he or she is able to hear the gospel message that God accepts sinners. As he will put it, the sinner 'repents himself back into himself' until he finds himself in God.[24] Consequently the knowledge as to what is truly 'sin' comes about as a *response* to revelation. 'Sin' is, in our pride, to take up a mistaken position in relation to God. Contrariwise faith is a letting go (a trusting in another); if an act, then a negative act as Kierkegaard will have it. Again the contrast with Catholicism should be noted. Whereas in Catholicism faith is Latin *fides* (belief), in the Lutheran case it is rather *fiducia* (trust). Though it could well be said that in Kierkegaard's case this is modified in so far as faith entails assent to the 'truth' of the Paradox, and indeed Danish *tro* has both connotations.

It is not however for Luther or equally for Kierkegaard that the stance of faith could become a settled estate once and for all. Rather does the human being once and again attempt to be adequate in him- or herself. Hence we are, as Luther expressed it, *semper peccator, semper penitens, semper justus* (always a sinner, penitent, just): living in a circle, we attempt to justify ourselves, responding to the revelation of the gospel we are penitent, and once again we look to Christ's righteousness.[25] Similarly Kierkegaard, speaking in a more epistemological context, likens faith to treading water; the Paradox is not to be appropriated but must constantly be actively related to as the truth. Given that faith is to look beyond ourselves to Christ, the 'future' is for Lutheranism a crucial category.[26] In the thought of the 20th-century Lutheran theologian Rudolf Bultmann 'future' and 'God' become concomitant. The relation to this future, to God, takes one outside oneself, whereas to rest on my laurels (my past) is of the essence of sin.[27] As we shall see, for Kierkegaard, relating to the idea of eternal life is existentially life-transforming. It follows that in this tradition there

---

[24] *E/O*, II, 216.

[25] *WA* 56.442.17.

[26] On the difference in this respect between the Catholic medieval tradition and Luther see David Steinmetz, *Luther and Staupitz: An Essay in the Intellectual Origins of the Protestant Reformation* (Durham, NC, 1980, and Philadelphia, PA, 1984).

[27] See for example 'Church and Teaching in the New Testament', in *Faith and Understanding; Collected Essays* I, L. P. Smith, trans. (London, 1969), 77–8; but this is a constant theme.

is little continuity of person, for once and again I must break myself open (in my self-satisfaction) as I consent to dependence on God. This will be mitigated in the later Kierkegaard as he comes to emphasize love for God as an 'other' to self and not just trust in God.

It follows naturally from what has been said that, within such a system of thought, the constitution of the self (in relation to God) is both prior and takes priority. Freed by God, such a self is in turn free to be present for the neighbour. Indeed, in Luther it is all one movement; giving us the acceptance and self-assurance we were in vain attempting to manufacture for ourselves, God turns us to the world in service. Thus within the Lutheran structure *person* leads to *works*, as *faith* to *love* (love being the word commonly used for the relation to the neighbour). It is never that through the world, or through the neighbour, we find God. The starting point is the revelation of God that we are accepted and it is that that is instrumental in our responding in the faith that is trust. Whereas previously we had been (mis)using others in the attempt to gain an adequate sense of self, now we are set free to serve others with disinterested love. The world is the field of human activity. The reigning characteristic of such a belief system is Christian freedom; free from having to justify ourselves we are set free to serve. Once again Kierkegaard stands a little apart from this, admitting to difficulty in 'rejoining' the world (which he well knows should be the concomitant and result of faith). As I shall postulate, this may be not unrelated to his sense of love of God and hence of standing before God as a centred self in relation to God.

Finally, to discuss one further matter fundamental to an appraisal of Kierkegaard's authorship. I refer to the recognition within modernity that nature and history, each and together, form a causal nexus. That is to say actions belong to a type and are interconnected, or in the case of those things that exist they belong to a category. I should clarify further: that this is the case is perhaps so obvious as not to be remarked upon, in that we have lost the pre-modern failure to comprehend this. To take a historical example. Whether or not Caesar crossed the Rubicon, it is comprehensible that he should have done so, in that there is a causal nexus within which getting on one's horse and crossing a river can take place; furthermore, there is a category 'crossing rivers', such that Caesar may have done so. To speak of a causal nexus—it should be noted—is not to take a determinist position: if Caesar crossed the Rubicon presumably he chose to do so. To take an example from nature. Seeing a black beetle we take for granted that it stands within what one may also call an open-ended causal nexus; its parents will likewise have been black beetles (though we now know nature to be evolving), it could not be that it is a one-off example of such a black beetle.[28]

Turning to Christian claims. A good definition of Christianity is that Christians believe a particularity to have occurred—let us say that we may make the definition as broad as possible—'in the events surrounding Christ'. This belief has of course been expressed in different ways. Thus the earliest such expression of which we know is the symbol ICHTHUS, in Greek an acronym for 'Jesus Christ God's Son Saviour' and (fortunately for those who designated themselves 'fishers' of men) the Greek word for 'fish'. These Christians did not proclaim that of any other. Meanwhile the author of the Book of Revelation designated Christ Alpha and Omega. With the translation of Christian belief into Greek categories, this claim to uniqueness has for much of Christian history been articulated in the confession that the second person of a triune God took the form of humanity, such that in one entity (Greek *hypostasis*—that which stands under, enabling to stand alone, Latin *persona*), Christ is in two natures, fully divine and fully human (the Definition of Chalcedon of 451). Subsequent to the breakdown in the Enlightenment of the meaningfulness of Greek thought-forms, Christians have attempted to express the claim to uniqueness in other ways. Thus one may count both Schleiermacher (the great liberal theologian of the 19th century) and Bultmann

---

[28] It may be useful to make a few further remarks. Of course we may not know at the boundaries of human knowledge and understanding what it is exactly that exists or is possible. Thus many credit extrasensory perception, or hold that prayer in the sense of focused, loving attention to another is efficacious. The point is however that if these things are so, are part of the way things are, then one takes for granted that this has always been the case. Thus, given that there are, as many think, spiritual healers today one might credit that Jesus was likewise one. But that water could change into wine is not possible given that, as we now know, wine contains carbon atoms and water does not. (Or, were this possible it would always have been possible and no miracle is involved.) Again, there is material relating to Tibetan Buddhist monks having a vivid sensation of the presence of a Master after his death. But, were this to be used to substantiate the claim that this is what Jesus' disciples experienced, any claim to a uniqueness having occurred is lost. Nor has anything essentially changed through the fact that, as we now believe, there is randomness at the subatomic level. If this is the case, then it has always been so; it did not commence, say, in the year 1080. Though theoretically in quantum theory it could be remotely possible that a randomness could occur at the macro level at which we live it would seem that this is not particularly relevant to the Christian case. It does not support a claim to a resurrection, which is a biological impossibility.

(the radical 20th-century theologian) Christians, in that they intended, each in their own way, to claim a uniqueness for Christ (and well knew that they must do so were they to be counted Christian).

Consequent to in particular the Newtonian revolution in the 18th century there came to be a problem with any claim to uniqueness. That there can be none such is equally the corollary of an (again 18th century) Linnaean[29] taxonomy, in which the natural world was classified according to type. However, the problem that confronted the Christian claim that a particularity had occurred in history may be thought to have been overshadowed (in that age not being fully recognized for what it was) by something that we have already discussed, the question of the disparity between what is 'eternal' and what 'historical'. Newton had found a place for God in the fact that the experimental observations were other than his calculations showed they should be; so God, thought Newton, must intermittently intervene to set the planets back on course. (With the discovery of Neptune the 'irregularity' of Uranus' orbit became in large part explicable, the further discovery of Pluto accounting for the remaining discrepancy.) During the course of the 18th century, however, it became incumbent on educated human beings to face the consequences of scientific discovery for theology. The idea of divine interventions or 'miracles' became dubious if not impossible. Hence the rise of deism. A question mark was placed against Christianity.

Now the problem that confronts Christianity is not straightforward. For the Christian claim is not that Jesus *qua* human being was in some way unique. As Kierkegaard depicts such a paganism—in an imaginative analogy—that would be as though to say that God had taken the form of a large green bird that whistles (*CUP*, 245). Christian doctrine is that, in Christ, God took on (full) humanity. Formulations of Christianity that appeared to deny this, as Apollinarianism or Eutychianism, were in the patristic era ruled out as heretical: the claim was not that Christ was God disguised as a human being. The problem arises however at the level of the claim that it could be said of one human being, in a way that this is true of none other, that his humanity is, in one *persona*, conjoined with a second and divine nature. Or, if the Christian claim to uniqueness is expressed in

---

[29] After Linnaeus (1707–78), the classifier of species.

terms of resurrection rather than incarnation, that it could be that one human being and one alone was raised from the dead (differentiating resurrection for example from the story of the raising of Lazarus). In whatever form Christians wish to express uniqueness, the claim that there has occurred a particularity in history clashes with the presuppositions of modernity. The Christian claim came in the 18th century to be known (I believe the term was coined by Christians) as the 'scandal' of particularity.

It is an interesting digression, not without relevance to our theme, to consider how thinkers of the late 18th and early 19th centuries responded to the Christian claim as to there having occurred a particularity, adapting (or discarding) Christianity in light of their disbelief. Would one could question Lessing in this regard, who in expounding his famous 'ditch', brackets the question of miracles (though he notes they are not occurring in 18th-century Germany). Kant (who was of sufficiently scientific bent that he had worked on phases of the moon) credits no particularity, postulating that human beings have projected onto Jesus the idea of a perfect man. Categorizing Christianity as a 'historical' or 'revealed' religion (one grounded in the belief that a particularity has occurred in history), he is politely contemptuous, leaving the matter to the theologians. Following Kant, Hegel will sublimate the idea of Christ into a concept, thereby abnegating any such claim. The interesting case is Schleiermacher. Coming straight out of the 18th-century Enlightenment and holding no warrant for particularity, in his early *Speeches* Schleiermacher avers 'to me all is miracle'.[30] However, twenty years later and now holding the Chair of theology in Berlin, wishing to be counted Christian while finding Greek thought forms obscurantist, Schleiermacher suggests that Jesus was uniquely possessed of an unclouded God-consciousness; whereas in the rest of us our God-consciousness is clouded by sin. The problem, however, is that if Christ was fully human—well, humans are not possessed of an unclouded God-consciousness!

We come to Kierkegaard. As a northern European living in a Protestant country after the Enlightenment one might well think he will not have believed in miracles. Indeed, as we shall see, in *Philosophical Fragments* Kierkegaard comments that, were a man to perform a

---

[30] Friedrich Schleiermacher, *On Religion; speeches to its cultured despisers*, trans. J. Oman (Harper Row, 1958), 88.

'miracle' in the street, the embarrassed bystanders would ask the conjuror to do the trick again that they might see how it is done (*PF,* 69–70). In fact however, as we shall see, Kierkegaard credited miracles.[31] Is it the case then that, when in that book as elsewhere, Kierkegaard speaks of the appearance of the God in human form he fully comprehends the problem with which the Christian claim that a particularity has occurred in history is confronted? On one level he surely does. As we have just said, he knows that Christianity does not claim that here was a divinized individual, immediately and evidently apparent as a peculiarity (in parallel with the large green bird). For Kierkegaard (as indeed also for Luther) God is always hidden in Christ. One could furthermore say that it is precisely in that Christ is accounted fully human that Kierkegaard's Paradox arises. (Though one senses that in Kierkegaard's case the basic dilemma that gives rise to the idea of the 'Paradox' is the problematic idea that the eternal entered time: on the title page of *Fragments* Kierkegaard places what is a near quotation from Lessing to this effect.) However it turns out (as I shall later discuss) that Kierkegaard apparently has very little hold on the idea that there is a regularity to nature. He would appear less than clear as to the nature of the problem for Christianity.

It is here that it will be useful to introduce an important theme, for my understanding of which I am indebted to the work of Julian Roberts.[32] Roberts suggests that, in this following Hamann, Kierkegaard subscribed to a notion known as 'figuralism'. That is to say there are 'figures' (or formations) which cyclically recur within history, upon each occurrence taking the figuration forward. Thus: foretold in the Hebrew Scriptures; the incarnation takes place in Christ; who will come again at the end of time. Roberts remarks on the windows of King's College Chapel in Cambridge in which are depicted a whole series of New Testament events together with the Old Testament events said to have prefigured them. The momentum drives forward towards salvation. If this is correctly surmised to be Kierkegaard's position (when we consider *Fragments* we shall see that there is good reason to think that it is), it is in the first place interesting as placing Kierkegaard as in some way in his age. Just as

---

[31] See pp. 88–9.
[32] Julian Roberts, *German Philosophy: An Introduction,* ch. 6, 'Kierkegaard' (New York, 1988).

for Hegel and Marx history is moving towards its *telos*, so also for Kierkegaard; the difference being that in Kierkegaard's case there is held to have occurred an irruption of the transcendent into temporal history. But what is of significance to us here is that, given the context of credence of figuralism, the idea of God entering history in Christ is not for Kierkegaard quite the a priori impossibility that it would be for one who is obliged to rule out any idea of incarnation in that there can be no such thing as a particularity of revelation.

We are ready to turn to Kierkegaard's texts. Of the first two texts that I shall consider, one in ethics (*Fear and Trembling*) and one in epistemology (*Philosophical Fragments*), it strikes me that they should not be read as their author having reached a settled account (they were published under pseudonyms). Rather are they an articulation in their respective fields of the gulf between on the one hand a humanist (or non-Christian) position and on the other Christian claims. (In attempting to synthesize the two Hegel muddies the waters.) In my opinion this early work is some of Kierkegaard's finest.

2

Fear and Trembling

Introduction

It was the convert Jew St Paul who admonished followers of Christ to work out their salvation 'with fear and trembling' (Phil. 2.12). Kierkegaard will pick up the phrase to elicit the nature of faith. To comprehend the text it is important to have understood something of Hegelian and of Kantian ethics and also to be apprised of the nature of Lutheran faith. These have been discussed in the opening chapter. Luther is a deeply Hebraic author who could well be said to have rediscovered sensibilities present in the Hebrew scriptures which had become lost in the ordered and humanistic thought world of Catholicism, bound up as it is with that of the pagan ancient world. I shall attempt to bring these themes to the fore. What 'answer' this enigmatic text gives to the dilemma that it poses, even what Kierkegaard himself thought, is not easy of elucidation. As Roger Poole commented, the book is constructed to be undecidable.[1]

Lutheran thought sets 'faith' over against 'reason'. The basic understanding is that the revelation is against expectation, in that it is revealed that God accepts sinners. Now Hegel had attempted to assimilate Christianity to human understanding (to reason), accommodating it within his system. Preceding Hegel, Kant had dismissed a

---

[1] Roger Poole, 'A Theory of Reading—Undecidability and "Filters"', Paper given to the Søren Kierkegaard Society of the UK, 6 May 2000.

faith that could induce persons to take actions that clearly transgress the ethical. Taking a stance against Hegel's adsorption of Christianity into philosophy, Kierkegaard will set faith—and one might say the human being—free. In many respects what Kierkegaard will attempt in relation to ethics in *Fear and Trembling* and in the field of epistemology in *Philosophical Fragments* published the following year run in parallel. Kant is contrasted with Hegel, his thought representative of what ethics should be, ethics being distinguished from that which is 'faith'. By comparison, Hegel's unholy confusion of that which is purely human with Christian faith is shown up for what it is. Kant and Hegel in common take for granted that one should abide by maxims that are cognate with human understanding as to the moral good, this taking precedence over any idea of 'revelation'. Whereas Kierkegaardian Hebraic and Lutheran faith stand in stark contrast with humanistic forms of thought.

It must be unsurprising that Kierkegaard chooses to open up what he will say through taking the *akedah*; the story in Genesis 22 of Abraham's 'binding' (the meaning of *akedah*) of Isaac with the intent to offer him up as a sacrifice. Fundamental to all three of the so-called 'Abrahamic' religions, in the Lutheran tradition the story had been closely associated with the understanding of faith. It will be good to recall the texts in the Christian scriptures which, in delineating the nature of faith, make reference to it. In the (non-Pauline) 'Letter to the Hebrews', faith is famously said to be 'the assurance of things hoped for, the conviction of things not seen' (Heb. 11.1); faith is future-orientated. Among the heroes of faith who are listed in that chapter Abraham is prominent. 'By faith Abraham obeyed ... By faith Abraham, when he was tested, offered up Isaac ... He considered that God was able to raise men even from the dead; hence, figuratively speaking, he did receive him back' (Heb. 11.8, 17, 19). Paul likewise speaks crucially of Abraham in depicting the nature of faith. We should recall that it was in reading his 'Letter to the Romans', chapter 1 verse 17, that Luther broke through to his novel understanding that those are accounted just who trust in Christ in God and it is not that we through works should attempt to become on our own account just.[2] Immediately following this verse it is Abraham who is held to be paradigmatic for faith: 'Abraham believed God, and it was reckoned to him as righteousness' (Rom. 4.3). It is an exact statement of the Lutheran understanding.

Kierkegaard must have known from childhood, in any case from his time as a confirmand, the pertinent passage in the 'Formula of Concord', the Lutheran confession of faith (1577). We know him to have had a copy of the work in his library, but how could he not have had. Pitting faith against reason, it tells of Abraham's unhesitating obedience to God.

Nor dare we permit any objection or human contradiction, spun out of human reason, to turn us away from these words, no matter how appealing our reason may find it. Abraham certainly had sufficient ground for a disputation when he heard God's words about offering up his son, because these words were patently contrary not only to reason and to divine and natural law but also the eminent article of faith concerning the promised seed, Christ, who was to be born of Isaac. He could have asked if this command was to be understood literally or if it was to receive a tolerable and loose interpretation. But as on the previous occasion when Abraham received the promise of the blessed seed of Isaac, although this seemed impossible to his reason, he gave God the honour of truthfulness and concluded and believed most certainly in his heart that what God promised he was also able to do. So Abraham understood and believed the words and command of God plainly and simply as the words read, and committed the entire matter to God's omnipotence and wisdom, knowing that God had many more ways and means of fulfilling the promises concerning the seed of Isaac than he could comprehend with his blind reason. In the same way we are to believe in all humility and obedience the explicitly, certain, clear and earnest words and commands of our Creator and Redeemer, without any doubts or arguments as to how it is to be reconciled with our reason or how it is possible.[3]

The text hardly fails to make evident what the human disposition should be.

Kierkegaard was furthermore aware of the passages in Kant where, taking issue with his Lutheran heritage, Kant judges Abraham's position unethical. Kant casts his objection in terms of duty, castigating those 'visionaries' (*Schwärmerei*) who would mistakenly follow

---

[3] *The Formula of Concord*, Article VII, 'The Lord's Supper', in Theodore G. Tappert, trans. and ed., *The Book of Concord: The Confessions of the Evangelical Lutheran Church* (Philadelphia, PA, 1959), 577–8.

religious whims. In his *Dispute of the Faculties* (a text, significantly, that considers only the dispute between philosophy and theology), Kant writes that Abraham should have replied to the allegedly divine voice: 'That I ought not to kill my good son is quite certain. But that you, this apparition, are God—of that I am not certain, and never can be, not even if this voice rings down to me from (visible) heaven.'[4] And again, in a longer passage in his *Religion within the Limits of Reason Alone*:

Take, for instance, an inquisitor...who has to pass judgement upon a so-called heretic...charged with unbelief. Now I ask whether, if he condemns him to death, one might say that he has judged according to his conscience (erroneous though it be), or whether one might not rather accuse him of absolute *lack of conscience*, be it that he merely erred, or consciously did wrong; for we can tell him to his face that in such a case he could never be quite certain that by so acting he was not possibly doing wrong. Presumably he was firm in the belief that a supernaturally revealed Divine Will... permitted him, if it did not actually impose it as a duty, to extirpate presumptive disbelief together with the disbelievers. But was he really strongly enough assured of such a revealed doctrine, and of this interpretation of it, to venture, on this basis, to destroy a human being? That it is wrong to deprive a man of his life because of his religious faith is certain, unless (to allow for the most remote possibility) a Divine Will, made known in extraordinary fashion, has ordered it otherwise. But that God has ever uttered this terrible injunction can be asserted only on the basis of historical documents and is never apodictically certain. After all, the revelation has reached the inquisitor only through men and has been interpreted by men, and even did it appear to have come to him from God Himself (like the command delivered to Abraham to slaughter his own son like a sheep) it is at least possible that in this instance a mistake has prevailed. But if this is so, the inquisitor would risk the danger of doing what would be wrong in the highest degree; and in this very act he is behaving unconscientiously. This is the case with respect to all historical and visionary faith; that is, the *possibility* ever remains that an error may be discovered in it. Hence it is unconscientious to follow such a faith with the possibility that perhaps what it commands or permits may be wrong, i.e., with the danger of disobedience to a human duty which is certain in and of itself.[5]

---

[4] Immanuel Kant, *The Conflict of the Faculties*, Mary J. Gregor, trans. (New York, 1979), 115 [1798].
[5] Immanuel Kant, *Religion Within the Limits of Reason Alone*, book IV, Theodore M. Greene & Hoyt H. Hudson, trans. (New York, 1960), 175; also *Religion and*

The stakes could not be higher.

The scene is set for *Fear and Trembling*. There has been much debate as to the significance of the pseudonymous author under whose name Kierkegaard issues the work: Johannes de Silentio. As we shall see, the Knight of Faith is necessarily silent. But it may also be a reference to Kierkegaard's relationship to his erstwhile fiancée Regine Olsen, much on his mind, his engagement to whom he had broken and whom he wonders whether he could from the hand of God regain. In a fairy tale by the brothers Grimm, Johannes is turned to stone rather than betray his secret despair but subsequently returned to life.

Exposition

Kierkegaard opens the book with a quotation from Hamann. It should be recalled that it was Hamann who, advocating a stance of faith in the face of reason, had enabled Kierkegaard when tempted to abandon Christianity as incompatible with philosophy to find his way back.[6] Hamann writes: 'Was Tarquinius Superbus in seinem Garten mit den Mohnköpfen sprach, verstand der Sohn, aber nicht der Bote.' (Literally translated: 'What Tarquinius Superbus in his garden with the poppy-heads said, understood the son, but not the messenger.') The story is that when a messenger arrived from his son asking for advice as to what to do about a rebellion, taking his stick in hand Tarquinius struck off the heads of the tallest poppies. When his action was reported to the son by the messenger, who himself failed to understand the gesture, the son understood that he should kill the leaders. Kierkegaard's intent in giving the quotation is presumably to imply that there is a silent communication between God and Abraham, unmediated by a world that is not party to comprehending it.

Rational Theology, The Cambridge Edition of the Works of Immanuel Kant, trans. & eds A. Wood & G. du Giovanni (Cambridge, 1996), 203–4.

[6] See pp. 19–20.

The Nature of Faith

Kierkegaard's book has come to be associated with what is known as the 'teleological' suspension of the ethical, its suspension in view of a higher *telos* (aim or goal). But we should note that, in a book of some 123 sides (in the Hongs' translation), Kierkegaard does not enter upon this consideration for the first 53 pages. What in the first instance concerns him is the nature of faith.

Kierkegaard will drive up the price of faith. Thus he tells of Dutch merchants who, that they may increase the price of spices, throw a cargo-load into the sea. He makes a quip at the expense of the Danish Hegelian theologian Hans Lassen Martensen, whom Kierkegaard sees as representing the epitome of what he is opposing. Martensen was wont to speak of 'going beyond' Hegel; Christianizing him in a bid to find a way forward for Christianity in the modern age. Writes Kierkegaard:

It is supposed to be difficult to understand Hegel, but to understand Abraham is a small matter. To go beyond Hegel is a miraculous achievement but to go beyond Abraham is the easiest of all.... All this [comprehending Hegel] I do easily, naturally, without any mental strain. Thinking about Abraham is another matter, however; then I am shattered. I am constantly aware of the prodigious paradox that is the content of Abraham's life, I am constantly repelled, and, despite all its passion, my thought cannot penetrate it....'[7]

Abraham's action is not to be assimilated to philosophy or comprehended through reason; for faith is quite other than anything of which Hegel has conceived.

For Kierkegaard the problem lies in the fact that the story of Abraham's binding of Isaac evokes no 'fear and trembling' in his contemporaries. When a member of his congregation who had heard the pastor preach on the *akedah* on Sunday thinks of emulating Abraham the pastor is outraged (28–9). Of Hegel's project of translating the specificities of faith into generalized concepts (*Begriffe*), Kierkegaard remarks that: 'Even though one were capable of converting the whole content of faith into the form of a concept it does not

---

[7] Howard V. Hong & Edna H. Hong, eds & trans., *Fear and Trembling and Repetition* (Princeton, NJ, 1983), 32–3 (henceforth 32–3, etc.).

follow that one has adequately conceived faith and understands how one got into it or how it got into one.'[8] Abraham in no way considers himself to have 'understood'; he simply trusts to the future and to God. Thus does Abraham respond to Isaac's question by stating simply that 'God Himself' will provide the burnt offering. Kierkegaard comments: 'He is not speaking an untruth, because by virtue of the absurd it is indeed possible that God could do something entirely different. So he does not speak an untruth but neither does he say anything for he is speaking in a strange tongue' (119).

Expressing what are profoundly Lutheran sensibilities, Kierkegaard majors on faith's future orientation and trust in what is possible for God. 'Everyone became great in proportion to his expectancy. One became great by expecting the possible, another by expecting the eternal; but he who expected the impossible became the greatest of all' (16). Judith Butler rightly grasps the sense present here: 'The task of faith is to continue to affirm infinite possibility in the face of events which appear to make existence itself a radically impossible venture.'[9] As Kierkegaard will say, employing the early 19th-century sense of 'possibility', it is faith which grants a future where there was none, allowing one to breathe. Faith opens up the otherwise closed nature of the world: 'Faith begins precisely where thought stops' (53). Kierkegaard presumably had in mind here not least his personal situation, fantasizing as to whether by some miracle he might 'regain' Regine, as did Abraham Isaac. 'But then the marvel happens; [the knight of faith] makes one more movement even more wonderful than all the others, for he says: "Nevertheless I have faith that I will get her—that is, by virtue of the absurd, by virtue of the fact that for God all things are possible"' (46). Faith is thus 'the paradox of existence' (47), something of which the Hegelians have not dreamt.

A Teleological Suspension of the Ethical?

We come to the main theme of the book, which follows naturally from the consideration of faith. Is it possible that the ethical could be

---

[8] Walter Lowrie, ed. & trans., *Fear and Trembling* and *The Sickness Unto Death* (Princeton, NJ, 1968), 24 (henceforth Lowrie, 24 etc.).
[9] Judith Butler, 'Kierkegaard's Speculative Despair', in R. C. Solomon & K. M. Higgins, eds, *The Age of German Idealism* [vol. vi of *Routledge History of Philosophy*] (London & New York, 2003), 384.

suspended or cancelled, superseded by that trusting and obedient relation to God that is faith? What relationship should exist between the ethical ideals of humanity and a faith exercised towards God? Kierkegaard will consider the matter in three *problemata* which follow logically the one from the other. The aim of these considerations is to force apart any unthinking elision of faith with reason. In each case Kierkegaard will commence from a Hegelian, or equally a Kantian, statement; in any case a position taken by the natural man, or which human culture presupposes. He comments that if this be the end of the matter, it follows that there is no such thing as faith. In which case it follows that Hegel is mistaken in thinking to have entered upon the domain of faith. There is a parallel here (as we shall see) to the procedure undertaken in *Philosophical Fragments*. There, first stating the Socratic (or Enlightenment) position, Kierkegaard is clear that, were it not for revelation, this position represents all that there is to be said. What is disallowable is the attempt to expand, to 'take further' (as would Martensen, or indeed Hegel), the internally consistent Socratic (or Kantian) paradigm, as though one could somehow incorporate faith.

Problema I: 'Is there a Teleological Suspension of the Ethical?' Says Kierkegaard: the ethical is the universal, a straightforward Kantian and Hegelian presupposition. We should note here that the German and Danish words rendered in English as the 'universal' are, respectively, *das Allgemeine / det Almene*—that which is held in common by all; the common weal or good we may say. Such a conception as to what is to be counted ethical is 'immanent in itself', having no *telos* beyond or other than itself. When one has considered what it is that is for the common good, that is the end of the matter. It must follow that 'as soon as the single individual asserts himself in his singularity [putting himself] before the universal he sins' (54). Kierkegaard makes reference to the section 'The Good and Conscience' in Hegel's *The Philosophy of Right*.[10] In the case of Hegel, there can be no question of any 'suspension' of his conception of the ethical in view of some other *telos* which should be allowed to take precedence over it. Another way of putting this is to say that humanity has no end beyond itself.

---

[10] T. M. Knox, trans. & with notes, *Hegel's Philosophy of Right* (Oxford, 1942), Second Part (iii), 86–104 [1820].

But if this is all there is to be said, then Hegel is wrong to speak of faith. For, says Kierkegaard:

Faith is namely this paradox that the single individual is higher than the universal—yet, please note, in such a way that the movement repeats itself, so that after having been in the universal he, as the single individual, isolates himself as higher than the universal (55).

We should note the caveat. The individual has first to have been in the universal, the ethical. Only then, through a suspension of the ethical, is the singularity of a particular case raised above the ethical. Were this not the case, that with which we should be faced would not be a teleological suspension of the ethical (a suspension in favour of a higher *telos*), but an action which was but a whim, an acting upon impulse without consideration of the ethical, thinking to put an idiosyncratic wish before the universal good. Faith is to be sharply distinguished from such a selfish pursuance of individual indulgence. Hence Kierkegaard adds: 'If this is not faith, then Abraham is lost, then faith has never existed in the world precisely because it has always existed' (55). That is to say, firstly, that if this is not faith then we are speaking of that which is not even ethical and, further, all that exists is the universal (but one should not mistakenly be calling such a universal 'faith').

Another way to put this is to say that: 'no categories are needed other than what Greek philosophy had or what can be deduced from them by consistent thought' (55). Kierkegaard adds naughtily: 'Hegel should not have concealed this, for, after all, he had studied Greek philosophy' (55). Paganism had no reason to speak of faith in the sense in which, with its concept of revelation, the Judaeo-Christian tradition does. In faith 'the single individual as the single individual stands in an absolute relation to the absolute' (56). It is on this account that he does not subordinate himself to the universal. Such an understanding 'cannot be mediated', stated in terms of a general principle evident to all, 'for all mediation takes place only by virtue of the universal' (56). But such a universalization, such a consideration as to what is the common good, is of the essence of (Kantian or Hegelian) ethics. To mediate is to consider others. Thus says Kierkegaard of faith: 'it is and remains for all eternity a paradox, impervious to thought' (56).

Problema II follows directly: 'Is there an Absolute Duty to God?' That is to say, is there any such thing as a suspension of the ethical in view of a higher *telos*? A *telos* to be indeed a *higher telos* and not simply a whim would have to be a duty exercised towards God.

Kierkegaard commences with his Hegelian statement: 'The ethical is the universal and as such it is also the divine' (68). Hegel has mediated the divine so that it becomes part of the universal, which is in effect to 'divinize' the universal. It is such a state of affairs from which Kierkegaard wishes to set faith free. He makes an exact statement of what is Kant's (pure) understanding as to what the ethical should be and what its implications for theology.

Thus it is proper to say that every duty is essentially duty to God, but if no more can be said than this, then it is also said that I actually have no duty to God. The duty becomes duty by being traced back to God, but in the duty itself I do not enter into relation to God. For example, it is a duty to love one's neighbour. It is a duty by its being traced back to God, but in the duty I enter into relation not to God but to the neighbour I love. If in this connection I then say that it is my duty to love God, I am actually pronouncing only a tautology, inasmuch as 'God' in a totally abstract sense is here understood as the divine—that is, the universal, that is the duty. The whole existence of the human race rounds itself off as a perfect, self-contained sphere.... God comes to be an invisible vanishing point, an impotent thought; his power is only in the ethical, which fills all of existence. Insofar, then, as someone might wish to love God in any other sense than this, he is a visionary, is in love with a phantom [Kant's position] which, if it only had enough power to speak, would say to him: I do not ask for your love—just stay where you belong. Insofar as someone might wish to love God in another way, this love would be as implausible as the love Rousseau mentions, whereby a person loves the Kaffirs instead of loving his neighbour (68).

Says Kierkegaard to the Hegelians: this is perfectly correct and logical. What is problematic is that, having said essentially nothing other than has Kant (i.e. not having spoken of revelation) you think to have spoken of the divine! If there is nothing 'incommensurable in a human life', nothing which fails to fit the talk of ethics and of humanity, as for Hegel there is not, then Hegel 'was not right in speaking about faith or in permitting Abraham to be regarded as its father' (68).

As in the case of the first *problema* so also here Kierkegaard distinguishes faith from what may be called a pre-ethical, aesthetic, realm. In this respect we should know that Hegel draws a distinction between *das Innere* (the inner, or inward), with which the child is to be associated (Kierkegaard's aesthetic, or pre-ethical, in which one thinks but of oneself), and *das Äussere* (the outer, or outward), attained to by the adult, which is the universal that is ethics. Comments Kierkegaard: 'But faith is the paradox that interiority is higher than exteriority' (69). Just as an action taken in obedience to God's command is not to be confused with an arbitrary whim (as we saw in *problema* I), so also is the inwardness of faith not to be confused with a pre-ethical, childish, subjectivity which has not considered the universal. Hegel counts a person at fault if he 'slips down again into the qualifications of feeling, mood, etc. that belong to interiority'; from which position Kierkegaard does not dissent. However: 'The paradox of faith is that there is an interiority that is incommensurable with exteriority, an interiority that is not identical, please note, with the first but is a new interiority. This must not be overlooked.' (69)

In distinguishing faith thus from immediacy Kierkegaard presumably has in mind the thought of Heinrich Jacobi or more especially of Schleiermacher, those who find the seat of religion in a pre-cognitive realm of awareness. Hegel had crossed swords with Schleiermacher over this, contending that all religion is mediated. Kierkegaard must agree with such a negative estimation of the religion of Romanticism.

Recent philosophy [Romanticism] has allowed itself simply to substitute the immediate for 'faith'... This puts faith in the rather commonplace company of feelings, moods, idiosyncrasies, *vapeurs* etc. If so, philosophy [such as Hegel's] may be correct in saying that one ought not to stop there. But nothing justifies philosophy [such as that of the Romantics] in using this language. Faith is preceded by a movement of infinity [the relation to God]; only then does faith commence, *nec opinate* [unexpectedly], by virtue of the absurd (68–9).

For faith there first has to be such a thing as revelation. Only then can we respond with faith, in an unawaited situation that by human standards must be classed absurd. The revelation is by its very nature unanticipated, demanding other than what human reason would expect. By making this distinction Kierkegaard will guard against what is mere subjectivity. He will make what is a parallel move again in the *Postscript* thinking it to guard Christian claims against a Feuerbachian reductionist conclusion. We know it is not simply a product of the human imagination because it is an absurdity, unexpected. Religion, Kierkegaard is contending, is not just a projection of the human mind.

Abraham cannot explain himself in terms of that which is comprehensible and thus held in common. How then is he to be distinguished from a person taking a pre-ethical position who, without consideration of the general good, acts on some private impulse? Of a so-called 'knight of faith' (such as Abraham), Kierkegaard has already under *problema* II commented:

He knows that it is beautiful and beneficial to be the single individual who translates himself into the universal, the one who [is] readable by all.... But he also knows that up higher there winds a lonesome trail, steep and narrow; he knows it is dreadful to be born solitary outside of the universal, to walk without meeting one single traveller (76).

If Abraham is a true knight of faith he would like nothing more than to return to the universal. For him it is the *universal* which represents a temptation he must resist. 'The knight of faith ... is kept in a state of sleeplessness, for he is constantly being tested, and at every moment there is the possibility of his returning penitently to the universal' (78). But our knight of faith also knows that, beyond the ethical, there winds a lonesome trail up higher. Thus he is 'constantly kept in tension' (79) as, with fear and trembling, he 'walks alone with his dreadful responsibility' (80). For him no mediation (seeing his situation in terms of the universal) is possible.

And a yet further question arises, *problema III*: 'Was it Ethically Defensible for Abraham to Conceal his Undertaking from Sarah, from Eliezer, and from Isaac?' As we have seen, faith by definition is subjective, non-communicable; in Hegelian terms not allowing of 'mediation'. For Hegel that which is private, hidden, which cannot be universalized, is essentially pre-ethical and Kierkegaard is in agreement (that is to say, unless we are speaking of a teleological suspension of the ethical in response to a command of God): 'If there is not a concealment which has its ground in the fact that the individual as the individual is higher than the universal then Abraham's conduct is indefensible' (Lowrie, 91). Again, if we are not speaking of a concealment that is on account of an individual obeying a *telos* higher than that which is the universal, such concealment is likewise indefensible. Abraham is rightly to be condemned.

Abraham remains silent; he cannot speak. For what should he say? That which he is about cannot be explained in universal human terms, communicable to another. Our 'knight of faith' is to be distinguished from a common murderer (who selfishly places a subjective desire or whim to kill above the common good). But he is also to be distinguished from the 'tragic hero', he who can explain himself in terms of the common good (and thus in this sense remain within the universal). The tragic hero's dilemma is that he must choose between two 'goods', subordinating that which he considers the lesser to the greater. Thus Agamemnon is comprehendible in his willingness to sacrifice his daughter Iphigenia that the fleet may sail to Troy. Likewise the case of Jephthah, in Judges 11. But, unlike in these cases, no greater good could possibly be served by slaying Isaac. Abraham is thus no 'tragic hero'. If he is not a 'knight of faith', he is indistinguishable from a common murderer.

A good test as to Abraham's genuineness in acting as a 'knight of faith' is to pose the question as to whether he loves Isaac. Presumably with Hegel's association of the ethical with societal forms (such as the family) in mind, Kierkegaard will remark: 'There is no higher expression for the ethical in Abraham's life than that the father shall love the son' (59). It follows once more that if there be no such thing as a knight of faith what we have here is but a murderer. In casting Abraham *qua* the 'father of faith' as 'ethical' Hegel speaks nonsense: 'If this is not Abraham's situation, then Abraham is not even a tragic hero but a murderer. It is thoughtless to want to go on calling him the father of faith' (66). Abraham does not have 'the middle term' (the universal, mediation) that saves the tragic hero (57). Either Abraham is the 'father of faith' in a wholly other sense than Hegel has allowed, or he is simply a murderer.

Regaining of the World

At what point then in the scenario that Kierkegaard is advancing does the ethical, that is to say the relation to the neighbour, come into play? At the point that is ever the case in Lutheran thought: the relation to God *issues* in the relation to the world. As Kierkegaard has it here, the ability to 'regain' the world (once having related to God) requires the exercise of a 'second faith'. As I have mentioned, in Kierkegaard's case there is envisaged to be a peculiar difficulty in making this movement. But that this is what one should be doing is consistently advanced in his writing from *Either/Or* (1843) onwards, being made much of for example in the *Postscript*.[11] It is of course never for Kierkegaard, a Lutheran, that the way to God lies *through* the world. Nor is it that the world is commensurate for God, in the sense that a person's God-relationship could issue in a resultant in the world, for example through becoming a monk. Kierkegaard's is neither a sacramental sense of the world, nor can there be a religious expression in the world for one's God-relationship. Rather does the Christian live *simul justus et peccator*, on the one hand relating to God, but meanwhile 'in' the world where (as we shall see) his God relationship leads to service of the world. The relation to God is exercised subjectively; personal and hidden from the eyes of the world, it is unmediated by the world. In his outward demeanour our knight of faith gives nothing away.

We hear of the ballet dancer who, making a high leap (the relation to God) succeeds in landing on the spot; although his wavering for a moment, says Kierkegaard, betrays that he is an alien in the world (41). The initial 'infinite resignation' of the world in order that one may make the God-relationship absolute (a situation Kierkegaard will discuss in *Postscript*), requires says Kierkegaard no more than human courage. It is the return to the world that is really demanding. The true knight of faith is the one who, having resigned everything, 'by virtue of the absurd' again grasps everything. 'But to be able to come down [as the dancer] in such a way that instantaneously one seems to stand and to walk, to change the leap of life into walking, absolutely to express the sublime in the pedestrian—only that the knight can do' (41). Fully 'of the world', our religious individual is incognito as the man of faith that he is. He may be a tax collector (39). What distinguishes such a one from he who has never embarked on the task of renouncing the world is that the finite is for him a matter of indifference (again, exactly as in *Postscript*). He enjoys as does the next his Sunday walk in the park. But when, on his arrival home, he finds his wife not to have prepared the dish on which he had looked to feast, it is neither here nor there to him (40).

---

[11] See p. 158.

Thus does the knight of faith, as though from the hand of God, receive back the world. Writes Kierkegaard: 'Through a double-movement [Abraham] had attained his first condition and therefore he received Isaac more joyfully than the first time.... He did not have faith that he would be blessed in a future life but that he would be blessed here in the world' (36). Again: 'only he who draws the knife gets Isaac' (38): only the one who in faith has related to God is able to fully relish the world for what it is. And again: 'only the one who was in anxiety finds rest' (27). Yet again: 'To be able to lose one's under-standing and along with it everything finite, for which it is the stockbroker, and then to win the very same finitude again by virtue of the absurd—this appals me, but that does not make me say it [faith] is something inferior, since, on the contrary, it is the one and only marvel' (36). Other than through faith, there is no true relation to the world. Kierkegaard's pseudonym expresses astonishment at the ability to do this: 'But to be able to lose one's understanding and along with it everything finite...and then to win the very same finitude again...' (36).

As I have mentioned, at the point that he wrote *Fear and Trembling* these thoughts are for Kierkegaard closely bound up with the ques-tion as to whether, the other side of having renounced her, there existed the possibility that he could through such a 'second' faith regain Regine. Interestingly in a remark in his *Journal* contempor-aneous with *Fear and Trembling* Kierkegaard remarks: 'If I had had faith I would have stayed with Regine.'[12] It seems that it was on account of his relationship to God that he had renounced her.[13] There is a problem for Kierkegaard in 'regaining' the world. He writes: 'What was the easiest for Abraham would have been difficult for me—once again to be happy in Isaac!—for he who with all the infinity of his soul... has made the infinite movement and cannot do more, he keeps Isaac only with pain' (35). Clearly with Regine in mind he writes: 'Here it is heaven itself that separates what heaven itself, after all, has brought together. Who would have suspected this? Least of all the young bride' (89). He makes mention of a case of which Aristotle tells in which the bridegroom *'to whom the augurs* [in Delphi] *prophesied a calamity that would have its origin in his*

---

[12] *JP* 5:5664 (*Pap.* IV A 107), 17 May 1843.
[13] See pp. 303–4.

marriage, suddenly changes his plans at the crucial moment when he comes to get his bride—he refused to be married' (89). But Kierkegaard also seems to suppose that by some miracle he may receive Regine back again, writing of the 'difficulties of finitude that, like evil spirits, want to separate the lovers, but love has heaven on its side and therefore this holy alliance triumphs over all enemies' (89). *Fear and Trembling* was largely written during a visit to Berlin. On returning to Copenhagen to his chagrin and astonishment Kierkegaard was to find that Regine had become engaged to a former suitor from whom he had wooed her. There is some evidence that he seemed to suppose that, unable to consummate their love, there would forever be a spiritual tryst between them. With his unexpected discovery Kierkegaard had rapidly to change the ending of the companion book that he was writing, his *Repetition*. The pseudonymous author of that volume was one Constantine Constantius!

Of the original print run of 525 copies of the book only 321 had sold three years later, the rest being remaindered. A review of the work, together with *Repetition*, commented that they 'are not for hasty readers and are not likely acquisitions for circulating libraries'.[14] Kierkegaard however predicted that after his death the book would be 'translated into foreign languages' and immortalize his name; that the reader would 'shrink from the frightful pathos'.[15]

Reception and Critique

Kierkegaard knew that he had raised vital issues for western theism and that he had done so in a way that could not be more striking. The book has indeed been translated into languages from Japanese to Hungarian. It has been commented upon from all manner of perspectives and taken up by widely differing schools of thought. What I shall endeavour to do here is to bring to the fore what it seems to me that Kierkegaard was about. I shall also enter into a fundamental dialogue with him.

---

[14] Howard V. Hong & Edna H. Hong, 'Historical Introduction', *FT*, xxxiv, xxxvi.

[15] *JP* 6:6491 (*Pap*. X^2 A 15), n.d., 1849.

The Hebraic/Lutheran Theme

Kierkegaard believes that an understanding for that which is God has in his day become lost. The peculiar circumstances in which this has come about we shall consider in the next section. Here we shall commence by drawing attention to the Hebraic (and Lutheran) sense of God that Kierkegaard attempts to evoke. One might say that it is precisely this God, in his wildness, otherness, and unpredictability which Luther in his day rediscovered, again in a situation in which 'God' had become domesticated, made to conform to the thought systems and machinations of humankind. In the late medieval situation God had become assimilated to a system over which human beings had control, able for example to contrive penalties and pronounce pardons, given that Catholicism believes in a continuing divine incarnation in the church and that that church had become corrupt. In the Catholic medieval understanding, inflected by the humanism of the Graeco-Latin world, God, conceptualized in philosophical terms, is part of an ordered whole to which we also belong; such that God is seen as (interchangeably) goodness or being and humanity understood as derived from God, there existing an *analogia entis* between God and humanity. Luther sweeps aside this world of thought in favour of a Hebraic direct and person-to-person relationship to God.[16] Conjuring up this Hebraic and Lutheran world cannot better be accomplished than through quoting Luther and modern Jewish commentators on Kierkegaard and on the *akedah*.

Here is Luther in his Genesis lectures. (The passage, culled from different parts of a lengthy disposition, has been put together in this form by Roland Bainton.)

Abraham was told by God that he must sacrifice the son of his old age by a miracle, the seed through whom he was to become the father of kings and of a great nation. Abraham turned pale. Not only would he lose his son, but God

---

[16] Coming from a Catholic context the Irishman Mark Dooley writes: 'The God of which Kierkegaard speaks is...more Jewish than Christian—if by "Christian" one means the God of Christendom, of the determinate, doctrinal, and confessional form of Christianity.' ('Kierkegaard and Derrida: Between Totality and Infinity', in Elsebet Jegstrup, ed., *The New Kierkegaard* (Bloomington, IN, 2004), 210–11). Dooley had better write 'Catholic Christian' and, equally, 'Jewish or Lutheran'. It is a good example of how little the Lutheran heritage is known.

appeared to be a liar. He had said, 'In Isaac shall be thy seed', but now he said, 'Kill Isaac'. Who would not hate a God so cruel and contradictory? How Abraham longed to talk it over with someone! Could he not tell Sarah? But he well knew that if he mentioned it to anyone he would be dissuaded and prevented from carrying out the behest. The spot designated for the sacrifice Mount Moriah, was some distance away; 'and Abraham rose up early in the morning, and saddled his ass, and took two of his young men with him, and Isaac his son, and clave the wood for the burnt-offering'. Abraham did not leave the saddling of the ass to others. He himself laid on the beast the wood for the burnt offering. He was thinking all the time that these logs would consume his son, his hope of seed. With these very sticks that he was picking up the boy would be burned. In such a terrible case should he not take time to think it over? Could he not tell Sarah? With what inner tears he suffered! He girt the ass and was so absorbed he scarcely knew what he was doing.

He took two servants and Isaac his son. In that moment everything died in him: Sarah, his family, his home, Isaac. This is what it is to sit in sackcloth and ashes. If he had known that this was only a trial, he would not have been tried. Such is the nature of our trials that while they last we cannot see to the end. 'Then on the third day Abraham lifted up his eyes, and saw the place afar off.' What a battle he had endured in those three days! There Abraham left the servants and the ass, and he laid the wood upon Isaac and himself took the torch and the sacrificial knife. All the time he was thinking, 'Isaac, if you knew, if your mother knew that you are to be sacrificed'. 'And they went both of them together.' The whole world does not know what here took place. They two walked together. Who? The father and the dearest son—the one not knowing what was in store but ready to obey, the other certain that he must leave his son in ashes. Then said Isaac, 'My Father.' And he said, 'Yes my son.' And Isaac said, 'Father, here is the fire and here the wood, but where is the lamb?' He called him father and was solicitous lest he had overlooked something, and Abraham said, 'God will Himself provide a lamb, my son.'

When they were come to the mount, Abraham built the altar and laid on the wood, and then he was forced to tell Isaac. The boy was stupefied. He must have protested, 'Have you forgotten: I am the son of Sarah by a miracle in her age, that I was promised and that through me you are to be the father of a great nation?' And Abraham must have answered that God would fulfil his promise even out of ashes. Then Abraham bound him and laid him upon the wood. The father raised his knife. The boy bared his throat. If God had slept an instant, the lad would have been dead. I could not have watched. I am not able in my thoughts to follow. The lad was as a sheep for the slaughter. Never in history was there such obedience, save only in Christ. But God was watching, and all the angels. The father raised his knife; the boy did not wince. The angel cried, 'Abraham, Abraham!' See how divine majesty is at hand in the hour of death. We say, 'In the midst of life we die.' God answers, 'Nay, in the midst of death we live.'[17]

The passage so closely resembles *Fear and Trembling* that it is tempting to think that Kierkegaard must have known it. At the very least it is deeply informative as to Kierkegaard's Lutheran heritage. There is the same drama, the same anthropomorphic attribution given to God. Yet God is not to be understood, his ways not ours. God is associated with 'future' and with 'promise'. Our response is to be one of utter obedience in that faith which is trust. God brings life out of death. Interestingly Luther as Kierkegaard has an onlooker, an outsider who cannot conceive of the scene. Abraham obeys no universal law. Nor, given what lies before him, can he communicate with any other.

Hardly unsurprisingly some Jewish commentators (whether religious or not) exhibit a fine sense for what is afoot. George Steiner writes:

Only the true God can demand of Abraham the sacrifice of Isaac. It is in the (sickening) unreason, in the incomprehensible enormity of precisely such an injunction that the believer will recognize God's authentic summons. It is the profound error of Kant and of Hegel to seek to identify the God of Abraham, Isaac and Jacob, the God who ordains the hideous death of His Son on the cross, with categories of human understanding and reasoned ethics.... Kierkegaard would have us discriminate unflinchingly between the *dieu des philosophes* and the living God, into whose hands it is indeed 'terrible to fall'. When men of war or guardians of civic virtue...sacrifice their children...they do so with intelligible, albeit mistaken or fanatical, motivations.... Such exemplary acts...are the very stuff of heroic chronicles...But they throw no genuine light on the matter of Abraham and Isaac. Nor does ethics.... Ethically considered, Abraham's acquiescence in God's commandment or indeed that of any man enjoined to carry out human sacrifice, is indefensible. Obedience may arise from fear of supernatural retribution, from superstition...None of these categories is moral. Where morality is at its most elevated, in a Socrates, in a Kant, inhumanity and irrational absurdity have no place. Confronted with God's demand, the response of the ethical must be one of counter-challenge....

[17] J. Pelikan & H. Lehmann, eds, *Luther's Works* (Philadelphia, PA & St Louis, MO, 1955–) 4, *Lectures on Genesis*, 21–5 (*WA* 43.202–20); Roland Bainton, *Hear I Stand: Martin Luther* (Tring, 1987), 382–4.

Kierkegaard is acutely cognizant of these arguments. He dwells with loving irony on their dialectical strengths. They are, he rules, wholly irrelevant to the *akedah*, to the overwhelming enigma and interpretation of Abraham's obedience. The sole pertinent rubric is that of absolute faith, of a faith which transgresses against and thus transcends all conceivable claims of intellectual accountability and of ethical criteria. Abraham's readiness to sacrifice Isaac... lies beyond good and evil. ... Abraham's actions are radiantly absurd. He becomes the 'Knight of Faith' riding forth like Don Quixote as God's champion in the face of humanist revulsion and ridicule. He dwells in paradox. His quantum leap of and into blinding faith isolates him completely. The heroic and the ethical can be generalized. They belong to arguable systems of values and representations. Faith is radically singular. The encounter with God as experienced by Abraham is, eternally, that of an individual, of a private being in the grip of infinity. ... No synagogue, no *ecclesia* [church/gathering] can house Abraham as he strides, in mute torment, towards his appointment with the Everlasting.[18]

Derrida likewise writes with panache:

God doesn't give his reasons, he acts as he intends, he doesn't have to give his reasons or share anything with us: neither his motivations, if he has any nor his deliberations, nor his decisions. Otherwise he wouldn't be God, we wouldn't be dealing with the Other as God, or with God as *wholly other*. ... One can understand why Kierkegaard chose, for his title, the words of a great Jewish convert, Paul, in order to meditate on the still Jewish experience of a secret, hidden, separate, absent, or mysterious God, the one who decides, without revealing his reasons, to demand of Abraham that most cruel, impossible, and untenable gesture: to offer his son Isaac as a sacrifice.[19]

This inscrutable God lies beyond ethics or reason. Kierkegaard never questions but that this transcendent, monotheistic God, the God of biblical revelation, is what God is.[20] It is given this context that we must attempt to evaluate or critique Kierkegaard's text.

---

[18] George Steiner, 'Wound of Negativity', 'Introduction' to *Fear and Trembling; The Book on Adler*, Walter Lowrie, trans., in J. Rée & J. Chamberlain, eds, *Kierkegaard: A Critical Reader* (Oxford, 1998), 107–8.
[19] Jacques Derrida, *The Gift of Death*, David Wills, trans. (Chicago and London, 1995), 57–8; the relevant chapter is reproduced in Rée & Chamberlain's *Kierkegaard*.
[20] See however pp. 214–16.

Opening up the Closed Nature of the World

What had happened in Kierkegaard's day was that the philosophical world had again become closed to transcendence. We should understand that what Kierkegaard is attempting is undertaken in the face of idealism.

Kierkegaard essentially agrees with Kant as to the options (simply suggesting that it would be possible to come down on the other side). 'Honest Kant', as Kierkegaard will refer to him,[21] had made the world of human beings self-contained. The ultimate corollary of his position is laid out in his *Religion*, a text Kierkegaard knew well. Denying the need, possibility or indeed morality of another taking upon him one's sins, Kant substitutes, for the second Adam that is Christ, the 'new man' which is our reformed selves who, symbolically, shall take on himself the sins of our previous selves.[22] This is simply a logical carrying through of Kant's ethics, whereby we alone are to be held imputable for our sin. Moreover, Kant takes for granted that there could be no particularity, such that Jesus is for him simply one human being among others, it owing to human projection that he is held to be a unique and perfect individual. Although Kant may have some vague sense of a transcendent God (more properly perhaps of the 'sublime'), religious concepts are for Kant but a useful imaginative horizon, encouraging us in our rightly held moral aspiration that the disjunction between the good and the actuality that we see will be righted. Kant in no way thinks it possible, nor could he wish, that there could be any kind of interventionary God. To think in these terms would constitute moral unbelief.

While Kant knows that one must choose between belief in Christian revelation and reason, Hegel has confused the issue. Speaking in terms of *Geist* (Spirit or Mind) rather than God, Hegel thinks the 'transcendent' dimension to be increasingly instantiated in the unfolding of the historical process. No more than for Kant is there any transcendent 'otherness'. Meanwhile the historical realm has been 'baptized'. Kierkegaard could not have known, as we do now with the

---

[21] *JP* 2:2236 (*Pap.* VIII¹ A 358), n.d. 1847.
[22] 'Dieser Selbst trägt für ihm, und so auch für alle die an ihn (pracktisch) glauben, als Stellvertrer die Sündenschuld.' (The English translators appear none too clear what is afoot, yet Kant's words are simply commensurate with his argument.)

publication of his early theological writings which Hegel had kept under the counter, that he had indeed interpreted Abraham in a manner exactly commensurate with what Kierkegaard suspected of him. Speaking in wholly negative terms of Abraham's abstraction of himself from human society Hegel writes:

With his herds Abraham wandered hither and thither over a boundless territory without bringing parts of it any nearer to him by cultivating and improving them.... He was a stranger on earth, a stranger to the soil and to men alike. Among men he always was and remained a stranger... He steadily persisted in cutting himself off from others, and he made this conspicuous by a physical peculiarity [circumcision] imposed on himself and his posterity.[23]

For Hegel there could be no possibility of a direct relationship on the part of an individual to a personal God. While for a man, setting himself against the mores of his society, to contemplate murdering his son is frankly immoral.

In telling his tale Kierkegaard is thus taking on and contradicting modernity. Minimally he will draw attention to the fact that, through the subversion that is Hegelian idealism, the Judaeo-Christian God of revelation has been lost. Kierkegaard simply poses the question as to what it would mean to be open to such transcendence. Hence the tenor of his work: Abraham does not know how to deal with something that is unassimilatable to the human world and which, if he is to respond to in obedience, must contradict human ethical presuppositions. Abraham has no language, no means of communication for that with which he believes himself confronted. Indeed Kierkegaard's text can do no more than indicate this beyond. He cannot translate it into the human framework. None has better grasped what is afoot here, with its radical challenge to Hegelian presuppositions, than the Hegelian scholar Judith Butler. Butler writes:

Kierkegaard's response will be that if there is an infinite that can never be resolved with the finite, then Kierkegaard's own texts will always *fail* to communicate the infinite. Indeed, Kierkegaard's response will be: 'My texts must fail to express the infinite, and it will be by virtue of that *failure* that the infinite will be affirmed. Moreover, that affirming of the infinite will not take

---

[23] G. W. F. Hegel, 'The Spirit of Christianity and its Fate', in T. M. Knox, trans., *G.W.F. Hegel: Early Theological Writings* (Chicago, IL, 1948), 186.

the form of a thought; it will take place at the limits of thought itself; it will force a crisis in thought, the advent of passion.'[24]

What if there exists a transcendence that, contrary to the Hegelian expectation, cannot be mediated into the historical? Thus also Pat Bigelow writes:

Whereas the power of the *Aufhebung* [the Hegelian dialectic, which enables resolution] is its ability to take up all differences as elements of selfsameness, the Kierkegaardian movement of transgression holds open the relation to the absolute other *in its unthinkable difference.*[25]

Kierkegaard's critique poses the question as to how we should be thinking about our reality. Denying the presuppositions of philosophical modernity, Kierkegaard will open up the possibility of another dimension.

The move that Kierkegaard makes here will be fundamental to his authorship. It will take all his art to find language, or literary form, to evoke what he will. Kierkegaard knows full well, after Kant (and also one may say Hume, whose thinking was mediated to him through German sources) that it is impossible to speak of knowledge of God or 'prove' God's existence. But given his heritage Kierkegaard would not think to attempt such proof even were it possible. He is, in his sense of God's incommensurability with the world, manifest only through God's revelation, a Lutheran. Kierkegaard will never commence theologizing speculatively 'from' the thought of God, as might indeed Calvin or Barth in the Reformed tradition; albeit in that tradition equally God is known through revelation. For Kierkegaard all that we have is on the one hand a phenomenology of the human being, one who is however open to the transcendent, and on the other hand biblical revelation. For any cognitive verifiability Kierkegaard will look to Christ. But in relation to Christ, as we shall see, there can only be the paradoxical relationship of faith, given that the finite cannot contain the infinite and that the two are in any case a contradiction in terms. Equally, Luther will always bring the human desire to speculate down to earth, pointing to the humility of Christ, 'the babe in the manger'.

[24] Butler, 'Speculative Despair', 375.
[25] Pat Bigelow, *Kierkegaard and the Problem of Writing* (Tallahassee, FL, 1987), 187.

The Question of Ethics

It will already have become evident that to think that the book is a consideration of whether there can be a teleological suspension of (Kantian) ethics, that is to say whether the universal can ever be bracketed on account of the demands of a higher *telos*, while not untrue is far from the totality of what Kierkegaard is about. His concern is for 'faith'. That is to say can a human being reaching beyond himself respond to a higher realm, the command of God? What would it mean to do this? But the idea of a revelation of God must always potentially involve that human ethics (the universal) is to be bracketed. Both Kierkegaard and equally Kant recognize this (which is why such a notion of God would for Kant be immoral, for it is potentially heteronomous). It was Hegel who had fudged the issue (and in attempting to go 'beyond' Hegel in the direction of Christianity, even more so Martensen in his postulating the wholly illegitimate notion of a Christian culture, one in which God was somehow instantiated, accommodated).

It is interesting to consider how Kierkegaard thinks of 'ethics'. Understood in the narrower sense, 'ethics' is for him axiomatically Kantian ethics. Kierkegaard will hedge around what he will say in order to make transparently clear what is at issue. Thus Abraham is not one who willingly overthrows Kantian ethics; he precisely longs to return to 'the universal', which for him represents the realm of comfort. Kierkegaard does not wish to open himself to the charge of immorality. If the call of the religious is a path that 'winds higher' than the commonality of human ethics, it does not thereby abolish ethics. Kierkegaard does not directly say that there could be a command from God to disobey the universal precept that one shall not kill. He is but raising a question. For as both he and Kant well see, if it is not even theoretically possible that God could command something other than the moral law, then the idea of God (at least the concept of God held by the Jewish and Christian traditions of revelation) is dead in the water. One might as well not speak of God but simply (as does Kant) of the 'idea' of God as an extrapolation of human ethics. It is Hegel who is mistaken in thinking that in postulating but one reality that encompasses both ethics and Christianity he can have his cake and eat it.

Understanding ethics in a broader sense, Kierkegaard could well be said to be what today would be called a 'virtue' ethicist. That is to say Kierkegaard thinks, as perhaps does any Lutheran theologian, that person comes before works, while issuing in works. Constituted by the relationship to God, the Christian turns to the world. From faith there flows love. What is problematic for Kierkegaard, as becomes evident in this book, is the second move of turning to the world. One senses that Kierkegaard knew of himself that he could not join the universal, which in his society would normally have entailed marriage. That this is a difficulty for Kierkegaard is bound up with his God-relationship and thus also with his conception of 'God'. As increasingly in the course of the authorship Kierkegaard comes to think in terms of a personal relationship with God, an 'other' whom he loves, it is possible that there comes to be a kind of competition between God and neighbour. But this is not evident at this early stage.

It is of interest in this connection to consider Jacques Derrida's take on *Fear and Trembling* in his *The Gift of Death*. As in so much of the ethics developed late in his authorship, Derrida reads the situation through what one may call Levinasian eyes. He sees the situation as a conflict of singularities or particularities. Is Abraham to obey God, or to relate as a dutiful father to Isaac? Abraham's 'sacrifice' to God, says Derrida, is 'the sacrifice of the most imperative duty (that which binds me to the other as a singularity in general) [to Isaac] in favour of another absolutely imperative duty binding me to the wholly other [God]'. This, Derrida concludes, but exemplifies the common human experience: there is always present a clash between one singularity and other singularities.

How would you ever justify the fact that you sacrifice all the cats in the world to the cat that you feed at home every morning for years? . . . What can be said about Abraham's relation to God can be said about my relation without relation to *every other (one) as wholly other [tout autre comme tout autre]*. . . . From this point of view what *Fear and Trembling* says about the sacrifice of Isaac is the truth.[26]

But is it not odd to think a 'duty' towards God in conflict with that towards another person, or to be analogous to that of conflicting duties towards two persons? It is an extraordinarily anthropomorphic notion of God, which is perhaps that of the Abrahamic religions. In

---

[26] Derrida, *Gift*, 71, 78, translation adjusted.

that that is the case Derrida has inadvertently put his finger on what is at stake, the notion of God.

Overcoming the Dilemma?

It is clear that the dilemma that Kierkegaard poses is the necessary corollary of Western theism. It could be said that if God is good by definition then it could not be that God should demand of Abraham that he should kill his son (and that Abraham is entertaining a delusion). But it should be noted that Kierkegaard himself does not say this, nor does he define God's will as necessarily the good when judged by human standards. (Such a statement is more likely to come from one of Catholic or Anglican disposition, or in the Anglo-Saxon tradition, who thinks there to be one moral order which pertains both to God and to ourselves.)[27] For Kierkegaard, if the term God is

---

[27] It may be worthwhile to comment here that much Anglo-Saxon discussion takes place in what may be thought really a rather different context than the primary concerns of *Fear and Trembling*. That it may be legitimate to pull a writer's thoughts into one's own ambit is of course another matter. Thus Kierkegaard is discussed in relation to the so-called 'Euthyphro dilemma'; from Plato's *Euthyphro*, in which he asks whether God wills morally good acts because they are good—that is to say God wills acts which we according to our criteria should consider good—or whether an act becomes 'good' through being willed by God. (See Martin Warner's editor's 'Introduction' to *Philosophy and Religion*, 1992, or Stewart Sutherland's discussion in his *Faith and Ambiguity* (London, 1984, 66–75)). What one may think much more problematic is when Kierkegaard's Lutheran context is so little understood that he is fully misread. Astonishingly the Kierkegaard scholar Alastair Hannay remarks: 'By adopting a *telos* outside the ethical [Kierkegaard] is not putting himself above morality so much as extending morality's universe.' (*Kierkegaard*, London, 1982, 78.) How can this be? It is frequently assumed that Kierkegaard equates God with 'the good'. But Kierkegaard is not thinking in these philosophical terms and it would be quite foreign for him to do so. Most problematic of all, Stephen Mulhall considers that the 'secret message' of the teleological suspension of the ethical is that space is made for a conception of the ethical that includes grace, remarking: 'Acknowledging Christ means acknowledging that [the] demands [of the ethical realm] must nevertheless be met, with help from a power greater than our own' (*Inheritance and Originality: Wittgenstein, Heidegger, Kierkegaard*, Oxford, 2001, 386). How is this vocabulary being employed? Kierkegaard is not a Catholic who thinks in terms of our receiving infused grace, enabling us to do what we could not do unaided. The Lutheran Reformation overturned such ways of thinking, shedding also the Aristotelian metaphysics through which alone it could make sense. Rather does Kierkegaard think, as does Luther, that 'having made the movements of infinity, [faith] makes the movements of finitude', (37); that is to say constituted through the relation to God, the human being turns to the world as the scene of human activity. On the other hand there would seem to be no reason to think that Kierkegaard is interested

not to be vacuous, and if God is held to be transcendent and conceptualized according to an anthropomorphic analogy, so that God could be said to have a will, it must potentially be possible that God could will something other than that of which humans have conceived. It becomes clear that any challenge to Kierkegaard's position will, of necessity, need to overturn the most fundamental presuppositions with which he in common with the Judaeo-Christian tradition as a whole is working. I think it should be said that the feminist challenge of recent years is of just such a magnitude.

In the first place it should be remarked upon that among feminists and others there has been a widespread expression of revulsion at and abnegation of the whole idea of 'sacrifice'. That feminists so universally raise questions here lends weight to the suggestion that God as portrayed not least in *Fear and Trembling* is a peculiarly male construct. As literature that suggests this one might want to cite such diverse material as Carol Delaney's devastating critique of the *akedah*, Mary Condren's discussion of the fatal admixture of 'sacrifice' in fuelling conflict in Northern Ireland, or Luce Irigaray's challenge to René Girard.[28] Interesting also is William Beers's study *Women and Sacrifice: Male Narcissism and the Psychology of Religion* in which he suggests (in somewhat inchoate fashion) that the fact that men clear the air, finding reconciliation through sacrificing (which on the face of it is bizarre), is a male narcissistic displacement of an unresolved relationship to the mother.[29] Certainly this would tie in well with Irigaray's response to Girard that it is

---

in an extreme form of what is sometimes called 'divine command ethics', as for example Seung-Goo Lee suggests ('The Antithesis between the Religious view of Ethics and the Rationalistic View of Ethics' in Robert L. Perkins, ed., *Fear and Trembling, International Kierkegaard Commentary* (Macon, GA), henceforth *IKC FT*, etc., 101–26). A post-Enlightenment, Western man, Kierkegaard does not give the impression that he thinks that human lives should moment by moment be beholden to God's latest, arbitrary command. We should consider here his measured response when Adolph Adler proclaimed himself the recipient of revelations from God.

[28] Carol Delaney, *Abraham on Trial: The Social Legacy of Biblical Myth* (Princeton, NJ, 1998); Mary Condren, *The Serpent and the Goddess: Women, Religion and Power in Celtic Ireland* (San Francisco, CA, 1989); Luce Irigaray, 'Women, the Sacred and Money', D. Knight and M. Whitford, trans., *Paragraph* 8 (Oct 1986, 6–18).

[29] William Beers, *Women and Sacrifice: Male Narcissism and the Psychology of Religion* (Detroit, MI, 1992).

actually the mother who is sacrificed. Delaney (an anthropologist) suggests that the story of the *akedah* derives from the time of, and seeks to legitimize, the establishment of patriarchal father–son religions in place of the more ancient matriarchal religions of the Mediterranean basin. But be these speculations as they may, they are only of interest to our present concern in suggesting that the presuppositions of the Abrahamic religions are not the only way in which one might conceive of God, and that they do not necessarily come naturally to women.

In this connection I should like to give brief consideration to the French philosopher Sylviane Agacinski's response to Kierkegaard in her 'We are Not Sublime: Love and Sacrifice, Abraham and Ourselves'. Agacinski finds herself 'suspicious of this exaltation of greatness, immensity and the absolute', of the 'formless and the faceless' too, as seemingly carrying a condemnation of finitude. While acknowledging that Kierkegaard 'recalls existing individuals to their finitude', she comments that 'the shape of the father or God' will always have 'marked' that finitude in advance. This is of course exactly correct. Agacinski remarks on those who are 'bewildered' by Abraham's faith, who have 'lost their capacity for the sublime:... who can no longer sustain any relationship with the absolute, the great and the eternal; or perhaps... who no longer need to sustain it'. They will say: ' "We have time; but we have nothing else. We are not sublime." ' Exalting the idea of a human transient love which does not depend on the sublime or answer in obedience 'here I am', she acknowledges that it implies 'something like the end of Abraham's faith... or, more generally, the end of our fear of something absolutely *external* to us which might be capable of exciting either devotion or respect'. Thus Agacinski concludes: 'To say that Abraham is sublime is to say that he has become a stranger to us.'[30] This may well be true of our world. It constitutes a revolution.

Kierkegaard wishes in this book to give space to the individual. He is wont to fulminate against the untoward passage in *The Philosophy of Right* where Hegel seems to deny such a position.[31] The real question

[30] Sylviane Agacinski, 'We are Not Sublime: Love and Sacrifice, Abraham and Ourselves', extract in Rée & Chamberlain, eds, *Kierkegaard*, 129, 130, 130–1, 135, 136, 144.
[31] See for example p. 267.

for ethics is whether, as Kierkegaard seems to suppose is the case, one must needs postulate a relationship to an unseen and transcendent God as the guardian of such individuality. Does belonging to society necessarily involve being placed under pressure to conform? Kierkegaard may perfectly correctly read Hegel as implying this. But I am reminded of Jessica Benjamin's depiction (in a book in which there is much discussion of Hegel) of what she names 'inter-subjective space'. Benjamin finds that: 'Women make use of the space in-between that is created by shared feeling and discovery'; believing that: 'the dance of mutual recognition, the meeting of separate selves, is the context for their desire'.[32] For Hegel the matter is clear: the tension involved in intersubjectivity will inevitably lead to a breakdown in relations, resulting in domination by one party of the other. But need that be? If one had a different reading of society maybe there would be no need for Kierkegaard's transcendent God. Could it not be that the space between human beings is a fount of creativity, allowing both of community and individuality? This, too, is where women might well be inclined to situate 'God', as that which passes between human beings, which is more than either of them individually. Such a way of thinking would overcome the fact that it is clearly problematic to place the idea of God in contradistinction to human ethics and values. The question that one must pose to Kierkegaard's depiction of Abraham is whether, in escaping the Hegelian universal through making recourse to the transcendent God of our imagination, we may not simply be replacing one heteronomy with another yet more ominous.

---

[32] J. Benjamin, *The Bonds of Love: Psychoanalysis, Feminism and the Problem of Domination* (New York, 1988), 130.

3

Philosophical Fragments

Introduction

In my estimation *Philosophical Fragments* is the most important text published in theology since the Enlightenment. Better than any other of which I am aware, it enables a consideration of the nature of Christian claims, and thus also the validity of Christianity given the epistemological context of the modern world. It is, however, by translating Kierkegaard's argument into a wider field, or equally one might say extrapolating from the way in which he casts his argument, that it best performs this function, proving its usefulness. Writing after the Enlightenment, Kierkegaard sees what it is that Christianity must claim if it is to be true to itself and the clash that this represents with modernity. Yet it also becomes apparent that he himself has not fully entered into modern presuppositions, such that he underpins a Christian position with an epistemological outlook that few would hold today. It is here that the dialogue with Kierkegaard is of the greatest fascination.

Though the book's prescience was scarcely recognized by Kierkegaard's contemporaries (after three years only 229 copies out of a print run of 525 had been sold),[1] it came at an opportune moment: Christianity was up against the wall. With the dawning of the

---

[1] Niels Thulstrup, 'Commentator's Introduction', in David Swenson, *trans.*, *Philosophical Fragments* (Princeton, NJ, 1967), xciv.

assumptions of modernity, the Christian claim that there could in Christ have occurred a 'particularity' in history was no longer feasible. (I have discussed this in chapter 1.) In consequence, veering away from Christological claims, the 18th century had embraced the abstract and universal God of deism. Following the work among others of Lessing, at the century's end Kant assumes the Christian myth to be but a vehicle that expresses in picturesque form truths that humans know about themselves. Much impressed by Kant on this score, denying all particularity, Hegel had subsumed the Christ event understood as a concept into the history of ideas; a history which reached its zenith not in Christianity but with his own philosophy. Meanwhile the theologian Schleiermacher, taking for granted the philosophical outlook of the 18th century which dealt in generalities and drawing on Romanticism, sought to awaken his contemporaries to a recognition of a spiritual dimension to the totality of nature and existence. To cap these developments, in 1835/6 David Friedrich Strauss's *Life of Jesus, Critically Considered* commenced on the path of dismantling the supernatural dimension of the biblical text, thereby undermining any positivistic basis on which the claims of Christian dogma could rest. It was a heady time.

Finally, most interestingly, we know that three months before publishing, on 20 March 1844 Kierkegaard purchased a copy of Feuerbach's *Das Wesen des Christentums* (*The Essence of Christianity*).[2] Feuerbach's book, which in the 'Preface' to the second edition of 1843 surveying the scene delivers the *coup de grâce*, may well have been instrumental in Kierkegaard formulating the challenge to modernity which his book represents in quite the way he does.[3] Rather than pertaining to a transcendent reality, Feuerbach charges, religion is but 'the dream of the human mind'. Far from being 'untrue', or to be reduced to concepts (as Hegel had wished to do) said Feuerbach, religion was in its concrete determinations 'true'; it was simply the story that man told about himself. Thus: 'I prove that the Son of God is

---

[2] H. P. Rohde, ed., *The Auctioneer's Sales Record of the Library of Søren Kierkegaard* (Copenhagen), 1967. (I owe this reference to Jon Stewart.)

[3] Hans Brøchner (see p. 86) tells us that on their walks together Kierkegaard would often refer to Feuerbach; that he appreciated the clarity and penetration with which Feuerbach had understood Christianity. ('Hans Brøchner's Recollections of Kierkegaard', quoted by Bruce Kirmmse, ed., *Encounters with Kierkegaard: A Life as Seen by His Contemporaries* (Princeton, NJ, 1996), 233.)

in religion a real son, the son of God in the same sense in which man is the son of man, and I find therein the *truth*, the *essence* of religion, that it conceives and affirms a profoundly human relation as a divine relation.' Theology becomes anthropology. Christianity, claimed Feuerbach, was as dead as a dodo, standing 'in flagrant contradiction with our fire and life assurance companies, our railroads and steam-carriages'.[4] As it must have seemed to Kierkegaard, were there to be any future for Christianity it must be given back its independent, tran-scendent reality. It must claim a revelation and speak of a commensur-ate faculty or disposition, which was not that of reason, which would allow of human response to this otherness. But all this must stand in contradiction to modernity.

Where to start? In a short tract that, tongue in cheek and with Hegel in view, he refers to as some mere philosophical fragments (the Danish is literally 'crumbs')[5], Kierkegaard (as he had in effect in *Fear and Trembling*) simply poses a question. But that question, if it be answered positively, must undermine the presuppositions of mod-ernity. Taking for granted that revelation and correspondingly faith have their own grounding (and therefore necessarily burst upon the scene), Kierkegaard denies the relevance of 18th- and 19th-century philosophical development. There had of course been a previous time when Christianity needed to shake itself free from the philosophical moorings to which it had grown accustomed and to which it had accommodated itself; namely in the Reformation. Luther proclaimed faith in the face of reason. But the situation had become more complicated. The reductionism implied by the whole development from Lessing through Kant and Hegel and crowned by Feuerbach's book posed a peculiar problem. Taking up the Lutheran position, Kierkegaard drives beyond anything that would have occurred to the Reformers to be necessary in terms of an absolute revelation from above, in which God in Christ is both what is revealed and also provides the means of its recognition. As 'the Truth' Christianity must declare the knowledge which is derived from human self-know-ledge (idealism) a falsehood.

---

[4] Ludwig Feuerbach, *The Essence of Christianity*, George Eliot, trans., (New York, 1957), pp. xxxix, xi, xvii.
[5] There is among Hamann's publications a title *Brocken* (*Fragments*) perhaps leading Kierkegaard to choose this title.

The Truth which is Christ that Kierkegaard will restore to its rightful place is that as formulated by the ancient Creeds: the second *persona* of a triune God is in two natures, fully human and fully divine (the Definition of Chalcedon). In considering this juxtaposition of human and divine Kierkegaard was strongly influenced by the thought of the 18th century. Following the heritage of the ancient world, Leibniz and later in the century Lessing had aligned the concept of God with that which was changeless.[6] Kierkegaard wished to say that the eternal had entered time in the particular: a paradox to thought exemplified by Lessing's famous ditch. Kierkegaard would attempt to cross the ditch with the aid of faith. As we have already considered,[7] Hamann had been instrumental at a crucial moment in Kierkegaard's development in suggesting to him that faith stood in the face of reason. Stemming likewise from Hamann, it must also be said that Kierkegaard held presuppositions concerning God's relationship to history and the possibility of God's acting in history that ill fitted the mechanistic understanding of cause and effect of a post-Newtonian world.[8]

Kierkegaard must cast his diatribe in compelling and original form. The problem was that his age counted itself Christian, an illusion which must first be destroyed. He must bring his contemporaries up short. There was a blatant irreconcilability between Christian claims and what passed in the culture as Christianity. Kierkegaard will strike at the unholy hybrid that is Hegelianism. In particular his target will be Martensen, who following an extended sojourn abroad had in 1838 returned to Copenhagen and, appointed to a position at the university, in immensely popular lectures attempted to find a way forward for Christianity by taking Hegelianism 'further'. There seems no question but that Kierkegaard was, not least, envious. As I have mentioned, there is a certain parallelism between *Philosophical Fragments* and *Fear and Trembling*. Whereas the earlier book challenges a Hegelian attempt to assimilate Christianity (or the Judaeo-Christian claims) to ethics, *Fragments* does the same for epistemology. In both cases Kierkegaard stands shoulder-to-shoulder with Kant in believing Christian faith incompatible with human ethics (*Fear and Trembling*) or the claims of reason (*Fragments*).

[6] See p. 15.   [7] See pp. 19–20.   [8] See pp. 91–2.

The book is what Kierkegaard will call a 'project in thought': he will present an abstract, ideal, case for his reader to think through logically. The text resembles a Greek drama with different scenes, even having an interlocutor who appears and comments on the action. The choice of 'Socrates' as a counter to Christ (the God/man never mentioned by name) proved inspired, bringing the contrast between humanistic and Christian 'truths' into stark relief. The theme had been with Kierkegaard for some time. The first thesis that he had chosen to defend in his examination for the magister (doctoral) degree in September 1841 read: 'The likeness between Socrates and Christ consists essentially in unlikeness.'[9] Socrates thus plays here the role that does Kant in *Fear and Trembling*. His is a pure form of idealism, standing over against the claims of Christianity. As in the earlier work, this shows up the Hegelian position for what it is, a confusion of the two. Employing a pseudonym, Johannes Climacus, seems to have been a last minute decision. It may be thought that Kierkegaard judged that the resultant distancing of himself from the work was what was required.

Exposition

Chapter I. A Project of Thought

The project stutters as it gets underway (compare *Fear and Trembling*.) On the title-page Kierkegaard makes reference to Lessing with a twist, asking how an eternal consciousness could be grounded in a historical point of departure. He quotes Shakespeare: 'Better well hanged than ill wed'; i.e. Hegel has 'wed' what he should not. And the chapter opens with the Socratic question as to whether the truth can be learned. All three references relate to major themes. The young Kierkegaard (just 31) may be alluding to giants that he may situate what he has to say within Western culture.

Kierkegaard first sets up the Socratic position. Socrates was ever his hero. In Plato's *Meno* Socrates asks how it is that—in fact *arête*, virtue (but Kierkegaard renders this 'truth')—can be learnt. For, in a

---

[9] Cf. Thulstrup, 'Introduction', lviii.

well-known conundrum, 'what a man knows he cannot seek, since he knows it, and what he does not know he cannot seek, since he does not even know what to seek'. What the *Meno* purports to show is that knowledge is essentially present within the human being, the teacher's role maieutic (pertaining to that of a midwife) drawing out what is already present. Asking a series of questions of an uneducated slave boy, Socrates brings him to the recognition that the area of the square on the hypotenuse (the diagonal across a square) is twice that of the original square; not the conclusion the boy would initially have jumped to. The Platonic understanding is that in a previous existence humans were possessed of knowledge; hence Kierkegaard speaks of 'the eternal' and the relationship to the eternal as given with the person himself. 'In the Socratic view, every human being is himself the midpoint and the whole world focuses only on him because his self-knowledge is God-knowledge'.[10]

This position is to be known as 'A'. (It occurs to me that it had been better only to name it 'A' when one has suggested that there can be anything other.) For 'A' we may of course 'read' not simply the Socratic world view but also the Enlightenment, particularly Kant, or indeed any humanist or religious position not predicated on revelation. All truth is already present, given with the world or with humanity, waiting to be uncovered. Of 'A' Kierkegaard comments that the following pertain to it: (i) That its 'truths' are true irrespective of when the learner comes to recognize them, any 'point of departure in time' being incidental, a mere 'occasion'. Thus also (ii) the person through whose help the learner comes to the knowledge is incidental to the truth, for in respect to the learner's eternal happiness this is 'given retrogressively' in so far as he was already in possession of the truth without knowing it (12). We should note that as an idealist Hegel of course in a sense thinks all truth 'given' ('from the beginning' we may say) and progressively realized in history. His system is a form of 'A' while he has in Kierkegaard's eyes wholly illegitimately gobbled up Christianity within it, loosing thereby what is of the essence of Christian faith.

The stage is set.

[10] Howard V. Hong & Edna H. Hong, eds & trans., *Philosophical Fragments and Johannes Climacus* (Princeton, NJ, 1985) 11 (henceforth 11, etc.).

Kierkegaard proceeds to pose the question around which the book will revolve. What would it mean to escape these presuppositions? That other scenario, which escapes the presuppositions present in 'A', Kierkegaard will name 'B'. In setting up 'B' Kierkegaard will again formulate an ideal case, the very opposite of 'A'.

The moment in time must have such decisive significance that for no moment will I be able to forget it, neither in time nor in eternity, because the eternal, previously nonexistent, came into existence in that moment (13).

That is to say in 'B' the truth is 'given' to the individual, or comes into existence for him at a particular moment in time. In other words we have the concept of a revelation in history, and a corresponding recognition in time as to its truth. This will now be thought through.

(a) The preceding (antecedent) state

The ideal state, the opposite of 'A', would have to be that the learner is devoid of the truth even in the form of ignorance: not even seeking the truth, he does not know that he lacks it. The learner is outside the truth, not coming towards it but going away from it; in 'untruth' (since he is outside the truth). (This must represent a 'Barthian' rather than what is commonly a Lutheran position, and other than the terms in which Kierkegaard will think elsewhere, a matter that we shall later consider.[11] It may be said to be the Kierkegaard by which Barth was profoundly influenced.)[12]

(b) The Teacher

The contact with the teacher must be such that the learner comes to see that the truth is not in him. That is to say there is a moment when the learner recognizes that in himself he is 'untruth'. He is further removed from the truth even than when he did not recognize this to be the case. Thus the teacher, who himself is one with the truth (for otherwise we return to the Socratic position, whereby the teacher is incidental to the truth, simply eliciting it), brings in his own self the truth to the learner. Moreover, given the learner is in untruth, the teacher must provide him with the condition for recognizing that this

---

[11] See pp. 128–9.   [12] See p. 129.

is the truth with which he is confronted. But one who provides the condition is not a Socratic teacher. We should call such a teacher, a Teacher, for he must 'recreate' the learner. 'But no human being is capable of doing this; if it is to take place, it must be done by the god himself' (14–15).

But consider. In so far as the learner is already 'created', it must be that the Teacher in the first instance endowed him with the condition for understanding the Truth (the Truth which is 'B'). That he is now destitute of it must owe to he himself; since it would be a contradiction that the God should deprive him of it. 'The untruth then is not merely outside the truth but is polemical against the truth' (15). Let us call this *sin*. Such a learner may appear free, 'for to be on one's own' apart from 'B' 'certainly is freedom' (i.e. presumably intended the kind of 'freedom' pursued in the secular Enlightenment). 'And yet [this learner] is...unfree,...bound and excluded, because to be free from the truth is indeed to be excluded, and to be excluded by oneself is indeed to be bound.' (As we shall discuss, in a tradition going back to the patristic era in a somewhat less absolute form, in Luther's thought one is bound either to God or the devil; to be bound to God is to be 'free'.[13]) Given that the learner bound himself, can he free himself? He must first will it. But if, recognizing that he had bound himself he could free himself, the moment in time would be of no significance. Thus we must say of this learner that he 'uses the power of freedom in the service of unfreedom'; he is the 'slave of sin' (17).

What should we call this Teacher who, giving the learner the condition for understanding that this is the Truth, is himself the Truth? A *saviour*, for he saves the learner from himself. 'And no one is so dreadfully imprisoned and no captivity is so impossible to break out of as that in which the individual holds himself captive!' (17). Such a Teacher can never be forgotten, for in that moment the learner would 'sink down into himself again' (17). (Note again the Lutheran context: to attempt independence, endeavouring to stand alone, is of the essence of sin.) Were the Teacher in another life to meet one who had not as yet received the condition he would be able to give it to him, but to the one who had already received it he would stand in a different relation. (So there is such a situation as being reprobate.) Such a teacher is *judge*. And the moment; should it not be called the *fullness of time* (Eph.1.10). (This is a jab at Hegel, who uses the term to suggest that the incarnation of the spirit which 'Christ' represents is the culmination of a gradual process taking place in time.)

(c) The disciple

(Note the Danish *Efterfølgelse*: literally one who 'after-follows'.)

On receiving the condition and the truth the learner does not become a human being for the first time, but he becomes a different person; a *new creation* (2 Cor. 5.17). Whereas previously he was constantly departing from the truth, he is turned around; a *conversion*. Conscious that he through his own fault was in untruth, he takes leave of his former state with sorrow; *repentance*. The change compares to a change from non-being to being, but since one who already exists cannot be born we may call it a *rebirth*. In the Socratic situation he gave birth to himself, owing nothing to anyone. By contrast, within 'B' he owes everything to his divine Teacher. In 'A' the person forgot the whole world on account of himself; in 'B' he forgets himself on account of his Teacher. (Compare the Lutheran understanding that to be a Christian is to transfer one's 'centre of gravity'.[14])

In conclusion we may say that in 'B' the moment is of decisive significance. Were it not to possess this character we should only be speaking Socratically, no matter what we said and however many strange words we employed (a swipe at Hegel, who in actuality remains in 'A' and has not entered upon 'B', though he wholly falsely speaks of Christianity) and even though we supposed we had gone 'beyond' (a swipe at Martensen, who embellishes Hegelianism to better Christianize it) that simple wise man (Socrates) who distinguished between the god, human beings, and himself. (That is to say if we are not speaking of 'B' then, willy-nilly, we remain with 'A', meanwhile having muddied the waters. In contrast with Socrates, Hegel and Martensen fail to make the proper distinctions.) In situation 'B' the person finds no pleasure in recollection (he was in sin, the truth not

---

[14] See p. 22.

in him); even less will he be capable of 'drawing the god over to his side' (you cannot Christianize what is essentially humanism) (20).

Is 'B' 'thinkable'? Why not? But who is supposed to think it? It can only be thought by the one reborn. (That is to say faith makes sense to he who possesses it, though only to him. We shall find this contention also elsewhere.[15])

In 'A' the person possesses the condition for comprehending the truth; thinking that since he is, so also is God. (God can be found through he himself, a natural theology.) Whether he can go any 'further' the moment must decide (a swipe at Martensen, who does not recognize this, speaking of no such moment) (20). If he does not understand this he is to be referred to Socrates (!), 'even though his opinion that he has gone much further will cause that wise man a great deal of trouble' (2). Kierkegaard compares such Hegelians to those who, when Socrates took some foolish notion away from them, became so exasperated that they positively wanted to bite him.

Chapter II. The God as Teacher and Saviour (A Poetical Venture)

The chapter is of a different ilk, setting out from another place; a further act in a play. Kierkegaard tells a story of the king who loves a lowly maiden (i.e. we are speaking of Christ's *kenosis*; Phil. 2.5–8).

What, asks Kierkegaard, moves the god to make his appearance? Love; 'for only in love is the different made equal, and only in equality or in unity is there understanding' (25). (Note the presupposition that God and humanity are radically other; as also we may say the structural sexism in so far as the one who condescends is presumed male, the other female.)

There exists a dilemma; for the god must convey that he is the god, and to do this become human; but that which he must convey is that he is not merely human but God. Consider the king's dilemma. Were he to appear to the maiden as king that might satisfy her but not him; she would be overwhelmed, whereas love makes equal. 'There was a people [the Jews] who had a good understanding of the divine; this people believed that to see the god was death' (30).[16] Not to disclose

---

[15] See p. 167.   [16] Cf. the discussion of *Anfechtung*, pp. 164–5.

itself is the death of love; to disclose itself the death of the beloved. It is a delicate moment; for the truth of the matter is that the learner owes everything to the god. 'That which makes understanding so difficult is precisely this: that [the learner] becomes nothing and yet is not annihilated; that he owes him everything and yet becomes boldly confident; that he understands the truth, but the truth makes him free' (30–1). Hence the god will appear in the form of a *servant* (cf. Phil. 2). 'But this form of a servant is not something put on like the king's plebeian cloak' (31–2). (Which would correspond to those heresies that suggested that God only *appeared* to be human, Apollinarianism, or Eutychianism.) How terrifying to sit with the god as his equal 'and yet the god's concern is precisely to have it so'.[17]

Chapter III. The Absolute Paradox (A Metaphysical Caprice)

Again, we change scene.

What Kierkegaard has to say is so out of kilter with what everywhere else is taken for granted that one wonders whether the chapter is some kind of prank—or metaphysical caprice? Reason, says Kierkegaard, comes up against a limit, 'the unknown'. If—as we may surmise—he has in mind Kant's 'first' *Critique* it must be said that this bears no comparison! What Kant there demonstrates is that there is a *limit* to our capacity to know, given that for knowledge to arise we must be in possession of sense perceptions. (With the implication that there are not the conditions in place for us to acquire 'knowledge' of God.) By contrast, Kierkegaard will conjure up a liminality as though there were a boundary of such a nature that there is that which 'exists' on the far side, an 'unknown' which is God. One might well say that if, as does Barth, Kierkegaard were to commence from revelation as a given, methodologically that would be fair enough (though simply circular if proving God's existence). But Kierkegaard here appears to commence not 'from above' (to employ the theological jargon, from revelation) but from 'below', from the human as knower. In which case the move is surely illegitimate? He then proceeds to hypostasize the divine (speak of it as though of an entity). But this is a sleight of hand.

---

[17] David Swenson, ed. & trans., *Søren Kierkegaard, Philosophical Fragments* (Princeton, NJ, 1967), 43 (henceforth Swenson, 43 etc.).

Kierkegaard remarks: 'One must not think ill of the paradox, for the paradox is the passion of thought and the thinker without... paradox is like the lover without passion.' (A swipe at Hegel, who will always resolve his dialectic, taking up both original opposing terms into a higher and more inclusive synthesis.) Every passion wills its own downfall (we desire resolution) and so also it is the ultimate passion of the understanding to will the collision [with the unknown] although the collision must be its downfall. (That is to say reason is incompatible with the Paradox; accepting the Paradox would be its downfall.) Thought wants to discover something it cannot think. Without really understanding itself, thought wills its own downfall. (How so one might say? This is no more than an assertion on Kierkegaard's part.) The unknown is not a human being (inasmuch as we know what man is); let us call it *the god* (39). (Thus (i) the unknown has been hypostasized; (ii) it has been assumed that God is that which is other than the human if also human; and (iii) it has been asserted, it would seem wholly illegitimately, that reason wills its own downfall.)

In some way Kierkegaard seems to take these points, commenting that it 'hardly occurs to the understanding to want to demonstrate that this unknown (the god) exists'. Living post-Kant, Kierkegaard knows that we cannot prove the existence of God. 'But if he does exist, then it is foolishness to want to demonstrate it, since I, in the very moment the demonstration commences would presuppose it not as doubtful' (39) (i.e. the only possible proof of God is an a priori ontological argument). Nor can one prove God's existence from his works. (Post-Hume, again as Kierkegaard knew full well, the argument from design falls and in any case Lutheran thought moves not from works to person, but from person to works.) Kierkegaard adds that it does not help 'to demonstrate that the unknown, which exists, is the god', for this is simply to develop the definition of a concept. (But one might comment that he has not yet shown that the unknown 'exists'...) One does not, says Kierkegaard, demonstrate the existence of a person from their works; rather the existence explains the works. (Exactly!) In the case of a person, no absolute relation exists between that person and his works, since someone else could have done the works. But in the case of the god an absolute relation pertains: 'God is not a name but a concept' (41). In classical theology one might say (and Kierkegaard refers to a statement in Spinoza) it is of the essence of God to exist.

But what are the works from which I would demonstrate the existence? Living post-Hume as he does, Kierkegaard comments: 'Are the wisdom in nature and the goodness or wisdom in Governance right in front of our noses? Do we not encounter the most terrible spiritual trials here' (42). Attempting to demonstrate God's existence from such eventualities I must live on tenterhooks lest something terrible happen, ruining my fragment of demonstration. How then 'does the existence of the god emerge from the demonstration?' (42).

Is it not here as it is with the Cartesian dolls [a toy]. As soon as I let go of the doll, it stands on its head. As soon as I let go of it—consequently, I have to let go... So also with the demonstration—so long as I am holding onto [it]... the existence does not emerge.... Yet this letting go, even that is surely something; it is... *meine Zutat* [German: that which I add]. Does it not have to be taken into account... It is a *leap* (42–3).

So faith is a leap, one that we take. Yet what an 'act', for precisely we let go (we trust). The existence (the recognition that this is the God presumably), says Kierkegaard, emerges from the leap (43). It would be good to think this through in relation to Luther's statement at the opening of his 'Greater Catechism', of which minimally from his catechetical training Kierkegaard was surely aware, where Luther asks (in relation to the Ten Commandments) 'What is it to have a God?' responding that to have a God is to trust in him; that in which I trust, says Luther, is my god.[18] It is a very 'subjective' statement as to how it is that we 'have a God'—in a tradition one might say that is to lead straight to Feuerbach! So perhaps we are not after all exactly hypostasizing God *qua* entity. But if that is the case one might well enquire (à la Feuerbach) how come it is not that God is a figment of the imagination?

There follows a discussion of this liminality between the understanding and the unknown. 'The paradoxical passion of the understanding is... continually colliding with this unknown, which certainly does

---

[18] R. H. Fischer, trans., *The Large Catechism of Luther*, WA 30, I. 133.1–134.6 (Philadelphia, PA, 1959), 9 [1529].

exist [in that the unknown exists] but is also unknown and to that
extent does not exist' (43). (Still illegitimate, so it would seem.) Kierkegaard comments that the understanding does not go beyond this; yet it
cannot stop reaching it and becoming engaged. The difference between
God and the human cannot be grasped. Every time one attempts it
there is an arbitrariness. (Exactly! Kierkegaard and I are on the same
page. One may add that there is in the Lutheran Reformation background a strong strain of recognition that left to itself the imagination
will manufacture its own gods; a Hebraic sense of idolatry. What is
actually 'God' lies beyond our conceptualization.)

So then: there exists a certain person (i.e. Christ, whose name
remains unmentioned) who looks like any other.

This human being is also the god. How do I know that? Well, I cannot know
it, for in that case I would have to know the god and the difference, and I do
not know the difference, inasmuch as the understanding has made it like
unto that from which it differs (45–6).

I encounter this man as though encountering (simply) a human
being. 'Just to come to know that the god is the different, man
needs the god' (46). In what does the difference, an absolute difference, consist? Sin. What was it Socrates lacked? The consciousness of
sin. (An astute comment on a fundamental difference between Greek
thought and Christian tradition.) 'Only the god could teach it', says
Kierkegaard; 'if he wanted to be a teacher.' So the teacher must bring
to prominence that absolute difference which is sin, wishing also to
annul this difference in equality.

The understanding objects. Yet it is also that in its paradoxical
passion it wills its own downfall. The Paradox likewise wills this
downfall of the understanding. (The ultimate anti-humanist position
one could take.) Thus the two are united in a mutual understanding.
But this 'understanding' is present only in the moment of passion
(48). As a metaphor for what he is saying Kierkegaard turns to erotic
love (as conceived of from a male perspective).

Self-love lies at the basis of love, but at its peak its paradoxical passion
wills its own downfall. Why then should the lover not be able to think this,
even though the person who in self-love shrinks from erotic love can
neither comprehend it nor dare to venture it, since it is indeed his
downfall (48).

Appendix: 'Offence at the Paradox (an acoustical illusion)'

There are two ways in which the understanding can encounter the
Paradox: that 'happy passion' (which Kierkegaard will later name
faith) and that unhappy encounter which is offence, comparable to
unhappy love.

Even when it thrusts down the object of love, even when it self-tormentingly
disciplines itself to callous indifference and tortures itself in order to show
indifference, even when it indulges in triumphant frivolousness over success
in doing this (this form is the most deceptive)—even then it is suffering (49).

Is that right? In a secular age like today? Are not many indifferent?[19]
The Lutheran sensibility is certainly the biblical sense that (like
Jonah) the human cannot escape his situation *coram deo*, before the
face of God, while in his desire for independence he restlessly
attempts to stand his own ground.[20]

No matter if the offended one is sitting crushed and staring almost like a
beggar at the Paradox, petrifying in his suffering, or even if he arms himself
with mockery and aims the arrows of his wit as if from a distance—he is
nevertheless suffering and is not at a distance (50).

Again, is this so today?

Thus we arrive at the statement, pregnant in all that has been said,
that the truth that is 'B' is *index sui et falsi* (the criterion of itself and
of the false). That is to say God's self-revelation is the truth, casting
into a position of untruth (of sin) that which is other than itself. This
is precisely the Lutheran dispensation. Far from being a *fulfilment* of
what preceded it (and thus unlike the Catholic dispensation in which
grace transforms nature), the relation to Christianity, following as it
does upon revelation, casts the natural man into a position that had
best be named sin. (In biblical terms, it is only in the light of his
recognition that this is the Christ—revelation—that Peter says
'depart from me for I am a sinful man', Luke 5.8.) Kierkegaard
comments that, though it might look as if the offence derived from
the Paradox (the God/man), the understanding taking offence at
what it cannot understand; in fact, arising from the human, it has
rebounded from the Paradox creating an acoustical illusion. Offence

---

[19] Cf. pp. 243, 250.   [20] Cf. pp. 243.

is 'the conclusion of untruth, with which the Paradox thrusts away'. (So we have some kind of blackmail, any humanist position or denial of the Paradox becoming a judgement on oneself?)

Recapitulating the position reached:

If we do not assume the moment then we go back to Socrates; and it was precisely from him that we wanted to take leave in order to discover something. If the moment is posited [the departure from 'A'] the Paradox is there, for in its most abbreviated form the Paradox can be called the moment. Through the moment, the learner becomes untruth; the person who knew himself becomes confused about himself and instead of self-knowledge he acquires the consciousness of sin etc., for just as soon as we assume the moment, everything [follows] (51).

'Offence' is the contention that there exists nothing but 'A'. From the Socratic viewpoint, the moment 'does not exist, has not been, and will not come'. Picking up on 1 Cor. 1.23, Kierkegaard comments that to such a one 'the moment of decision is *foolishness*' (52). The Paradox's claim that it is human understanding that is the absurd resounds as an echo in offence at the Paradox.

Kierkegaard flings a final barbed comment at Hegelianism.

When the understanding wants to have pity upon the Paradox and assist it to an explanation, the Paradox does not put up with that but considers it appropriate for the understanding to do that, for is that not what philosophers are for—to make supernatural things ordinary and trivial? (53).

In that happy passion (which is faith) the difference is on good terms with the understanding. It is not that the understanding comprehends the Paradox, but it understands that this is the Paradox. The difference is necessary in order to be united in some third (a somewhat Hegelian move!). The understanding surrenders itself while the Paradox bestows itself ('*halb zog sie ihn, halb sank er hin*': German, literally half dragged she him, half sank he thither).

Chapter IV. The Case of the Contemporary Disciple

By 'contemporary' is to be understood the one who lives contemporaneously with the God.

So the god has made his appearance as a Teacher in the form of a servant. The god's presence is not incidental to the teaching: it *is* the teaching. He must make himself known. How shall he do this; for that to which he would alert the learner is the difference—that this human is furthermore the god. Were the learner to *learn* something, we should have returned to the Socratic. The appearance of the God is 'the news of the day' (58). (We shall have something to say of this in the Critique.) For the true learner 'it is the eternal, the beginning of eternity' (58). The god providing the condition, the historical becomes the point of departure for the learner's 'eternal consciousness' (58). (Compare Lessing's scepticism on this point.) The learner comes to an 'understanding' with the Paradox when, in the moment, 'the understanding steps aside and the Paradox [bestows] itself'. Kierkegaard names this happy passion *faith*.

We should note that—as Kierkegaard points out—were a contemporary to follow the Teacher everywhere, documenting all that he does, he is not thereby a disciple. By contrast were a person to arrive on the scene at the last moment his historical ignorance would pose no obstacle to his becoming one. Given that he can observe the teacher, the person whose life falls contemporaneously with that of the god would appear to hold the advantage. But if he 'believes with his eyes' he is in fact deceived, 'for the god cannot be known directly' (63). The form of the teacher is of no importance; were he, meeting him by chance, not to recognize him (a reference to the Emmaus story, Luke 24.13) he would not thereby cease to be a believer. For, as that story tells us, precisely as Kierkegaard would have it: 'The god gave to the disciple the condition that enables him to see him, opening for him the eyes of faith' (Swenson, 80).

Kierkegaard introduces an interlocutor who comments on the action. This interlocutor remarks that it appears, then, that the contemporary is not advantaged? Consider this. In the case of an emperor who celebrates his wedding with great festivities the contemporary who sees the spectacle must be fortunate. But suppose the magnificence is not something to be seen directly. What then does it mean to be a 'contemporary', without the contemporaneity existing in time? Were the chronological contemporary in a later life to appeal to his contemporaneity, saying 'We ate and drank in your presence, and you taught in our streets', the god will respond 'I tell you, I do not know where you come from; depart from me, all you workers of iniquity!' (cf. Luke 13.26–7). But of the one who comes later as, equally, of the chronological contemporary who receiving the condition from the God believes, we must say that 'he is a contemporary, a genuine contemporary—which indeed only the believer is and which every believer is' (69).

Interlude

Kierkegaard distinguishes between truth (presumed changeless) and historicity.[21] What, then, would it mean for the changeless to come into being? [The incarnation.]

Hegel believes that the necessary must actualize itself, come into being; consequently, no distinction is to be made between that which exists and the real. Kierkegaard profoundly disagrees, thinking such a proposition to undermine freedom. The incarnation is an act of God freely undertaken on account of his love for humankind. Kierkegaard remarks: 'Nothing whatever comes into existence by way of necessity' (74). (This is a strange comment if Kierkegaard intends it in relation to the *physical* universe, meaning that God is behind every event in such a way that there is no necessity that events conform to the causal nexus, as we shall consider.) And further: 'The actual is no more necessary than the possible' (75). (That of course is fine in relation to *human actions*, in that, contra Hegel, there is no reason for that which is possible necessarily to come into being.) As Kierkegaard says: 'The change of coming into existence is actuality; the transition takes place in freedom' (75). Coming into existence represents the change, taking place in freedom, of coming into actuality (77). Hegel is mistaken in contending that history is the concretion of the Idea (with its apparent determinism).

But asks Kierkegaard (in view of the proposition that truth is changeless) when change is involved how can we be said to have *knowledge*; that is to say knowledge of a *coming into being*? (Note that this discussion actually goes back to Parmenides, early 5th century BC, who thought that either a thing is or it is not; thus a thing cannot be understood to come to be, the implication of holding that the real is changeless.) Kierkegaard takes as read that 'immediate sensation and immediate cognition cannot deceive' (81). But, he says, 'the historical intrinsically has the *illusiveness* of coming into existence, it cannot be sensed

---

[21] For the background to this distinction see p. 15.

directly and immediately' (81). He picks up the distinction in Aristotle between a 'change' which consists in a coming into existence (*kinesis*) and a change which presupposes existence (*alloiosis*) (what we might call a change taking place within the causal nexus). The first of these is a change from non-being to being (whereas the second is not). Now, given the definition of God as eternal, there is a problem: 'It is... the perfection of the eternal to have no history and of all that is, only the eternal has absolutely no history' (76). We would appear to be in a fix and this on two counts: how can one have knowledge of coming into existence; besides which the eternal is changeless, does not come into being.

Kierkegaard takes an example. The perceiver sees a star. (That presents no problem: he has an immediate sensation and so cognition.) However, 'the star becomes dubious for him the moment he seeks to become aware that it has come into existence' (81). (We should recall the 19th-century context; there being no conception that a star is formed from intergalactic dust, nor indeed that energy is interchangeable with matter, the star has apparently 'come into being'.) The organ for the historical, says Kierkegaard, must correlate to the historical: it 'must have within itself the corresponding something by which in its certitude it continually annuls the incertitude that corresponds to the uncertainty of coming into existence' (81). Now this is the nature of *tro* (Danish trust—i.e. faith or belief indifferently). *Tro* is other than knowledge. 'Trust/belief believes what it does not see; it does not trust/believe that the star exists for that it sees, but it trusts/believes that the star has come into existence' (81; my alteration for clarity).

Kierkegaard now contends that we relate to *every* event in this way, remarking: 'Immediate sense perception and cognition do not have any intimation of the unsureness with which belief approaches its object, but neither do they have the certitude that extricates itself from the incertitude' (82). This to modern ears must be astonishing: we relate to *any* event with *tro*, *tro* having about it a certitude that allows of an extrication from the incertitude attached to change. (Incidentally, there would appear to have been little point in initially drawing attention to Aristotle's distinction between the change that is a coming into existence and change that presupposes existence?) I shall return to this in the Critique.

The Greek sceptic *willed* to doubt. 'Belief is not a knowledge but an act of freedom, an expression of will' (83). The contemporary to an event 'cannot *know* immediately and directly that it has come into existence... for the first mark of coming into existence is... a break in continuity'. (83–4, emphasis mine). 'The conclusion of belief is no conclusion but [rather] a resolution and thus doubt is excluded' (84). Belief and doubt are not two kinds of knowledge, for neither is a cognitive act; they are 'opposite passions'. Belief is 'a sense for coming into existence', while doubt 'a protest against any conclusion that wants to go beyond immediate sensation and immediate knowledge' (84). Of the person whose life is not contemporaneous with the historical event we may say that he has the report of contemporaries (85). Both generations alike must relate to the event through *tro*.

APPENDIX

Kierkegaard rules out the Hegelian dialectic, whereby an apparent contradiction can be *aufgehoben*, raised to a higher level, having in itself the power to produce a third thereby resolving the contradiction. He affirms that a paradox is indeed a paradox. He continues that a distinction is to be made. What has been said in the 'Interlude' pertains to normal historical facts. However in relation to the idea of the eternal coming into being one must say that it 'has a unique quality in that it is not a direct historical fact but a fact based upon a self-contradiction' (87). It follows that, to a heightened degree, no distinction is to be made between the situation of the person who is contemporary to the event and the person who comes later; for one is 'face to face with a self-contradiction and the risk entailed in assenting to it'. It is 'a historical fact, but only for faith'. Here faith (*tro*) is to be understood in the first instance in its ordinary sense as pertaining to the relation to any historical fact; but secondly it 'must be taken in [a] wholly eminent sense' (87). One does not have *faith* that the God *exists* (that is to say eternally); that would be a wrong use of language. Socrates did not have *faith* that the god *existed*; 'what he *knew* about the god he attained by recollection and for him the existence of the god was by no means something historical' (87, my emphases). However, in the case of the god coming into existence, no one can in the immediate sense be contemporary with this historical fact: 'Because it involves coming into existence it is the object of faith.... It is not a question here of the *truth* of it but of assenting to the god's *having come into existence* (87).[22] Such a historical fact is historical to the first power, requiring faith in the ordinary sense; and furthermore to the second power since it is based on a contradiction requiring faith in the eminent sense.

Chapter V. The Disciple at Second Hand

Consider then the present-day disciple (the disciple at second hand).

The contemporary disciple 'saw a human being in a lowly form who said of himself that he was the god' (93). So—according to Kierkegaard—he has been given the jolt. The decision remains to be taken as to whether he will believe.

Of later generations, it could be said that they are advantaged in being able to consider the far-reaching consequences of the appearance of the god. What stands to their disadvantage is that the essence of that which is to be related to becomes dimmed. Kierkegaard believes his generation to have lost all sense of what is at stake.

> Or is not Venice built over the sea, even if it became so solidly built up that a generation finally came upon the scene that did not notice it; and would it not be a sad misunderstanding if this last generation made the mistake of permitting the piles to rot and the city to sink? But consequences founded on a paradox are humanly speaking built over a yawning chasm and their total content, which can be transmitted to the individual only with the express understanding that they rest upon a paradox, are not to be appropriated as a settled estate for their entire value trembles in the balance (Swenson, 123).

Observing the consequences for world history (as do Hegelians), this later generation fails to comprehend that that which is to be believed is built over an abyss (is in itself a Paradox).

Every succeeding generation is placed in like situation as is the contemporary: 'The absolute fact is a historical fact and as such the object of faith' (100). Just as his presence to the historical event becomes the occasion for the contemporary to become a follower 'by receiving the condition, please note, from the god himself (for otherwise we speak Socratically)', so the report of this event by contemporaries is the occasion for those who later become followers

---

[22] We see how misleading is for example Murray Rae's speaking of 'knowledge [*sic*] [which] is acquired in the moment of faith' (*Kierkegaard's Vision of the Incarnation*, Oxford, 1997, 61).

'by receiving the condition, please note, from the god himself' (100). Were it to be that the contemporary gave the condition (as one might contend pertains in Catholicism) to the one who came later, it would follow that the latter would come to believe in the contemporary! (Thus any belief via the church is ruled out.) 'One human being, in so far as he is a believer, is not indebted to someone else for something but is indebted to the god for everything' (101–2).

What, then, may a contemporary do for one who will come later? He can leave record that he himself has believed. He should say: 'I believe and have believed that this happened, although it is folly to the understanding and an offence to the human heart' (cf. 1 Cor. 1.23). In that way he prevents others from making up their minds on account of his belief. Further, he can report the content of the matter: 'the historical fact that the god has been in human form' (103). Other historical details are of nil importance. Had the contemporary generation recorded no more than that 'we have believed that in such and such a year the god appeared in the humble form of a servant, lived and taught among us, and then died', this would suffice (104). Indeed, the New Testament (which Kierkegaard does not refer to by name) suggests it to be to the disciples' advantage that the god depart (John 16.7). If the one who comes later understands himself 'he must wish the contemporary's report to be not too prolix and above all not to be couched in so many books that they could fill the whole world' (cf. John 21.25) (106).

All human beings are in the same situation: 'the god himself is the reconciler' (106). Would he put some human beings at an advantage? That would indeed bring conflict. Christianity, comments Kierkegaard, is the only historical phenomenon which, in being historical, has made the historical the individual's point of departure for his eternal consciousness. (In the terms that I shall discuss this, Christianity is grounded in the wager that there has occurred a particularity in history.) Kierkegaard comments: 'No philosophy (for it is only for thought), no mythology (for it is only for the imagination), no historical knowledge (which is for memory) has ever had this idea— of which . . . one can say . . . that it did not arise in any human heart' (cf. 1 Cor. 2.7–9) (109). (Kierkegaard thus implies that, that this man is the god, has been made known by revelation and is not simply a human projection.)

MORAL

Kierkegaard sums up.

> The projected hypothesis indisputably makes an advance upon Socrates, which is apparent at every point. Whether it is therefore more true than the Socratic doctrine is an entirely different question, which cannot be decided in the same breath, since we have here assumed a new organ: Faith; a new presupposition: the consciousness of Sin; a new decision: the Moment; and a new Teacher: the God in Time. Without these I certainly never would have dared present myself for inspection before that master of Irony, admired through the centuries, whom I approach with a palpitating enthusiasm that yields to none. But to make an advance upon Socrates and yet say essentially the same things as he, only not nearly so well—that at least is not Socratic (Swenson, 139).

The book is an experiment in thought: a projected hypothesis. In one sense, clearly, it makes 'an advance' upon the Socratic, this being apparent at every point: the Teacher is other than the Socratic teacher, and so forth. Whether, however, the 'advance' in which 'B' consists is *more true* than the Socratic must be an entirely different question, not to be decided in the same breath, since we have enlisted quite other assumptions (which can be expressed in different ways, mutually implying one another—a new organ, faith, and so forth). Were it not that he, the author of *Fragments*, had moved into a new key, speaking of something essentially at variance with the Socratic, he would never have dared present himself before Socrates. Socrates would have held it mere twaddle had someone (Hegel/Martensen) thought that an 'advance' could be made upon the Socratic while remaining with the Socratic presuppositions—meanwhile saying these things not nearly so well.

Critique

Kierkegaard's Christology

We have already touched on the fact that given that he lives in modernity, willy-nilly Kierkegaard's 'Christ' may well not be the Christ of Chalcedon. What it would seem important to consider here is the philosophical context within which classical Christology was formulated, what it enabled the Fathers to say, and what sense it lent to their definitions. That context was the universalism of Neoplatonism. That is to say the universal was accorded a greater reality than the particular example of it; whereas living as we do after the rise of Nominalism in the late Middle Ages, doubting the existence of universals in the ancient sense, we think that the real is what they would have called the particular example of that universal. In attempting to convey the concept of 'real universals' I cannot do better than repeat the example through which (in its implications for Christology) it was explained by the late Donald MacKinnon in a seminar I attended. Consider shirts on a washing line. Some are pink and some are blue, some have pockets and some do not. But they all participate in what we may call 'shirtness' (what it is to be a shirt): the universal.

The implications for Christology are considerable. If what is being said by the Fathers is that in the incarnation God in Christ took on 'humanity' and by 'humanity' is intended a universal, then all other examples of that universal (ourselves) participate in what has been taken on by God in Christ. It is important to be clear here. It is not being said that in taking on the universal, humanity, God in Christ became some kind of general (or umbrella) concept that harbours all of us. To conform to the universal there must be a particular example of it (a shirt has to have a colour and have or not have pockets). But one is not deifying the colour and the pockets. Other shirts equally exemplify shirtness and are in all cases related to the first one *qua* shirt, though in their particularities they may differ. In thinking about what difference this makes, consider for example how reality looks to Gregory of Nyssa (d. 385/6), the man often credited with being the architect of the doctrine of the trinity. In his tract 'On Not Saying that there are Three Gods'[23] Gregory instances Peter, James, and John as three exemplifications of what it is to be 'human'; that is to say as holding a common *ousia* or nature, the universal. Thus the argument goes that in parallel with what it is to be 'human' there are not three gods. By contrast we would surely tend to employ this example

[23] E. R. Hardy & C. C. Richardson, eds, 'That We Should Not Think of Saying There Are Three Gods', *Christology of the Later Fathers* [vol. 3, *Library of Christian Classics*] (London and Philadelphia, PA, 1954), 256–67.

to exactly the opposite effect: the three people would indicate a threeness.

Given that Kierkegaard is thinking within the context of modernity, his Christ must look very different from that of Chalcedon and this in two respects. What Kierkegaard takes as his presupposition as to what it is that Christianity contends is that in one *persona* Christ is in two natures, human and divine. But firstly it must be said that if the concept of universals—lending the possibility that both we and Christ having a nature shared in common participate in the universal 'humanity'—falls away, Kierkegaard's Christ could be thought to become a lone figure. Again it makes much less sense naturally today to hold that, through participating in our nature, Christ raises us up to his divinity. Christ becomes a somewhat extraordinary being, one of a kind. This is not to say that earlier Christians did not believe in the uniqueness of Christ, they did. But the emphasis is different. Secondly it must be said that, with what Max Weber termed the 'disenchantment' of the world in modernity, such that people are seen as a whole person rather than a synthesis of physicality with the spiritual, this divine Christ sticks up like a sore thumb in a world otherwise devoid of divinity.

Now Kierkegaard of course knows very well that Christian doctrine is not that one man 'is' God, or should we say 'a god', collapsing the two natures into one. That would be paganism. As he well says, referring to a German children's story widely known in Denmark, Christ is not 'a divine Mr. Goodman'[24] (*PC*, 36). Nevertheless he cannot but give the impression, so alien as a possibility to modernity, that this man and he alone is God. The lack of a Trinitarian sense in Kierkegaard (who, as is Luther, is deeply Christocentric) only reinforces this impression. Gregory tells us that the trinity resembles a chain; if you draw on one link you bring the others with it.[25] By contrast Kierkegaard's book is entirely taken up with this man, who is God. Of course Christians have ever proclaimed the truth of that which the Greeks deem foolishness (1 Cor. 1.23). Nevertheless the way in which Christ's singularity is accentuated by Kierkegaard, in a modernity which knows of no examples unique in kind, makes Christ

---

[24] An English rendering of the Danish 'Godmand'; Lowrie has 'Uncle George'.
[25] 'On the Difference between Ousia and Hypostasis', in Maurice Wiles & Mark Santer, eds, *Documents in Early Christian Thought* (Cambridge, 1975), 43.

an oddity in a way in which this was less evidently so of the original doctrine. In the midst of a crowd this man alone—did one but know it, for he appears just like any other—is possessed of a second and divine nature.

We should dwell a little longer on the difficulty that arises for Christology with the Enlightenment and the rise of Romanticism. When one has come to have a modern sense of subjectivity and what it is to be a unique individual it becomes all the more surprising to say of one individual that in a second nature he is God. It may well be thought that the reason why kenotic Christology came into vogue in the 19th century was precisely because people could no longer envisage what it could mean to say that this man had a consciousness of himself as being God; a consciousness quite other than that of which the rest of us are possessed. (Kenotic Christology, predicated on the *kenosis* or self-emptying of Christ, cf. Phil. 2.8 where this word is used, seeks to explain how one who was God could become human and thus for example not omniscient.) At the start of the century, judging that these Greek concepts no longer made sense to his contemporaries, Schleiermacher is already abandoning the classical Christian categories of 'substance' and 'nature', attempting to express Christ's uniqueness in other ways. Thus he speaks in terms of Christ's self-awareness as a person, one of ourselves, however, in Christ's case having a 'unique' because unclouded consciousness of God.

Thus it should not be lost sight of that it is in the midst of modernity and subsequent at least to Schleiermacher that Kierkegaard attempts to resurrect a traditional Christology. Yet he can no longer say what in effect a patristic author would say, for the philosophical context lacks. Meanwhile to state a patristic doctrine within modernity conveys a different message, jarring with the culture, in a way that this was not necessarily true of the original.

Kierkegaard and Biblical Criticism

Kierkegaard clearly aims to have advanced a position that is not vulnerable to being undermined by historical and textual criticism of the biblical documents. One believes in Christ through faith. Historical details about the god, so we are told, are of even less importance than were we concerned with one who was simply a historical individual. Kierkegaard's position is further assured by the contention that it is only as the god gives the condition that the eyes of the believer are opened. At the same time it is clear that he has a fairly literal view of the biblical text, supposing it to be historically accurate in a way that few who have been through the mill of historical and textual criticism could hold today. How he compares with his contemporaries in general in this regard it is not for me to judge. But it is clear that among those contemporaries there were some who were beginning to supply a historical contextualization to the biblical documents with which Kierkegaard did not really want to come to terms. As I have mentioned, astonishingly there is no evidence that he either owned or read Strauss's famous book.[26] Such an omission—on the part of a reader as voracious as Kierkegaard—must be striking.

We have fascinating historical insights in this regard from a few years subsequent to the writing of *Fragments*. Kierkegaard was well acquainted with a distant relative, Hans Brøchner, seven years younger than he, who was the translator into Danish of the later work of Strauss. The two would take walks together. After Kierkegaard's death Brøchner committed his memories of their conversations to paper. Brøchner records:

Once, in 1851 I believe, [Kierkegaard] asked me what I was working on at the moment. I replied that I was reading the New Testament. That seemed to please him, but it did not please him when I added that I was reading it mostly with this end in view: to find primitive Christianity in the received texts and follow the successive development of the Christian dogmatic concepts. To him such an investigation bordered on the offensive. Although he deals so little with dogma in his writings and adheres everywhere to what is central to Christianity, he was nonetheless unable to relate himself to the Scriptures in such a way that they became the object of critical investigations. He could not do this in part because the Scriptures were to him a whole, an integral expression of Christianity into which he would not introduce any distinctions and in part because when made the object of scholarly investigation the Scriptures became an object of knowledge rather an object of faith.[27]

And again:

---

[26] Cf. N. H. Søe, 'Christ', in Niels Thulstrup & Marie Mikulová Thulstrup, eds, *Theological Conceptions in Kierkegaard* [vol. 5, *Bibliotheca Kierkegaardiana*], 55.
[27] Bruce Kirmmse, *Encounters*, no. 40, 243.

I expressed my conviction that a great many people read his writing with genuine seriousness and that the silence of our press, which I more or less interpreted as the critics' sense that the works were beyond their powers of criticism, was by no means a sign that he had encountered indifference among the wider public among whom I believed he had already had significant influence. But I added that, with respect to attitudes toward Christianity, the effect had been just as much negative as positive.... His definition of Christianity was just the sort that might perhaps repel many people from it. Such had been the case with me and it was capable of doing so precisely because of the separation it proposed between Christianity [on the one hand] and nature and concrete human life [on the other].... He became serious, gave me his hand in silence and left me [they were about to part] but with a kind look on his face.[28]

And yet again: 'I once spoke quite zealously about how no positive religion [i.e. religion based on historical claims] could be tolerant, precisely because, with its claim to be revealed religion, it must insist that it is the only true religion, and it would have to consign the others to untruth.' Brøchner had repeated the phrase 'in general', saying that a positive religion 'in general' (i.e. as a universal religion) is a non-entity. Kierkegaard responds: 'Yes, and so is a chamberpot in general!'[29]

What one has to say is that these snippets of conversation give evidence of a real inability on Kierkegaard's part to come to terms with what was afoot. He will not enter into a consideration of the questions that the young Brøchner (aged 31 in 1851) is pondering. Kierkegaard stops the conversation short, is displeased, or evades the issue with a witty (but irrelevant) remark. Brøchner and others are asking uncomfortable questions as to the basis on which Christian doctrine might be built. In Brøchner's case there has furthermore arisen a moral problem about the exclusivity of Christian claims following from its claim to particularity. Kierkegaard seems obtuse. Brøchner can neither epistemologically allow the proposed separation between nature (how the natural world otherwise is) and Christian belief, nor ethically the fact that a positive, historical, religion consigns others to being outsiders, is intolerant. Kierkegaard is clarifying for him and others what it is that Christianity entails and the effect is 'just as much negative as positive'. Brøchner's personal story

[28] Kirmmse, *Encounters*, no. 42, 244.
[29] Kirmmse, *Encounters*, no. 41, 243–4.

is that, unable on account of conclusions he had reached to take his qualifying examinations in theology, he became instead a professor of philosophy.

What are the caveats in Kierkegaard's position? In the first place one should note that Kierkegaard's Christological polemic is grounded in the presupposition that Jesus of Nazareth stood there and (in however ambivalent a manner) proclaimed himself God. In an unpublished work, *Johannes Climacus*, probably written in late 1842 and early 1843 (thus a year previous to *Fragments*) Kierkegaard remarks: 'Unless it were assumed that it makes no difference whether it was Christ who declared that he was God's Son...' (*JC*, 151), implying thus that he thought Christ did indeed declare this. But such a proposition must seem most unlikely. A generation before Kierkegaard, Schleiermacher had thought John's gospel the earliest on account of the great dialogues in its central chapters. Today it must be a rare scholar who considers that the words attributed to Christ as he speaks of his relationship to his Father are reports that came from the mouth of the historical Jesus. Rather is that gospel a meditation on the significance of Christ that arose from the belief of the early church. But such a conclusion undermines the foundation of Kierkegaard's position.

Secondly Kierkegaard fails to take account of the *Weltanschauung*, or world picture, of the context in which the gospels were written. The significance of this difference in *Weltanschauung* was brought to attention in particular through the work in the mid-20th century of the New Testament scholar Rudolf Bultmann. Kierkegaard writes as though contemporaries of Jesus simply reported on what they witnessed, no account being taken of the fact that they 'saw' what they did with pre-modern eyes. Consider the different sense of reality to ours which in the patristic period Origen displays in pointing to other instances of virgin birth in nature and purportedly among humans in contending for the virgin birth of Christ, or Augustine in citing other instances known to him of a miraculous bringing back to life following death.[30] In one sense Kierkegaard is cognizant that there is a disparity between what is recorded and what possible. Of miracles, he comments that bystanders would be likely to ask the conjuror to do the trick again that they might the better see how it was done (69–70). But

---

[30] Origen, *Against Celsus* I, 37; Augustine, *The City of God*, XXII, 8, 8 (trans. H. Bettenson, Harmondsworth, 1972, pp. 1042–3).

his presupposition is clearly that a miracle did indeed take place. Miracles play the vital role for Kierkegaard of alerting the contemporary that something is afoot.[31] Presumably we should today put a rather different interpretation on what transpired.

Finally, there is no recognition on Kierkegaard's part that, given that the gospels are in effect faith statements that arose in the early church, they are a different genre of literature than simply eyewitness accounts. Kierkegaard writes: 'When a freethinker applies all his acumen to prove that the New Testament was not written until the 2nd century, it is precisely inwardness he is afraid of and therefore he must have the New Testament placed in the same class with other books.'[32] But this is unfair. One is not necessarily avoiding 'inwardness' because one tries to arrive at the truth of the matter. The boot is on the other foot: it is rather that Kierkegaard is evading what in his day and age is becoming evident, with its startling implications for Christian faith. Scholars now take for granted this difference in genre; that the ultimate chapter of John's gospel is full of magic numbers, that the feeding of the five thousand is a play on the eschatological feast which according to Jewish midrash will take place at the end of time, and so forth. The gospels are not straight historical reportage. In the ancient world less distinction would have been made between fact and embellishment than in ours.

Of course Kierkegaard can respond, as in the face of such critique he surely would, by declaring the biblical documents inspired. But as he well understood (as we shall discuss in conjunction with *Postscript*) this is simply to pass the buck, for then one has to have faith that the bible is inspired! Such a move is of no avail. Again one might well say that Kierkegaard is but conducting an experiment in thought: what is it that one would have to say that one might escape the presuppositions of modernity? Again, that the book was published under a pseudonym. But these responses are beside the point. If it comes to be comprehensible how, over a period of time and within a certain cultural context, the belief could have arisen that this

---

[31] Cf. 'Mynster [in his sermon] ... put up a strong argument against something I also take issue with—naturalism! "Unfortunately we know far too well what people in our day think of miracles."' *JP* VI 6692 (*Pap.* X³ A 564), n.d., 1850.
[32] Reidar Thomte, ed. & trans., *The Concept Angst* (Princeton, NJ, 1980), 142–3 (henceforth *CA*, 142–3 etc.).

man in a second nature in one *persona* was the second person of a triune God, it becomes not very sensible to undertake a wager of faith that this is the case, nor is there reason to pen such a book as Kierkegaard's. Indeed, the Christian contention may come to seem so improbable that one thinks no further of it (presumably where a large majority of the population of secular Europe stands today). Kierkegaard's contention, indeed Christian dogma, is a castle built on insecure foundations indeed.

Causality and Particularity

If we are to comprehend Kierkegaard's Christology we must consider his epistemology. We can best do this by tackling the opaque 'Interlude', which turns out to be opaque largely because Kierkegaard is working with something other than modern presuppositions. That Kierkegaard thinks in this way gains the importance that it does as his epistemology lends support to his Christological contentions. If today we think very differently about reality such support falls away.

Thinking in terms of 'coming into existence' (as, we may say, do either Aristotle or Hegel) Kierkegaard writes: 'Everything which comes into existence proves precisely by coming into existence that it is not necessary'. This is non-problematic: by 'not necessary' here Kierkegaard means contingent, as opposed to God who would be considered 'necessary'. (We have already mentioned in conjunction with the discussion of 18th-century thought the distinction between that which is eternal and necessary and that which is historical and contingent).[33] Kierkegaard is here challenging Hegel and we may think perfectly rightly. Hegel believes that 'possibility' will axiomatically bear fruit in 'actuality', in history (come into being). This is indeed a kind of determinism. Kierkegaard contends that in coming into existence the contingent precisely proves that it is not necessary (in the sense that God is necessary). He proceeds to allude to Aristotle's distinction between a coming into being *ab initio*, which Aristotle names *kinesis*, and change taking place within that which already exists (what we should call change within the causal nexus), which Aristotle names *alloiosis*. Again this is fine. Kierkegaard's

---

[33] See p. 15.

example of the *first* kind of change is the star coming into being; an example which, given Kierkegaard's 19th-century context, would be an obvious example. (We should see this as representing the *second* kind of change, given that we now know stars to form from interstellar gas clouds.)

Now, says Kierkegaard, in relation to the *first* kind of change (the coming into being *ab initio* of the star) we must exercise *tro*, Danish trust, belief, or faith). Immediately a question arises for us as to whether there are indeed examples of the kind of change which consists in a 'coming into being' *ab initio*. Perhaps the beginning of the universe itself alone exemplifies the category; though in this case also we learn from astronomers that it is perhaps 'thinkable' as having occurred through a quantum fluctuation. But we may comprehend Kierkegaard. Now however a problem arises. Kierkegaard makes what is a wholly unjustified elision, one would have thought also for others in his day and age. He says that *tro* is needed in relation to *any* kind of change, thus also changes that occur within what I have called the causal nexus, the type of change that Aristotle names *alloiosis* which occurs within what already exists. Now it would of course be possible to say that God is the power behind all and thus behind all change taking place within the universe, whether I push my pencil off my desk or water changes into ice. But for us such change takes place within a causal nexus; not, as we shall see, the terms in which Kierkegaard is thinking. We are already alerted that something strange is afoot through the fact that he does not appreciate that there is any real distinction between the two kinds of 'change'. All change for him is in effect as the star's coming into being.

It transpires that Kierkegaard, writing in the 1840s, 150 years after Newton, has actually little sense of the regularity with which change takes place in predetermined fashion within a causal nexus. (When I use the word predetermined here I do not of course mean that changes have to take place, that there is no free will, but if I choose to push my pencil off the desk it will fall according to the law of gravity.) To say that change takes place within a causal nexus is of course not to say that any particular change will take place; Kierkegaard is surely right here against Hegel. Nor is it to say that we do not need to exercise 'trust' in relation to the belief that an action took place in the past. We might discover that there was no such man as Alexander who conquered half of Asia (Lessing's example). But if there *was* such a man who did so, then he had to mount his horse and get it to put one foot in front of the other, which is part of the causal nexus, belonging to the category of mounting one's horse and conquering half of Asia. Here is Kierkegaard writing in *Either/Or*, vol. I:

> Yet... I wanted to say something rather general about the occasion or about the occasion in general. Very fortunately, it so happens that I have already said what I wanted to say, for the more I deliberate on this matter, the more I am convinced that there is nothing general to be said about it, because *there is no occasion in general*. If so, then I have come just about as far as I was when I began. The reader must not be angry with me—it is not my fault; it is the occasion's (*E/O* I, 239, my italics).

Kierkegaard thinks the world a kind of random place in which just about anything can happen, presumably because God is behind each individual action. He lacks a sense for the regularity of nature, that as I have put it things take place according to certain laws within a causal nexus.

There have of course been Kierkegaard scholars who have recognized this (though in general one may say it has been given scant recognition and its implications not thought through). Patrick Sheil writes of 'Kierkegaard's bemusement at the idea of our ever being able to see one event as the certain consequence of another', commenting 'he is terribly puzzled by this idea' and further remarking on Kierkegaard's 'breezy scepticism in the face of all explanation and all attribution of supposed effects in the world as such'.[34] While Robert Perkins tells us, of Kierkegaard:

> The only authors he refers to with approval in epistemological matters are Hume and the Greek sceptics. These several allusions are sufficient to show the preference Kierkegaard has for empiricism as opposed to a Kantian critical idealism.... All objective knowledge for Kierkegaard is empirical, and it is in every sense an approximation.[35]

I am fishing in the dark here, but it would seem that the following is the case. Hume's scepticism was turned upside down by Hamann as compared with what Hume thought were its implications for

[34] Patrick Sheil, *Starting with Kierkegaard* (London, 2011), 19.
[35] Unpublished comments quoted by Stephen Crites, *In the Twilight of Christendom: Hegel vs. Kierkegaard on Faith and History* (Chambersburg, PA, AAR Studies in Religion, 2, 1972), 22, note.

Christianity: Hamann contended that Hume's position allowed a loophole for a Christian like himself to think that, in his transcendence, God could influence causality (or to put it another way, one need not think in terms of any causal nexus and God can intervene in the world at will). Subsequently, Kierkegaard acquired from Hamann such a view of how the world works. Of course, the historical line of development was that Kant countered Hume's scepticism, as Perkins indicates, and in his critical idealism assumes a causal nexus even when we cannot prove it. This strain of thought then feeds into scientific modernity.[36]

And there is yet something else afoot here. Hamann thinks that faith must take precedence over reason, writing: 'Faith is not a work of reason and therefore cannot succumb to any attack by reason; because believing happens as little by means of reasons as tasting and seeing.'[37] Hamann quotes Hume against himself. Hume had written, with irony:

So that, upon the whole, we may conclude that the *Christian religion* not only was at first attended with miracles, but even at this day cannot be believed by any reasonable person without one. Mere reason is insufficient to convince us of its veracity; and whoever is moved by *Faith* to assent to it, is conscious of a continued miracle in his own person, which subverts all the principles of his understanding, and gives him a determination to believe what is most contrary to custom and experience.[38]

---

[36] One is tempted to think that (not unnaturally) causality becomes the more evident as human knowledge increases. Thus Hume, who finds Locke (of an earlier date) wrong in saying that it is 'only probable' that all men will die or that the sun will rise tomorrow, writes: 'Though there be no such thing as Chance in the world; our ignorance of the real cause of any event has the same influence on the understanding, and begets a like species of belief or opinion.' (D. Hume, *An Enquiry Concerning Human Understanding*, ed. P. H. Nidditch & L. A. Selby-Bigge (Oxford, 1975), section VI 'Of Probability', 56.) Yet, arguing that we had best proceed from experience, he comments that 'Adam' could not have known through his rational faculties that water would suffocate him nor fire consume him. 'Nor does any man imagine that the explosion of gunpowder... could ever be discovered by arguments a priori' (Section IV 'Sceptical Doubts concerning the Operations of the Understanding', 27). Indeed, not a priori. But since Hume's time we have so far expanded our knowledge of the causal nexus that it is fully comprehensible to us at a molecular level as to why these things should be the case.

[37] Georg Hamann, *The Memorabilia of Socrates*, ed. & trans. Ronald Gregor Smith, *J. G. Hamann, 1730–1788: a study in Christian existence; with selections from his writings* (London, 1960), 56.

[38] Hume, *Enquiry*, section X 'Of Miracles', 131.

Hamann chose to read this straight, to the effect that indeed there exist such miracles. Kierkegaard finding this in Hamann takes it on board.[39] One can see how this exactly comports with the procedure that he follows in *Philosophical Fragments*: the teacher who is the God not only performs miracles which alert but also provides the condition (a continuous miracle in the disciple's own person) which allows of the disciple's assent. Faith is indeed a kind of miracle, the condition for apprehending the Truth given by God.

Furthermore again, the context in conjunction with which Kierkegaard thought in such a way was what we have already discussed,[40] his belief in figuralism, again acquired from Hamann. It will be good to take this elucidation further. In 19th-century parlance, Kierkegaard is a 'supernaturalist', not a 'naturalist'. He thinks God to have a controlling hand in history (and not either that it is just chaos or that it simply unfolds from within itself). In a world in which as we have already seen he conceives that God is behind every action, significant acts take place in history. (It must be much easier to credit the second of these if one's general view of causality is already the first.) It would seem that such significant acts are held either to repeat in such a way as to magnify, or to undo, previous occurrences. Thus Christ is the 'second' Adam, who undoes the sin of the first. As Julian Roberts comments, the repetition of the figure, representing 'an irruption of the transcendent into the temporal continuum', brings about a genuine newness.[41] In thinking in this manner Kierkegaard is part of a long tradition. In the patristic period it would have been called recapitulation. In the Middle Ages it was held that one could 'read' history backwards ('allegorically') and forwards ('anagogically'). Kierkegaard likewise comments in *Fragments*: 'In our project...everything is forward looking and historical' (Swenson, 121). (For example, presumably the incarnation could be held proleptic of the eschaton.) Again, in *Repetition*, 'The modern view...must seek freedom forward, so that here eternity opens up for him as the true repetition forward'

---

[39] Louis Pojman, *The Logic of Subjectivity: Kierkegaard's Philosophy of Religion* (Tuscaloosa, AL, 1984), 131 suggests Kierkegaard was unaware of its provenance in Hume's scepticism, but Patrick Gardiner, *Kierkegaard* (Oxford, 1988, 77) quotes Kierkegaard commenting on Hamann's attribution of the passage to Hume.
[40] See pp. 29–30.
[41] Julian Roberts, *German Philosophy: An Introduction*, ch. 6, '*Kierkegaard*' (New York, 1988).

(*Repetition*, 317). And in *The Concept Angst*: 'Christ alone is an individual who is more than an individual. For this reason he does not come in the beginning but in the fullness of time' (*CA*, 33, footnote).

What one must say is no more, but also no less, than this. If one thinks in these terms no wonder it becomes 'possible' to conceive that there could be an incarnation. It forms part of what we may call a whole theo-historical belief system. But together, I take it with most 21st-century Europeans, I lack any such. This matter of causality is of course the question of particularity in another guise. If, for Kierkegaard, each happening comes from the hand of God, or can come from the hand of God, there existing no ordered regularity, then it is not difficult to credit that there can be all sorts of one-off happenings which, one of a kind, form no part of a causal nexus. To a person who thinks in such a way the contention that, for example, there can have been no such thing as a resurrection, for there is no category of things 'resurrections', cuts no ice. Again, neither does the contention in relation to incarnation that it could not be that one person and one alone is possessed of a second and divine nature. But once persons start thinking in terms of things as belonging to categories and take for granted that there is a causal nexus, as they did with the dawn of modernity, such a recognition presumably becoming well established subsequent to Newton, then Christians are in problems. If they would be Christian they must proclaim, in some way or another, the uniqueness of Jesus as the Christ (the 'scandal' of particularity). Of course Kierkegaard recognizes that there is this scandal, but he also has a whole epistemology that backs up its possibility.

Finally, it will be helpful here to consider something that I mentioned at the outset. Kierkegaard set up his experiment in thought in terms of the battle with Hegelian idealism. It suited him thus to juxtapose Christ with Socrates (who represents a pure form of idealism, incompatible with Christianity). He can thereby highlight the illegitimacy of the confusion that Hegel's hybrid represents. Given that Plato thinks that proof of the immortality of the soul is to be arrived at through the movement inwards which is recollection (*Phaedo*, 72e ff.), Socratic idealism well represents a position the exact opposite of Christian belief in revelation. But had Socrates not suited his purposes so well Kierkegaard could equally have taken Kant as exemplifying the counter position to Christian revelation. However, the relevance of what Kierkegaard has to say need not be confined to the battle with idealism.

Thus we may usefully cast the issue with which Kierkegaard's book confronts us in more expansive terms. Consider our proverbial person on a desert island and let him be Einstein. Potentially at least he is able (i) to elucidate mathematics, (ii) to discover the laws that pertain to the empirical world, and (iii) to arrive at moral principles and insights. That is to say on model 'A' all knowledge and wisdom, not simply that acquired through 'recollection', but mathematical, empirical, and moral is available to humankind; implicit to human beings, or given with the founding of the world. Now set against this Christian claims. Our islander could know nothing of such 'Truths' unless a missionary were to arrive. It was this that Kant understood exactly in proclaiming Christianity a 'historical', 'positive' religion. Christian 'Truth' is quite unlike anything that our islander could come to conclude for himself. As Kierkegaard recognized, Christianity is predicated upon revelation, given to humankind at a moment in time. Equally it is in the moment that our islander, learning of the good news, is confronted with the question as to whether he will believe (in the face of reason). At the end of the day the issue is that as to whether we think there could be any such eventuality (that is to say whether anything other than 'A' could possibly be).

The implications of 'B' (that is to say in Kierkegaard's terms any departure from 'A') being correct are of course extraordinary. In the first place we have introduced a thoroughgoing heteronomy, which many will think morally dubious. As the human being looks to Christ rather than being centred in himself human autonomy is undone. This is justified through the belief that Christ is God. As we have seen, such a 'Truth' carries the implication that left to him- or herself the human being is in 'sin'. Sin becomes a position (autonomy we might say). Furthermore what is not always appreciated is the profound epistemological implication. What humankind has come to take for granted is mistaken; there has occurred in history an unthinkable particularity. In Kierkegaard's case it becomes more 'thinkable' through the epistemological presuppositions to which he holds. But for us everything we thought we knew about how the universe functions (since Newton or before) is undone. This too has moral implications. Should we think that human reason is in this manner nullified? How should we then conceive of ourselves? What would this mean for our self-understanding? Many (I am assuming) would rather abide by human moral integrity and by confidence in our ability to discover how the world works.

Did Kierkegaard Leap Lessing's Ditch?

The short answer to this question must be that neither was the ditch the same, nor was Kierkegaard's manner of crossing it one that could have satisfied Lessing. It is worth thinking this through.

Lessing's ditch consisted in the impossibility of predicating the existence of absolute and eternal truths on contingent truths of history (occurrences which might or might not have happened). Since the ancient world, the idea of 'God' had of course been analytically (i.e. integrally, internally), related to the idea of the 'eternal' and of 'change-lessness', which had in turn been held to involve 'perfection'. Thus one could well hold that the root cause of the conundrum that is the eternal/time dichotomy is the human propensity to imaginatively construct that which is the contrary to, or other than, the human experience of life as contingent and historical. What is problematic is the idea, derived from the ancient world, that there exists that that is perfect/eternal/changeless (what Derrida would designate with the ascription 'full presence'). If one agrees with this latter contention one would presumably also hold that Hegel rightly contested tran-scendent absolutes; for him reality can always be mediated (resolved) into the historical. One would then have to say that, living in the midst of modernity and post-Hegel, Kierkegaard invites us in the face of Hegel (for this is his clear intent) to hold to a traditional notion of God. It is this move which creates for him the Paradox; since one who is living in time is held to be God (by definition eternal) and thus a paradox in terms. In this sense Kierkegaard recreates, or abides by, Lessing's dichotomy.[42]

---

[42] Whether the incarnation is in fact a paradox in terms is an interesting question. Some years ago a debate was conducted through the pages of *New Blackfriars* in which the Dominican theologian Herbert McCabe argued that to be a human being and to be God are certainly not incompatible in the sense in which for example being a sheep and a human clearly are; being one of which rules out being the other as alternative kinds of mammal. (There were patristic arguments

In regard to the postulation that there is that which is God, existing as it were outside our time–space continuum, Kierkegaard, as we have seen, makes some extraordinary (one might think farcical) moves. Thus he postulates that we come up against an 'unknown'— which is God. How come? Why is there any such? To conclude that, beyond the boundary to what we can know (which Kant delineated) there lies an 'unknown', then furthermore hypostasizing it (making of it a something, God), has to be a category mistake. Does Kierkegaard or does he not think with Thomas Aquinas (or perhaps Descartes), that we can reason from the world to that which lies 'beyond', to God? Has he not grasped, with Kant, that an extrapolation from that which lies within the world to a presumption of *knowledge* of anything 'beyond' is illegitimate? One would have thought he fully grasps this. Kierkegaard always speaks (notably in the *Postscript*) about the human *response* to God (to the 'idea' of eternal life), rather than speculating about the beyond. His theology is a phenomenology of human faith, in this at one with his Lutheran tradition which (unlike Catholic or English, analytic, philosophy of religion) has been averse to speculation as to the existence or nature of God. On the other hand one would have to say that the *import* of belief in Christ as the Paradox is that God is eternal. Again it must be said that today profound questions are raised for Kierkegaard and for classical Christian theology in thinking in such terms at all. In a world in which, as physicists and astronomers tell us, time/space has no 'outside', should we even metaphorically continue to employ the language of 'outside' and 'before' in speaking of God? One would have to say that, in this respect at least, it is Hegel who is a better 'fit' with modernity.

Kierkegaard's leap of faith, allowing him through crediting the Paradox to bridge the gap between the eternal and that which exists in time, we may think not something that Lessing would have countenanced as solving the problem that he posed. What Lessing seeks is certainty of knowledge. Kierkegaard's move to a different

---

along the same lines.) To which the patristic scholar and theologian Maurice Wiles responded that being 'eternal' and being 'in time' must surely be held incompatible. (Herbert McCabe & Maurice Wiles, *New Blackfriars*, 58, no. 691, Dec 1977). But be that as it may: Kierkegaard (who thinks in terms of the eternal/time dichotomy) holds that the God/man is indeed a Paradox which cannot be thought (that is to say related to through reason).

organ of apprehension that is faith seems illegitimate: as he well knows faith is not knowledge. Such a 'resolution' may be triumphantly proclaimed by those who (as Kierkegaard would appear to), contend that the Paradox is perfectly 'reasonable' to the one who has faith. But we may think this the somersault that, on his deathbed, Lessing valiantly refused to make (as Kierkegaard well knows).[43] Kierkegaard has substituted for the quest to know a passionate movement of willing to let go. Not least in this connection do questions arise as to whether we could possibly think moral a God who demands of us that we forego our reason. Kierkegaard's becomes the ultimate anti-humanist stance. He may be perfectly correct in thinking that, in the light of modernity, this is the only move left to Christians. Indeed, he may applaud it as of the essence of faith. The value of *Fragments* is that it becomes evident that adherence to Christian 'Truth' must undermine all that, epistemologically, we thought we knew, together with annulling our self-understanding as possessed of a rationality which should allow us to adjudicate on questions of truth.

Thus it could be said that Kierkegaard's Johannes Climacus has succeeded brilliantly. If what he wishes to show is that Christian claims are incompatible with modernity he has certainly done so. Minimally, the Hegelian attempt to assimilate Christianity to 'the system' as, equally, what has often been the Catholic attempt to think together faith and knowledge, as though Christian claims could be all of a piece with our reason, have been laughed out of court. Kierkegaard has shown that there is no way in which we can move directly into Christianity, as in putting a hand into a glove (to employ an analogy of his). One must—in bafflement—be brought up short before a Paradox. It is a Paradox moreover to which is intrinsic the claim that there has occurred a particularity. We are here not simply speaking of what the Greeks might have thought inconceivable, that one particular instance of humanity is raised to the status of an absolute truth. We are speaking of what is an 'unthinkable' particularity, in the sense that, were such an incarnation to have occurred, it must presumably be counted one of a type, belonging to no category. Faced with such a contention one either takes the a priori position (as does the present author) that (quite apart from the

---

[43] See p. 147.

question as to whether the Paradox is or is not in itself paradoxical and unthinkable) there can be no such particularity. Or, despairingly, one lets go of reason in Kierkegaard's 'leap' of faith.

All that has been said in this Critique does not, of course, prove that Kierkegaard is necessarily wrong in postulating the possibility of an incarnation. It merely suggests that he is unlikely to be right. What Kierkegaard's own stance may be (though one may think that one knows) does not figure in the text. What one should, however, note is that Kierkegaard puts forward this important book simply as a 'project of thought' in which he will think out what Christianity implies. As he comments in his draft for the 'Preface': 'It is by no means my intention with this project to be polemical, to defend something or to combat something' (183). And he returns to such a thought in *The Concluding Unscientific Postscript*, where he says of *Fragments*: 'I only repeat once again: whether Christianity is in the right, I do not decide. In that pamphlet, I have already said what I continually confess, that my fragment of merit, if there is to be any mention of that, is to state the issue' (*CUP*, 369). We should be clear how today that issue looks.

4

The Concept Angst

Introduction

The intellectual background behind Kierkegaard's *The Concept Angst* is extraordinarily complex. Of all Kierkegaard's works this book may owe the most to other people. A medley of ideas derived from diverse sources had made their impact upon him. Yet the book, both a compilation and a novel synthesis arising out of a tradition of thought, has about it a sparkling originality. We have before us a work of genius as Kierkegaard plumbs the depths of human consciousness.

We may commence by considering the understanding of original sin that came with the cultural baggage that all the thinkers who we shall here be considering inherited. Enunciated by Augustine, it had been passed down through Western culture. In *The City of God* Augustine writes:

Man [i.e. Adam] was willingly perverted and justly condemned, and so begot perverted and condemned offspring. For we were all in that one man, seeing that we all *were* that one man who fell into sin through the woman who was made from him before the first sin. We did not possess forms individually created and assigned to us for us to live in them as individuals; but there already existed the seminal nature from which we were to be begotten. And of course, when this was vitiated through sin, and bound with death's fetters in its just condemnation, man could not be born of man in any other condition. Hence from the misuse of free will there started a chain of disasters: mankind is led from that original perversion, a kind of corruption at the root, right up to the disaster of the second death, which has no end. Only those who are set free through God's grace escape from this calamitous sequence.[1]

Generated from the male semen alone, human beings were present in Adam's loins and sin (so it was believed) was transmitted through sexual intercourse from one generation to the next. Humankind was held collectively to be a *massa peccati*, a lump of sin. Unless redeemed by Christ, human beings were irrevocably warped and justly condemned to death. Dying unbaptized an infant was headed for damnation. It may be difficult for us today to conceive of what it meant to be saddled with such a mindset.

In the Reformation the doctrine in this stark form passed over into Protestantism. As the (Lutheran) 'Augsburg Confession of Faith' (1530) has it:

Since the fall of Adam all men who are propagated according to nature are born in sin. That is to say they are without fear of God, are without trust in God, and are concupiscent. And this disease of vice of origin is truly sin, which even now damns and brings eternal death on those who are not born again through Baptism and the Holy Spirit.[2]

Hamann, Kant, Hegel, and Kierkegaard, all Lutherans, were brought up on the Lutheran confessions of faith, possessing one and all a deep knowledge of theology. Schelling, whom we have not yet considered, was the son of a learned pastor. He had first met Hegel at the well-known seminary the Tübinger Stift.

It was this inheritance that, by the 18th century, had been unsettled by new biological knowledge.[3] Furthermore, it ill fitted the spirit of

---

[1] Augustine, *The City of God*, XIII, 15, 14 (trans. H. Bettenson, Harmondsworth, 1972, p. 523); see also XIV, 11, 11 (Bettenson p. 569).

[2] Theodore G. Tappert, ed. & trans., *The Book of Concord: The Confessions of the Evangelical Lutheran Church* (Philadelphia, PA, 1959), 29.

[3] In a book published in Amsterdam in 1748, Benoît de Maillet argued that the church was mistaken in its claim that the earth was no more than 6,000 years old. In 1756 George-Louis Leclerc, Comte de Buffon (1707–88), in his *Histoire Naturelle* challenged Linnaeus's taxonomy of species, arguing that species are not immutable. Leclerc opined that there was no strict boundary between the animal and vegetal kingdoms and further, pointing to their similarities, speculated as to the common ancestry of humans and apes. In 1803 in a speech given to a scientific institution created by the French Revolution, Jean-Baptiste Lamarck went so far as to suggest that modifications in organisms could be brought about by environmental circumstances. While Etienne Geoffroy Saint-Hilaire, in his *Influence du monde ambiant pour modifier les formes animales* (*Influence of the Surrounding*

the age. The idea that original sin was passed down from an ancient ancestor increasingly appeared both unrealistic and ethically over-deterministic. (It should be noted that the German for 'original sin' *Erbsünd*, as also the Danish *Arvesynd*, connote quite literally the 'sin of the ancestors'.) Kant's influential *Religion within the Limits of Reason Alone* (1793), built around the story of the Fall and redemption of man, is a full-blown statement of a novel conception. (Kant published his work outside Prussia to evade Prussian censorship.) Interestingly, he does not deny a 'radical evil' in humankind, but he writes:

However the origin of moral evil in man is constituted, surely of all the explanations of the spread and propagation of this evil through all members and generations of our race, the most inept is that which describes it as descending to us as an inheritance from our first parents; for one can say of moral evil precisely what the poet said of good: *genus et proavos, et quae non fecimus ipsi, vix ea nostra puto.*' [Ovid, *Metamorphoses*, XIII, 140–1: 'Race and ancestors, and those things which we ourselves have not made, I scarcely account our own.']⁴

Every sinful action, Kant concluded, 'must be regarded as though the individual had fallen into it directly from a state of innocence'. Whatever natural causes might influence him, his action is yet free and hence he must be judged to have made an original use of his will. We cannot thus 'enquire into the temporal origin of this deed, but solely into its rational origin'.⁵

Schleiermacher, the theologian, thought in many respects likewise, writing of Adam and Eve: 'We have no reason for explaining universal sinfulness as due to an alternation in human nature brought about in their person by a first sin'. Indeed, as he points out, Adam must

World in Modifying Animal Forms), published in Paris 1833, wrote: 'The external world is all-powerful in alteration of the form of organized bodies; ... these [modifications] are inherited and they influence all the rest of the organisation of the animal, because if these modifications lead to injurious effects the animals which exhibit them perish and are replaced by others of a somewhat different form; a form changes so as to be adapted to the new environment.' It was a short step to Darwin. (I owe this summary to Bettina Bergo's 'Evolution and Force: Anxiety in Kierkegaard and Nietzsche', *The Southern Journal of Philosophy* 41, no. 2, 2003, cf. p. 163, footnotes 14, 15, 16. Bergo is a laudable exception among Kierkegaard commentators, who inexplicably neglect this vital context.)

⁴ Immanuel Kant, *Religion within the Limits of Reason Alone*, ed. Theodore M. Greene & Hoyt H. Hudson (New York, 1960), 35.
⁵ Kant, *Religion*, 36.

already have been sundered from God before his first sin 'for, when Eve handed him the fruit he ate it without even recalling the divine interdict'. The universal sin that precedes each actual sin was not to be considered as derived, rather was our situation identical with that of our first parents.[6] In Hegel's case 'Adam', understood as humanity, could act as a precise illustration of his belief that the Judaeo-Christian myth is but a concrete representation of what are indeed true concepts. The first act of disobedience, thought Hegel, was but 'something contingent or accidental', remarking, 'The story is the eternal history of humanity'.[7]

We must consider the heritage furthermore if we are to comprehend the way in which in the first half of the 19th century thinkers shaped their consideration of other questions: freedom, sin, angst, the nature of the self and the relationship to God. In what is Luther's most famous theological exposition, his *On the Bondage of the Will* (1525), one of the few works of his he thought worth preserving, Luther thunders back at Erasmus, who had in fact been encouraged to attack him by others. To assume (as did Erasmus in his liberal *On the Freedom of the Will*) that the human being has a free will, a so-called *liberum arbitrium*, as though he stood in some kind of a neutral place, able equally to choose good or evil, was, said Luther, wholly to misconstrue the situation. Rather (adopting and developing an ancient pseudo-Augustinian metaphor) are we a horse ridden either by God or the Devil, the horse (in Luther's case) having no choice as to its rider. For God to be the rider was to be 'free'. To Luther's ears Erasmus's position sounded simply Pelagian (and indeed the fate of Erasmus's tract was, on this account, to land up on the Index). In his early years Augustine had been inclined to think in terms of just such a freedom of choice, but subsequent to his spat with Pelagius had foregone any such optimistic view.

This 'positive' understanding of freedom (to employ later vocabulary) is fundamental to Luther's theology. The human does not possess an essentially independent basis, but (whether he knows it or not) is always *coram deo*, before the face of God. As Luther tells Erasmus, quoting Homer, God has not gone off to 'an Ethiopian

---

[6] Friedrich Schleiermacher, *The Christian Faith*, §72 (New York, 1963), 291, 295.
[7] Peter Hodgson, ed., *Lectures on the Philosophy of Religion*, III, *The Consummate Religion* (Berkeley, Los Angeles, & London, 1985), 104, 105, 106.

banquet'[8] but is present as God. Either one acknowledges dependence on God, the rightful relation of creature to Creator, or one is involved in a wilful bid for independence (the story of the Fall) that is sin. Thus the 'freedom' that is independence and choice comes to be associated in the tradition with the Fall, sin, and angst. It was this angst from which Luther found himself delivered as he came to understand 'justification' not as becoming in and of oneself 'good', but rather as that 'transfer of gravity' (as we have described it)[9] whereby the Christian's will becomes one with God's (positive freedom). It is this sense of freedom as identity that passes into German idealism. Kant is very close to Luther translated into secular terms. It is notable that, whereas in his earlier moral philosophy Kant holds to a 'positive' understanding of freedom as being tied to the good, in his *Religion* he develops a sense for the *failure* of the will (*Willkür*) to make the moral law the maxim of its actions. By contrast Socrates had thought that no man could willingly do evil.

Yet there is also present in the tradition a sense for what is often known as the 'fortunate Fall', *felix culpa*. It was after all in his disobedience in eating the apple that Adam came into his own, possessed of the knowledge of good and evil. The freedom that is freedom of choice comes to be aligned not only with the possibility of sin but also creativity. Hegel can accordingly appropriate the story of the Fall into his dialectic. The Fall, thought Hegel, represents a cleavage, in itself evil. Nevertheless, in this cleavage is first found conscious human cognition, the knowledge of good and evil. Represented by the first man, it is humanity as a whole that enters into this cleavage. Now the cleavage contains within itself the potential of being sublated. 'The confirmation of the fact that the knowledge of good and evil belongs to the divinity of humanity is placed on the lips of God himself' who says 'Behold, Adam has become like one of us, knowing good and evil' (Gen. 3.22). Thus the Fall forms part of the necessary history of humanity, which however will be reconciled in a higher rational standpoint, such that true freedom for Hegel is positive freedom.[10]

---

[8] J. I. Packer and O.R. Johnston, eds, *Martin Luther on The Bondage of the Will* (London, 1957), 200; cf. *Odyssey* i.22.f, *Iliad* i.423ff.

[9] See p. 22.

[10] Cf. Peter Hodgson, ed., *Hegel: Lectures on the Philosophy of Religion*, I, *Introduction and the Concept of Religion* (Berkeley, Los Angeles, & London, 1984), 276.

It was this totalization present in idealism, the identity of freedom and rationality (truth), together with the necessary nature of the Fall for Hegel (rather than it having occurred through man's freewill) that was so worrisome to those who turned against Hegel, whether Schelling or at a later date Kierkegaard. Schelling voiced his disquiet already in his so-called *Freiheitsschrift* (*Vom Wesen der menschlichen Freiheit*), *On the Nature of Human Freedom*, of 1809, with which Kierkegaard was familiar. Idealism allowed neither for actuality (the contingency of historical occurrences) nor—at the end of the day—for freedom in the sense of freedom of choice. The crux of the problem was that there was no real way to speak of evil as a positive force; in idealism evil was but an appearance, the contrary of that reality which is the good. For Schelling this creates a theodicy problem.[11] He comes to envisage that there must be a radically free creation (hence the possibility of evil), and that this freedom must consist in a falling away from freedom understood as identity posited by idealism. Human autonomy is the tragic, Promethean, attempt of man to plough his own furrow in the face of God. It was this concern for 'actuality' which made the young Kierkegaard's heart leap for joy (he was 28) as, in 1841, he listened to the elderly Schelling lecture in Berlin.[12]

Meanwhile already in the 18th century there is a developing interest in human subjectivity. In a sense that we seem irrevocably to have lost (perhaps since the acceptance of evolution changed humankind's self-image), there is held to be that of the 'divine' within man, who was created by God. Thus human evil is conceptualized as the obverse of the capacity within the human being for God. Kierkegaard finds this in Leibniz (of whose theodicy we know him to have made an intensive study in 1842–3),[13] noting that, as Leibniz writes, 'the ground of evil is

---

[11] Cf. Martin Heidegger: 'The system [Hegelianism] is split open by the reality of evil.' Martin Heidegger, *Schelling's Treatise on the Essence of Human Freedom*, trans. Joan Stambaugh (Athens, OH, 1985), 98, quoted by Timothy Dalrymple 'Adam and Eve: Human Being and Nothingness' in Lee Barrett & Jon Stewart, eds, *Kierkegaard and the Bible, Kierkegaard Research: Sources, Reception and Resources*, 1, 1, *The Old Testament* (Farnham, 2010), 20, note 99.

[12] Cf. Hannay, 145 (*Pap.* III A 179). Kierkegaard's knowledge of the later Schelling was very considerable. Although he did not remain in Berlin to hear the lectures on revelation, in 1843 he made a careful study of those lectures as reported on by others. (Cf. Dalrymple, 'Adam and Eve', 19.)

[13] Cf. Dalrymple, 'Adam & Eve', 21.

not to be sought in matter but in the ideal nature of creation'.[14] In a dawning Romanticism, moreover, there is present a sense for an angst encountered by the human together with his awareness of his freedom. Such a sense is found in Hamann, who may well be held the first Romantic. Kierkegaard notes in his *Journal* in 1842:

In Vol. VI, p.194 of his works, Hamann makes an observation which I can use, although he neither understood it as I wish to understand it nor thought further about it: 'However this angst in the world is the only proof of our heterogeneity. If we lacked nothing, we should do no better than the pagans and the transcendental philosophers, who know nothing of God and like fools fall in love with lovely nature, and no homesickness would come over us. This impertinent disquiet, this holy hypochondria'.[15]

This angst, this dis-ease, is in fact a 'holy' hypchondria, a homesickness that we possess on account of our divine origin, which also forms our *telos*. Angst, Kierkegaard concludes, is proof of our heterogeneity, of the fact that we have a higher destiny.[16]

If angst correlates with the human capacity for the divine, Kierkegaard notes in *The Concept Angst* that Schelling also speaks of a melancholy that is spread over nature (59). Kierkegaard was sarcastic about secular notions of 'the sublime', judging them an 'aesthetic accounting' for transcendence.[17] That is to say such Romanticism had substituted for the fact that the human is created for divinity a false attempt to fill our capacity. For Kierkegaard as for Schelling the gulf that, in the human quest for freedom, opens out between the human and God is a source of tension and tragedy. Yet, as we have already noted, it is also the prerequisite for human creativity.

---

[14] *JP* 3:2364 (*Pap.* IV C 30), n.d., 1842–43. Cf. Leibniz *Theodicy* (London, 1951), 140–1.

[15] *JP* 1:96 (*Pap.* III A 235), n.d., 1842; J. Nadler, ed., *Werke* (Vienna, 1949–53), quoted by Ronald Gregor Smith, *J.G. Hamann* (London, 1960), 49.

[16] Cf. Kierkegaard's remark written in 1845: 'I understand perfectly well what Plato [in fact Aristotle, *Ethics* II, 6] said so well, that an animal will produce an animal of the same species, a plant a plant of the same species, and so a man will give birth to a man; but by this nothing is explained, thought is not satisfied, only a vague feeling is aroused; for an eternal being cannot be born.' (*Stages on Life's Way*, Lowrie, 58).

[17] *Pap.* X⁵ A 126 (1853), quoted by Bruce Kirmmse, 'Kierkegaard and 1848', *History of European Ideas*, 20 (1995), 170. Cf. Jørgen Bukdahl: 'the human spirit's mightiest attempt at self-redemption since the Renaissance'. (*Søren Kierkegaard and the Common Man*, Bruce Kirmmse, trans. (Grand Rapids, MI, 2001), 2.) Cf. also John Milbank, 'Kierkegaard reinscribes transcendence within the terms of sublimity' ('The Sublime in Kierkegaard', *The Heythrop Journal*, 37 (1996), 310.)

Kierkegaard writes of this 'split' (Danish *splid*), 'for even the split in man has more significance than immediate innocence'.[18] It is in angst that the human being first awakens to possibility: that is the dilemma. In the course of his authorship (it is already presaged in this book), Kierkegaard will attempt to find a way to speak both of human autonomy, that the self shall come to itself, while also construing the relationship to God as fundamental to the synthesis of the self. For (from Luther forwards) it is only in overcoming the sin of separation and consenting to be grounded in God that the human can be healed. Such was the fertile intellectual soil out of which Kierkegaard developed *The Concept Angst*.

Kierkegaard will undertake a phenomenological study, probing that psychological predisposition in which sin occurs. He will throw a line across from such an experiential analysis to Christian dogmatics. As he puts it, his task is: 'To explain how my religious existence comes into relation with and expresses itself in my outward [everyday, experiential] existence' (105). I have already commented on the close relationship between the two in the Lutheran tradition: faith rescues one from angst; or conversely, angst results from a falling away from the relation intended by the Creator. The exploration of this existential state thus forms a prolegomena to dogmatics. Kierkegaard had long been interested in what we should call phenomenology, as a student musing in his *Journal*: 'genuine anthropological contemplation... has not yet been undertaken'.[19] This judgement notwithstanding, he was not wholly without guidance. The philosopher F. C. Sibbern, who had been his teacher and with whom he remained in conversation, had in 1819 (and 1828) published a philosophical study of the emotions, *Menneskets aandelige Natur og Vaesen: Et Udkast til en Psychologie* (*Man's Spiritual Nature and Being: A Proposal for a Psychology*). Sibbern thought a psychologist should be a poet.[20] Furthermore Kierkegaard's former teacher, friend, and mentor Poul Martin Møller, to whose memory the book was dedicated, had been interested in experimental psychology.

---

[18] *JP* 1:41 (*Pap.* IV C 33).
[19] *JP* 1:37 (*Pap.* III A 3), 5 July 1840.
[20] Cf. Roger Poole, 'Dizziness, falling... Oh (dear)!... Reading *Begrebet Angest* for the very first Time', *Kierkegaard Studies Yearbook* 2001 (Berlin & New York, 2001) 207.

Finally, it is worth remarking that, in undertaking such a study, Kierkegaard was tackling something in which it may be thought that there was much at stake for him. As early as 1835 when he was 22, he had remarked in the so-called Gilleleje letter that a person must 'first learn to know himself before knowing anything else'.[21] Kierkegaard's youth had been clouded by his father's belief that, on account of some sin he had committed, the whole family lay under a curse, such that all his children were destined to die before him. By the time Kierkegaard wrote five of the seven siblings were dead, leaving only Kierkegaard's elder brother, Peter Christian, and he himself, the youngest. In *Stages on Life's Way* (published ten months subsequently) Kierkegaard remarks:

If it were thinkable that the father had influence upon the son, that the father's nature was a postulate from which the son's nature could not liberate itself, the contradiction comes from another side; for then the thought is so dreadful that there is nothing on earth so dreadful as to be a father (Lowrie, 58).

It was presumably a matter of some urgency to Kierkegaard to establish that sin was not inherited. We should, furthermore, be aware of an enigmatic remark in his *Journal* for May 1843: 'for it was, after all, angst which brought me to go astray'.[22] What this refers to is unknown. There are entries in relation to his broken engagement that might lead one to think that, as a young man in a drunken state, Kierkegaard had (?) visited a prostitute.[23] Whatever it was, it was not until his religious experience of the spring of 1848 that Kierkegaard convinced himself that God had not only forgiven but forgotten.

In calling his book *'The Concept' Angst* Kierkegaard is making a deliberate jab at the Hegelians. In his study as to the particular Hegelian that Kierkegaard has in his sights in his various books, Jon Stewart concludes that *The Concept Angst* has in mind Adolph Adler.[24] Nevertheless, it would seem clear that the snub is directed at

---

[21] Hannay, 35 (also translated in *JP* 5:5100), 1 Aug. 1835.

[22] *JP* 5:5664 (*Pap.* IV A 107), 17 May 1843. See also *JP* 5:6133 (*Pap.* VIII A 645): 'As yet, at least, I cannot come to such heights of faith, I cannot yet win such cheerful confidence of faith that I can believe that painful memory away.'

[23] This would not have been an unusual occurrence in the world in which he lived in which men customarily married late.

[24] In a draft for the book Kierkegaard names both Heiberg and Adler (*CA*, Supplement, 180; *Pap.* V B 49:5, n.d., 1844). Cf. Jon Stewart's comments, *Kierkegaard's Relation to Hegel Reconsidered* (Cambridge, 2003), 400–1.

the eminent literary critic and socialite J. L. Heiberg, the man who had introduced Hegel to Denmark and to whose circle the young Kierkegaard had briefly belonged. Heiberg had written what Kierkegaard gauged a hurtful review of *Repetition*, leading him to commit many pages of response to his *Journal*, which however he forbore to publish. He makes some reference to this affair in the introduction to the book. *Qua* Hegelian, Heiberg distinguished sharply between concepts, which alone allowed of rational investigation, and mere affectivities, moods and emotions: he had given lectures along these lines at the Royal Military High School in 1832, which Martensen had duly reviewed.[25] Provocatively, Kierkegaard calls his work *'The Concept' Angst*. His book will diverge markedly from a Hegelian text, which would typically have proceeded by making deductions from first principles.

We should also remark that Kierkegaard's angst (the Danish meaning is identical to the German) is ill-rendered in English as 'anxiety'. Kierkegaard's earlier English-language translator Walter Lowrie tried 'dread'. This is good in so far as it conjures up the context of Romanticism. Kierkegaard can speak of a 'sweet angst' that tantalizes or invites. Angst, he will say, is 'a sympathetic antipathy and an antipathetic sympathy' (42). Philosophically the distinction between angst and anxiety (or fear) is said to be that whereas fear has an object, angst is devoid of any such. Animals can know fear, while the human may possess unfocused angst. Angst, more particularly, is future-orientated. I have concluded that the word is now sufficiently well known in English to employ it.

Exposition

Introduction

Kierkegaard depicts the nature of disciplines. **Ethics** is a science (i.e. a *Wissenschaft*; the equivalent Danish is used)[26] concerned with ideality.

---

[25] Cf. Roger Poole, *Kierkegaard: The Indirect Communication* (Charlottesville, VA, 1993), 98–9.
[26] The German term, well known in English, has wider connotations than the English 'science': concerted and ordered thought.

It must assume (cf. Kant) that 'every man possesses the requisite conditions', not permitting itself 'to be distracted by the babble that it is useless to require the impossible' (16–17). It is abstract, not phenomenological. Sin belongs to it only insofar as that it is upon sin that it is 'shipwrecked'. By contrast, **psychology** is phenomenological (descriptive); it loves to portray the contours of a phenomenon. So now sin. Whereas innocence may be called a *state*, in that it could well remain, sin is no state but rather 'again and again' (15).

Sin shows itself not accidentally to the individual, leading to a presupposition 'that goes beyond the individual': **hereditary sin**. A category lying beyond the reach of ethics has appeared. Thus the situation is 'still more desperate'. We have come up against a presupposition that cannot be explained. Kierkegaard notes that the symbolic books (of Lutheran faith), the 'Smalcald Articles', 'Augsburg Confession' and 'Formula of Concord' declare the impossibility of explanation. He quotes the first of these: hereditary sin 'cannot be comprehended by human understanding, but must be known and believed' (26). Unlike Hegelian practice, the book will know how to distinguish between what can and what cannot be understood (!).

Hereditary sin belongs to **dogmatics** and it is in this realm that the solution will be found to what is uncovered. Unlike ethics (which depicts an ideality), dogmatics proceeds from actuality. It 'does not deny the presence of sin;...it presupposes it and explains it by presupposing hereditary sin'. Through repentance and faith, dogmatics will raise actuality up to ideality (19). Psychology can reach the point where it seems as though sin were there, and that human nature is so constituted that sin is possible is quite correct. But wanting to make sin constitutive of the human is revolting to ethics and sounds like blasphemy to dogmatics (22). Just as freedom is never *possible* but rather *is* when it is actual, so also with sin.

As soon as psychology is absorbed in the possibility of sin, it is unwittingly in the service of another science, dogmatics, which will assist it with the explanation (23). Like ethics, dogmatics is a theoretical subject, but unlike ethics it has sin within its scope. Now dogmatics must not 'explain' hereditary sin; rather does it presuppose it 'like that vortex about which Greek speculation concerning nature had so much to say, a moving something that no science can grasp' (20).

Chapter I. Angst as the Presupposition of Hereditary Sin and as Explaining Hereditary Sin Retrogressively in Terms of Its Origin

Note the title.

§1. *Historical Intimations Regarding the Concept of Hereditary Sin*

Is hereditary sin identical with the first sin (Adam's sin)? Kierkegaard will give a complex response. In remarks commensurate with Kant's *Religion*, he comments that when thought met with difficulties an expedient was seized upon: in order to explain at least something 'a fantastic presupposition was introduced', innocence, the loss of which constituted the Fall (25). But this explanation introduced another problem: the doubt that such a state ever existed. 'The history of the human race acquired a fantastic beginning. Adam was fantastically placed outside this history' (25).

To rephrase our question: 'Does ... the particular individual participate in inherited sin only through his relation to Adam and not through his primitive relation to sin?' (26). (In other words, should not the Augustinian, hereditary, scenario be questioned.) According to the second option 'Adam's sin is more than something past' (26). Kierkegaard will want to say both. On the one hand (the second option) we sin as did Adam; or as Kierkegaard puts it, sin posits itself, each first sin arising out of a person's direct relation to sin, there being no previously extant state determining that we shall sin. (This constitutes a considerable break with the Reformation confessions.) On the other hand there is what we may call 'hereditary' sin; a certain solidarity with the race, such that sin has a history. Bringing these together, Kierkegaard will say that the individual is 'simultaneously himself and the whole race' (28), finding in this man's perfection. But it is also a contradiction, which the book will explore. In strikingly Hegelian fashion Kierkegaard writes, 'a contradiction is always the expression of a task, and a task is movement' (29). We may say: 'As the history of the race moves on, the individual begins constantly anew, because he is both himself and the race' (29).

§2. *The Concept of the First Sin*

Possessed of a Lutheran context, Kant and Kierkegaard both take for granted that 'person' precedes 'works' and not *vice versa*.²⁷ Luther had turned on its head the medieval–Aristotelian understanding of the *habitus*, whereby practice (works) brings about in a person conformity with that which he practices. Rather does the good tree (person) bring forth good fruit (works) (Matt. 7.17).²⁸ Thus the first sin (the Fall) is a *qualitative* step (in accord with the biblical story), from which sins, particular acts, proceed. [Kant, we should note, speaks of a propensity, a subjective determining ground of the will, preceding all acts; in respect to 'original sin' making the ingenious suggestion that it may be conceptualized as so far back in our life that it could be considered to lie in the noumenal realm, corresponding to the original sin of Adam which is, as it were, outside history.²⁹] Kierkegaard writes: 'That the *first* sin signifies something different from *a* sin . . . is quite obvious. The first sin constitutes the nature of the quality. . . . The new quality appears with the first, with the leap, with the suddenness of the enigmatic' (30). But, while wishing with Kant to hold the individual imputable, Kierkegaard's position differs from Kant's in his holding sin to bear a relation to the history of the race. As Kierkegaard was clearly aware, there had in the consideration of original sin been a tradition, on which he can draw, of employing universals. He comments: 'Man is individuum and as such simultaneously himself and the whole race and in such a way that the whole race participates in the individual and the individual in the whole race'³⁰ (28).

---

²⁷ See p. 25.
²⁸ 'The Freedom of a Christian', in Dillenberger, ed., *Selections*, 70. Ignorant as to the structure of Lutheran thought, the Catholic Philip Quinn remarks: 'It seems natural to think of those character traits for which we hold people morally responsible as bad habits brought about by the effects an extended course of bad actions has in shaping or moulding innate endowments [the Catholic *habitus*]. Looked at from this perspective, Kant has got the cart before the horse. [Indeed from this perspective he would have! He has the Lutheran ordering.]' ('Does Anxiety Explain Original Sin?', *Noûs*, 24 (1990), 231.)
²⁹ Kant, *Religion*, 17, 26, 27.
³⁰ Lee Barrett tells us that the understanding of Adam as a 'real universal' was prominent in post-Reformation theology ('Kierkegaard's "Anxiety" and the Augustinian Doctrine of Original Sin', *IKC CA*, 51).

Kierkegaard advances his double proposition. On the one hand, to say that inherited sinfulness changed everything would be to make the individual into the race; whereas every individual is himself and the race. Rather must we say with the Genesis story: 'Sin came into the world by a sin' (32). That is to say, each person's first sinning is imputable. Were the first sin of each who lives subsequent to Adam brought about by an extant quality, sinfulness, his sin would be his only in a nonessential way, having rather 'its serial number in the universal sinking fund of the race' (31). Each individual makes the leap that 'posits the quality' (sin) (32). Such an idea causes offence. Unable to shoulder responsibility, the leap (which Kierkegaard construes as a circle) is made into a straight line, as though sin were to be explained by some pre-existent state of 'sinfulness'. In fact 'sin presupposes itself'; it is always a leap. Yet it must also be said that, since the race does not begin anew with each individual, the sinfulness of the race acquires a history; a history which proceeds by 'quantitative determinations' (sin increases) (33). In summary we may say sin 'proceeds in quantitative determinations while the individual participates in it by the qualitative leap' (33). With an eye presumably on Kant, Kierkegaard comments that this view 'is not guilty of Pelagianism, which permits every individual to play his little history in his own private theatre unconcerned about the race' (34).

§3. The Concept of Innocence

Kierkegaard excoriates those who waste time pondering what would have been had Adam not sinned (the subject of a famed medieval dispute): 'When the guilty asks [this question], he sins, for in his aesthetic curiosity he ignores that he himself brought guiltiness into the world and that he himself lost innocence by guilt' (36).

§4. The Concept of the Fall

Sinfulness 'is not an epidemic that spreads like cowpox'; we each leap originally. The bible has often had a harmful effect in that, wanting to find an explanation for sin, people refer back to the Genesis story 'as if the whole matter were something foreign' (40).

§5. *The Concept Angst*

So to angst. We may say that: 'innocence is ignorance. In innocence man is not qualified as spirit but is psychically qualified in immediate unity with his natural condition' (41). Kierkegaard is clearly influenced by Romanticism here. In that one cannot yet speak of spirit man may be compared to the beast; nevertheless 'the spirit in man is dreaming'.

In this state there is peace and repose, but there is simultaneously something else that [cannot be called] contention and strife, for there is indeed nothing against which to strive. What, then, is it? Nothing. But what effect does nothing have? It begets angst.... Dreamily the spirit projects its own actuality.

Angst is 'a qualification of dreaming spirit' and as such integrally related with what it is to be human (41). It is not to be equated with the fear that refers to something definite. Rather is it 'a *sympathetic antipathy* and an *antipathetic sympathy*': one cannot look away, yet one dreads. Hence one speaks of a strange or bashful angst (42). Kierkegaard comments: 'This anxiety belongs so essentially to the child that he cannot do without it' (42).

He who becomes guilty through angst is indeed innocent, for it was not he himself but angst, a foreign power, that laid hold of him, a power that he did not love but about which he was anxious. And yet he is guilty, for he sank in angst, which he nevertheless loved even as he feared it (43).

Kierkegaard concludes: 'That angst makes its appearance is the pivot upon which everything turns.'

Of the human being we can say the following. 'Man is a synthesis of the psychical and the physical' (43). However a synthesis requires a third which unites them; this third is spirit. (This formulation will be the subject of *The Sickness unto Death*.) In the dreaming state the spirit 'constantly disturbs' the relation between soul and body, a relation that is liable to fall asunder. So how does spirit relate itself to a synthesis of the psychical and physical? Negatively, inversely, as angst. Since spirit is constitutive of what it is to be human it cannot be done away with. Nor can man sink into the vegetative state, for he is qualified as spirit (44). What we have then is an ignorance, which is angst, qualified by spirit. Such innocence 'has ... reached its uttermost point' (so that it may give way, turning into something else). Of Adam, Kierkegaard comments: 'The prohibition [that he shall not eat the apple] induces in him angst, for the prohibition awakens in him freedom's possibility;... the anxious possibility of *being able*. Adam 'has no conception of what he is able to do' (44). Kierkegaard avers: 'further than this, psychology cannot go' (45).

§6. *Angst as the Presupposition of Hereditary Sin and as Explaining Hereditary Sin Retrogressively in Terms of Its Origin.*

'Possibility' is to be able. The intermediate term is angst; but angst 'no more explains the qualitative leap than it can justify it ethically'. For angst is 'neither a category of necessity nor a category of freedom; it is entangled freedom, where freedom is not free in itself but entangled, not by necessity, but in itself' (49). So we must say sin is not determined, yet neither does it proceed from a will which is free. Were it the case that sin had come into the world by an act of an abstract *liberum arbitrium*[31] there could be no talk of angst.

Chapter II. Angst as Explaining Hereditary Sin Progressively

With sinfulness, sexuality was posited. In that moment the history of the race began. As the sinfulness of the race moves in quantitative determinations so also does angst. Hereditary sin manifests itself in the single individual as angst. In the state of innocence inherited sin must also have 'that same dialectical ambiguity' out of which guilt breaks forth by a qualitative leap. Kierkegaard tells us: 'Angst will be more reflective in a subsequent individual than in Adam, because the quantitative accumulation left behind by the race now makes itself felt in that individual.' Angst is not in itself an imperfection, but sinfulness in the subsequent individual has 'attained a greater power' and 'hereditary sin is growing' (52). Coming about through anxiety, sin in turn induces new anxiety. Leaping forward Kierkegaard remarks: 'Only in the moment that salvation is actually posited is this anxiety overcome. ... When salvation is posited, anxiety, together with possibility, is left behind' (53).

---

[31] See p. 104.

§1. Objective Angst

By 'objective' angst is intended that angst which is the reflection of the sinfulness of generation. Kierkegaard speaks of 'the great significance of Adam above that of every other individual in the race'. Orthodoxy teaches that, through Adam's sin the world of nature was brought under sin. However in the case of nature we cannot say that sin 'entered in as the quality of sin'. Romans 8.19 speaks of 'the eager longing of creation'; such a 'longing' presupposes that nature is in a state of imperfection. It is angst from which creation longs to be delivered.

§2. Subjective Angst

This is the angst present in the state of innocence. Kierkegaard writes:

One may liken angst to dizziness. He whose eye chances to look down into the yawning abyss becomes dizzy. But the reason for it is just as much his eye as it is the precipice. For suppose he had not looked down.

Thus angst is the dizziness of freedom which occurs when the spirit would posit the synthesis and freedom gazes down into its own possibility, grasping at finiteness to sustain itself. In this dizziness freedom succumbs. Further than this psychology cannot go and will not. That very instant everything is changed, and when freedom rises again it sees that it is guilty. Between these two instants lies the leap, which no science has explained or can explain. He who becomes guilty in angst becomes as ambiguously guilty as it is possible to be. Angst is a womanish debility in which freedom swoons. Psychologically speaking, the fall into sin always occurs in impotence. But angst is at the same time the most egoistic thing and no concrete expression of freedom is so egoistic as is the possibility of every concretion. This again is the overwhelming experience which determines the individual's ambiguous relation, both sympathetic and antipathetic. In angst there is the egoistic infinity of possibility, which does not tempt like a definite choice, but alarms (*aengster/* makes anxious) and fascinates with its sweet anxiety (*Beaengstelse*) (Lowrie 55, adapted).[32]

---

[32] It is tempting to think that Kierkegaard must have known the following passage in Kant: 'He [man] discovered in himself a power of choosing for himself a way of life, of not being bound without alternative to a single way, like the animals. Perhaps the discovery of this advantage created a moment of delight. But of necessity, anxiety and alarm as to how he was to deal with this newly discovered power quickly followed ... He stood, as it were, at the brink of an abyss. Until that moment instinct had directed him toward specific objects of desire. But from these there now opened up an infinity of such

To repeat. Angst is the 'dizziness' of freedom, which occurs when the spirit would posit the synthesis and freedom becomes aware of its own possibility. (Such a synthesis would be for the self to be itself; to be healed.[33]) In the moment, the human grasps at finiteness to steady himself and freedom succumbs. When it rises again it sees that it is guilty. As Kierkegaard remarks in a draft: 'Psychologically speaking the first sin always takes place in impotence.'[34]

We shall then proceed to consider this angst present in the subsequent individual (a) as consequent upon generation and (b) as the consequence of the historical relationship.

(A) ANGST AS CONSEQUENT UPON GENERATION

Sensuousness becomes sinfulness on each occasion that sin enters the world. That sensuousness *became* sinfulness is the history of generation, but that it *becomes* sinfulness is the qualitative leap of the individual.

There follows a consideration of woman. That which is derived (woman derived from Adam's rib) is less perfect than the original; though says Kierkegaard this is true only of the human race, in animals every subsequent specimen is as the first. Woman is weaker than man, anxiety more reflexive in her and women more sensuous. It follows that angst will in her find greater scope. That woman is more sensuous is apparent in her physicality; her ideality lies in her beauty. Where beauty is concerned, we have a synthesis from which spirit is excluded.

Venus is essentially just as beautiful when she is represented as sleeping, possibly more so, yet the sleeping state is the expression for the absence of spirit.... If on the other hand Apollo is to be represented it would no more be appropriate to have him sleep than it would be to have Jupiter do so (66).

Woman's 'greatest wisdom' and 'highest beauty' is to be found in silence. Ethically her ideality consists in procreation. Therefore Scripture says

---

objects, and he did not yet know how to choose between them.' 'Conjectural Beginning of Human History', *On History*, ed. & trans. Lewis White Beck (Indianapolis, 1963), 56.

[33] See p. 128 and pp. 226–30.

[34] Quoted Thomte, 'Entries from Kierkegaard's Journals and Papers', *CA*, 188.

that 'her desire shall be for her husband' (Gen. 3.16). In a draft Kierke-gaard remarks: 'She is more sensate than man; for were she more spiritual she could never have her culmination point in another. Spirit is the true independent.' And further: 'The Seducer's secret is simply that he knows that woman is anxious' (189).

Picture an innocent young girl; let a man fasten his desirous glance upon her and she becomes anxious. . . . On the other hand, if I picture a young woman fastening her desirous look upon an innocent young man, his mood will not be anxiety but disgust mingled with modesty, precisely because he is more qualified by spirit (67).

The sexual is the expression for the contradiction that the immor-tal spirit is determined as sex; that it has to take the form of being male or female. It is as though the human does not know what to do with the sexual drive; is made modest, anxious, or covered with shame. As soon as spirit is posited the erotic is done for. Hence in paganism the erotic, seen as comical, is neutralized by irony. While in Christianity it is suspended. When the spirit becomes anxious about putting on the concretion of sexual difference the person leaps away: it is this that feeds into monasticism. But why this anxiety? On account of the fact that the spirit cannot participate in the culmin-ation of the erotic; it feels itself a stranger here.

(B) THE CONSEQUENCE OF THE HISTORICAL RELATIONSHIP

In the subsequent individual sensuousness may signify an obscure knowledge of sinfulness. Further, there may be a mistaken appropri-ation of the *de te fabula narratur*. (As had Kant, Kierkegaard makes reference to Horace: *mutae nomine de te fabula narratur*—change but the name, of you the tale is told.)[35] The individual forgets that the leap takes place not of necessity but owes rather to himself. Again, we are inclined to think a child's behaviour consequent upon its environment, failing to impute responsibility.

Subsequent to the advent of Christianity, whereupon redemption was posited, sensuousness was seen in a light not found in paganism,

---

[35] Kant, *Religion*, 37; Horace, *The Satires, Epistles and the Art of Poetry*, trans. J. Conington (Charleston, SC, 2006), 23.

serving to confirm the relationship of sensuousness to sin. Sensuousness is not sinfulness, but sin makes sensuousness sinfulness. The task is to bring the sexual into conformity with the spirit.

The realization of this is the victory of love in a person in whom the spirit is so victorious that the sexual is forgotten and recollected only in forgetfulness. When this has come about sensuousness is transfigured in spirit and anxiety is driven out (80).

When such an understanding has triumphed, as compared with Greek culture more has been gained than lost. Something of Greek *jouissance* is lost, but a spirituality unknown to Greek culture gained. Those who really lose out are they who live as though sin entered the world 6,000 years ago—a curiosity which does not concern them. They do not gain Greek erotic enjoyment; meanwhile the sexual fails to be qualified by the eternal, which is spirit.

Chapter III. Angst as the Consequence of that Sin which is Absence of the Consciousness of Sin

The chapter will consider the question of time, transition and the moment.

Hegel has subverted the category of the eternal. Why furthermore does he employ the category of transition so cavalierly? The Hegelian system is supposed to be presupposition-less, but Kierkegaard does not know what a presupposition is if the terms transition/negation/mediation are not presuppositions. By contrast, Plato knows of the moment: we should not forget that the new comes about through a leap (is not simply a transition).

There follows a complex passage to which I shall pay attention in the 'Critique'.

The human being (as we have said) is a synthesis of psyche and body. But he is also a synthesis of temporal and eternal. These syntheses are differently formed, in that the former can only come about when a third, the spirit, is posited; whereas the latter has but two factors. Where is the third asks Kierkegaard (the Hegelian), for a synthesis requires a third. Time is correctly defined as an infinite succession, but it is incorrect to think the succession 'implicit in time itself' (85). Because each moment is a process, no moment is a present.

Now the eternal is seen as an 'infinitely contentless present'. In representation, time is expanded into an illusionary view of an infinite. But on the contrary, 'the present is the eternal, or rather the eternal is the present, and the present is full' (86). (That is to say the eternal is present in each moment in succession.)

> The moment signifies the present as that which has no past and no future... The eternal also signifies the present as that which has no past and no future, and this is the perfection of the eternal.... If... time and eternity touch each other, then it must be in time, ... the moment (87).

An atom of time is 'but an atom of eternity... stopping time' (88). Thus the synthesis of time and eternal is not another synthesis but an expression of the first synthesis. 'The moment is that ambiguity in which time and eternity touch each other... whereby time constantly intersects eternity and eternity constantly pervades time' (89).

In a certain sense the future is the whole, of which the past is a part; thus the future can signify the whole (i.e. figuralism).[36] The Greeks did not have a concept of the future; the 'eternal' lies behind as past.

> If there is no moment the eternal appears behind as the past.... If the moment is posited but merely as a *discrimen* [division] then the future is the eternal. If the moment is posited [cf. *Fragments*] so is the eternal, but also the future which reappears as the past [figuralism] (90).

These three represent respectively the Greek, Jewish, and Christian views. 'The pivotal concept in Christianity, that which made all things new, is the fullness of time, but the fullness of time is the moment as the eternal, and yet this eternal is also the future and the past.' Kierkegaard comments that if this is lost sight of 'not a single concept can be saved from a heretical and treasonable admixture that annihilates the concept' (90). The future is not a simple continuity with the present, whereby the concepts of resurrection and judgement would be destroyed. By assimilating Christ to time, Hegel and Christendom have, in a 'treasonable admixture', brought about what is a travesty of Christian faith.

Kierkegaard will proceed to cash this out in relation to our present consideration. Angst will be discussed under various headings.

---

[36] See pp. 29–30 and pp. 84–5.

§1. The Angst of Spiritlessness

In spiritlessness (the condition of which Kierkegaard accused his contemporaries) there is no angst: it is too happy and contented for that. Paganism is absence of spirit; in this differing from spiritlessness and much to be preferred. When the salt has lost its savour (bourgeois society has lost Christianity) wherewith shall it be salted? Even though spiritlessness lacks angst, angst is waiting.

§2. Angst Defined Dialectically as Fate

What is the object of angst? Nothing. In paganism that nothing is posited as fate. The tragic nature of paganism lies in the pagan not daring to forbear taking counsel from the oracle. The concepts of guilt and sin do not in paganism emerge in their deepest sense. Had they done so, paganism would have perished through the contradiction that one became guilty by fate.

§3. Angst Defined Dialectically as Guilt

In Judaism the object of angst takes the form of guilt. Judaism is further advanced than Greek culture. (Not least a swipe at Hegel?) To the oracle in paganism corresponds the sacrifice in Judaism. What would help the Jew would be 'the cancellation of the relation of angst to guilt and the positing of an actual relation' [to Christ] (104). Lacking this, sacrifice becomes ambiguous, expressed by its repetition.

'Every human life is religiously designed': i.e. we are spirit; the relation to God fundamental to our constitution (105). Consider the religious genius, one who does not remain in immediacy.

The first thing he does is to turn toward himself. Just as the immediate genius has fate as the figure that follows him, so he has guilt. In turning toward himself, he *eo ipso* turns toward God and there is a ceremonial rule that says that when the finite spirit would see God it must begin as guilty.

Whether he will at any time turn himself outward remains for him a subsequent question.[37] Note the Lutheran structure; the relation to

---

[37] See pp. 44 and 158.

God begins through guilt. 'The greater the genius' says Kierkegaard 'the more profoundly he discovers guilt' (107). In turning inward he discovers freedom. He does not fear fate for he is not concerned with an outward task. His bliss is to know of himself that he is freedom. However, with freedom another figure comes into being: guilt. To the degree that he discovers freedom, so does he know angst. He fears guilt for it alone can deprive him of freedom. As soon as guilt is posited, freedom returns as repentance (108–9).

Now it becomes apparent in what sense there is more angst in the subsequent individual than in Adam: guilt is conceived of more concretely in the face of freedom. 'At last it is as if the guilt of the whole world united to make him guilty.' [A good description of Luther's state of mind prior to his grasping his revolutionary understanding of justification.]

Just as fate at last captures the immediate genius, . . . the moment when by himself he collapses before himself by fate, likewise does guilt capture the genius who is religious and this is the moment of culmination, the moment when he is greatest, not the moment when the sight of his piety is like the festivity of a solemn day of rest but when by himself he sinks before himself in the depth of sin-consciousness (110, supplemented by Lowrie, 98).

Again the Lutheran structure. It is not ethical behaviour, when 'the sight of his piety [resembles] . . . the festivity of a solemn day of rest', but the guilt in which 'he sinks before himself in the depth of sin-consciousness' that is prerequisite for entrance into the religious.

We are in a position to consider faith, but chapter IV will intervene.

Chapter IV. The Angst of Sin or Angst as the Consequence of Sin in the Single Individual

By a qualitative leap sin enters the world, constantly. One would think that, sinning, angst would be cancelled. Further, the leap is to actuality; so it would seem that possibility is annulled [Hegelian *aufgehoben*]. But no. Angst returns in relation to what was posited and in relation to the future. Now, however, it has a definite object, its 'nothing' an actual something, since the distinction between good and evil is postulated '*in concreto*' (111–12). 'To speak of good and evil as the objects of freedom finitizes both freedom and the concepts of good and evil. [That is to say it is to speak of freedom as a *liberum arbitrium*, which it is not.] Freedom is infinite and arises out of nothing' (112).

Angst will be considered under two rubrics: angst about evil and angst about the good (the demonic).

§1. Angst about Evil

No matter how deep an individual has sunk he can sink deeper; this 'can' is the object of anxiety. 'Angst wants to have the actuality of sin removed, not entirely but to a certain degree, or to put it more exactly, to a certain degree it wants to have the actuality of sin continue—but note, only to a certain degree' (114). The angst (i) concerns the actuality of sin, out of which sophistry brings forth possibility and (ii) it is, in view of the future possibility of sin. 'Sin advances in its consequence; repentance follows it step by step, but always a moment too late' (115). The individual is dragged along; sin conquers. 'Anxiety throws itself despairingly into the arms of repentance. Repentance ventures all. It conceives of the consequence of sin as suffering penalty and perdition' (115). (We may say this represents both the thought of the natural man and a 'Catholic' situation.) 'In other words repentance has gone crazy' (116).

But repentance cannot make him free; in that he is mistaken. The occasion comes; anxiety has already discovered it. Every thought trembles. Anxiety sucks out the strength of repentance and shakes its head. . . . Already he has a presentiment of the prostration of freedom (116).

Says Kierkegaard: 'Men use one or another prudential device to abort this embryo of the highest life; . . . the most effective means of escaping . . . spiritual trial [*Anfægtelse*, German *Anfechtung*][38] is to become spiritless and the sooner the better' (117). That is to say that, with the failure of the ethical (the attempt once and again to repent), and the despair that this brings, two ways are open: to plunge into immediacy, spiritlessness; or (what we are about to consider) to take the step of faith.

Thus 'ethically the point is to get the individual rightly placed in relation to sin' (117). The individual must know himself a failure, falling

---

[38] See pp. 164–5.

down in guilt before his own eyes. 'As soon as this is accomplished, the individual stands repentant in sin . . . . In that very moment he has been brought to dogmatics.' Repentance is the 'highest ethical contradiction' since ethics requires ideality but 'must be content to receive repentance' and further given that repentance is 'dialectically ambiguous with regard to what it is to remove', an ambiguity that dogmatics removes in the Atonement (117–18). Of atonement Kierkegaard comments that in it hereditary sin becomes clear; presumably that is to say that Christ, the second Adam, atones for all history.

§2. *Angst about the Good*

Whereas the bondage of sin is an unfree relation to evil, the demonic is an unfree relation to the good; an anxiety about the good and in consequence its denial or shunning. The good signifies the restoration of freedom, or redemption/salvation. 'Freedom is posited as unfreedom, because freedom is lost; . . . the demonic is unfreedom that wants to close itself off. This, however, is . . . an impossibility' (123). (That is to say the relationship to God, which is freedom, is posited as unfreedom, given that a supposed 'freedom' of independence will be lost. Recall that in the Lutheran tradition freedom consists in being bound to the good, while sin consists in closing one's self off in the attempt to maintain oneself apart from God.) When this in-closing reserve comes into contact with what is truly freedom it becomes anxious. In the New Testament the demonic says to Christ 'What have you to do with us?' (Matt. 8.29), suggesting that Christ has come to destroy him. Or he implores Christ to go another way (Matt. 8.31).

What an enclosed person conceals in his in-closing reserve 'can be so terrible that he does not dare to utter it, not even to himself' (128); as though were he to utter it he might be tempted to repeat what he has done. Such a repeating is most likely to occur when a person is not master of himself. 'Similarly a person in an intoxicated state may have done what he only faintly remembers, yet he knows that it was such a wild thing that it is almost impossible for him to recognize himself'[39] (128). Kierkegaard comments that what determines whether

---

[39] Presumably a reference to Kierkegaard's own behaviour, see p. 109.

the phenomenon is demonic is 'the individual's attitude toward disclosure', whether he will accept it in freedom. If he will not the phenomenon is demonic (129). In-closing reserve is liable to result in involuntary disclosure; the unhappy man blurts out his secret. Thus does the demonic shun contact with the good that will help him. He replies in a reply 'that expresses all the horror of this state: Leave me alone in my wretchedness'. Or, looking back to a point in the past: 'At that time I could probably have been saved—the most dreadful reply imaginable' (137). Neither punishment nor thunderous tirades against him make him anxious, 'yet every word that is related to the freedom scuttled and sunk in unfreedom will do so' (137).

In an intellectual sense the content of freedom is truth and truth sets a person free. Unbelief and mockery of religion relate not (as is commonly believed) to content but to certitude. The thought of eternal life in its weightiness creates a responsibility in the acceptance of it and may involve a change in life that is feared. Thus a person will seek to sooth his soul by producing a new proof. Yet what is this 'but a "good work" in a purely Catholic sense!' (an evasion of the relation with God). Of attempts to prove the truth/untruth of religion one may say, 'when a man of rigid orthodoxy applies all his diligence and learning to prove that every word in the New Testament derives from the respective apostle, inwardness will gradually disappear' (142); but likewise when a freethinker attempts to prove that the New Testament was not written until the 2nd century.[40] The most refined form of such self-objectivization, reflecting the defiance and arrogance of unbelief, is 'the one that becomes interesting to itself by wishing itself out of this state while it nevertheless remains complacently in it' (144).

Everyone who has lost inwardness can say 'the wine of life is drawn' (Macbeth), for 'inwardness is...the fountain that springs up unto eternal life' (John 4.14) (146–7). Inwardness is 'the constituent of the eternal in man' (151). When the eternal is denied, the individual becomes demonic.

If the eternal is posited the present becomes something different from what a person wants it to be. He fears this and thus he is in anxiety about the good. He may continue to deny the eternal as long as he wants but in so doing he

---

[40] Cf. pp. 144–5.

will not be able to kill the eternal entirely. . . . No matter how much he denies it he cannot get rid of it.

There is always present a 'restless disturber' which nevertheless is the 'true rest'—eternity (152). As the way to hell is paved with good intentions, so is eternity best annihilated by mere moments (aesthetic existence, living for immediacy). 'Men are not willing to think eternity earnestly but are anxious about it and anxiety can contrive a hundred evasions. And this is precisely the demonic' (154).

Chapter V. Angst as Saving through Faith

Kierkegaard writes:

This is an adventure that every human being must go through—to learn to be anxious in order that he may not perish either by never having been in anxiety or by succumbing in anxiety (155).

He comments: 'Whoever has learned to be anxious in the right way has learned the ultimate.' Were a human being either a beast or an angel he could not have angst. It is consequent upon the fact the human is intended to be a synthesis, a synthesis brought about by spirit, that he has angst. The more profoundly he experiences angst, the greater the person. We are not speaking of fear as related to something external 'but in the sense that he himself produces the angst' (155).

Angst occurs on account of freedom's possibility. Such angst is 'absolutely educative', consuming all finite ends. 'Whoever is educated by angst is educated by possibility and only he who is educated by possibility is educated according to his infinitude' (155–6). Possibility is the weightiest of all categories. It is true that we often hear the opposite stated [by Hegelians], that possibility is light whereas actuality heavy. But this is said by those who know not what possibility is, associating it with happiness, fortune, etc. The one who truly knows what is possibility will praise actuality, for even when it rests heavily upon him he will remember that it is far lighter than possibility. Finite things only educate finitely. If he does not defraud the possibility that wants to teach him he will receive everything back; 'for the disciple of possibility received infinity and the soul of the other expired in the finite' (158).

There is however a danger to which the one educated by possibility is exposed: not that of going astray but self-slaughter. 'If at the beginning of his education he misunderstands the anxiety, so that it does not lead him to faith but away from faith, then he is lost' (159). If however he will remain with angst, so that it 'enters into his soul and searches out everything and anxiously torments everything finite and petty out of him' (159), it will lead him where he wants to go. 'Whoever does not wish to sink in the wretchedness of the finite is constrained in the most profound sense to struggle with the infinite' (160). So too with guilt: whoever learns to know guilt only by analogy to judgements of the police court 'never really understands that he is guilty, for if a man is guilty he is infinitely guilty' (161). The one who has truly learnt to be in angst 'will dance when the anxieties of finitude strike up the music and when the apprentices of finitude lose their minds and courage' (161–2).

'He who with respect to guilt is educated by angst will therefore repose only in atonement' (Lowrie, 145). Thus we have completed the deliberation: 'As soon as psychology has finished with anxiety it is to be delivered to dogmatics' (162).

Critique

Methodology

In the first place it would be good to draw attention to the seeming methodological incompatibility between this book and *Fragments*. This is the more remarkable given that Kierkegaard worked on the two books concurrently. Given that both books were published pseudonymously, Kierkegaard did not of course need to write compatible books. Pseudonymity may indeed have enabled him to explore problems one at a time without reference to what he said elsewhere. But then one has to ask whether there is such a thing as a Kierkegaardian position. It may well be that this incompatibility is the more in evidence subsequent to certain issues having come to the fore in the 20th century; but to say this does not really help. The problem is this. In *Fragments* the human has no prior awareness of his or her need for the 'truth' that is given in revelation, the revelation not only being the Truth but also bestowing the condition for its recognition. By contrast, *The Concept Angst* discusses a perceived need, angst, which it is suggested is overcome through the relation to God, a line of thinking that will be carried through in *The Sickness unto Death*.

In the 20th century Barth was to draw attention to this conundrum present in Kierkegaard's authorship. Have we here a theology that commences from 'below', an answer to perceived human need, or from 'above', with the unexpected revelation of God which discloses our need to us? In his 'Preface' to the second and revolutionary edition of his *Römerbrief* (*Letter to the Romans*) of 1922, Barth, who in that book famously speaks of revelation coming 'straight down from above', acknowledges a debt to Kierkegaard.[41] But Barth was to become less sure that Kierkegaard was an ally in this. In his 1933 debate with Emil Brunner who, within the context of the Third Reich, had suggested that characteristics of human life such *Volk* might provide a 'joining point' (*Anknüpfungspunkt*, attachment point) for reception of the gospel, Barth responded in no uncertain terms in a reply simply headed '*Nein!*'. Barth contends that God's revelation, creating its own channel (the position put forward in Kierkegaard's *Fragments*), awaits in the human no 'joining point', neither positive nor negative. In speaking of a 'positive' joining point Barth surely has in mind Catholic theology, in which nature is transformed by grace; in speaking of a 'negative' joining point presumably the Lutheran tradition, which typically has had a prior propaedeutic as to human angst. (Barth was of course himself Reformed, Calvinist.) Lecturing in Copenhagen in 1965 on the occasion of his collecting a prize, Barth voiced his worries, asking whether in his perceived subjectivity Kierkegaard may not have compromised the utter freedom of the coming of the gospel.[42]

What is one to say? It could well be contended that such a confusion (if that is what it is) pervades the Lutheran tradition, being by no means peculiar to Kierkegaard. Augustine's thought

---

[41] Karl Barth, 'The Preface to the Second Edition', *The Epistle to the Romans* (Oxford, 1933), 4, 10.

[42] Karl Barth, 'A Thank You and a Bow: Kierkegaard's Reveille', trans. H. Martin, *Canadian Journal of Theology*, xi (Jan 1965) [Ger. orig., 'Dank und Reverenz', *Evangelische Theologie*, 23 (1963)].

would be a fine example of a theology which employs a 'negative' joining point; his unquiet heart finding satisfaction in that good which is the revelation of God in Christ (Augustine's Neoplatonism). But where is Luther? On the one hand, in contradistinction to the Augustinian tradition, he commences from an unexpected revelation; on the other he speaks of an angst which is overcome through the message of acceptance which is the gospel. Likewise Kierkegaard. Again in the 20th century the Lutheran theologian Bultmann on the one hand, as an existentialist, commences from human inauthenticity, on the other is sometimes accorded the designation of being a fringe dialectical theologian for whom revelation is key. In relation to Kierkegaard on this score it is worth remarking that Schelling in his late lectures (commentary on which we know Kierkegaard to have been reading in 1843, thus immediately prior to writing both *Fragments* and *The Concept Angst*), appears to have this dual starting point. (Again he is a Lutheran.) For Schelling on the one hand a revelation breaks through as the only epistemological solution possible to the impasse reached through the fact that post-Kant we are aware that we cannot gain knowledge of God through human reason, nor yet (as Schelling thought) reach God through experience; while on the other hand the human can (as he believed) only have his need met by a direct personal relation to God.

Biology and Theology

There is furthermore not simply tension between this book and other work but, on another score, present within the book itself. On the one hand Kierkegaard desires to release the conception of original sin from a traditional Augustinian conception, confirmed in the Lutheran confessions, in favour of individual human responsibility; yet on the other he wishes to claim that sin has a social dimension, and not only that, but furthermore to cast this social dimension in classical biblical terms. In regard to the need for a social dimension (bracketing for the moment how this social dimension shall be conceived of) Kierkegaard writes: 'Christianity has never assented to give each particular individual the privilege of starting from the beginning in an external sense' (73). We may sympathize with his dilemma! No more than he have we solved the question as to individual responsibility and thus imputability for sin, versus the recognition that we do not sin in isolation from the community of which we are a part. Are we to be tough on crime or tough on the causes of crime? But Kierkegaard causes unnecessary problems for himself by casting this social dimension in the quasi-biological terms of hereditary sin. That he did this raises interesting questions as to what factually (biologically and historically) he believed to be the case.

Prior to Kierkegaard, as we have seen, Kant, Hegel, and Schleiermacher had all understood the Genesis story as myth, one that nevertheless imparted 'truths' about human beings. Kierkegaard, too, had made the move to such a conception, writing (in what may be counted an exact definition): 'Myth allows something that is inward to take place outwardly' (47). Such an insight was presumably embedded in his theological training. In a book published in Copenhagen in 1825 the theologian H. N. Clausen used the word 'myth' of the Genesis account.[43] Kierkegaard took a course on Kant and Schleiermacher with Clausen in 1833–4. No less than Kant it would seem, Kierkegaard wished to hold humans imputable for their actions. His comments on the responsibility even of children for their acts are striking. Yet Kierkegaard also appears to give credence to the biblical story, whether understood metaphorically (thus simply on account of wishing to remain in continuity with the tradition) or conceived to be historically true is unclear. Kierkegaard may be well aware of the tension in his work. At a later date (1850) he was to comment in his *Journal* on the 'composite of qualitative heterogeneous categories. "Hereditary" is a category of nature. "Guilt" is an ethical category of spirit. How can it ever occur to anyone to put these two together, the understanding says—to say that something is hereditary which by its very concept cannot be hereditary'.[44]

It is difficult to surmise what Kierkegaard, living in Copenhagen in the early 1840s, may have thought the truth of the matter to be. (And Kierkegaard scholars take scant interest in this.) As we have seen, he paid little attention to biblical historical criticism, and as we shall yet discuss he was sceptical as to the relevance of scientific discovery for the study of humankind.[45] But the idea that an intelligent individual, who read German periodicals and frequented the coffee bars of Copenhagen,

[43] *CA*, Supplement, 233, note 22.
[44] *JP* 2:1530 (*Pap.* X A 481), n.d., 1850.
[45] See p. 306.

had by this date not come up against speculation about evolution is scarcely credible.[46] Published in Britain in the same year as Kierkegaard's book, Robert Chambers' *Vestiges of the Natural History of Creation and other Evolutionary Writings*, was a sell-out, creating a stir. The fact that Kierkegaard chose to cast in hereditary–biological terms his sense for the importance of the social ambience as the setting in which the fall into sin occurs left him vulnerable. What when there could no longer be conceived to be a single ancestor as Kierkegaard had surmised (writing that 'nature does not favour a meaningless superfluity' (46)?) Is Kierkegaard working phenomenologically, considering the present, or making deductions from a priori historical–biological beliefs? Thus what possible evidence could substantiate his contention that sin increases through the generations? Perhaps, in thus contending, he is simply seeking to needle the Hegelians who held that *Geist* is progressively instantiated in history! Yet, on the other hand, Kierkegaard will judge the idea of a Fall taking place outside time 'fantastic' (25).

A particular instance of the problem is Kierkegaard's depiction of 'woman'. Since the 17th century there had been various theories abroad as to the relative contributions of spermatozoa and ovum to the fertilized embryo or homunculus. Kierkegaard finds the idea of a Fall outside time 'fantastic'. And is the idea that Eve was formed from Adam's rib not 'fantastic'? He betrays a deeply engrained social prejudice. Thus he tells us that 'Eve is a derived creature' (47). Further we hear that, unlike what is the case in other species, in the case of humanity that which is derived is less perfect than the original. He wishes to see the individual human being in his or her societal context. Yet when it comes to woman's angst he apparently lacks any social analysis. Why wouldn't a young woman be anxious, in a patriarchal society in which there were few guards against a woman being raped, if a young man fastens a desirous look upon her? Moreover, in the 19th century pregnancy (as had been the case for Kierkegaard's sisters) not infrequently ended in

---

[46] John Elrod tells us that Darwin's *Origin of the Species* published in 1859 'found immediate and enthusiastic acceptance among Danish academics who were themselves already at work both empirically and speculatively on an evolutionary accounting of the emergence of the species'. ('Introduction', *Kierkegaard and Christendom*, Princeton, NJ, 1981, xiv.)

death. Kierkegaard finds that the more profoundly a human possesses angst, the greater that human. If, as he tells us, angst distinguishes human beings from beasts and (as he observes) woman has more angst than man, how come that it is not she who stands at the pinnacle of creation?

If truth were told Kierkegaard simply stands as a pertinent example in a long tradition stretching down to the present day in which woman fails to be seen as a fully articulate, self-actualizing human being in her own right. Venus, so Kierkegaard informs us, is just as beautiful when sleeping. We recall the frequency with which in Western art or literature woman is portrayed as faceless, inert, sleeping or dead.[47] Indeed, Kierkegaard's is an exact articulation of that which, associating it with woman, Jean-Paul Sartre depicts as what it is to be *en soi*; inert in its completion. Woman's self-expression he remarks is that of a 'totality with no history' (66). Kierkegaard's comments are pathetic; in terms of his argument uncalled for. Whatever his biological misunderstandings, one would have thought such an outlook profoundly at odds with his sense for each person's inherent integrity *coram deo*. Kierkegaard argues that, woman inhabiting more exclusively than does man the physical aspects of the synthesis between body and spirit, this gives greater scope for anxiety in the cleft between the elements of the synthesis. On the contrary, one might well think from phenomenological observation (quite apart from research showing that the left and right sides of the brain become integrated at a younger age in girls) that women are on the whole more integrated as between the mental/spiritual and physical than are men.

Faith, Time, and Angst

The work under consideration concerns angst, the contrary of faith. Nevertheless there is a passage in which the concept of faith is considered—and this passage is pivotal to comprehending Kierkegaard's

---

[47] Cf. 'lovely in death as in life' (Howard V. Hong & Edna H. Hong, eds & trans., *Love's Deeds* (otherwise known as *Works of Love*), Princeton, NJ, 1995, 313) (henceforth *LD* 313, etc.). Witness Elisabeth Bronfen's depiction of the frequency with which Western drama and art take place over her dead body (Elizabeth Bronfen, *Over Her Dead Body: Death, femininity and the aesthetic*, Manchester, 1992).

authorship. Kierkegaard has a fully worked out epistemology that allows of the truth of Christian propositions. Far from faith being some unjustified leap into the blue, it may well be that this epistemology is held by him to be a necessary foundation if one is to accept the truth of Christianity. In any case it must be said that Kierkegaard supplies the epistemological undergirding to his theology; he does not just leave Christianity hanging in the air, an impossibility unsupported by any structure of thought. That Kierkegaard explores this epistemological position in depth indicates how well he realizes that Christian 'truths' do not fit with other ways of seeing reality; not the Greek, nor the Jewish, and we may say not the Catholic (for which we may translate that which seems axiomatic to the natural man), nor the Hegelian which in this has something in common with this latter. Rather does the way in which Kierkegaard thinks fit precisely with a Lutheran *simul justus et peccator*. It holds as conceivable 'interventions' in time, whether incarnation, resurrection or judgement. I shall consider this with reference to the passage on time in chapter III.

If time is conceived to be an infinite succession, one moment giving way to the next, then it comes naturally to think of the eternal as an 'extension' of time, situated at its 'end'. As Kierkegaard puts it, we represent it spatially. The Hindus speak of a line of kings that has ruled for 70,000 years; the 70,000 years 'are for thought an infinite vanishing' (86). And indeed in the Catholic way of thinking, which became normative in the West, eternity was conceived of in this manner as somehow an extension of time. Not so, says Kierkegaard; the eternal is different in kind. Thus the eternal irrupts each moment into time. The human is (i) both in himself in time and eternal and (ii) a synthesis of body and mind (the Danish *Aand* as also the German *Geist* having the connotations of both 'mind' and 'spirit'), which synthesis only comes about as the third which is spirit is posited; so these two are in effect one and the same synthesis. This understanding of the how self becomes a self is paralleled by the understanding of the incarnation, which again is a synthesis in the moment of the eternal with that which is temporal. Were one to cease to think in this way says Kierkegaard, one would botch all that Christianity claims. In holding as does Hegel that the eternal is mediated (transformed) into time, any sense of that otherness which is the eternal and which enters time in the moment is lost. For Hegel there is essentially no moment, only continuity. In speaking of the 'fullness of time' (Gal.

4.4), he simply intends that the progress of history had reached the point at which it was appropriate that Christ should come (of course seeing this advent in purely conceptual terms). Not a bit of it responds Kierkegaard; the incarnation is a moment in which the eternal is joined to time (the 'fullness of time'), this in parallel with what is the case in each moment.

But such a way of thinking is nothing if not a perfect fit with the Lutheran understanding that we are *simul justus et peccator*; that is to say we live 'from' the future, or God, in the present. The two are joined in the person in the moment. Now this state of affairs is not, for the Christian, a stable situation.[48] (Once and again we fall back into the way of thinking of the natural man, corresponding to time being but a succession from past to future.) Thus faith must be repeated in each moment enabling the self to be synthesized in the moment, nothing (other than purely nominally) being carried forward. There is a profound discontinuity of self. As Bultmann will have it, I relate to my past as to sin (while I live from the future, as for Bultmann I do). In this tradition there can be no *habitus*, nor good works on which I build, taking me forward into the future. But Kierkegaard also brings to this arena, as we have discussed, the idea of figuralism. History is making for a *telos*. It is not however the *telos* in terms of which Hegel (or Marx, a materialist Hegelian) think, in which there will be a consummation of present history, of time as we know it. Judaism and Catholicism, Kierkegaard avers, hold a similar notion. Rather does 'progress' consist in an in-breaking of the eternal in an ever-increasing crescendo, as the 'figure' of God's intervention brings about fulfilment. Hence, as Kierkegaard says, all history is in some sense contained in that future. As a human act, once and again repeated, faith relates to this reality.[49] The two correspond: the reality that is believed in and the faith that believes in it.

Another way of putting which would be to say that we receive ourselves 'in the moment' from God. Angst occurs when we fail to trust this (fail to exercise faith), such that the self falls apart. Most of the time, in a bid to hide our angst from ourselves, we bury ourselves in the present (the aesthetic way of life). Or we try desperately, in

---

[48] See p. 24.

[49] In relation to this discussion see Stephen Crites, *In the Twilight of Christendom: Hegel vs. Kierkegaard on Faith and History* (Chambersburg, PA, AAR Studies in Religions, 2 1972), 66–75, but Crites fails to point to the Lutheran context.

Kierkegaard's language despairingly, to come to ourselves by our-selves that we may feel good about ourselves (the ethical way of life). We think that of our own volition we can constitute ourselves in relation to the present and the world in which we live. But neither the aesthetic not the ethical way of life will do the trick and faced with the recognition of this we suffer angst. This is the moment that is ripe with a kind of pregnancy. As Kierkegaard will have it, angst is supremely 'educative' (156). Now we are faced with a choice. Either we can, in faith, submit to dependence on God, recognizing that we can only come into our own as the spirit forms the synthesis, which will be for the self to 'rest transparently in God'[50]. Or else in the moment of anxiety, freedom (which we may call the possibility of self-actualization in relation to God) swoons and, submerging our-selves in the aesthetic, we attempt to forget our divine possibility, that we are spirit. Kierkegaard's understanding of the human being as both spirit and carnal in nature is thus the axis of his anthropology, corresponding to his theology and indeed his metaphysics.

Reception

The book received no review.

However by 1881 the Danish critic and man of letters Georg Brandes (who cannot but have had this text in view) was recom-mending to Nietzsche that he read Kierkegaard, 'one of the most profound psychologists who ever lived'.[51]

Subsequent to the turmoil of the Great War, the European Contin-ent was to enter an age of angst and Kierkegaard's text came into its own. In three footnotes in his *Being and Time* (1927), Martin Hei-degger, not given to acknowledging his sources, pays tribute to Kierkegaard, remarking that it was he who had 'gone farthest in analysing the phenomenon of anxiety [*Angst*]'.[52] For Heidegger it is angst which discloses the 'facticity' of human existence, the human being's thrownness (*Geworfenheit*) in the world in which he is not at home (*nicht zu Hause*). It is also however, as in Kierkegaard's case,

---

[50] See p. 239.
[51] Paul Krüger, ed., *Correspondence de Georg Brandes*, I–VI (Copenhagen, 1966), III, 448, quoted by Thomte, 'Historical Introduction', *CA*, xiv.
[52] Martin Heidegger, *Being and Time*, trans. John Macquarrie & Edward Robinson (Oxford, 1962), 492.

that we have angst that presents us with the possibility of achieving authenticity (*Eigentlichkeit*, literally a coming to own ourselves). Where Heidegger, however, differs from Kierkegaard is in the lack of divinity. Whereas for Kierkegaard such 'authenticity' (the self coming to itself) is only to be achieved through the relation to God, Heidegger recommends 'resoluteness'. A latter-day Pelagian (or 'ethical' individual), he believes that at least ideally we can come to ourselves by ourselves. Interesting also is that in the case of Heidegger (who incidentally was a fine Luther scholar, known in his early years for the depth of his Luther scholarship), it is 'the future', in his case in the form of death, which forms that horizon from which we live (one might say by inverted existence)[53] in our present. Kierkegaard must turn in his grave as Heidegger amputates that which he, Kierkegaard, believes gives 'possibility' to human existence, which is God. Heidegger's is a far harsher doctrine.

Partly through Heidegger and partly directly Kierkegaard was also important for French existentialism. Called up for military service, in December 1939 Jean-Paul Sartre writes to Simone de Beauvoir requesting that she send a copy of *The Concept Angst*.[54] After consuming it (and finding it bafflingly theologic), he tells her that she will see in the book what Heidegger owes to Kierkegaard. What evidently interests Sartre is 'the relation [of] anxiety to its object, to something that is nothing (linguistic usage also says pregnantly: to be anxious about nothing)'.[55] Thus does Kierkegaard feed into the Sartrean conception of angst in the face of nothingness and, as in the case of Kierkegaard, our inauthentic behaviour is an attempt to cope with this (in Sartre's vocabulary our bad faith, *mauvais foi*). Albert Camus was likewise deeply influenced by Kierkegaard. His novel *The Fall* depicts a classic case of a man brought face to face with his inauthenticity, his self-understanding as an ethical individual (he had been an advocate) shattered as he fails to rescue a woman who

[53] See p. 218.
[54] Lee Fahnestock & Norman MacAfee, trans., *Letters of Jean-Paul Sartre to Simone de Beauvoir, 1926–1939* (Harmondsworth, 1994), 378.
[55] Quintin Hoare, trans., *War Diaries: notebooks from a phoney war, November 1939–March 1940* (New York, 1984), 124–5, quoted by J. Stewart, 'France: Kierkegaard as a Forerunner of Existentialism and Poststructuralism' in Jon Stewart, ed., *Kierkegaard's International Reception, Kierkegaard Research: Sources, Reception and Resources*, 8, 1, *Northern and Western Europe* (Farnham, 2009), 435.

commits suicide, throwing herself into the Seine. When we encounter our protagonist he is drowning himself in the aesthetic, living a down-and-out existence among the pimps and the prostitutes of Amsterdam. (Compare Kierkegaard: 'Forget that you were a child, that there was piety in your soul and innocence in your thought, . . . doze your life away in the glittering inanity of the soirées, forget that there is an immortal spirit within you; and when wit grows mute there is water still in the Seine' (*E/O* II, 211).) Yet this man keeps in a cupboard the stolen panel from the van Eyck triptych that shows the just judges 'on their way to meet the lamb'. As he knows, after ethical failure there is always the possibility of repentance and entry into the religious. But, in the last line of the novel 'it'll always be too late'.[56]

In a quite different intellectual context in 1939–40, giving Gifford Lectures in Edinburgh, the American political thinker and theologian Reinhold Niebuhr was to draw on Kierkegaard's book. It is reliably reported in Scotland that the audience could hear the first German bombs falling on the docks at Leith as he spoke. Niebuhr portrayed German hubris as arising out of angst. In true Kierkegaardian style he tells us:

Man, being both free and bound, both limited and limitless, is anxious. . . . Anxiety is the internal precondition of sin. It is the inevitable spiritual state of man, standing in the paradoxical situation of freedom and finiteness. Anxiety is the internal description of the state of temptation. It must not be identified with sin because there is always the ideal possibility that faith would purge anxiety of the tendency toward sinful self-assertion. . . . That is why Christian orthodoxy has consistently defined unbelief as the root of sin, or as the sin which precedes pride.[57]

And Niebuhr quotes Luther 'in conformity with the general Christian tradition' as saying in his 'On the Freedom of a Christian', referring to Sirach 10:14: 'The beginning of all sin is to depart from God and not to trust Him'. What is interesting and most significant about Niebuhr's take on Kierkegaard's thought is the emphasis on human creativity and not simply sin as arising out of the 'paradoxical situation of

---

[56] Albert Camus, *The Fall*, trans. Justin O'Brien (Hamondsworth, 1963), 95, 108.
[57] Reinhold Niebuhr, *The Nature and Destiny of Man*, I, 'Human Nature', ch. VII (New York, 1964), 182–3.

freedom and finiteness' in which human beings find themselves. Given angst, human beings write symphonies.[58]

By the 1960s Kierkegaard's text, now available in English translation, was firmly in the public eye. Every angst-ridden student was attracted—at least to the title. What people derive from this opaque book must be a matter for curiosity. Perhaps its dreamlike nature encourages them to make of it what they will, taking from it what they can. The book fed into existential psychotherapy. It influenced the work in theology and cultural theory of the German immigrant to the United States Paul Tillich.[59] *The Concept Angst* has been the most influential of Kierkegaard's texts (excepting perhaps the existential import of the *Postscript*). Considering its Christian context it is interesting that its major impact has been in secular fields. What has proved seminal, whether in philosophy, psychoanalysis, or literature, has been the analysis of the phenomenon of angst. How remarkable that this apparently arcane book (a deliberation on original sin) has proved perhaps more able than any other of Kierkegaard's texts to stand the test of time. So long as humans struggle and survive, wrestling with their predispositions, we may think that it will continue to fascinate and engage.

[58] Niebuhr, *Nature and Destiny*, 182.
[59] Cf. Thomte, 'Historical Introduction', xvi.

5

Concluding Unscientific Postscript to *Philosophical Fragments*

Introduction

As is the case with all Kierkegaard's work, the *Concluding Unscientific Postscript to 'Philosophical Fragments'* is precisely named, its organization wholly logical. Nevertheless, one should grasp that both title and organization, with boxes within boxes as subsection is divided into subsections, are in their convolution a joke at Hegel's expense. This is Kierkegaard's major anti-Hegelian text. It is, logically, published under the name of Johannes Climacus of *Fragments* fame.

The interface with the book to which the work is advisedly a 'postscript' is not exact. In the present book Kierkegaard will introduce the thought that, quite apart from the Paradox which is Christ, given that 'the eternal' stands in a paradoxical relation to time a natural or 'Socratic' religion must necessarily be related to out of one's subjectivity. To be Christian is to take a yet further step, as that which must be related to subjectively is the eternal present in time, and thus in itself a Paradox.

The book is divided into two parts. By far the longer, Part II concerns subjectivity and the subjective relation to the thought of the eternal (a) within religion in general (b) specifically within Christianity. By way of a foil for Part II, Part I discusses the mistaken attempt to hold an 'objective' relation to Christian truth. There is extensive polemic against Hegel, more particularly the 'Hegelianism' present in Copenhagen as represented by Martensen. Indeed the book may in part have been fuelled by anger and resentment on Kierkegaard's part. At the precise time that it was composed, effecting a reconciliation with the Primus of the Danish Church, Jacob Peter Mynster, the two having previously found themselves on opposite sides in the debate over Hegel, Martensen had been appointed to the coveted post of Court Preacher. Kierkegaard, for whom his relationship with Mynster was of considerable moment and who, at least as far as Hegelianism was concerned, would have seen Mynster as standing on his side of the debate, felt decidedly left out. It is in large part this book, widely influential, that has given Kierkegaard the epithet of being the ur-father of existentialism. It is through and through Lutheran.

It may be useful at the outset to attempt to pin down what it is that Kierkegaard finds so impossible about Hegel and Hegelianism. His fear is that, in the attempt to 'modernize' Christianity, enabling it to be commensurate with the present ethos, its essence has been lost. Hence the book focuses on the offence and otherness of Christian claims. The corollary of relating to these claims is that one is uprooted from the world and from one's natural self. (Note the Lutheran sense that a Christian is uprooted from being centred in self, from what is comfortable and comes naturally.) In consequence, Christian claims should challenge the bourgeois Christianity of Kierkegaard's time. Now Hegel appears precisely to wish to affirm the *Sittlichkeiten* or ethical mores of society. Hegelian religion à la Martensen is thus only too at home in the world. Kierkegaard, moreover, suspects (and now that we have available, as he did not, Hegel's early essays on religion, we may think rightly) that Hegel believes very little at all. He simply wants to take the forms or concepts, the *Begriffe*, of the religion and show them (as did Kant in *Religion within the Limits of Reason Alone*) to be a useful illustration of what he would in any case say. Hegel will cement the society through what must sound to Kierkegaard like a *Volksreligion*. By contrast Kierkegaard is adamant that it is *qua* individual that one exercises one's relationship to God. It is that relationship which must take priority in one's life, leading in turn (as we shall see in considering *Love's Deeds*) to service of others. Thus there is present a basic clash of positions, presumably irreconcilable.

Fundamental to this difference of philosophy is a disparate understanding of the relationship of history to faith. With the increasing recognition of the category of 'history' in the early 19th century, not least through the work of Hegel, Christian 'truths' come to be qualified. They are marked as coming from a particular era, bearing the imprint of their time. The thought must occur that one should adjudicate as to their relevance to the present age. Not only Hegel, but also for example Schleiermacher and not least Martensen, come to put great emphasis on 'Christian history' (in the case of those who are theologians, on the Christian church in its continuity through history). In Hegel's case this takes the form of a belief in the onward march of civilization, in which the life of Christ is a major turning point but not in any sense absolute. Hegel thinks that by an act of diremption and mediation, societal, or theological thought differentiates itself and is then reintegrated in a higher resolution or sublation. Thus although we are in need of abstract thought forms that we may understand ourselves in relation to that thinking as it were set over against ourselves, ultimately it will be reintegrated into human self-understanding. History is the progress of *Geist*, or spirit. It has about it an inevitability, novelty occurring when the time is ripe. Kierkegaard thinks quite otherwise. For him also, as we have seen, the eternal 'enters' history, but in the moment, paradoxically, for the eternal and time are contraries. For Kierkegaard there can be no 'divinization' of history itself, which is rather taken forward by that which is other than history, which is God. (Neither man, we should note, thinks the historical process simply chance or chaos.)

Correspondingly, for each thinker the individual must be placed in a differing relationship to this process. From Kierkegaard's perspective, in Hegel's case the individual is swallowed up in the history of the society. He or she relates to the divine (if one can use this term at all) through his or her relation to his or her culture and time. As we have already seen in conjunction with the consideration of *Fear and Trembling*, there will in consequence be some real issues around liberty of conscience and non-conformity. For Kierkegaard this is anathema. Increasingly during the 1840s, but this was always present, he came to see his 'category' as 'the individual'. The task of life is to come to oneself and one achieves this individuation in the first place through one's God-relationship. This is not necessarily an insular view of the human being (as we shall see in the next chapter). In one sense Kierkegaard with his sense of individual conscience is close to Kant. But there is more than that involved. The individual has in view his eternal destiny and there must be a transformation of his mode of living in relation to that destiny. In this sense one could say that Kierkegaard is Augustinian; but he is also very different from Augustine, in as much as life is not conceived of as a transformation of self but rather a looking to another, and in that what is at stake is not a consummation of present circumstances but the in-breaking of another order. Kierkegaard is ultimately Lutheran, not Augustinian Catholic.

Kierkegaard will in this book be at pains to stress the 'suffering' which is a corollary of the juxtaposition involved as the individual with the thought of the eternal lives 'meanwhile' in this world. The jarring of the eternal and of history is taken to exaggerated lengths as Kierkegaard attempts to unhinge Hegelianism. This brings us to the role that 'the thought of Lessing' plays in the book for Kierkegaard. Lessing, with his ditch, precisely forbore to synthesize history with the eternal. He can thus be employed as a weapon against Hegel. Lessing's deathbed scene as recounted by Jacobi (which Kierkegaard relishes, reciting it with great aplomb) is a valiant refusal on Lessing's part, in the face of Jacobi's admonitions, to take any easy path into the religious life. In his last known words, Lessing would rather abide by his integrity.[1] Kierkegaard admires that. He thinks Hegelianism slippery; in danger of losing any sense for the eternal—while no one quite notices what has transpired. It is that sleepwalking into oblivion on the part of Christianity that he so fears. But where the Kierkegaardian position has a soft under-belly is in the refusal to recognize that the Christian absolutes with which Kierkegaard will counter a Hegelian position were constructed within history. By the mid-19th century it is becoming increasingly difficult to think anything other

---

[1] See p. 148.

of the declarations of Nicaea and Chalcedon. This we have already considered.[2]

Exposition

Introduction

The book (as in *Fragments*) is an experiment in thought, its presupposition that each has an 'infinite interest' in his eternal happiness.

Part I. The Objective Issue of the Truth of Christianity

Chapter I. The Historical Point of View

Since there must always be uncertainty surrounding historical facts, the attempt to secure one's faith objectively through historical scholarship is misplaced. To counter the difficulty, people resort to holding the bible inspired, but this simply transfers the problem since that the bible is inspired is a matter of faith. Or they make recourse to the church. Kierkegaard has in mind here (given the phrases he picks up) his contemporary N. S. F. Grundtvig and the Grundtvigians, who countered the uncertainty of looking to the bible by according authority to the church. But this also must involve 'approximation'— any security gained is inadequate to making the 'infinite decision' on which an eternal happiness is based (a person asked to base his eternal happiness on the fact of his baptism must despair). Or people point to 'the evidence of the centuries'; but this proves nothing.

To become more and more 'objective' is actually to regress, bringing a person no closer to faith, for 'faith does not result from straightforward scholarly deliberation' (29).[3] Can a demonstration as to the problems harm a believer? No. Why then mount a demonstration? It is when faith loses its passion that demonstrations are

---

[2] See pp. 16–17, 26.
[3] Howard V. Hong & Edna H. Hong, eds & trans., *Concluding Unscientific Postscript to 'Philosophical Fragments'*, vol. I (Princeton, NJ, 1992), 29 (henceforth 29 etc.).

thought necessary. But it is 'a misunderstanding to want to assure oneself objectively and thereby avoid the risk in which passion chooses' (42). One who holds to Christianity objectively is a pagan, 'because Christianity is ... a matter of spirit and of subjectivity' (43). ('Pagan' since the person thinks he has got 'a god' to which he can directly relate.)

Chapter II. The Speculative Point of View

The speculative point of view (i.e. Hegelianism) considers Christianity a historical phenomenon which becomes 'true' by permeating it with concepts. Christianity is part of an unfolding *Geist*, its historical specificity (i.e. particularity) becoming lost. Kierkegaard further attacks the reduction of Christianity to mere ethics and civilized behaviour. The good wife tells her husband, uncertain whether he is a Christian, that he is a subject of the Danish Lutheran state, so of course he is a Christian. Kierkegaard addresses Martensen, 'Mr Speculative Thinker': 'Are you a Christian or are you not? The question is not whether you are going further' (52). The problem is not idealism *per se* (Hegel) but its introduction into the church. The speculative thinker makes himself light; the one interested in his eternal happiness 'as subjectively heavy as possible' (57).

Part II. The Subjective Issue, The Subjective Individual's Relation to the Truth of Christianity, or Becoming A Christian

SECTION I. SOMETHING ABOUT LESSING

Chapter I. An Expression of Gratitude to Lessing

Kierkegaard compares himself to one perched in a garret on top of a vast building (Hegelianism) having the dim suspicion that there is something wrong with the foundations, watching those who redouble their exertions to beautify or enlarge the structure (Martensen et al.), who makes the acquaintance of a man 'whose fame was ... like a smile of fortune in the midst of his loneliness'. He finds his 'difficult thoughts' touched upon, such that he comes to have 'the hope first of understanding the nature of the difficulty [the ditch] and then perhaps of being able to overcome it'. (Swenson /Lowrie, 59)[4]. For Kierkegaard, Lessing's stance puts a spanner (American wrench) in the works of Hegelianism.

Kierkegaard clearly delights in Lessing, admiring (it would seem) his courteousness, honesty, and perspicacity, savouring meanwhile his wit and economical use of the German language. Lessing, says Kierkegaard, avoided the 'meaningless situation' whereby his God-relationship would be at second hand through another. In this he compares Lessing with Socrates—in Kierkegaard's book the ultimate accolade. (Cf. *Fragments* where Kierkegaard comments that no man dare make himself 'a god' for another, but every disciple must be at first hand.)[5]

Chapter II. Possible and Actual Theses by Lessing

Note the humour! It is, rather, Lessing's outlook that counts. 'Just as he himself is free, so, I think, he wants to make everyone free in relation to him' (72); the secret of communication 'hinges on setting the other free' (74). (Exactly as in the case of Socrates' maieutic teaching.) Communication becomes 'a work of art' (79). Thus must it be when it is a matter of becoming.

Kierkegaard refers to well-known sayings of Lessing's: (i) *that contingent historical truths can never become a demonstration of eternal truths of reason;... that the transition whereby one will build an eternal truth on historical reports is a leap* (93).[6] That he may focus on this difference in categories Lessing will allow that reports of miracles are as reliable as other historical reports. Kierkegaard notes however the difference from his own position; namely that for he himself when it comes to a relation to what is itself a Paradox contemporaneity doesn't help, since there is 'no direct transition'; were there to be, this would constitute 'unbounded injustice' to all who come later (97). Thus the problem is not actually the breadth of the ditch (the inability of historical events to prove the eternal), but

---

[4] David Swenson & Walter Lowrie, trans. & eds, *Concluding Unscientific Postscript* (Princeton, NJ, 1968), 59 (henceforth Swenson/Lowrie, 59 etc.).
[5] The theme of *Fragments*, ch. 5; see 100–2.
[6] Cf. Gotthold Lessing, 'On the Proof of the Spirit and of Power' in Henry Chadwick, ed., *Lessing's Theological Writings: Selections*; discussed p. 15.

rather the need for 'dialectical passion'; the lack of which makes the ditch infinitely wide.

Kierkegaard turns to the deathbed scene reported on by Jacobi. To his horror Jacobi had discovered Lessing to be some ilk of Spinozist or pantheist. Concerned for his soul, he attempts to inveigle Lessing into (we may say) leaping the ditch. There follows one of the most delicious passages in Kierkegaard. Lessing responds: 'Gut, sehr gut!...Ich begreife wie ein Mann von Kopf auf diese Art Kopf-unten machen kann, um von der Stelle zu kommen; nehmen Sie mich mit, wenn es angeht.' [Good, very good!...I grasp how a man with a good head (a smart man) can in this manner make a head-under (a somersault) (i.e. lower his good head) to get moving; take me with you if that's possible!] Comments Kierkegaard: Lessing's irony beautifully reveals his recognition that, when it is a question of leaping, one must do it alone. 'His urbanity and his partiality for Jacobi are truly admirable, also his conversational artistry in courteously stating "take me along—if at all possible"' (102). Jacobi responds: 'Wenn Sie nur auf die elastische Stelle treten wollen, die mich fortschwingt, so geht es von selbst.' [If you will just step on the elastic spot that propels me it will come about by itself.] Kierkegaard remarks that Jacobi thus seems inclined to transform the leap into something objective. Lessing replies, with what are his last known words: 'Auch dazu gehört schon ein Sprung, den ich meinen alten Beinen und meinem schweren Kopf nicht mehr zumuten darf' [That also involves a leap which I can no longer ask of my old legs and my heavy head] (102).

Kierkegaard finds Jacobi's remark 'just step on this elastic spot' pious fraud. When someone is averse to making the leap [Danish *Spring*], so averse that this passion makes the ditch infinitely wide, then the most ingeniously contrived springboard [Danish *Springemaskine*] is of no avail. Lessing knows well that the leap, as decisive, does not allow of approximation. His reply is dialectically correct and personally evasive—he excuses himself on account of his old legs and heavy head. Enjoying Lessing's irony, Kierkegaard remarks that it goes without saying that one with young legs and a light head can easily make the leap. Lessing 'reposes in himself and feels no need of companionship; therefore he parries ironically and slips away from Jacobi on his old legs' (103). Despite all his apparent enthusiasm on behalf of others, Kierkegaard finds Jacobi self-seeking. Kierkegaard crowns his estimate of Lessing in citing the latter's famous remark that, were God to hold all truth in his right hand and in his left only the forever striving for truth and were to say 'Choose', humbly falling at his left hand he would say, 'Vater, gieb! die reine Wahrheit is ja doch nur für dich allein!' [Father, give! Pure truth is indeed for you alone!]

SECTION II. THE SUBJECTIVE ISSUE, OR HOW SUBJECTIVITY MUST BE CONSTITUTED IN ORDER THAT THE ISSUE CAN BE MANIFEST TO IT

Chapter I. Becoming Subjective

Objectivity tempts. Wishing to evade the pain and crisis of decision, the individual wills to make the issues objective—so that he can decide upon them. In this way it becomes possible to evade the decision; one awaits yet further evidence. But in the situation with which we are concerned the question of 'truth' has precisely to do with the manner of the subject's acceptance of it: 'An objective acceptance is paganism or thoughtlessness'(130). Christianity teaches that the way is to 'become subjective, that is, truly to become a subject' (131). It wills to intensify passion to its highest pitch; and faith is 'the highest passion of subjectivity' (132).

Becoming subjective is 'the highest task assigned to every human being' (133). Of such a person—Kierkegaard has Socrates in mind— one could say: 'Even in death he would *will* not to know that his life had had any significance other than that of having ethically prepared the development of his soul' (135). Socrates 'was occupied solely with himself' (147). Thus Kierkegaard contrasts Socrates, as he has Lessing, with those (considered in Part I) who, making it into an objective issue, attempt to take distance from the question as to the truth of Christianity. 'To become subjective should be the highest task assigned to every human being, just as the highest reward, an eternal happiness, exists only for the subjective person or, more correctly, comes into existence for the one who becomes subjective' (163). This last we shall discuss.

Chapter II. Subjective Truth, Inwardness; Truth is Subjectivity

Kierkegaard throws down a gauntlet in the face of Hegelianism. One must attend to what is to be understood by 'being'; 'what it is to be an existing human being'. He remarks that 'the fantastical disregard of this' has caused confusion (189). Truth is 'in the process of becoming' (190). In the case of God thinking and being may be co-eval, but that is not true of existing human beings who are becoming. An existing spirit presumably asks after truth because he wants to exist in it! The truth under consideration is thus 'truth' in a different sense than objective, scientific, truth. What we have here is the truth of appropriation, of inwardness. Truth, says Kierkegaard, is a redoubling (a personal assimilation). While the objective way 'is of the opinion that it has a security that the subjective way does not have', in actual fact 'to exist' and 'objective security' are incompatible. 'Pencil-pushing modern speculative thought takes a dim view of passion and yet, for the existing person, passion is existence at its very highest—and we are, after all, existing persons. . . . All essential knowing pertains to existence' (197).

Kierkegaard contends that 'truth as a paradox corresponds to passion'; further, that the truth appears paradoxical lies in its relating to an existing subject (199). There is a distinction between asking after objective truth, reflected upon objectively as an object to which the knower relates himself, in which case he relates himself not to the relationship but to the objective truth; and asking 'the question about truth' subjectively, in which case what concerns us is the individual's inner stance. Take knowledge of God. What is reflected upon objectively is that this is the true God. Subjectively 'the individual relates himself to a something *in such a way* that his relation is in truth a God-relation' (199). Pursuing the objective way the individual enters upon an approximation process, by which it is proposed to bring God objectively to light. 'But this is in all eternity impossible, because God is a subject and therefore exists only for subjectivity in inwardness' (Swenson/Lowrie, 178). By contrast, choosing the subjective way the individual understands the dialectical difficulty of finding God objectively, feeling the pain of every moment wasted in which he lacks God. 'That very instant he has God, not by virtue of any objective deliberation, but by virtue of the infinite passion of inwardness' (Swenson/Lowrie, 178–9; cf. *CUP,* 199–200).

For the person who knows what it means to think dialectically the road 'swings off' (Swenson/Lowrie, 179). The only way in which an existing person enters into a relationship with God is:

When the dialectical contradiction brings passion to despair and assists him in grasping God with 'the category of despair' (faith) so that the postulate [as to God], far from being the arbitrary is in fact *necessary* defence, self-defence; in this way God is not a postulate, but the existing person's postulating of God is—a necessity... If the problem is to calculate where there is more truth, ... whether on the side of the person who only objectively seeks the true God ... or on the side of the person who is infinitely concerned that he in truth relate himself to God with the infinite passion of need—then there can be no doubt about the answer for anyone who is not totally botched by scholarship and science (200–1). [Swenson/Lowrie: 'who has not been demoralized with the aid of science' (i.e. *Wissenschaft*) (179).] ...

If someone who lives in the midst of Christianity enters, with knowledge of the true idea of God, ... the house of the true God, and prays, but prays in untruth, and if someone lives in an idolatrous land but prays with all the passion of the infinite, although his eyes are resting upon the image of an idol—where, then is there more truth? The one prays in truth to God although he is worshiping an idol; the other prays in untruth to the true God and is therefore in truth worshiping an idol (201).

If one enquires objectively into immortality while another 'stakes the passion of the infinite on the uncertainty—where then is there more truth and who has more certainty?' (201). The first has entered 'upon an approximation that never ends', since in fact 'the certainty of immortality is rooted in subjectivity' (201).

Consider Socrates. He poses the question objectively as to whether there exists immortality. Does it follow that he is a doubter? No. 'He stakes his whole life on this "if"; he dares to die and, with the passion of the infinite, he has so ordered his whole life that it might be acceptable—*if* there is an immortality' (201). By contrast, those who have the 'three demonstrations' as to the existence of God do not so order their lives. The uncertainty helped Socrates 'because he himself helped with the passion of infinity' (202); whereas the demonstrations are dead, failing to demonstrate anything. 'The Socratic ignorance was thus the expression, firmly maintained with all the passion of inwardness, of the relation of the eternal truth to an existing person; and therefore it must remain for him a paradox as long as he exists' (202). By contrast the attempt to arrive at an objective truth through a demonstration is never done with; unable, moreover, to arouse subjective passion.

Thus can Kierkegaard speak of 'the passion of the infinite' as being 'the very truth'. Now 'passion of the infinite is precisely subjectivity and thus subjectivity is truth' (202). Within the objective point of view there exists no infinite decision; 'only in subjectivity is there decision'. Wishing to become objective is 'untruth'. Kierkegaard concludes: 'The passion of the infinite, not its content, is the deciding factor, for its content is precisely itself.' The subjective 'how' and subjectivity are 'the truth'. Given that the subject exists this 'how' is 'dialectical' in relation to time. In the passion of decision the existing person is in the temporal realm, such that 'the subjective "how" is transformed into a striving ... motivated and repeatedly refreshed by the decisive passion of the infinite'. So now a definition: '*An objective uncertainty, held fast through appropriation with the most passionate inwardness, is the truth,* the highest truth there is for an *existing* person' (202). Objective knowledge 'is suspended'. Objectively all the person has is uncertainty; but it is the uncertainty that intensifies the passion of inwardness. 'Truth is precisely the daring venture of choosing the objective uncertainty with the passion of the infinite' (203).

In other words, to be in truth is the step of faith: 'without risk, no faith' (204). Faith is the 'contradiction between the infinite passion of inwardness and the objective uncertainty' (204).

If I am able to apprehend God objectively I do not have faith; but because I cannot do this, I must have faith. If I want to keep myself in faith, I must continually see to it that I hold fast the objective uncertainty, see to it that in the objective uncertainty I am 'out on 70,000 fathoms of water' (204).

That subjective inwardness is truth is apparent from Socratic wisdom, 'the undying merit of which is to have paid attention to the essential meaning of existing, of the knower's being an existing person' (204). So we may say that 'in his ignorance, Socrates was in the truth in the highest sense within paganism' (204). It is the misfortune of speculative thought to have forgotten this, avers Kierkegaard.

Is there a category of thought that truly 'goes beyond'? (In contrast with Martensen's 'advance' upon Hegel.) Subjectivity, inwardness, is truth. Is there a *more inward* expression for it? That is to say a 'going beyond'. Yes: were one to say 'Subjectivity is untruth' (207). Kierkegaard distinguishes his move from a Hegelian idealism, which holds subjectivity to be untruth on account of the fact that objectivity is truth. To say that subjectivity is untruth 'puts barriers in its own way at the very moment it wants to begin, which makes the inwardness so much more inward ... The work goes backward, that is, backward in inwardness' (207). Given that the subject cannot be presupposed to have been in untruth eternally, we must say that a change 'so essential has taken place in him that he in no way can take himself back into eternity by Socratically recollecting' (207–8). As in *Fragments*, where Kierkegaard has made this same move, he proposes that we call this untruth 'sin'. The individual is born in sin; 'hereditary sin'. 'If existence has in this way obtained power over him he is prevented from taking himself back into eternity through recollection' (208). The back door of recollection closed, inwardness acquires depth. 'He must go forward' (209).

To go forward then! 'Let us assume that the eternal, essential truth is itself a paradox' (209). How does such a paradox emerge? By placing the eternal truth together with existing: 'The eternal truth has come into existence in time. That is the Paradox' (209). The subject, who on account of sin was prevented from Socratically taking himself back into eternity is now unconcerned with this, for the eternal truth 'has come in front of him' (209). Given the objective uncertainty and the ignorance of the person the eternal repels, but in that the eternal is not *in itself* paradoxical it does not repel sufficiently intensely. When, however, the eternal truth comes into existence, is *in itself* paradoxical, it repels by virtue of its absurdity to the individual, to which the corresponding passion of inwardness is faith: '...without risk no faith; the more risk the more faith; the more objective reliability, the less inwardness' (209). As compared with the strenuousness of faith, 'the Socratic existential inwardness resembles Greek nonchalance' (210).

What then is the absurd? That the eternal truth has come into existence in time. That which actually 'goes beyond' the Socratic 'must essentially have a mark of standing in relation to the god's having come into existence' (210). Faith *sensu strictissimo* (in the strictest sense)—compare *Fragments*—is that which relates to a coming into existence (*PF*, 81). Now we see that, in as much as the absurd contains the element of coming into existence, the route of approximation is inappropriate in that it will confuse the object of faith with a simple historical fact for which it seeks historical certainty.

By contrast the absurd contains the contradiction that something (the eternal) that can only become historical in direct opposition to all human understanding has become historical. 'This contradiction is the absurd, which can only be believed' (211). Thus: 'Christianity has proclaimed itself... as *the Paradox* and required the inwardness of faith with regard to what is an offence to the Jews, foolishness to the Greeks [1 Cor. 1.23]—and an absurdity to the understanding' (213). We may say: 'It cannot be expressed more inwardly that subjectivity is truth than when subjectivity is at first untruth [i.e. sin] and yet subjectivity is truth [i.e. faith]' (213).

Kierkegaard concludes with an attack on a Hegelianism which, thinking to have 'gone beyond' Hegel in order to be Christian (Martensen), has dissolved the Paradox (so losing Christianity).

Suppose that speculating is temptation, the most precarious of all. Suppose that the speculator is not the prodigal son, for this is what the concerned God presumably would call the offended one whom he continues to love nevertheless, but the naughty child who refuses to stay where existing human beings belong, in the children's nursery and the education room of existence where one becomes adult only through inwardness in existing, but who instead wants to enter God's council, continually screaming that, from the point of view of the eternal, the divine, the theocentric, there is no paradox (214).

Kierkegaard adds: 'Has being human now become something different from what it was,... is the condition not the same: to be an individual *existing* being' (214–15). Thus does he maintain a distinction between the Kantian/Socratic individual (or Lessing) who is offended—the prodigal son whom God nevertheless loves; and the Hegelian (Martensen) who in his hubris thinks to 'go beyond' the Paradox, proclaiming that from the point of view of the eternal there is no paradox; and who has thereby lost Christianity.

Chapter III. Actual Subjectivity, Ethical Subjectivity; the Subjective Thinker

Kierkegaard will consider what it is to exist in actuality, as an individual human being *sub specie aeternitatis*; the Lutheran sense of being placed *coram deo*, before God. The difficulty lies in the person's being composed of both eternal and temporal (cf. *The Concept Angst*). The Hegelian is correct that *sub specie aeternitatis* there is no either/or, but for one who exists it is a different matter. For an existing person, eternity is not eternity but the future. And the future has to do with decision. Where the eternal relates itself as future to the person who is in a process of becoming there is an 'absolute disjunction' (307).

Pure thinking (Hegelianism) is useless when the truth needed is that in which to exist. It compares to travelling in Denmark with a small map of Europe on which Denmark is but a pinpoint. (It is not the right scale.) Says Kierkegaard, the immorality of the age might be said to consist in a 'debauched contempt for individual human beings' (355). People cling together *en masse*. Whereas: 'Every human being must be assumed to possess essentially what belongs essentially to being a human being' (356).

Chapter IV. The Issue in *Fragments*: How Can an Eternal Happiness Be Built on Historical Knowledge?

The reference is to Kierkegaard's rephrasing of Lessing's question on the title page of *Fragments*. The chapter consists in two divisions. Division 1, 'For Orientation in the Plan of *Fragments*', has three subsections which contrast the Socratic and the Christian. Division 2, 'The Issue Itself', has two sections: section 'A', 'Pathos', considers in three subsections the nature of that 'suffering' in which the relationship to the eternal consists, followed by an 'intermediate clause' between 'A' and 'B'; section 'B', 'The Dialectical', again in three subsections, together with an appendix, considers the specifically Christian. We enter into a dense (and hilarious) jungle, designed to send up the smooth contours of Hegelianism and easy platitudes of contemporary Christian existence.

Division 1. For Orientation in the Plan of Fragments

Recall here the book's 'Introduction': the presupposition is that 'Christianity... wants to make the single individual eternally happy' and that 'precisely within this single individual [there is] this infinite interest in his own happiness'. From *Fragments* we learned that the mark of the essentially Christian is that the question as to an eternal happiness is decided in time, the criterion being the relation to something historical. Surely, says Kierkegaard, no one reading the

New Testament will deny this? Such a qualification (what I have called the claim to particularity) 'forms the sharpest contrast to paganism' (369). Whether Christianity is in the right Johannes Climacus will not decide: the aim is to state the issue. Hence it is perfectly possible to know what Christianity *is* without being a Christian. But to know what it is *to be a Christian* is something else. This he will now consider.

Division 2. The Issue Itself

The individual's eternal happiness is decided in time through a relation to something historical that furthermore is historical in such a way that its composition includes that which according to its nature cannot become historical and consequently must become that by virtue of the absurd (385).

Such is Christianity's claim. Kierkegaard will take us on a journey in which we shall consider what it is to hold a subjective relation to the truth, first Socratically, then in the Christian sense. To relate to an 'eternal happiness' while in time is (in either case) 'plain and simple pathos'; pathos has however fallen into discredit 'in our philosophical nineteenth century' (385).

'A' PATHOS

As stated, the section consists in three sub-sections, considering the 'initial', 'essential', and 'decisive' expressions of existential pathos. The writing is permeated by Lutheran themes together with a critique of a 'Catholic' position (the Middle Ages), which sought a solution through 'the monastery'. For what I have called the 'Catholic' position we may read not simply what, historically, people did but what it comes naturally to human beings to do. We are not concerned with a critique of 'monasteries' *per se*; one could as well hold a subjective relation to an objective truth while a monk as in any other occupation. Rather does 'the monastery' represent a mistaken turning, in that the felt need to do something adequate to one's relation to the eternal is channelled into something outward. But at least in the Middle Ages people were attempting to make the Absolute absolute, and in that that was the case they were doing better than Kierkegaard's contemporaries, for whom 'an eternal happiness' has become relative, one good among others.

§1. The Initial *Expression of Existential Pathos*

The idea of an 'eternal happiness' must transform the whole of existence. The person must come to relate to the Absolute absolutely; it cannot be a relative *telos*, one among others. Ergo, what is involved is a 'dying away from immediacy'. (Note that Plato's Socrates conceives of the relation to the absolute in these terms.)[7] Now such a dying away from immediacy is a suffering. If a single hard spot remains, anything that for the sake of 'eternal happiness' the individual is not prepared to forego, he has no relationship to it. By contrast, the parson treats religion as though it had a *telos* in time: if one does such and such one will be rewarded—one's business will flourish and so forth. But by definition an 'eternal happiness' is not to be had in time.

Now to the person prepared to let immediacy die away the monastery becomes a temptation. Could one not in a monastery fulfil the task? But 'to be a monk' is equally 'to be something' as 'to be a councillor'; one has mediated with the world. By contrast, to have succeeded in the task would consist in remaining in the finite while having severed one's roots in it. Such an individual compares to an adult who, playing with children, does not play as do they for his actuality lies elsewhere. Again consider that the woman in love (a metaphor for relating to God) would not think it meritorious to need to be with her lover in each moment (the monastic attempt).

Maintaining an absolute relation to the Absolute *telos* is a correspondence of like with like. The kingdom of heaven resembles a pearl hidden in a far country (Matt. 13.46). Foregoing all else one must set out on 'an enthusiastic venture in uncertainty' (Swenson/Lowrie, 355). For an eternal happiness as the absolute good 'has the remarkable quality that *it can be defined only by the mode in which it is acquired*' (427). The discourse about this good consists in saying: 'Venture everything' (427). By contrast the 'tortured self-contradiction of worldly passion' arises from the attempt to maintain an absolute relationship to relativities. To seek for assurances is to ditch the venture, for it is the act of faith that is transformative.[8] 'To obtain a proof of the resurrection [would seem to be] a tremendous help—if it

---

[7] Cf. Plato, *Symposium* and *Phaedrus*.
[8] Cf. Heb. 11.1, 8: 'Faith is the substance of things hoped for, the evidence of things unseen... By faith Abraham... went out'.

were not for the fact that the very existence of this proof [would constitute] the greatest difficulty of all' (Swenson/Lowrie, 384).

§2. *The* Essential *Expression of Existential Pathos: Suffering*
Our individual has now succeeded in the initial task: he relates absolutely to the absolute and relatively to the relative. He no longer knows that suffering which accompanies an uprooting from the finite. Lo and behold, another form of suffering overtakes him! For 'the Infinite' which now confronts him is not the natural element of the finite creature. Kierkegaard will here make reference to the Lutheran concept of (German) *Anfechtung*, (Danish) *Anfægtelse* (literally being 'fought against': the terror and claustrophobia of being confronted and feeling confined by the Infinite). Suffering stands in what is but an accidental relation to the life of immediacy: if things go well one is happy, encountering misfortune one suffers. By contrast the religious individual has suffering constantly with him. When Juliet (who lives in immediacy) on account of her loss of Romeo sinks in impotence, the religious orator will proclaim new suffering—and Juliet rise again.[9]

Consider that 'suffering' which is the 'essential expression' of the religious life. We stand *coram deo*, before God. (Luther well knows that no one can so stand; Climacus likewise.) To be known by God in time makes life 'acutely strenuous'. Paul speaks of being caught up into a third heaven (in Kierkegaard's terms, he relates absolutely to the Absolute). What does he discover? A thorn in the flesh![10] *Anfechtung* expresses 'the reaction of the limit against the finite individual' (410), 'the opposition of the absolute itself' (411). In temptation 'it is the lower that tempts;... in *Anfechtung*... the higher that... tries to frighten him back' (Swenson/Lowrie, 410). Climacus comments that *Anfechtung* will be unknown to one who is not very religious; he himself knows nothing of it. The task of the individual is to understand that before God (*coram deo*) he is nothing. This discomforts (*Anfechtung*). Such an individual will hit on the strangest things to do (as though there could be an outward resultant) to please God!

---

[9] Cf. *CA*, 161: The one who has truly learnt to be in angst 'will dance when the anxieties of finitude strike up the music'; cf. also Paul: 'I have learned, in whatsoever state I am, therewith to be content. I know both how to be abased and I know how to abound' (Phil. 4.11–12).

[10] Cf. 2 Cor. 12.7.

What, however, could one do commensurate to the Infinite? Our individual should bear this in mind when considering taking an outing to the Deer Park. (There is such on the outskirts of Copenhagen, to which Kierkegaard was wont to take carriage rides.) Once again the monastery tempts. Would it not be possible twenty-four hours a day to hold to the Absolute absolutely? The Middle Ages well understood the incommensurability of the world with the thought of God; hence the monastery. 'If the religiousness of our time has gone further' (is more advanced—a jab at Martensen's mistaken notion) this consists in it being 'capable of holding the thought of God together with the flimsiest expression of the finite' (473). Experiencing *Anfechtung*, now contemplate the idea of going to the Deer Park! It must seem incommensurate with one's relation to the Infinite. The task becomes 'with God to be capable of it' (486). The monastery consists in superhuman exertion. But that is presumptuousness, hubris. By contrast an excursion to the Deer Park represents the humblest expression for the God relationship! One best expresses the *difference* between being human and the eternal. To the Deer Park? And does our individual enjoy himself? Of course, for it is human to enjoy oneself! The only resultant in the world of such an individual's religiousness is humour. The God-relationship is inward and unmediated.

§3. *The* Decisive *Expression of Existential Pathos: Guilt*
The 'decisive' expression of what it means to be an existing person is guilt. Not guilt about this or that, but a comprehending of oneself as essentially guilty. It is placing this together with the idea of an eternal happiness which points up the infinite, qualitative, difference between oneself and God. While the discovery of guilt would appear to be a backward movement inasmuch as going deeper is going forward it is in fact a movement forward. (Cf. the Lutheran context.) Guilt traps (*Anfechtung*). Consciousness of guilt belongs to the sphere of immanence: it arises from the *idea* of the eternal. (In this it differs from the consciousness of sin.) In the Middle Ages it was naively thought that what was needed was penance for sin, thereby making the matter outward—as though certain 'sins' had been committed against God, such that a situation pertained analogous to a court. But no third party can help. The guilt itself is worse than any punishment. Equally inappropriate is self-flagellation as having the effect of finitizing guilt.

The Middle Ages so to speak let God have a hand in the game, but this is to make God into a fantastic figure.

INTERMEDIATE CLAUSE BETWEEN 'A' AND 'B'

That which has been set forth is a matter of existence, pathos-filled and dialectic insofar as it concerns the relation of an existing person to the idea of the eternal. Kierkegaard will call it Religiousness 'A'. We shall now proceed to discuss the specifically Christian, Religiousness 'B', which is dialectical in a sense not yet entered upon. It will entail a new pathos. Religiousness 'A' is by no means undialectical (it concerns the qualitative difference between the human and God) but it is not paradoxically dialectical. Christianity has often been made into aesthetic gibberish: a 'titbit for dunces', because it cannot be thought. But the very fact that it cannot be thought is 'the most difficult of all to hold fast when one is to exist in it, . . . especially for brainy people'. It is, says Kierkegaard, 'equally difficult for every human being to relinquish his understanding and to concentrate his soul on the absurd' (557). If he stakes his life on this absurd, his life is lived by virtue of the absurd. 'But if he understands that it is not the absurd [i.e. if he is a Hegelian], then *eo ipso* he is no longer a believing Christian' (558). Kierkegaard speaks of the 'martyrdom' of faith and of 'crucifying' the understanding (559).

Christianity is a 'relating to the pathos-filled' 'A', 'as an impetus for new pathos' 'B' (559). It is when, in 'A', 'the eternal happiness' has become for the individual the only comfort, and furthermore when owing to guilt-consciousness it has become a repelling relation—and yet this relation means more than anything else—that the time has come to begin the dialectic. One does not prepare oneself for Christianity by reading books or by world-historical surveys (Hegel) but by immersing oneself in existing. Given Christianity is an existence-communication, 'any other preliminary study is bound to end in misunderstanding' (560). 'The paradox is that this apparently aesthetic relationship, that the individual relates himself to something outside himself is, nevertheless, to be the absolute relationship with God' (561). Within immanence (deism or some kind of natural religion) God is not 'a something, but everything and is infinitely everything', the up-building consisting in his being within the individual. The paradoxical up-building (Christianity) corresponds to God in time as an individual human being, the individual relating himself to something outside himself. This relation to the God in time cannot be thought. If the Paradox is not in this manner held fast then Religiousness 'A' is the higher, for Christianity has become aesthetic.

'B' THE DIALECTICAL

Because an individual relinquishes the understanding in faith he should not think poorly of the understanding. He makes 'daily efforts' to exercise faith, which 'presses forward against the understanding' like rolling a weight up a mountain (565). 'The believing Christian both has and uses his understanding, respects the universally human, does not explain someone's not becoming a Christian as a lack of understanding and...uses the understanding—in order to see to it that he believes against the understanding' (568).

§1. *The Dialectical Contradiction that Constitutes the Break: To Expect an Eternal Happiness in Time through a Relation to Something Else in Time*

It is not that the existing individual comes in time to relate himself to the eternal ('A'), but that *in time* he relates himself to the eternal *in time*. This runs directly counter to all thinking. In Religiousness 'A' the eternal is *ubique et nusquam* (everywhere and nowhere) but hidden by the actuality of existence. In the paradoxical–religious the eternal is present at a specific point (particularity); in this lies the break with immanence. If the individual, himself undialectical, has his dialectic outside himself, what we have is an aesthetic interpretation of Christianity. (Presumably intended that he will have made the God/man into a fantastic object.) If the individual is paradoxical–dialectical then we have the paradoxical–religious. (Christianity.) The break makes the inwardness the greatest possible. By contrast, in Religiousness 'A' there is no historical point of departure: the individual, in time, 'reflects upon his being eternal' (573).

§2. *The Dialectical Contradiction that an Eternal Happiness is based on the Relation to Something Historical*

For thinking (i.e. idealism) the eternal is higher than the historical, since the eternal (*Geist*) is the basis of all else. In the religiousness of immanence the individual must transform his existence in accordance with his relation to the eternal. In the dialectical paradoxical relation the contradiction lies in basing one's eternal happiness on an approximation. 'The subjective individual at the peak of his subjective passion is to base his eternal happiness on...historical knowledge' (575). The research scholar occupies himself objectively and academically, it making no difference to his subjective existence. But in 'B' the problem is overcome. 'The existing person must have lost continuity with himself, must have become someone else...and now, by receiving the condition from the god [cf. *Fragments*], becomes a new creation' (576). That is to say: 'The contradiction is that becoming a Christian begins with the miracle of creation and that this happens to someone who is created' (576). (The Lutheran break in continuity of self-understanding.) Every Christian 'is Christian only by being nailed to the paradox of having based his eternal happiness on the relation to something historical' (578). By contrast 'to transform Christianity into an eternal history, the god-in-time into an eternal becoming-of-the-deity etc.'—i.e. Hegelianism—'is nothing but evasion and playing with words' (578).

§3. *The Dialectical Contradiction that the Historical under consideration here is not Something Historical in the ordinary sense but consists of That Which Can Become Historical Only against its Nature, Consequently by Virtue of the Absurd*

That the eternal comes into existence in time, is born, grows up, and dies is a break with all thinking. If however the coming-into-existence of the eternal in time is supposed to be an eternal-coming-into-existence (Hegelianism) then Religiousness 'B' is abolished: 'all theology is anthropology' (a reference to Feuerbach)[11] (579). (That is to say, in Hegelianism the moment, particularity, is abolished.) The person who understands Christianity directly (the Hegelian) will 'confuse Christianity with something that has arisen in man's, that is humanity's, heart, confuse it with the idea of human nature and forget the qualitative difference that accentuates the absolutely different point of departure: what comes from God and what comes from man' (580). Faith, Kierkegaard concludes, is a 'totally unique sphere'

[11] Cf. Ludwig Feuerbach, 'Preface' to the Second edn, *The Essence of Christianity*, George Eliot, trans. (New York, 1957): 'the true sense of Theology is Anthropology', xxxvii. See pp. 61–2.

that, 'paradoxically,...accentuates the actuality of another person [Christ]' (580). Ethically it is heteronomous. It is this that is the Paradox; not 'the unusual in a direct (aesthetic) sense, but the apparently familiar and yet the absolutely strange' (581).

Appendix to 'B'. The Retroactive Effect of the Dialectical on Pathos
  Leading to a Sharpened Pathos and the Contemporaneous Elements
  of This Pathos

Religiousness 'A' is the individual's own pathos-filled transformation of existence. Oriented toward the purely human, it assumes that every human being participates in this eternal happiness and finally becomes eternally happy (581). By himself the individual is unable to gain consciousness of sin, only guilt-consciousness, since guilt-consciousness is 'a change of the subject within the subject himself' (584). The subject's self-identity is preserved. By contrast the consciousness of sin is 'a change of the subject himself which shows that outside the individual there must be [a] power that makes clear to him that he has become a person other than he was by [his] coming into existence; that he has become a sinner' (584). This power is the god in time. Again, in Religiousness 'A' the individual sees all humankind as standing in relation to the eternal, a relation of which every human being is capable, while the eternal is everywhere; such that 'no time is spent waiting or in sending a messenger' (584). By contrast in Religiousness 'B' the believer does not know that the whole race is to be saved, in that the single individual's salvation depends on his being brought into relation to that historical event which, on account of being historical cannot be everywhere at once but becomes known to human beings in time. (Particularity is of the essence of 'B'.) Through no fault of their own countless generations continued to be unaware of the god's having existed. To have one's existence qualified in this way says Kierkegaard, is 'sharpened pathos', both because it cannot be thought and because it is isolating (584–5).

Christianity is the only power that truly can cause offence. 'For the believer, offence comes at the beginning, and the possibility of it is the continual fear and trembling in his existence' (585).

Chapter V. Conclusion

Kierkegaard comments on the misunderstanding he has exposed as to what is Christianity. A Christian is one who accepts Christian doctrine. Of the person who has refused Christianity, Kierkegaard comments (admonishing such a one to keep silent) that one can respect that which one cannot force oneself into. Being a Christian involves conformity to the 'how' of Christianity, which must fit the absolute Paradox. The Christian holds fast to an objective uncertainty with the passion of inwardness.

A FIRST AND LAST EXPLANATION

In an appendix to the book Kierkegaard acknowledges that he is the author of all the pseudonymous works adding: 'Thus in the pseud-onymous books there is not a single word by me' (626).

Critique

God's Transcendence and Revelation

The aim of the *Postscript* is, in the first instance, in giving God back God's transcendence to counter Hegelianism. This has nothing spe-cifically to do with Christianity. But secondly, to find a valid way to speak of the truth of Christian claims in the face of a Hegelian and Feuerbachian reductionism.

What Hegel has done is to subsume God, or rather *Geist*, within history. Kierkegaard will turn the clock back and set God free. Such an outlook belongs to his Lutheran tradition, but behind that quite fundamentally to the Hebraic and, in so far as eternity is juxtaposed with time, one might say also to the Greek tradition. The problem that confronts Kierkegaard is how he shall do this in modernity, subsequent to the Enlightenment and specifically to Kant. It is no longer possible to employ reason to attain to God (and in any case the idea that God could be reached through ratiocination is wholly foreign to Kierkegaard's tradition). Kierkegaard fully accepts the Kantian epistemological recognition that one cannot speak of know-ledge other than that achieved through the synthesizing power of the human mind exercised in relation to the empirical world. (In this he is simply at one with the whole post-Kantian philosophical and theological German tradition.) Schleiermacher had tried to find a way forward through drawing attention to another faculty, human awareness or feeling, which he claimed was the province of religious sensibilities. But Kierkegaard (as Hegel) is suspicious of a religious immediacy (which incidentally can lead straight to a Feuerbachian reductionism). Faced with the same dilemma, the elderly Schelling turns to a study of human religious traditions, postulating that the transcendent God's self-disclosure is in some way captured through the human response. Kierkegaard's approach to the conundrum (in this not unlike Schelling) is to focus on a phenomenological depiction, in his case, of the human response to the 'idea' of eternal life: eternal life presumably rather than 'God' since he is concerned with the phenomenology of the human being, who in respect to eternal life is an interested party.

Attempting through speaking of the human response to God to conjure up a Hebraic sense of the God's otherness, Kierkegaard turns to the Lutheran concept of *Anfechtung*. In the Hebraic background there is, notably, the young Isaiah in the temple who, confounded by the vision of God, cries out 'Woe is me! For I am undone' (Isa. 6.5). Luther speaks of human angst *coram deo* as being so acute that a whole army turns tail in terror at the sound of a 'rustling leaf' (Lev. 26.36).[12] Kierkegaard has horrendous descriptions of *Anfechtung*. Thus in *Fragments*, repeating this in the present work, he will say with reference to Moses that the Jews were a wise people, they understood that to see God is to die (*PF*, 30; *CUP*, 484). In the *Postscript* Kierkegaard compares the situation of the human before God to that of a fish out of water, for (as he says) infinity is not the natural element of the human as air not that of the fish. Again, he speaks of a bird caught in a cage (484), reminiscent of Luther's sense that there can be no escaping God, which in turn looks back to Jonah.

One might consider this tradition profoundly masculinist, possessed of a transcendent father-figure God, before whom the son squirms, found out, laid bare, in his smallness and inadequacy. One could further comment on the fact that both Luther and Kierkegaard had human fathers of whom they had had good reason to

---

[12] *WA* 19.226.16. For *Anfechtung* in Luther see Gordon Rupp, *The Righteousness of God* (London, 1953), 106–15. See also my *Christian Contradictions: The Structures of Lutheran and Catholic Thought* (Cambridge, 2001), 30–2, 139, 255–6.

be afraid, who, if loving, could be unpredictably wrathful. It is interesting that *Anfechtung* as a response to God is not in the same way present in the peopled universe of Catholicism, with Mary, all the saints, and Christ himself negotiating the space between God (the father) and humanity. Moreover there is in that tradition held to be some far-off analogy between God and humanity. *Anfechtung* as a response to God is Hebraic and Lutheran. At other times however (as we have yet to consider)[13] Kierkegaard would appear to have a conception of God that is quite otherwise inflected: God is conceived of as ubiquitous rather than present as a transcendent 'Other'.

But if Kierkegaard conjures up the otherness of God he also puts in place an epistemological structure (as we have considered)[14] which allows him to speak of revelation. An interesting comparison may be made here with Hegel or more specifically with Marx. All three men come out of a Hebraic or Lutheran tradition, in which the future is a vital category. In Kierkegaard's case as in Marx's 'the future' qualifies the present. However Marx speaks of a *telos* that is to be attained to by a transformation of present circumstances; in Kierkegaard's case there is an in-breaking of another order. Thus for Kierkegaard human history is relativized in view of the future; it becomes a 'meanwhile'. Yet that in-breaking is also in some way proleptic of another reality. In this sense Kierkegaard's speaking of God performs the role of a transcendental in relation to which our present may be judged. One may make a comparison also here with Kant. For Kant the idea of the *summum bonum*, as also for Marx the idea of a classless society, lead us to aspire to the hope that that which is unjust about our present circumstances will be righted. By contrast, in Kierkegaard's case the in-breaking of the future is disruptive of the present; the eternal does not bring mundane history to a successful conclusion but is rather of another order of historicity. It is here that Kierkegaard will counter Hegel. For Kierkegaard the Christian lives in two realms; the Lutheran *simul justus et peccator*. He lives 'from' the future or God (that other reality giving him his self-understanding), while present in the world. In the 20th century Bultmann has a similar structure in his dialectic between what he names *Geschichte* (ultimate meaning) and *Historie*.

---

[13] See pp. 214–16.   [14] See pp. 90–5.

Within the Lutheran tradition the counter to God's otherness lies in incarnation, as God makes himself known through the humility of the Christ child in the manger. It follows that in Kierkegaard *Anfechtung* is connected with a natural religion or Judaism, religiousness 'A', which will be turned on its head through religiousness 'B'. (Though Kierkegaard is capable of saying in *Fragments* of the incarnation that it is 'less terrifying to fall upon one's face while the mountains tremble at the god's voice than to sit with him as his equal' (*PF*, 35–6). The truth of Christianity, so Kierkegaard surmises, will be secured by its paradoxicality, its unthinkability (to human ways of thought). It is as though the very clash with human reason has as consequence that this revelation must come from God, for it would never have occurred to human beings. Whether this move is of any avail must however be doubtful. It leaves Kierkegaard wholly vulnerable (again as we have considered),[15] as he did not want to face, to the contention that this paradox was constructed within history and thus of human making. In attempting to secure Christianity against a Feuerbachian reductionism by speaking of an unexpected revelation, he has laid himself open to the possibility of historical reductionism.

Faith and Subjectivity

That for which the *Postscript* is best known is Kierkegaard's exposition of subjectivity. It is this, together with the emphasis on human existence as a subject of study, which has passed into existentialism. One should comprehend what Kierkegaard is up to in this respect, or the book may come over as an endless, if hilarious, discussion of an individual's queer existence in relation to a postulated conception of God. In the first place what we have here is an attack on the abstractions of Hegelianism as a way of doing philosophy. Kierkegaard will restore the individual to his rightful place at the centre of any consideration of human life or the human relation to God. That relation remains hidden for God is 'hidden', not objectively present as an item that can be immediately related to (to think in terms of this latter is to have an aesthetic relation to an idol). Thus the individual's relationship to God is necessarily subjective. That Christian faith is belief in a paradox likewise entails that Christianity is not a doctrine, in the sense of an item of knowledge

---

[15] See pp. 85–90.

that takes its place among other items of knowledge as though it were an objective 'fact'. The relation to it must be dialectical, not immediate. Faith comes to be a venture, undertaken in relation to an objective uncertainty. Such a venture takes an individual outside him- or herself as he or she relates to that goal. Moreover, no individual can venture for another.

This does not have as consequence that there is nothing 'objective' about the Christian claim, as though all we were concerned with is an inward disposition. To be a Christian is to exercise a 'subjective' relation of faith in relation to that which is held to be an 'objective' truth; not of course a truth which one could appropriate, for it is a paradox, but nonetheless a truth which, on account of its paradoxicality must necessarily be related to subjectively. Whether the Paradox that is Christ is indeed a contradiction in terms is an interesting question. (In conjunction with the discussion of *Fragments*, I have suggested that that can be argued either way.)[16] Kierkegaard believes that Christ on account of being the eternal in time is a Paradox in terms. He does however suggest—this is a rather different point— that the Paradox is not 'paradoxical' to the one who has faith. Thus he writes in his *Journal*:

The absurd is the negative sign. When I believe, then assuredly neither faith nor the content of faith is absurd. O, no, no—but I understand very well that for the person who does not believe faith and the content of faith are absurd (and in doubt they begin to become absurd for me).[17]

The one who believes has somehow turned a somersault. But as far as reason is concerned, the object of faith is necessarily a Paradox.[18]

---

[16] See p. 97 n. 43.   [17] *JP* 6598 (*Pap.* X⁶ B 68) n.d., 1850.

[18] There has been considerable debate as to whether and in what sense the relation to the Paradox (and thus Christianity) involves irrationalism. Working in the analytic philosophical tradition, the American Louis Pojman argued in papers (see his 'Kierkegaard on Justification of Belief', *International Journal for Philosophy of Religion*, 8/2 (1977)) and in his *The Logic of Subjectivity* (1984) that faith and the object of faith in Kierkegaard form part of a rational system of beliefs. To which Gregory Schufreider responded persuasively ('Kierkegaard on Belief without Justification', *International Journal for the Philosophy of Religion*, 12/3 (1981)), that it would be a misunderstanding to suppose Kierkegaard to think we could speak of subjective *knowledge*, or that to the one who has faith the Paradox is somehow not a Paradox after all. Kierkegaard, said Schufreider, is wishing to engage a non-cognitive aspect of the human being. 'The absurd cannot be mediated by understanding at any point, for in every moment faith must rediscover the paradox as its absolute condition.' To which Pojman replied (in the same issue) qualifying his position but contending that Schufreider is working with too

The risk that is faith is not however to be decried. It is precisely this that gives faith its life-transforming character. As Kierkegaard considers, while seeming to be a tremendous help, to obtain proof of the resurrection would in fact constitute the greatest difficulty of all.[19] In this sense Christianity is an 'existence communication' and, as Kierkegaard says, 'not a doctrine' (by which he means a factual statement about an objective reality which can simply be appropriated and so moved beyond). It is the uncertainty involved which has as consequence that the step of faith is a movement which must be undertaken once and again in the moment. Luther too has exactly this sense: as he puts it, what is grasped in faith becomes in the next instant sin (as once and again I come to be settled in myself). I rest on

narrow a definition of 'knowledge': what Kierkegaard would argue is that subjectivity is 'truth directed'. Now the latter may well be the case but would seem to be beside the point. Going beyond Schufreider, Karen Carr has argued that it is not that, as some have contended, that Kierkegaard is an irrationalist or 'suprarationalist' (as though for the believer there is no paradox), but rather antirationalist, the antagonism with reason continuing after the life of faith has been embraced. The problem is the corruption of reason by a sinning will. She quotes Kierkegaard in his *Journal*: 'The matter is very simple: will you or will you not obey, will you submit in faith to his divine authority, or will you take offense—or will you perhaps not take sides—be careful, for that, too, is offense.' (*JP* 3026 (*Pap.* VIII[2] B 15), n.d., 1847). I fear Carr is right in this: one has faith in the face of reason, it being this which gives faith its passion.

A related question is that as to the relationship between Religiousness 'A' and Religiousness 'B'. As over against the Episcopalian Walter Lowrie, Kierkegaard's indomitable translator, J. Weldon Smith III argued ('Religion A/ Religion B: A Kierkegaard Study', *The Scottish Journal of Theology*, 15 (1962)) that there is radical discontinuity marked by a qualitative leap between the two. Religiousness 'A' is a religion of inwardness, Kierkegaard writing that while it is 'by no means undialectical ... [it] is the dialectic of inward transformation'. It can exist in paganism and is the religiousness of everyone within Christendom who is not decisively Christian. 'God is neither a something—He being all and infinitely all—nor is He outside the individual, since edification consists precisely in the fact that He is in the individual' (*CUP*, Lowrie, 494, 498). Smith comments: it is 'the individual's own self-definition and self-transformation of existence, before God'. By contrast religiousness 'B' is a 'paradoxical religiousness', conditioned by a 'definite something', the individual coming into relation with the eternal *in time* ('Religion A/B', 255). There is, thus, a breach with immanence, sin being the name for the fact that an alteration has taken place within the individual, such that, receiving the condition from the God he becomes a new creature. This is clearly right. Further, Kierkegaard's position is surely to be distinguished from a volitionist view. Faith for Kierkegaard might be called an 'anti-volitionist' volitionist view in that it is a letting go (see p. 72).

[19] In the 20th century Bultmann, the Lutheran New Testament scholar and theologian, thinks exactly the same way in this regard.

my laurels. Kierkegaard speaks of faith as treading water; once I stop I've lost it. Therefore also faith is a passion, for in passion I am taken outside myself. If I once cease to exercise faith, I am self-satisfied, secure in myself, shut up in a self-enclosure (which is quintessentially to hold myself apart from God). The whole tradition is in this sense highly ecstatic and existential.

In order to highlight the nature of faith Kierkegaard has a debate going within *Postscript* with what is the natural human disposition (which would conform also to Catholicism). The discussion of 'the Middle Ages' and 'the monastery' act as a foil against which he will pit a profoundly Lutheran position.[20] The temptation that the 'monastery' represents is the temptation to think that one could find an outlet for one's subjectivity by pouring it into some outward resultant in the world. One might further say that what 'the monastery' represents is an attempt to get faith under control. Being a monk is something one could live up to. It becomes a task, as is being a councillor. But if that is the case then 'being a monk' becomes a good work—and God superfluous. Such an individual does not essentially need God except to reward him. He remains centred in himself. Thus the ethical life is a form of 'sin', an evasion of God. It should be recalled that in this tradition there is no sense in which one could see God through the world; the world is not diaphanous of God. Faith is the response to a revelation that, in taking one outside oneself, gives one a 'double' existence as one lives 'meanwhile' in the world. But does our individual enjoy himself in the Deer Park?[21] Of course, for it is human to enjoy oneself. That the God-relationship is other than the world allows the human to be human and the world the sphere of humans. It is not for the human *qua* human to attempt to rise to God, for example through some kind of mysticism. It is in exercising one's humanity that one best exemplifies the *difference* between what it is to be human and God. It is not for us to become in ourselves gods: as Luther puts it 'a holy man is a fiction'.[22] God escapes human categories. Christianity does not confirm my past self but gives me a radically different sense of self as by faith I am caught up beyond myself into God.

---

[20] See pp. 155, 156, 158. [21] See p. 158.
[22] WA 40, II.347.9–10.

It is here that Kierkegaard's controversial discussion of the pagan at prayer becomes interesting. Of our pagan at least it may be said that he prays 'in the truth' (even though he should pray to an idol). As Robert Solomon has well remarked, the contrary of being subjectively 'in the truth' is not falsity (as in believing something false, as does the pagan) but rather inauthenticity.[23] It follows that the question must be posed as to whether it matters if what one believes to be objectively true is in fact so as long as one stands in a 'true' relationship to it. Thus the Catholic philosopher Alastair MacIntyre has charged that for Kierkegaard 'the criterion of both choice and truth is intensity of feeling'.[24] But this judgement is inadequate. Kierkegaard never suggests anything other than that the 'truth' of the God/man is the fundamental fact which, incompatible with reason, puts reason in its place. It can however only be 'the truth' in an existential, life-transforming, sense for the one who stands in a true relationship to it. Moreover we are far from speaking of some (interior) intensity of 'feeling'; precisely is it that faith takes one outside oneself to the reality of another. Nevertheless, what is true is that Kierkegaard may have been forced into taking up an 'anthropomorphic' stance; precisely what he sought to counter in staking out a claim for the truth of Christianity in the face of Hegelian reductionism. Kierkegaard's whole reason for speaking of the response of the human to God rather than simply postulating an 'objective' God has been that he is fully aware that the latter position leaves him open to being a sitting duck which the Feuerbachians can shoot down, contending that such a God is but a human projection. Now, again, he opens the door to reductionism.

It is interesting finally to ponder with what intensity Kierkegaard apparently needs the assurance and security which faith gives. Of course he writes under a pseudonym, but his *Journals* do not suggest anything other: as early as 1838 he is remarking that the Christian life consists in 'an unshakeable sureness, an unshakeable certainty about one's relationship to God'[25]. Such an understanding of faith and the Christian life was of course fundamental to his tradition. In 1845, the year in which he wrote the *Postscript*, Kierkegaard remarked in his *Journal*:

---

[23] Robert Solomon, *From Hegel to Existentialism* (Oxford, 1987), 84.
[24] P. Edwards, ed., *Encyclopaedia of Philosophy* (New York, 1967), iv, 338.
[25] *JP* 1:434 (*Pap.* II A 252), 23 Aug 1838.

When one reads Luther one gets the impression, rightly enough, of a sure and certain mind ... And yet it seems to me there is something disturbing about his certainty, which is in fact uncertainty. It is common knowledge that a particular state of mind often tries to conceal itself beneath its opposite. One encourages oneself with strong words, and the words become even stronger because one is hesitant. That is not deception, but a pious wish. One does not even wish to express the uncertainty of fear, one does not wish (or dare) even to name it, and one forces out the very opposite mood in the hope that it will help.

Perhaps there is a certain self-knowledge here on Kierkegaard's part? What is fascinating is that he immediately continues:

Thus Luther makes paramount use of that which is used with such moderation in the New Testament: the sin against the Holy Ghost. (Matt. 12.31–2 and parallels.) In order to encourage himself and the believer he makes immediate and draconian use of it on every occasion with the result that ultimately there is not a single man who has not committed the sin against the Holy Ghost not only once but many times. And the New Testament says that it cannot be forgiven; so what then?[26]

So Kierkegaard would seem to be critical of Luther in this. Yet by the time he writes *Sickness unto Death* in the spring of 1848 (amended in 1849) he takes up just such a drastic stance himself as we shall see. The sin against the Holy Spirit, in Kierkegaard's terms declaring Christianity to be a lie and untruth, becomes the ultimate form of offence, the highest intensification of sin.[27]

The point is that classically for the Lutheran tradition Christianity revolves around a freedom attained to on account of one's sureness as to one's acceptance by God. Thus in asserting one's faith one must possess utter assurance or the act of faith would bring no relief.[28]

---

[26] Alexander Dru, ed. & trans., *The Journals of Søren Kierkegaard: a selection* (Oxford, 1938) (henceforth Dru), no. 540 (*Pap.* VI A 108), n.d., 1845.

[27] See p. 243.

[28] Catholicism is very different here. Catholics have been suspicious of the Lutheran emphasis on the need for assurance. Thus among the Canons appended to the Tridentine 'Decree Concerning Justification' (1547) we find: 'If anyone says that in order to obtain the remission of sins it is necessary for every man to believe with certainty and without any hesitation ... that his sins are forgiven him, let him be anathema.' (Canon 13, 'Decree Concerning Justification' in John Leith, ed., *Creeds of the Churches*, revised edition Richmond, VA (1973), p. 422.) Catholicism has a doctrine of hope, which is where faith (in the Catholic case the objective dogma of the church) becomes personal: I dare to hope that I too am among those who will be saved. But this in turn implies a different view of the person, who is

Hence Luther tells Erasmus: 'Take away assertions and you take away Christianity.'[29] However as we have said one will need to take the step of faith (trust in another and not in ourselves) once and again. As Stephen Crites puts it: 'The project of faith ... implies a constant crisis of decision.'[30] It should be remembered here that in Luther's case he came straight out of the volitionist emphasis of the late Middle Ages. But such an emphasis is present in Kierkegaard too: one must, in what I have called an anti-volitionist volitionism, let go.[31] Yet Kierkegaard also knows such a willing out of one's subjectivity to be fraught with danger. Precisely the issue arises as to the objectivity of the truth of God. Thus in *Fragments* Kierkegaard writes, 'deepest down in the heart of piety lurks the mad caprice which knows that it has itself produced the God' (Swenson/Lowrie, 56). Or again, in the present work: 'But freedom, that is the wonderful lamp. When a person rubs it with ethical passion, God comes into existence for him' (138). On the one hand it must be that the object of one's faith is objective to one; it is that which, in faith, takes one outside oneself. On the other hand the step of faith in relation to that truth (doubly so in the case of a Truth which is a paradox) must by the very nature of the case be taken out of one's subjectivity. Faith for Kierkegaard is thus a subjective relation to a Truth which one takes to be objectively the case.

Does Kierkegaard Foster Irrationalism?

One may think it is pre-eminently on account of this book that the question has arisen as to whether Kierkegaard's authorship may not have fed into the cult of irrationalism which, in the political sphere, had such dire consequences in the mid-20th century. Perhaps the best

able (through infused grace) to stand of him- or herself before God. It was such a sense that Luther lacked; faith (trust in a righteousness not his but Christ's) delivering him from fear. As we shall see in the later authorship Kierkegaard does come to have a sense that, through God's love, one can stand before God. But it is never the substantial sense of self that with its high doctrine of creation and its understanding of infused grace one finds in Catholicism. The Lutheran sense of faith remains quite fundamental to Kierkegaard, albeit it is qualified by a greater epistemological element, belief in the truth of the Paradox. See further pp. 251–3.

[29] WA 18.603.28–9; Dillenberger (ed.), *Selections*, 168.

[30] Stephen Crites, *In the Twilight of Christendom: Hegel vs. Kierkegaard on Faith and History* (Chambersburg, PA, AAR Studies in Religion, 2, 1972), 76.

[31] See p. 72.

way to approach this emotive question is to break it down into a series of sub-questions, attempting to speak to them in turn. However, by the very nature of the case we may not arrive at a clear-cut answer.

In the first place, is there something held in common, a certain attitudinal stance, as between Kierkegaard's understanding of 'faith' and fascist ideology? The answer is clearly 'yes' or the question would never have arisen. In a nutshell it consists in this. Kierkegaard thinks that the human being needs to achieve absolute certainty, that this alone makes life tolerable. Thus when the desired result cannot be achieved through reason (and in any case reason would not give rise to the passion of faith) Kierkegaard speaks of passion in relation to what is an objective uncertainty. Further, he speaks of the human in exercising this passion as caught up in an act of 'choosing' in which the whole person is existentially involved. The choice involves allegiance to another, while making this choice takes one outside oneself in such a way that one's self-understanding is bound up with another who has mastery over one's life. This revolutionary act is a drastic step, undertaken by one who would otherwise find himself in despair; a wager at achieving meaning and authenticity. The talk is of an existence–communication rather than of living in accord with ratiocination. One can see what the problem is and why not a few, including Kierkegaard scholars otherwise inclined to find themselves at one with him, have found it worrisome.

The second question logically to pose should then be whether in fact, historically, Kierkegaard's thought fed into 20th-century fascism? This question is difficult of adjudication. Certainly it is the case that it was principally the right in Germany that first exhibited an interest in his work as it appeared in German translation. (Translation commenced in the 1860s, a collected edition in twelve volumes being published between 1909 and 1922; thus a whole generation before Kierkegaard came onto the Anglophone scene.) The exception to this is perhaps theological interest in Kierkegaard: notably Barth was of left-wing disposition. Although there is no direct connection, and we do not know him to have read Kierkegaard, there is some evidence that Nietzsche may indirectly have known of his thought through secondary sources.[32] In the 1920s a leading Kierkegaard scholar was Emanuel Hirsch, his influential *Kierkegaard-Studien* appearing in three volumes

[32] Cf. T. H. Brobjer, 'Nietzsche's Knowledge of Kierkegaard', *Journal of the History of Philosophy*, 41/2 (2003), 251–63.

between 1930 and 1933. This was exactly the time when Hirsch was developing National Socialist 'German Christian' thinking. What attracted Hirsch was what he referred to as the *Wagnis-Charakter*, risk (or dare) character of Kierkegaard's 'leap' of faith which he found conducive to a National Socialist framework of thought.[33] No wonder the young Theodor Adorno, a member of the Frankfurt school and of Marxist orientation, was so exercised by Kierkegaardian thought, publishing his highly critical (and misleading) *Kierkegaard: Konstruktion des Ästhetischen* (*Kierkegaard: Construction of the Aesthetic*) in the spring of 1933. But the history of Kierkegaard reception does not of course answer the question as to whether his thinking has been rightly interpreted.

So, thirdly, we should ask what Kierkegaard himself thought of nationalism and political fanaticism. Here the answer would seem unequivocal: he despised it. Kierkegaard had no time at all for the kind of folkish outlook which others around him (including for example Grundtvig) saw fit to cultivate. In 1848 he stood squarely opposed to the patriotic fervour whipped up in Denmark against Germany in the dispute over Schleswig and Holstein (Danish Holsten), Denmark's half-German and German speaking provinces. In regard to Kierkegaard's opinion of what he judged mob behaviour let the following quotation from his *Journal* suffice.

In contrast to what was said about possession in the Middle Ages and times like that, that there were individuals who sold themselves to the devil, I have an urge to write a book *Possession and Obsession in Modern Times*, and show how people *en masse* abandon themselves to it . . . This is why people run together in flocks—so that natural and animal rage will grip a person, so that he feels stimulated, inflamed, and *ausser sich* [beside himself]. The scenes on Bloksberg[34] are utterly pedantic compared to this demonic lust, a lust to lose oneself in order to evaporate in potentiation, so that a person is outside of himself, does not really know what he is doing or what he is saying or who it is or what it is speaking through him, while the blood rushes faster, the eyes glitter and stare fixedly, the passions boil, lusts seethe.[35]

---

[33] Cf. Marcia Morgan, 'Adorno's Reception of Kierkegaard: 1929–1933', *Søren Kierkegaard Newsletter*, no. 46 (2003).
[34] Bloksberg: Mephistopheles escorts Faust there. Presumably the reference is to the gaggle of witches present.
[35] *JP* 4:4178 (*Pap.* X^2 A 490), n.d., 1850.

There could hardly be a more prescient depiction of what was to overtake Europe in the mid-20th century. Kierkegaard must have been horrified had he lived to see National Socialism. His category was that of the individual, pitted against the mob. He hated all collectivity. And he was much exercised about Hegel's discussion of the state in his *Philosophy of Right.*[36]

But finally a way to think through this question, perhaps more telling than any other, is to consider that Christianity which Kierkegaard influenced. No theologian of his generation was more taken up with Kierkegaard than the young Dietrich Bonhoeffer. The spring semester of 1933 saw Bonhoeffer lecturing on Christology at the Humboldt University in Berlin. We have the substance of what he said, compiled after his death from notes taken by his students. The lectures are prefaced by a quotation from Kierkegaard: 'Be silent, for that is the absolute.'[37] Working on Hitler's personal papers in the Bundesarchiv (national archive) in Koblenz and sending for a volume for 1933: 'Kirchliche-Angelegenheiten: Evangelische Kirche' (Church Affairs: Protestant Church), I was struck when one of the first documents was a letter from Bonhoeffer complaining about the aggressive behaviour of members of the SA in the university courtyard. Naïve maybe to think it efficacious to write to the Reichskanzlei, but what other German pastor was so quick off the mark? Bonhoeffer was to lose his life through his political opposition to the regime. That for him was the cost of discipleship, the title of his 1937 book *Nachfolge* (the one word connoting both 'consequences' and 'disciple').[38] That Kierkegaard's disciple Bonhoeffer was so clearly opposed to the Third Reich has sometimes been rolled in as evidence that a Kierkegaardian outlook does not necessarily lead to a fascist disposition.

There is however more to be said. Consider again those lectures of 1933. Brilliant and powerful, they consist in a demolition of everything for which the Enlightenment stood in favour of a (non-rational) allegiance to Christ. At this stage in his career Bonhoeffer may well be said to have been more Barthian than Barth; alone

---

[36] See p. 267.

[37] Bonhoeffer, Dietrich, *Christology*, trans. J. Bowden (London, 1966), 27.

[38] The title was taken from an entry on Kierkegaard in the German encyclopaedia *Die Religion in Geschichte und Gegenwart.* (Information given to me by his friend Franz Hildebrandt who was with Bonhoeffer when he chose it.).

I believe in this allegiance among his colleagues on the Berlin faculty. Bonhoeffer does nothing whatever to dismantle 'National Socialist' modes of thought (if that is what they are): he replaces Hitler with Christ. But then in this Bonhoeffer was simply at one with the Confessing Church (*Bekennende Kirche*), of which he was a leading light. The members of that church got to their feet (as had not earlier been the custom) to say the Creed, 'I believe in God'; in a totalitarian context a political statement, in that it was markedly not to say 'I believe in Hitler'. Consider again. When towards the end of the war news reached the Dutchman Willem Visser't Hooft, General Secretary of the World Council of Churches in Process of Formation in Geneva (and a friend of Bonhoeffer's) that many in the United Kingdom were speaking of rebuilding European values and civilization on the basis of a natural law theology (interest in which was at the time widespread, extending from Catholicism to the Free Churches), Visser't Hooft wrote to Bishop George Bell of Chichester that their friends in the Confessing Church were opposing Hitler not on the grounds of the Greeks and Romans but on biblical grounds.[39] The Confessing Church was scarcely fuelled by humanism.

At the worst point of the war in 1941, the English philosopher and social activist Dorothy Emmet published an article of the greatest interest: 'Kierkegaard and the "Existential" Philosophy'.[40] Translations of Kierkegaard had begun to appear in English. Emmet averred: 'To make Søren Kierkegaard spiritually responsible for the present war would have as little, and perhaps as much, truth in it as the facile explanations which made Hegel responsible for the last one.' The article was in tone measured. Both Nazi apologists and Confessional opponents, she commented, 'are consciously or unconsciously moved by a way of thinking which puts the decision of the individual ... above any objective or universal norm of ethics or of reason by which it can be either justified or criticised'. And so she continued by pointing out that something very different was afoot from liberal or democratic values. It was Emmet's conviction that 'until we have

---

[39] Papers of the World Council of Churches in Process of Formation, Archives of the WCC, Geneva. Quoted by Peter Ludlow, 'Kirchenkampf und Oekumene', paper lent to me by the author and at that time unpublished. Letter dated 15 Dec 1943; quotation from letter given in my *Christian Contradictions*, 151.

[40] Dorothy Emmet, 'Kierkegaard and the "Existential" Philosophy', *Journal of the Royal Institute of Philosophy*, 16 (1941), 257–71.

faced those "existential" religious categories and come to terms with them, we shall not know how to speak to that in the German spirit of which Nazism is a perversion'. Emmet evinces (considering the early date) a rather thorough grasp of Kierkegaard; she had access also to German sources. She hoped through her article to have 'brought home some idea of [Kierkegaard's] importance to any who may not have realized his decisive influence on recent trends in theology and in German philosophy'.[41] Her article is in many ways not unsympathetic—and she loves Kierkegaard's humour. Nonetheless this is a very different world from the Anglo-Saxon milieu with which she is familiar.

Does Kierkegaard foster irrationalism? Some have thought so. Herbert Marcuse comments that Kierkegaard's was the last great attempt to restore religion as that instrument which would liberate humanity from oppressive social conditions; an interesting comment in view of *Love's Deeds* as we shall see. But, says Marcuse, his concentration on the individual led him to attack universal concepts that would 'uphold the essential equality and dignity of man'. While in no way directly accusing Kierkegaard for what was to follow, Marcuse notes that this 'anti-rationalist attack on universals' became increasingly influential in European thought, 'existentialism playing an important part in this attack'. This led to a rejection of universal, rational norms; laws were to be based rather on supposed existential needs, such that particularities such as race could be exalted.[42] The Hungarian thinker György Lukács, who had a lifelong love/hate relationship with Kierkegaard, came to similar conclusions.[43] As we see the question is not easy of adjudication. And Kierkegaard is not present to posterity to answer for himself.

In *Fragments* Kierkegaard writes: 'In the Socratic view, every human being is himself the midpoint and the whole world focuses only on him because his self-knowledge is God-knowledge' (*PF*, 11). And again: 'Socrates had the courage and self-collectedness to be sufficient unto himself' (*PF*, 11). Kierkegaard understood very well

---

[41] Emmet, 'Kierkegaard', 256, 257, 258, 270.

[42] Herbert Marcuse, *Reason and Revolution* (New York, 1941), 264, 266, 267.

[43] György Lukács, *The Destruction of Reason*, trans. Peter Palmer (London, 1980) [1954]. On Lukács on Kierkegaard see András Nagy, 'Abraham the Communist' in George Pattison and Steven Shakespeare, eds, *Kierkegaard: the self in society* (Basingstoke, 1998).

what was at stake. Christianity is not humanism and not to be reached through the interiority of recollection. It is a religion predicated on revelation, which thereby potentially (as Kierkegaard recognized) imparts another 'truth', demanding of us something other than can be arrived at through reason. If this is not the case, as Kierkegaard would say, then one should return repentantly to the Socratic, from which one should never have departed. A Russian who visited Kant noted (it having impressed him) that Kant had said: 'Reason commands us to believe in it.'[44] That is a quite other creed.

---

[44] A. Gulyga, *Immanuel Kant: His Life and Thought* (Boston, MA, 1987), 190f, quoted by Jack Verheyden, 'The Ethical and the Religious as Law and Gospel' in D. Z. Phillips & Timothy Tessin, eds, *Kant and Kierkegaard on Religion* (Basingstoke, 2000), 155.

6
Love's Deeds

Introduction

Situated within a different field, *Love's Deeds* is again deeply Lutheran. But it is Luther with a difference and the difference is informative about Kierkegaard. The Lutheran understanding is that God loves with an agapeistic love; a love which loves because it is love's nature to love, loving irrespective of the goodness or desirability of that which is loved. Such disinterested love is spontaneous, uncalculating. The supreme insight of Lutheran faith must surely be that of itself love brings about change in the one who is so loved. To say that we are 'justified by faith' is to say that we stand in right relation to God; accepted, as we trust in God's acceptance of us. The corollary of such acceptance (irrespective of merit) is that freed from the insecurity of concern about our acceptance we are in turn set free to love the neighbour with a like love to that with which God has loved us, without preconditions.[1] In Luther's case it is one movement: his gratitude spills over in a spontaneous love of neighbour. Thus 'person' (constituted through God's acceptance) issues in 'works' (love of neighbour); as also we may say faith (the relation to God) leads to love (the relation to neighbour).

---

[1] There is a good discussion of this in Gerhard Ebeling, *Luther: An Introduction to his Thought*, trans. R. A. Wilson (London, 1972), chs 9, 10. Cf. Mark Taylor: 'In traditional Lutheran terms, Kierkegaard can argue that faith makes love possible.' ('Love and Forms of Spirit: Kierkegaard vs. Hegel', *Kierkegaardiana* 10 (1977), 111.)

Steeped in this framework of thought, Kierkegaard comments in a *Journal* entry: 'No; infinite humiliation of grace, and then a striving born of gratitude—this is Christianity.'[2] That is to say, in no way on account of anything about the way I am but on account of God's sheer graciousness am I accepted, this issuing in a striving (for the neighbour) born of gratitude; and he adds 'this is Christianity'. Such is the dynamic through which in the Lutheran tradition the relationship of God, self and neighbour are understood. *Love's Deeds* is a thinking through of the multifaceted nature of these relationships. Recognizing that Christian love is a spontaneous agapeistic acting in relation to the other, Kierkegaard writes: 'What love does, that it is; what it is, that it does—at one and the same moment' (280). Where Kierkegaard is unusual in terms of his tradition is in the degree to which he emphasizes that we are commanded also to love God. Of course one may say that love is implicit in that trust which is faith. But in Kierkegaard it is explicit that, as 'centred' selves, we may dare to love (even) God. One may well think that it is the corollary of this very orientation, in which God is conceived of as an 'other' whom one shall love, rather than thinking in terms of a trust which is a displacement of self to God, that Kierkegaard experiences difficulty in the subsequent move of turning to the world. Love of neighbour for him becomes a duty.

It is important to consider Danish vocabulary. Rather than translating the title of the book (as is customary) *Works of Love*, I find it right to reflect the Danish title *Kjerlighedens Gjerninger, Love's Deeds*, or *Works*. This alone retains the Lutheran understanding that it belongs to the very nature of love to perform works. Love is not static or contemplative, but busy, present in the world, acting for the neighbour. To say *Works of Love* fails quite to catch this, seemingly simply differentiating such (loving) works from others. Danish words for love are incommensurate with the Greek tripartite division *eros*, *philia*, *agape*. Danish *naestekjerlighed* (*naeste*, next, being also the biblical word for the neighbour, *kjerlighed*, love) is equivalent to Greek *agape*. Danish has a distinct word, *elskov*, for erotic love. The *opposite* of that love which loves irrespective of the worthiness of that which is loved (which is *kjerlighed* or *agape*), is preferential love

---

[2] *JP* 1:993 (*Pap.* X³ A 734), n.d., 1851.

(*forkjerlighed*), the Danish prefix 'for' being equivalent to German 'vor', as in *Vorliebe* (preferential love). Thus of both Greek *eros* (that love which is desire) and Greek *philia* (love of the brother) it may be said that they are *forkjerlighed*, preferential love. (Aristotle says of *philia* that I love the other on account of the likeness to myself that I see in him.)[3]

To say something of the circumstances which elicited this beautiful book. After a drawn-out engagement, Regine—his one and only 'queen' as Kierkegaard was wont to say—was preparing to marry. He must consider the nature of that love which he might continue to exercise toward her. We may well think that the work was written for he himself and for her (given that she and her fiancé read his books together) as much as for any third party. But Kierkegaard was struggling also on other counts. The previous year, 1846, there had erupted what is known as the '*Corsair* affair'. *The Corsair*, a scurrilous Copenhagen broadsheet, demolished the rich and powerful—while the populace laughed. Kierkegaard, acting out of a sense of public duty, had attacked it, whereupon the ire of the editor was turned against him. Month after successive month he must endure being pilloried in public. The experience left Kierkegaard indescribably lonely. It had been his habit as he walked the streets of Copenhagen to engage with the common people. Now he could not as much as descend from a carriage he had taken into the countryside without the locals staring, laughing, and pointing at his trousers. Kierkegaard, who had a walking impediment, was commonly depicted in cartoons with one trouser leg shorter than the other. In 1847 he notes in his *Journal*: 'One must really have suffered a great deal in the world, have been very unhappy, before there can be any question of beginning to love one's neighbour.'[4]

But it is not simply Kierkegaard's personal situation that finds reflection in this book. We learn something of the social and political circumstances around him. It will be good here to fill in some of the background. At first neutral in the Napoleonic Wars, Denmark had subsequently backed the losing side, emerging in consequence scarred and impoverished. In 1813, the year of Kierkegaard's birth, the state had almost gone bankrupt. Only in the 1840s, the so-called

---

[3] Aristotle, *Nichomachean Ethics*, book IX, ch. 10.
[4] *JP* 4:4603 (*Pap.* VIII[1] A 269), n.d., 1847.

Danish 'golden age' and Kierkegaard's most productive period, was real recovery evident. Denmark was as yet an undeveloped economy, though the countryside was fast changing.[5] The system of bonded labour (serfdom) to which Kierkegaard refers had only recently been abolished. In the towns there remained deep poverty. The son of a *nouveau riche* merchant with a grand house on the most fashionable square in town, Kierkegaard was raised in a highly privileged situation. Yet this same father, the child of peasant parents, had himself been freed from bonded status. In 1847 Denmark was an absolute monarchy, and Kierkegaard could scarcely have foreseen what lay around the corner in the European revolutions of the following year. Nevertheless his writing breathes a prescience of incipient social unrest.

Kierkegaard admonished his readers to read his pastoral writing contemplatively, preferably out loud. Of *Love's Deeds* he comments: 'These Christian deliberations, which are the fruit of much deliberation, will be understood slowly but then also easily, whereas they will surely become very difficult if someone by hasty and curious reading makes them very difficult for himself' (207). And it is indeed only as one pauses to grasp the intuitive moves that he makes, or the changes in emotional disposition he attributes to others, that the work shines forth. Kierkegaard depicts himself a 'master spy' or observer of humankind. One fears a modern editor would have cut the book by half—and we should have lost so inestimably much. But this length and complexity may have resulted in the book not having attained to the status of the Christian classic it should be accounted. For one must surely judge *Love's Deeds* edifying writing of the first order. Replete with wisdom and insight, it does not however lack a cutting edge. As Kierkegaard himself commented, it was written 'to arouse and to vex' not to 'assuage and comfort'.[6] Such is the nature of Christian discipleship.

Thus it was amid much turbulence, personal and potentially social—the marriage of his beloved, a depth of personal isolation, the

---

[5] For a fascinating depiction of the social conditions pertaining in Denmark on the eve of the 1848 revolution see the early chapters of Bruce Kirmmse, *Kierkegaard in Golden Age Denmark* (Bloomington & Indianapolis, 1990).

[6] Hannay, 272 (*Pap.* VIII[1] A 293). See also Alastair Hannay, *Kierkegaard: A Biography* (Cambridge, 2001), 358.

poor at his door, and rising resentment over class and gender inequality—that Kierkegaard forged this serene text. As he puts it: 'But to speak figuratively, to sit in the kettle the coppersmith is hammering on and then to understand the same thing, the highest' (79). The writing would seem to reflect a new maturity on Kierkegaard's part. We sense his despair and savour the means of his healing. *Love's Deeds* is the only one of Kierkegaard's major works published under his own name. The Copenhagen public were to reward him for his labour, the book becoming one of a handful of his thirty-eight titles to run to a second edition (1852) in his lifetime. Not an overtly philosophical book, it has found little resonance in the world of scholarship. Among Kierkegaard scholars it has met with increasing interest in recent years, disproportionately it would seem among women.

The book consists in two sets of discourses. Built around the pattern of Lutheran thought (and thus more theoretical), the first set was completed in April 1847. Consisting in a series of vignettes which in some way serve to illustrate these considerations, the second set was finished by August. In a *Journal* note written the day of the book's completion Kierkegaard comments: 'No matter how hopeless things have often seemed, I scrape together the most blessed thoughts I can muster of what a loving person is and say to myself: that is how God is every instant.'[7] The book appeared on 29 September. On 3 November Regine married. Kierkegaard notes:

That girl caused me enough trouble. Now she is—not dead [a reference to Regine's threat of suicide when he had called off their engagement]—but happily and well married. I said that would happen on the same day (six years ago) and was declared the basest of all base scoundrels! Remarkable![8]

The very act of penning the book may have been efficacious. Kierkegaard further noted 'I am becoming more calm'.[9] He was to spend the autumn sorting out his affairs, and in December finally sold the family house.

[7] *JP* 5:6032 (*Pap.* VIII[1] A 219).
[8] *JP* 5:6083 (*Pap.* VIII[1] A 447), n.d., 1847.
[9] *JP* 5:6035 (*Pap.* VIII[1] A 220), n.d., 1847.

Exposition

Some Christian Deliberations in the Form of Discourses: First Series

I. Love's Hidden Life and Its Recognizability by Its Fruits

Luke 6.44: Every tree is known by its own fruit, for figs are not gathered from thorns, nor are grapes picked from a bramble bush

Kierkegaard starts where logically he should. It is God's agapeistic love which is the wellspring behind humans loving in this manner.

> Just as the quiet lake originates deep down in hidden springs no eye has seen so also does a person's love originate even more deeply in God's love. If there were no gushing spring at the bottom, if God were not love, then there would be neither the little lake nor a human being's love. Just as the quiet lake originates darkly in the deep spring, so a human being's love originates mysteriously in God's love.... But the quiet lake can dry up if the gushing spring ever stops; the life of love, however, has an eternal spring (9–10).

The source of a human's agapeistic love is hidden. It is made manifest (see the title) by its fruits (Luke 6.44). Kierkegaard may well have in mind Luther's use of this metaphor in his 'The Freedom of a Christian';[10] but after all this is the logical biblical reference for either of them to cite. This as we have said is the structure of Lutheran thought: person leads to works. As God loves us so do we love the neighbour. But then Kierkegaard (continuing the plant analogy) will say something which encapsulates an emphasis which is peculiarly his. 'It is said of certain plants that they must form a heart. In like manner one may also say of a person's love: "If it is actually to bear fruit and thus be known by its fruit, it must first of all *form a heart*".' It is out of that centredness that a person loves the other. Kierkegaard remarks on how rarely the eternal gets 'so much control over a person' that love forms their heart (12).

---

[10] We know Kierkegaard (unsurprisingly) to have had at least second-hand acquaintance with the essay since his student days. (Craig Hinkson, 'Will the Real Martin Luther Please Stand Up: Kierkegaard's View of Luther versus the Evolving Perceptions of the Tradition', *IKC For Self-Examination* and *Judge for Yourself!*, 42, note 8, citing *Pap.* I C 1, p. 9.).

II. A. You *Shall* Love; II. B. You Shall Love *the Neighbour*; II. C. *You* Shall Love the Neighbour

Matt. 22.39: But the second commandment is like it: You shall love your neighbour as yourself

Kierkegaard will expound the whole structure of what he would say. Recall that the biblical word for 'neighbour' in Danish is *naeste* (the next one, the one near to you); cf. German *Nachbar*.

II. A. *You* Shall *Love*

Presupposing that a person loves himself, Christianity adds that you shall love your neighbour as yourself. The scripture does not say you shall love God as yourself but 'with all your heart and all your soul and all your mind'. A person should love God 'unconditionally *in obedience* and love him *in adoration*' (19). Without proper self-love neither can a person love the neighbour. Most people have not learnt to love themselves. 'To love yourself in the right way and to love the neighbour correspond perfectly to one another; fundamentally they are one and the same thing' (22). Failing to love themselves, one is suicidal, another wastes time in inconsequential pursuits.

Kierkegaard moves to the distinction basic to the book between 'the love of preference' and Christian love (Danish *Kjerlighed*, Greek *agape*). *Agape* is marked by the 'change of eternity'. No more than do Luther before him or the Swedish 20th-century theologian Anders Nygren after him, does Kierkegaard conceive that God takes up and transforms human love.[11] It is revelation that makes apparent what love is, while in its light *eros* and *philia* are found wanting: Christianity 'did not arise in any human being's heart' (24). The love of the

---

[11] Anders Nygren, *Agape and Eros*, trans. Philip S. Watson (New York, 1953) [Part I 1930, Part II 1936]. Thinking in an Augustinian mould Catholics (or Anglo-Catholics) have often misread Nygren here (see my *Christian Contradictions: The Structures of Lutheran and Catholic Thought*, Cambridge, 2001, ch. 4 'Nygren's Detractors') and thus would also be inclined to misread Kierkegaard or Luther. In a word the false assumption is that 'eros' equates with Catholic 'creation', such that it can then be said that 'agape' transforms 'eros' as 'grace' transforms 'nature'. But upon a Lutheran model 'eros' has nothing to do with 'creation'. If God loves with an agapeistic love then God also creates out of agape. We are not speaking of a Neoplatonist reorientation of the self, but of a dichotomy (see the discussion of the structure of Lutheran thought in ch. 1, or for more detail *Christian Contradictions*, ch. 1, 'Luther's Revolution').

beloved (*eros*) or the friend (*philia*) are 'soaring' loves, based on preference. By contrast it is our duty to love the neighbour. To choose a beloved or find a friend is a complicated business, but if one will only acknowledge one's duty the neighbour is easy to find. The love which 'self-ignites' can turn to hatred or jealousy, while the love arising from God's love endures (cf. 1 Cor. 13). The love of desire is dependent on the other; the love of duty liberating.

There is a falseness about an independence which, feeling no need to be loved, is simply in need of another to love, thereby gratifying its self-esteem. Rightly ordered love 'certainly feels a need to be loved' (39). But loving another with adoration is a mark of despair. Despair 'is not something that can happen to a person, an event such as good fortune and misfortune'. It is 'a mis-relation in a person's innermost being' (40).[12] The only security against despair is 'to undergo the change of eternity through duty's *shall*' (40): you must not love another in such a way that the loss of that other would make evident that in actuality you were in despair. Does this mean you should not love? Far from it. What secures against despair at the loss of the other is not 'feeble, lukewarm grounds of comfort—that one must not take something too hard, etc.' (41). When you know not what to do the command of eternity will counsel 'so that all turns out well nevertheless' (43).

II. B. *You shall Love* the Neighbour

Whereas *philia* and *eros* were forms of love known to paganism, the recognition of *agape* owes to Christianity.[13] It is made to appear as though the relationship were that of high to higher. But this is not so: Christianity is an offence to the natural man. Christianity has thrust from the throne loves based on drive and inclination placing *agape* in their stead. The praise of preferential love belongs to paganism, while of love of neighbour in paganism 'no intimation is to be found' (44). The love of passion (*eros*) is an either/or. Only bungling and confusion result when it is thought that, while teaching a higher love, Christianity 'in addition' praises *eros* and *philia*. The New Testament

[12] Cf. Howard V. Hong & Edna H. Hong, eds & trans., *The Sickness Unto Death* (Princeton, NJ, 1980) (henceforth *SuD*).
[13] Cf. Nygren, *Agape*, who argues that this is historically the case.

says no word of the *eros* the poet celebrates; no verse concerns the *philia* which paganism cultivated (45). Is the poet then no Christian? That has not been said, but he is not Christian *qua* poet. *Eros* is based on a drive that has its highest expression in this: there is only one beloved in the whole world and this only one time of *eros* is everything. Its essence lies in its unconditionality. Christian love teaches us to love all people, unconditionally all. If one makes a single exception of a person whom one does not wish to love the love is not Christian. Passion excludes the third; the third means confusion. The disparity could not be starker. Shut your door and pray to God; when you open it 'the very first person you meet is the neighbour, whom you *shall* love' (51).

Christianity, it has been held, has something against *eros*. But this is a misunderstanding.

Because paganism never had an inkling of self-denial's love for the neighbour, whom one *shall* love, it divided love this way: self-love is abhorrent because it is love of self, but erotic love and friendship, which are passionate preferential love, are love. But Christianity, which has made manifest what love is, divides otherwise: self-love and passionate preferential love are essentially the same, but love for the neighbour—that is love. To love the beloved, asks Christianity, is that loving?—and adds, 'Do not the pagans also do the same?'...

If someone thinks that the difference between paganism and Christianity is that in Christianity the beloved and the friend are loved faithfully and tenderly in a quite different way than in paganism, this is a misunderstanding. Does not paganism offer examples of erotic love and friendship so perfect that the poet looks back to them for instruction? But no one in paganism loved the neighbour; no one suspected that he existed.

What paganism called love, distinguishing it from self-love, was actually preference. But passionate preference is 'essentially another form of self-love' (cf. Aristotle). One sees the truth of the saying: 'the virtues of paganism are glittering vices'[14] (53).

What is decisive is love for God; from which flows love for neighbour. Of this paganism 'had no inkling' (57). Omitting God and thinking *eros* and *philia* love, paganism abhorred what it thought self-love. Now the lover is in actuality 'relating himself to himself'. *Eros*

---

[14] Attributed to Augustine, though the expression is not his; see Howard V. Hong & Edna H. Hong, eds & trans., *Works of Love* (in this book known as *Love's Deeds*) (Princeton, NJ, 1995) (henceforth *LD*), 'Notes', 502, note 73.

and *philia* constitute 'the very peak of self-esteem, the *I* intoxicated in the *other I* ' (cf. Aristotle's *Nichomachean Ethics*).[15] In the beloved and the friend it is not the neighbour that is loved, but the other 'I', or one might say the first 'I' again but more intensely. Given the neighbour is 'the *first you*' we do not come a step closer (56). One loves the neighbour on the basis of an equality before God (*coram deo*). Every person equally has this equality and has it unconditionally. 'In erotic love and friendship, preferential love is the middle term; in love for the neighbour, God' (57–8).

II. C. You *Shall Love the Neighbour*

But who is the neighbour? Kierkegaard turns to the beloved (i.e. the one who in this context we should be unlikely to consider). From the category of 'neighbour' no one, least of all the beloved, is excluded. Likewise the friend. It is the love for the other *qua* neighbour which is the 'sanctifying element' (keeping relationships right). Ask the poet how disconsolate it is to live alone without a beloved (63). But 'heaven has a new, . . . more blessed joy in readiness for the sorrowing'. Christian consolation swallows up the pain. The neighbour cannot be taken from you, since it is your love 'that holds the neighbour fast'. Lose everything in erotic love and friendship, 'you still retain the best in loving the neighbour' (65).

Kierkegaard discourses on the nature of *agape*, that love which loves without respect to the worthiness of that which is loved.

Have you never thought about God's love? If it were love's excellence to love the extraordinary, then God would be, if I dare say so, in an awkward position, since for him the extraordinary does not exist (65).

The excellence of being able to love only the extraordinary is 'more like an accusation'.

Because the neighbour has none of the perfections that the beloved, the friend, the admired one, the cultured person, the rare, the extraordinary person have to such a high degree, for that very reason love for the neighbour has all the perfections that the love for the beloved, the friend, the cultured person, the admired one, the rare, the extraordinary person does not have. . . . Erotic love is

---

[15] Aristotle, *Nichomachean Ethics*, book IX, chs 4, 7–9.

defined by the object; friendship is defined by the object; only love for the neighbour is defined by love (66).

Kierkegaard speaks of the anxiety of *eros* and *philia*, deriving as they do from their dependence on their object. By contrast the person who loves with an agapeistic love loves also his enemy.[16] 'Shut your eyes, remember the commandment to love, then you love—your enemy— no, then you love the neighbour, because you do not see that he is your enemy' (68). Further, with shut eyes you see not the dissimilarities of earthly life. The equality of neighbourly love is something other than social equality.

> Well intentioned worldliness . . . rejoices when it succeeds in making temporal conditions the same for more and more people, but it acknowledges itself that its struggle is a pious wish, that it has taken on a prodigious task, that its prospects are remote—if it rightly understood itself, it would perceive that this will never be achieved in temporality, that even if this struggle is continued for centuries, it will never attain the goal (72).

Oblivious to the dissimilarities of earthly life, taking 'the shortcut of eternity' Christianity loves the neighbour. It is the truly revolutionary.

The mob form an 'ungodly alliance' against the 'universally human'. Thus it is thought treasonable to wish for fellowship with all people. These people (the mob) will 'perhaps misunderstand it' if someone (like Kierkegaard), who does not hold in common with them what they have sides with them. [A fascinating remark in view of what was to come.] Kierkegaard speaks out against serfdom (so recently abolished): the times are past when only the powerful and prominent were human beings. Significantly, he thinks the change only commensurate with Christianity. 'The inhumanity and the un-Christianness in this consists in . . . wanting to deny kinship with all people' (74). Thus Kierkegaard comments also, with delicious irony, on the behaviour of some of his class: 'the distinguished corruption' of the 'distinguished person' who, fleeing 'from one distinguished circle to another' takes care not to look at these other people 'lest he should meet a fellow being' knows no bounds. The world has changed and corruption also.

It is the measure of a person 'how far he is from what he understands to what he does' (78). Kierkegaard speaks of human evasion:

---

[16] This is often held the mark of *agape*; see Nygren *Agape*, 101–2, 154, 731.

'At a distance everyone recognizes the neighbour' (79–80). The lowly say of their betters: 'Be cautious . . . because these enemies still have so much power that it could be dangerous to break with them.' Again, there is 'suppressed envy in the acclaim that honours the powerful' (cf. Nietzsche). Were such a lowly person to give earthly advantage its due his peers 'would perhaps push him away as a traitor, scorn him as slave-minded', while 'the privileged would perhaps . . . deride him as a climber'. This spells trouble for the Christian who acts out of Christian equality. What is regarded as 'too lowly' for the distinguished (to love the neighbour) is regarded as 'too presumptuous' for the lowly (to love the neighbour)! (80–1). Imagine one who, preparing a banquet, invites the lame, the blind, cripples, and beggars (cf. Luke 14:12–13). He says to a friend 'yesterday I gave a great banquet!' Upon discovering who were the guests the friend might say: 'It is a strange use of language to call that kind of a gathering a banquet.' Now suppose the man, quoting the Gospel were to say: 'But I thought I had language on my side' (81–2). 'So scrupulous is Christian equality and its use of language that it requires not only that you shall feed the poor; it requires that you shall call it a banquet. . . . The one who gives *the banquet* sees the neighbour in the poor and lowly—however ludicrous this may seem in the eyes of the world' (83).

Christianity cuts across the grain of the world. Moreover (given his experience in the *Corsair* affair) Kierkegaard knows the Christian to meet with derision. It is pleasant, he comments, for flesh and blood to avoid opposition, but is it of comfort in the hour of death? The only comfort lies in not having avoided the opposition but having suffered on account of it. It is for the Christian simply and solely to obey, to put himself in the position where Governance (Kierkegaard's term for God) can use him. In the hour of death he is to say: 'I have done my part; whether I have achieved anything, I do not know . . . but that I have existed for [others] that I do know and I know it because of their derision' (85). He ponders whether there can be a single one whom Governance has used as an instrument in the service of truth who 'has arranged his life in any other way than to exist equally for every human being' (86).

Thus Kierkegaard speaks of the equality of all *sub specie aeternitatis*. In the theatre of life we wear different costumes, but when the curtain falls all are one and the same—actors. Now eternity is 'not a stage, . . . it is truth' (87). On the stage of eternity you will see what people essentially were as you did not see it on account of the dissimilarity which you saw.

Take many sheets of paper, write something different on each one; then no one will be like another. But then again take each single sheet; do not let yourself be confused by the diverse inscriptions, hold it up to the light, and you will see a common watermark on all of them.

'The neighbour' is the watermark all have in common 'but you see it only by means of eternity's light when it shines through the dissimilarity' (89). True devotion is to be willing to give up all earthly advantage in conformity to the claim that God and eternity have on the individual. Such a one 'is on the point of loving the neighbour' (90).

III. A. Rom. 13.10 Love is the Fulfilling of the Law; III. B. Love is a Matter of Conscience

Chapter III concerns the difficulty involved in loving the neighbour and the clash with the world it brings in its train.

Under the heading 'love is the fulfilling of the law' (Rom.13.10), Kierkegaard considers what is the Lutheran understanding of 'law' (as opposed to 'gospel'). Failure to fulfil the law and thus falling down before one's own eyes makes a person open to the gospel message. Of the prodigal son Kierkegaard comments that his awareness that he was not doing his father's will brought him closer to God (94). What concerns us is the *doing* of the works; love in action. Kierkegaard tackles evasion. 'Busyness' and 'worldliness' are inseparable. To be busy is to be divided, scattered; a multiplicity in which it is impossible for a person to be whole. The one who occupies himself with the eternal is never 'busy'. Perhaps with what he considered his squandered youth in mind Kierkegaard remarks that 'wasted time precedes every human beginning' (102).

What counts is the priority given to the relationship with God. 'To love God is to love oneself truly; to help another person to love God is to love another person; to be helped by another person to love God is to be loved' (107). Kierkegaard is concerned that persons should not appropriate or misuse others, seeing another in relation to her- or himself rather than to God. Likewise it is for us to put our relationship to God first, differentiating between that relationship and a relation to another that would be inappropriate. In such an instance Christianity may bring not peace but a sword: *eros* and *philia* can easily take a wrong turning. Each person is God's bondservant; therefore 'he dare not belong to anyone in love unless in the same love he belongs to God and dare not possess anyone in love unless the other and he himself belong to God in this love' (107–8). Were a love relationship the most blissful attachment, if it does not lead me to God it is not true love. Christianity asks whether a love relationship stands in relation to God; if not it will split it up. If only one person understands this, he will be faced with the 'horror of a collision' (108). The Christian must be able to hate father, mother, sister, brother.

Kierkegaard is concerned lest recognition of the right relationship to God become lost through societal changes. The 'abominable' era of bond service is past 'and so there is the aim of going further—by means of the abomination of abolishing the person's bond service in relation to God' to whom each human being is bound by his creation *ex nihilo* (115). We are to love God in adoration and obedience, 'receiving our orders' from God (117).

There follows a fascinating discussion of what happens when people make 'gods' of others. Unmindful of 'eternity's equality', throwing herself away the vulnerable woman will abase herself before the arrogant man, naming as 'love' her craving that he 'inhumanly should demand everything of her' (125). Were she to be told that for God the dissimilarities between people were 'jest and trumpery', such that she should honour herself, she would call this selfishness. Likewise the one who exists for the ruler, craving that he 'will step on him so that he can joyfully praise the ruler's gracious love and kindness' (126). Persons can desire to make themselves indispensable not only on account of their power but also through their weakness.[17] Whereas Socrates (Kierkegaard's model human being) 'did not let himself in any way be spellbound by temporality or by any human being' (129).

Thus under 'Love is a Matter of Conscience' Kierkegaard further discusses social hierarchy. Christianity 'has never been a friend of the trumpery of novelty'; it has not wanted to topple governments to place itself on the throne nor 'contended . . . for a place in the world'.

---

[17] This chimes in well with feminist discussion of the fact that woman's 'sin' typically consists in self-abnegation not hubris. Kierkegaard is observant.

What it has done is to make the relation between persons 'a matter of conscience' (135). Accordingly, of a charwoman he writes:

From the Christian point of view... she has the right to say, as she is doing her work and talking to herself and to God... 'I am doing this work for wages, but that I do it as carefully as I am doing it, I do—for the sake of conscience.'... If the woman becomes displeased because no one wants to listen to such talk, this merely shows that she is not of a Christian mind... there are certain things, among them particularly the secrets of inwardness, that lose by being made public... Christianity's divine meaning is to say in confidence to every human being, 'Do not busy yourself with changing the shape of the world or your situation, as if you (to stay with the example) instead of being a poor charwoman perhaps could manage to be called "Madame". No, make Christianity your own and it will show you a point outside the world and by means of this you will move heaven and earth; yes, you will do something even more wonderful, you will move heaven and earth so quietly, so lightly, that no one notices it' (136).

In the divine sense, Christianity makes everyone one of a kind. While the king 'should and ought to be the only one who rules according to his conscience', it is granted to everyone to obey for the sake of conscience.

See, the world makes a great noise merely in order to achieve a little change, sets heaven and earth in motion for nothing, like the mountain that gives birth to a mouse—Christianity quietly makes infinity's change as if it were nothing. It is very quiet, as nothing of this world can be;... what else is Christianity but inwardness! (137).

Likewise in marriage. Each is asked whether he or she has consulted with God and with his or her conscience. This is 'infinity's change' in *eros*, taking place in a person's hidden inwardness.

What abominations has the world not seen in the relationships between man and woman, that she, almost like an animal, was a disdained being in comparison with the man, a being of another species. What battles there have been to establish in a worldly way the woman in equal rights with the man—but Christianity makes only infinity's change and therefore quietly. Outwardly the old more or less remains. The man is to be the woman's master and she subservient to him; but inwardly everything is changed, changed by means of this little question to the woman, whether she has consulted with her conscience about having this man—as master, for otherwise she does not get him (138)....

In the name of Christianity fatuous people have fatuously been busy about making it obvious in a worldly way that the woman should be established in equal rights with the man—Christianity has never required or desired this. It has done everything for the woman, provided she Christianly will be satisfied with what is Christian; if she is unwilling, then for what she loses she gains only a mediocre compensation in the fragment of externality she can in a worldly way obtain by defiance. . . .

Christianity does not want to make changes in externals; neither does it want to abolish drives or inclination—it wants only to make infinity's change in the inner being. (139).

And to men Kierkegaard has this to say: the man who does not see in his wife the neighbour and only secondly the wife never comes to love his neighbour no matter how many people he loves—for he has made of his wife an exception.

What Christ said of his kingdom, that it is not of this world, holds true of everything Christian. There have been times when Christians thought it necessary to give Christianity a worldly expression—so they thought to abolish marriage and live in the cloister. But that is a childish way to distinguish Christianity; like a child who hides himself—in order that he may be found. It is the hiding place of inwardness which 'keeps the secret of faith' (1 Tim. 3.9). 'Christianity does not bring about any external change at all in the external sphere; it wants to seize it, purify it, sanctify it, and in this way make everything new while everything is still old' (145). Worldly relations are but an interlude, for it is to God that the heart must be bound.

When the couch of death is prepared for you, when you go to bed never to get up again and they are only waiting for you to turn to the other side to die, and the stillness grows around you—then when those close to you gradually leave and the stillness grows because only those closest to you remain, while death comes closer to you; . . . and then when the last one has bent over you for the last time and turns to the other side because you yourself are now turning to the side of death—there still remains one on that side, the last one by the deathbed, he who was the first, God, the living God—that is, if your heart was pure, which it became only by loving him (150).

The relationship with God is the most infinite, the most confidential.

IV. Our Duty to Love the People We See

1 John 4.20: If anyone says, 'I love God', and hates his brother, he is a liar; for how can he who does not love his brother, whom he has seen, love God, whom he has not seen?

What we have in all its parts is a profoundly Lutheran statement. The person must first love the unseen God that he may learn what is love. (The relation to God comes first, it is not that he or she learns to love God by loving the neighbour.) 'But that he actually loves the unseen will be known by his loving the brother he sees.' (The relation to God results in and becomes visible through love of the neighbour.) God 'continually points away from himself, so to speak, . . . saying "If you want to love me, then love the people you see; what you do for them, you do for me"' (160). Thus does God turn us to the neighbour. There follows a polemic against mysticism. The 'most dangerous of all escapes' is 'wanting to love only the unseen or that which one has not seen' (161). Christian love 'comes down from heaven to earth' (173); mysticism's direction is the opposite.[18]

Continuing in a Lutheran vein, Kierkegaard depicts *agape* as that love that loves irrespective of the worthiness of that which is loved. It is love that brings about change; it is not conditional upon change.

Christ's love for Peter was boundless . . . He did not say, 'Peter must first change and become another person before I can love him again'. No, he said exactly the opposite, 'Peter is Peter, and I love him. My love, if anything, will help him to become another person'. Therefore he did not break off the friendship in order perhaps to renew it if Peter would have become another person; no, he preserved the friendship unchanged and in that way helped Peter to become another person (172).

It is this that lies at the heart of the Christian gospel. God's love in Christ is revealed to be quite unlike human love, whether *eros* or *philia*. Whereas human life continually flies away with the beloved's perfections (*eros*), Christian love 'grants the beloved all his imperfections and

---

[18] Compare Luther who, pointing to the incarnation, opposes mysticism. Of Philip who has said 'show us the Father and we shall be satisfied' (John 14.8), a mystical text, Luther comments: 'Away he goes with his own thoughts and flutters up into the clouds.' He thinks Christ to rebuke Philip: 'He who has seen me has seen the Father' (John 14.9) (*WA* 45.512.6f.).

weaknesses and in all his changes remains with him, loving the person it sees' (173). If a friend does not respond to the request of another, says Kierkegaard, that other may let the friendship cease—until perhaps the friend does respond. 'Is this a relationship of friendship?' he asks (172). (An example exactly parallel to a pre-Reformation understanding of how God will treat us; we must become good before we can stand in relation to God.) The one closer to helping an erring one is he who calls the other a friend even though an offence has been committed against him. (As God accepts us irrespective of our merits.) Humans speak of finding the perfect person that they may love them; 'whereas Christianity speaks about being the perfect person who boundlessly loves the person he sees' (174). Thus has Christianity taught us what is truly love, agape.

V. Our Duty to Remain in Love's Debt to One Another
Rom. 13.8: Owe no one anything, except to love one another

Kierkegaard will speak of the training required to love and the suffering which ensues. Note again in this passage the Lutheran context: *agape* does not calculate, whereas in the Catholic under-standing God had been thought to 'calculate'.

Human ways of acting, 'book-keeping arrangements', whereby a tally of wrongs are kept, comments Kierkegaard, is 'the greatest abomination to love' (178). 'God knows what trivialities, which . . . are . . . very carefully collected and very carefully hoarded, give us human beings either immediately or, what is just as sad, after a long time, an occasion for accusing someone or other' (168). Such accounting is only possible within a finite relationship; the one who loves does not calculate. Says Kierkegaard: love's element is, 'infinitude, inexhaustibility, immeasurability'. The source of such love is God; 'it continually remains in its element by means of the infinitude of the debt'. (180). (That is to say God loves us irrespective of our debt, which example we follow. Christianity goes against the grain of the world. Again, in that 'the law', calculation, is overcome in Christ.)

But in the world it will go badly for the Christian; 'the good is rewarded with hate, contempt and persecution' (192). It is not a question of hatred of the world, of a secret desire to be persecuted; the world's opposition does not stand in an accidental relation to

Christianity. A pagan at his death may consider himself fortunate in not having encountered adversities. A Christian would be obliged to be dubious 'because Christianly the world's opposition stands in an essential relationship to the inwardness of Christianity' (194). At the moment of choosing Christianity a person must understand what it entails: a two-edged sword is handed over rather differently than a bunch of flowers. Being a divine good, Christianity is a dangerous human good: 'it is an offence, a foolishness' (198).

And Kierkegaard—as he is wont to do—takes the Lutheran dialectic into the epistemological sphere.[19] 'When Christianity came into the world it did not need to point out ... that it was contending with human reason, because the world discovered this easily enough.' (It was foolishness to the Greeks.) But now, says Kierkegaard, when Christianity has for centuries lived with reason, when a fallen Christianity (like those fallen angels who married mortal women) has married human reason (i.e. Hegelianism), when they are in a familiar relationship, it is for Christianity to pay attention to the obstacle. 'Woe to the one who first hit upon the idea of preaching Christianity without the possibility of offence' (200). Christianity offers people the choice of being offended or of accepting it. Meanwhile, without so much as noticing the offence, the world has appropriated Christianity; then proceeding to take offence at authentic Christianity.

Some Christian Deliberations in the Form of Discourses: Second Series

I. Love Builds Up
1 Cor. 8.1: But love builds up

In a fine piece of writing, building on the thought that thinking the best of another in itself promotes change, Kierkegaard comments that to be loving is to presuppose love in the other. Instinctively we want first to pull out the splinter (Matt. 7.3–5); but 'the one who judges ... that the other person lacks love—he takes away the foundation' (220). Citing the parable that best illustrates the Lutheran and New Testament sense of *agape* Kierkegaard writes:

[19] See pp. 19–20.

See, the prodigal son's father was perhaps the only one who did not know that he had a prodigal son, because the father's love hoped all things. . . . The father won back the prodigal son simply because he, who hoped all things, presupposed that love was present in the ground (220).

With great insight Kierkegaard remarks: 'If anyone has ever spoken to you in such a way or treated you in such a way that you really felt built up, this was because you very vividly perceived how he presupposed love to be in you' (222). And drawing attention to the tenderness and maturity of love he concludes: 'Love is not a being-for-itself quality but a quality by which or in which you are for others' (223). Nothing could better illustrate the contrast between *agape* and *eros* or *philia*.

II. Love Believes All Things—and Yet Is Never Deceived
1 Cor. 13.7: Love believes all things

The question is whether there is 'mistrust or love in you' (228). The one who loves without demanding reciprocity cannot be deceived. (Compare Paul's speaking of *agape* as a love which, enduring all things, never fails: 1 Cor. 13.7–8.) Remarks Kierkegaard, such a love can easily be confused with weakness; but the 'powers of eternity' are in this powerlessness. The one who loves has the 'courage to believe all things'; and Kierkegaard adds—presumably with the *Corsair* affair in mind—'courage to bear the world's contempt and insults' (244).

III. Love Hopes All Things—and Yet is Never Put to Shame
1 Cor. 13.7: Love hopes all things

Kierkegaard turns to 'possibility', a category which gains in importance for him as circumstances seem to close in around him.

Possibility, this marvellous thing that is so infinitely fragile (the most delicate shoot of spring is not so fragile!), so infinitely frail (the finest woven linen is not so frail!), and yet, brought into being and shaped with the help of the eternal, stronger than anything else, if it is the possibility of the good! (251).

He who lives without possibility is in despair. 'He breaks with the eternal and arbitrarily puts an end to possibility; without the consent of eternity, he ends where the end is not' (252). There follows an example of 'reduplication', which I shall discuss. Says Kierkegaard, unless he be loving, a person cannot hope 'because the good has an infinite connectedness' (255). Indeed: 'In the same degree to which he hopes for others, he hopes for himself, because in the very same degree to which he hopes for others, he is one who loves' (255). And—employing typical vocabulary of his—this is 'eternity's like for like' (256). Whereas in the world disappointed expectancy leads to shame (whereupon we know it was not hope but a craving) love hopes all things—and yet is never put to shame.

IV. Love Does Not Seek Its Own
1 Cor. 13.5: Love does not seek its own

Christian love is a revolution. There is a 'you' and an 'I', but no mine and yours. The one who loses his soul will gain it (a 'redoubling'). Whereas, lacking the flexibility to comprehend others, the domineering person wants everyone to conform to his pattern for human beings.

Whether he is a tyrant in an empire or a domestic tyrant in a little attic room essentially makes no difference; the nature is the same: domineeringly refusing to go out of oneself, domineeringly wanting to crush the other person's distinctiveness or torment it to death (270–1).

The person who has not come into his own in relation to God is unable to let others be themselves. Just as such a rigid person only looks out for himself, so also with small-mindedness and imperious envy. Such an attitude is incompatible with God, 'who lovingly gives *all things* and yet gives all things distinctiveness' (271).

The greatest thing that one person can do for another is to enable the other to stand on his or her own ground. Suppose a lover (Kierkegaard is viewing himself in relation to Regine), seeing to his delight that he was loved, realized that a relationship would be damaging to the beloved's distinctiveness. While erotic love would be unable to make the sacrifice, *agape* (that love which is self-sacrificing, loving each in his or her distinctiveness) would do so. In the social world we distinguish between those who are their own masters and those who are dependent 'and we wish that everyone might at some time be in a position to become his own master' (274). Likewise in spiritual things to become one's own master is the highest. 'In love to help someone... to become himself, free, independent, his own master, to help him stand alone', is the greatest gift (274). Thus Socrates designated himself a midwife. But Socrates did not love the one he wanted to help (the concept of *agape* was absent from the ancient pagan world). The one who loves agapeistically has understood that every human being 'stands by himself—through God's help' (278). Annihilating himself, he is an instrument in God's hand that the other not be hindered in his or her God-relationship.

V. Love Hides a Multitude of Sins
[1 Pet. 4.8]

The person who loves gives others confidence. We love to be near someone who loves, for they cast out fear. Such a person will choose the most lenient explanation, a mitigating explanation which hides a multitude of sins, suspending judgement until, sure enough, a little circumstance comes to light that gives him the clue. He is victorious with his explanation, acquired through immersing himself in another's life. He sees the sin, but believes that forgiveness takes it away. 'Only love has sufficient dexterity to take away the sin by means of forgiveness' (295). Forgiveness deprives sin of sustenance. Sin can become furious at love, raging against it; but in the end it cannot hold out.

VI. Love Abides
1 Cor. 13.13: So... love abides

Again Regine is in mind. 'When despondency wants to deaden all of life for you ... —oh, then bear in mind that love abides!' (303). For we are speaking of God's love, of *agape*. If a broken relationship ceases to be loving, then in truth it has never been.

The one who truly loves never falls away from love; for him, therefore, it can never come to a break, because love abides.... By abiding... he maintains the upper hand over the past; ... [transforming] what... is a break into a possible relationship in the future.... But that requires the powers of eternity, and therefore the loving one, who abides, must abide in *love*; otherwise the past gradually acquires the power and then little by little the break comes into view (305).

It was such a continuing relationship that he longed should be possible with her. There follows a discussion of 'woman' (perspicacious, but also outrageous, as we shall discuss). Of the woman who waited for the man who never came, he remarks that it is 'a noble womanly deed, a great and glorious work' for such a woman to remain true to herself in her love. 'She faded away—a sacrifice to erotic love' (310). *Qua* human being this is the highest that can be said, that one is sacrificed. Lovely in death as in life, it remains the case that *eros* had been her highest. But, concludes Kierkegaard, 'erotic love is not the eternal' (313).

VII. Mercifulness, A Work of Love Even If It Can Give Nothing and Is Able to Do Nothing.

Kierkegaard discusses alms-giving. (It may be useful here to know his own practice. Given his overall expenditure as recorded in his accounts the amounts he gave were trivial. However, he quite possibly gave away more quietly; there is some evidence that this is the case.[20])

The incessant talk about giving money is almost merciless, whereas Christianity speaks of mercifulness. If one is merciful, generosity will follow. We are atrociously unfair to poverty and misery in failing to comprehend that they can practice mercifulness. For as an attitude mercifulness is a work of love, even though unable to give or do anything. Of the poor widow Christ says that she 'gave out of her poverty' (Mark 12.44). Mercifulness is infinitely unrelated to money. Consider eternity! Of all the things that it would not occur to you to find there is money.

What comfort the poor person can derive from being merciful. He cries out 'oh be merciful', but actually is asking for generosity. We should use language correctly were we to say to him:

Oh, be merciful! Do not let the envious pettiness of this earthly existence finally corrupt you so that you could forget that you are able to be merciful...Be merciful, be merciful toward the rich! Remember what you have in your power, while he has the money! (322).

---

[20] Cf. Joakim Garff, *Søren Kierkegaard: A Biography*, trans. Bruce Kirmmse (Princeton, NJ, 2005), 534.

Commenting that the life of the poor man is a 'dangerous protest against loving Governance', such that the man 'has the power to alarm the rest of us', Kierkegaard asks:

Which is more merciful: powerfully to remedy the needs of others or quietly to suffer and patiently to watch mercifully lest one disturb the joy and happiness of others? Which of these two loves more: the fortunate one who has sympathy for the suffering of others, or the unfortunate one who has true sympathy for the joy and happiness of others? (326).

The world does not understand eternity.

Temporality has a temporal and hence a bustling conception of the need... [saying] 'The poor one, the wretched one could in fact die—therefore the most important thing is that help be given'. No, answers eternity, the most important thing is that mercifulness be practised... 'Provide money for us, provide hospitals for us, that is the most important!' No, says eternity, the most important is mercifulness. From the point of view of eternity, that someone dies is no misfortune, but that mercifulness is not practised certainly is (326).

Of the rich man who loudly proclaims how much he has given, eternity will ask whether he has been merciful: 'Mercifulness is *how* it is given' (327).

VIII. The Victory of the Conciliatory Spirit in Love, Which Wins [*Vinde*] the One Overcome [*Overvunde*]
[*Eph. 6.13: To continue to stand after having overcome everything*]

To overcome evil with good is to fight *conciliatingly*, that the good may be victorious in the unloving person. Long before the enemy thinks of seeking agreement the loving one is 'already in agreement with him' (335). (Again, love is the motor of change.) To win the one who has been overcome must entail a peculiar difficulty, in that he will feel humiliated. It would not be loving to allow the unloving one to believe himself right in the evil he did; rather is it love's work that it become 'entirely clear to the unloving one how irresponsibly he has acted so that he deeply feels his wrong' (338). At the same time one wants to win the one overcome 'for the truth and himself' (339). The solution lies in the relationship passing through a third party, God. Lacking a third party human relations become unhealthy, either too ardent or embittered. The one who loves 'is too loving to face the one overcome directly and be himself the victor who savours the victory—while the other is the one overcome' (339). Before the third both are humbled. 'The one who loves humbles himself before the good, whose loyal servant he is, and, as he himself admits, in frailty; and the one overcome does not humble himself before the loving one but before the good' (340). (Again what insight into human relationships!) That he may prevent humiliation, the one who loves does not look at the one overcome. But in another sense he does look at him.

Would that I could describe how the one who loves looks at the one overcome, how joy beams from his eyes, how this loving look rests so gently on him, how it seeks, alluring and inviting, to win him! ... This is the way the loving one looks at him and besides is as calm as only the eternal can make a person (342).

The loving one seeks to gain the love of the one overcome. The one overcome asks 'Have you really forgiven me now?' The one who loves answers 'Do you truly love me now?' He is not replying to what is asked. 'He does not even want to answer the question about forgiveness, because this ... could easily make the matter too earnest in a damaging sense. What a wonderful conversation!' (344). Finally the other will be broken of the habit of asking about forgiveness. 'Thus he, the one who loves, has conquered, because he won the one overcome' (344).

IX. The Work of Love in Recollecting One Who is Dead

As in the previous two deliberations, the heart of the matter is the interior disposition. The ultimate test of love's presence is how a person relates to one who is dead; that is to say the case in which there can by definition be no reciprocity. (It is we may say Paul in 1 Cor. 13 taken to its ultimate point.) Kierkegaard has previously remarked that one can tell how a mother relates to her child through observing how she regards it as it sleeps.

We certainly do have duties to the dead says Kierkegaard. The work of love in recollecting the dead is the most faithful, the most unselfish love. 'The child cries, the pauper begs, the widow pesters, deference constrains, misery compels, etc.' (351); such extorted love is not free. But to love the dead is to love freely. The proverb runs 'Out of sight, out of mind'. Proverbs speak of how things go in the world; in the Christian sense every proverb is untrue! Loving the dead, we learn to love the living, unselfishly, faithfully. 'In the relationship to one who is dead, you have the criterion by which you can test yourself' (358).

X. The Work of Love in Praising Love

Kierkegaard reflects on himself *qua* author. Nothing is so swift as a thought.

And now to be out on the sea of thought . . . Before one learns to be able, when night comes, to sleep calmly, *away from* the thoughts in the confidence that God, who is love, has them in abundance, and to be able to wake up confident to the thoughts, assured that God has not been sleeping! (363).

That which a human can by himself know of love is superficial, deeper love he must come to know from God. 'Thus every human being can come to know . . . that he, like every human being is loved by God' (364). (We have returned to where the book commenced.) Kierkegaard once again contrasts Christian love with that understanding natural to the human. Socrates thought that to love was to love the beautiful, speaking in jest of loving the ugly. 'And what is *the ugly*? It is the *neighbour*, whom one *shall* love.' Of the neighbour Socrates knew nothing. True love is not to find the lovable object (the Platonist *eros* or Aristotelian *philia*) 'but to find the unlovable object lovable' (*agape*, which loves irrespective of worth) (373–4). Once more we are confronted with the novelty of Christian *agape*.

Conclusion

The apostle says 'Beloved, let us love one another (1 John 4.7). To love others is the only thing worth living for; without this you are not really living.

Christianity has abolished the Jewish like for like (an eye for an eye, a tooth for a tooth). (Again, 'gospel' stands over against 'law'; thus in Lutheran thought Christianity tends to be pitted over against Judaism.) It has replaced it with eternity's like for like ('redoubling'). Christianity, says Kierkegaard, turns our attention away from the external to the inward, making every relationship into a God-relationship. In a Christian sense it does not concern you what others do to you, you have to do only with what you do to others, or how you take what others do to you.

If you refuse to forgive you make God hard-hearted. If you cannot bear people's faults against you, how should God be able to bear your sins against him? If there is anger in you, then God is anger in you; if there is leniency and mercifulness in you, then God is mercifulness in you. . . . If there is a word you would rather not hear said to you, then watch your saying of it . . . because echo promptly repeats it and says it to *you*. . . . God repeats the words of grace or of judgement that you say about another (384–5).

Thus does Kierkegaard speak of 'the rigorous like for like' (386).[21]

Critique

It may be thought hardly surprising that the book has enjoyed a mixed reception. There are those (myself included) who, while not uncritical, count this their favourite Kierkegaard text. Nor to my knowledge is it unknown for persons navigating deep waters to find it pastorally efficacious. But the book has also met with wrath and incredulity on account of Kierkegaard's social views and general political incorrectness. Any evaluation can only gain through placing the book in context and that I shall attempt. A social conservative, Kierkegaard was nevertheless a radical conservative. Indeed one may think to see in embryonic form in this text some of the complex judgements which, in the years following its publication, were to lead to his preparedness to put himself on the line in his opposition to church and society.

The Individual

The base point of Kierkegaard's deliberation is the individual's rela-tion to God. The depths of a human being are found in the depths of God. It is through the relationship to God (not to society, church or other persons) that we are constituted. It was this that Kierkegaard found lacking in Hegel and (as we shall in the next chapter consider)

---

[21] For other examples of redoubling see pp. 281–2, 380.

his position challenges a Hegelian position whereby the self is constituted though societal relationships. Moreover, given that others are also constituted in the first instance through their relationship to God this will impact on one's relation to others. Integrity is given to each individually. Furthermore, that each person is so constituted confers an equality on persons *sub specie aeternitatis*, as we shall shortly consider. The fundamental nature of the relation to God may be said to give a certain relativity to inter-personal relations. But this need not imply callousness; it can enable persons to accord to others their proper independence. It is on all accounts a deeply Protestant standpoint.

Given the emphasis accorded to the constitution of the person Kierkegaard's ethical outlook could be classified a 'virtue' ethics. His position is deontological (ethical behaviour deriving from the prior constitution of the person) rather than consequentialist (holding that that choice should be made of most consequent benefit). 'Person' precedes while issuing in 'works': as is the person, so will be their works. As Luther proclaimed in that revolutionary essay 'The Freedom of a Christian' (1520), making reference to Matthew's Gospel, the good tree bears good fruit, and again (making reference to Aristotle, as though to chide the medieval theologians) the good builder builds a good house (and not vice versa).[22] But one wonders whether Kierkegaard may not have gained this outlook which may be classed a 'virtue ethics' as much from his awareness of Greek philosophy as from his Lutheran heritage.[23]

Such a position is predicated upon a presupposition as to the maturity and self-awareness of individuals. 'To become one's own master' writes Kierkegaard 'is the highest' (274). In the months before writing, Kierkegaard had received a painful schooling in this regard on account of the *Corsair* affair. Aware of the integrity of his position, he had needed to muster the strength to stand alone. It would seem of crucial importance in such a situation to possess a decent sense of self. That Kierkegaard majors on this is noteworthy, in that one might have surmised that, given his background and context, he would

---

[22] Aristotle, *Nichomachean Ethics*, book II, ch. 1.
[23] See for example Plato, *The Republic*, trans. F. M. Cornford (Oxford, 1941), 138–9.

be weighed down by an exaggerated sense of sin. Nor does it strike me
that structurally the Lutheran tradition has been helpful in this matter
of self-integrity. Quoting Luther, Nygren, whose classic *Agape and
Eros* so closely mirrors the discussion of agape in *Love's Deeds*, speaks
of the self as a (mere) 'channel' between God and neighbour. Kierkegaard expresses himself quite otherwise.[24] We have a self-integrity,
accountability, and responsibility to ourselves. The person who wastes
his or her time on trivialities is failing in love for him- or herself; an
interesting take on time management. Kierkegaard expects of us great
inner strength.

This emphasis impacts on our relations to others. The quotation
from Kierkegaard given immediately above continues: 'And in love
to help someone... to become himself free, independent, his own
master, to help him stand alone—that is the greatest beneficence'
(274). It is the nature of love to build up. To love another is to help
the other cultivate his or her God-relationship, given it is for that
other to stand in his or her relation to God as do we. Anything
else is exploitation; we should not attempt to play 'god' to another.
(As we saw in conjunction with *Fragments*, no individual can
mediate God to another; in that sense there are no priests or saints.)
Nor can we allow another to play 'god' to us. We must exercise
sufficient integrity neither to misuse others, distorting them in
relation to our neediness; nor mistakenly stand in for God for
them. Kierkegaard will enable Regine to find her feet apart from
him. (Though he had scarcely been pleased when she had promptly
done so, becoming engaged to another!) Domineering behaviour, as
equally erotic worship, fails to grant another dignity of personhood.

Kierkegaard had an astute awareness of the peculiar individuality
of each. This would well fit with what in recent times has been a
characteristic of virtue ethics: a concern for the practice of 'attentiveness'. Kierkegaard was markedly attentive. He could hardly have given
us his lively depictions of all and sundry, filling his works with such
anecdotes, had he not been possessed of an observant (and often
mischievous) eye. It is upon such attentiveness on the observer's part
to slight shifts in disposition, for example on the part of the one in

[24] See p. 252.

the wrong, that is predicated consequent action in winning that person over. If strict with himself, Kierkegaard advocates a loving kindness towards others, a slowness to judge, and readiness to forgive. He has absorbed the (not least Lutheran) insight that love and forgiveness release in the one given such acceptance forces for growth and change. Hence he advises patience and tolerance; a waiting and observing, until some small piece of information comes our way enabling us to give context to the other's bad behaviour. One may think that modern psychiatry has confirmed so much of what Kierkegaard has to say, if not expressing it so vividly or persuasively. In all their perversity and unreasonableness, their weakness and their pain, Kierkegaard will find in other people a lovability. He is fundamentally optimistic, both discerning and fostering strength.

Kierkegaard knows that what he has to say of the healing nature of the relation to God will sound like pious pretentiousness. What other comfort, says he, compares with that of eternity? He simply recommends that his readers try it out! Clearly it is this relationship that, in his hour of need, prevented he himself from becoming unhinged. That their relation to God can play this role for an individual is we may think for Kierkegaard consequent upon the fact that it is through this relation that a human being is constituted. As we have seen and shall further consider, a person is in a quite fundamental sense spirit, the eternal constitutive of their being. Thus to turn to God is for that person to find again his or her groundedness. Kierkegaard will give this understanding its rightful priority.

The Individual and Society

We turn to wider questions of individual and society. Before mounting a critique (for a critique must surely follow), we should do well to recognize that the position Kierkegaard adopted could, in his society, alienate others of his class. It was Kierkegaard's practice to give copies of his publications to Mynster, primus of the Danish church, who had been a formative influence in his life.[25] Subsequent to his delivering *Love's Deeds*, Kierkegaard called to see Mynster. He recorded:

[25] See p. 257.

He said he was very busy so I left immediately. But he was also very cool towards me. Probably he is offended by the latest book. That's how I understood it. I could be wrong...I have always boggled at writing what I know might offend, indeed infuriate him. I assume that has now happened....I have never done the slightest thing to gain his support and consent but it would have pleased me indescribably to have him agree with me[26]

Love's Deeds exhorted the privileged to take account of those of whose existence they might prefer to be unaware. Such an admonition, published at a time when social turbulence was gaining momentum, could well smack of radicality.

As did others of his class, Kierkegaard in 1847 believed in or took for granted a monarchical constitution. Denmark had no representative assembly and no real landed aristocracy with whom the monarch shared power, though a cultured urban élite, whose wealth had been built up through Copenhagen's pre-eminence in the carry trade as a shipping port. It was not so much that Kierkegaard had a 'catholic' belief in the divine right of kings. Rather was he a-political (if not naïve), believing in minimalist government. Were his peers to rule, so thought Kierkegaard, they would be much more likely to interfere in what was alone his business. Furthermore, the Danish context was that ever since fearing social disorder Luther had sided with the princes against the peasants, Lutheran thought had exhibited a marked predilection for a biblical view, based on Romans 13, that one should obey rulers and those placed in authority. Kierkegaard held that it was for the king to govern; that was his calling. Thus in many ways politically and socially conservative, Kierkegaard was by sentiment adamantly opposed to what he sarcastically referred to as government by the numerical; democracy.[27]

But first and foremost, Kierkegaard had theological concerns leading him to think as he did. He worried that, were attitudes of deference and obedience in the political sphere to be overthrown, subtle changes in the human disposition toward God would follow. Observing that the monarchical constitution had served as a bulwark for the Christian religion, he feared that its demise would leave the

---

[26] Hannay, 274–5 (*Pap.* VIII[1] A 390), 4 Nov 1847.
[27] *Pap.* X[5] A 126 (1853), quoted by Kirmmse in 'Kierkegaard and 1848', *History of European Ideas*, 20 (1995), 169–70.

worship of God high and dry. (Who is to say he was wrong?) Kierkegaard—who by chance had sat in the same lecture theatre as Friedrich Engels listening to the elderly Schelling in Berlin in 1841— was lacking in any kind of messianic or revolutionary fervour. Superficially at least, 1848 was to find him far removed from the clamour of the streets, writing a tract on the structure of an individuated self in relation to God. Yet one could judge this a *political* response to the world around him. Kierkegaard saw the whipping up of sentiment by 'the mob' as undermining individual responsibility. He noted that such groups were inclined to set themselves against others as a perceived enemy. The other side of this coin was that Kierkegaard was scathing of the behaviour of members of his own class; of the distinguished person who flees from one distinguished circle to another with closed eyes lest he should meet another human being. And he thought serfdom, whereby one man in effect owns another, an abomination. There was a sense then in which, judged by his own criteria, Kierkegaard was all of a piece.

It is in the context of such a subtly differentiated outlook that Kierkegaard takes the positions that he does in this text. He tells the beggar that he, too, recognizing that his presence may disturb those more privileged than he, can exercise the quality of mercy. Not possessed of much else to contribute, this at least a beggar can bring to the situation: his conduct and behaviour. He is not to be excluded from what can be expected of persons. (May it not also be that Kierkegaard recognizes that, caught in circumstances over which one has little control, anger and envy of others can be profoundly self-destructive?) Kierkegaard seems to want to value the worth and speak to the wholeness of each human being—to the point that (as we may think) he becomes blind to other issues.[28] In a world in which Kierkegaard and those around him believe in an afterlife, it apparently becomes more important that the beggar keep his integrity, guarding his relationship to God, than whether he live or die. It is such passages which led the 20th century left-wing social theorist Adorno to mount a full-scale (and in some ways unfair) attack on *Love's Deeds*, portraying Kierkegaard's outlook as 'spiteful' and speaking of his 'stubborn maintenance of the "givenness" of the social

---

[28] One should not however underestimate Kierkegaard's recognition of the problem, see p. 213, n. 32.

order... ready to lend its arm to oppression and misanthropy'.[29] One can understand such a judgement.

We should also consider in this regard a further passage. Advising the charwoman that she should not aspire to call herself 'Madame', Kierkegaard comments that as she works she may say 'regally to herself before God' (136) that it is for the sake of conscience that she performs this work to perfection. *Coram deo*, before God, no one is her superior. In this context we should remember that it owed to Luther that the term *Beruf*, calling, became the common German word for occupation; according to Reformation principles everyone's occupation was a calling. Kierkegaard's outlook is well captured by words of the 17th-century English poet George Herbert.

> Teach me, my God and King,
> In all things thee to see,
> And what I do in any thing,
> To do it as for thee.

Further:

> A servant with this clause
> Makes drudgerie divine:
> Who sweeps a room, as for thy laws,
> Makes that and th' action fine.

And the poem, named 'The Elixir', concludes:

> This is the famous stone [the philosopher's stone]
> That turneth all to gold;
> For that which God doth touch and own
> Cannot for less be told.[30]

Within his framework of thought, Kierkegaard will accord dignity to the cleaning lady. Who is to tell if she, too, saw herself and her situation in these terms?

What one may say by way of critique is surely this. In the first place one may question whether, as a member of the privileged class,

[29] Theodor Adorno, 'On Kierkegaard's Doctrine of Love', *Studies in Philosophy and Social Science*, 8 (1940). Reproduced in Daniel W. Conway, ed., *Søren Kierkegaard: Critical Assessments of Leading Philosophers*, 2 (London & New York, 2002), 7–21, quotation p. 14.
[30] George Herbert, 'The Elixir' from *The Temple* (1633).

Kierkegaard has the right to dictate how others shall see their lot (even if he means to give good and comforting advice). Secondly it is surely difficult—to the point of scandalous—to think that, on account of some idea of an afterlife, the physical needs of the beggar in this life should be neglected. In our day some of us may have felt this way upon seeing a crippled beggar lying on a dirty pavement in India, while an apparently oblivious world walks by: talk of reincarnation just doesn't do the trick. But thirdly—and this is more complex—we should perhaps recognize how recent is our present sense that social engineering can and should be used to mitigate the lot of the poor. As Kierkegaard wrote, Marx's 'Communist Manifesto' still lay a year away; let alone the vast efforts for social improvement undertaken in European cities during the latter half of the 19th century. Kierkegaard is living in that laissez-faire world depicted in the early novels of Charles Dickens, of whom he was an almost exact contemporary. Sylvia Walsh rightly remarks, both of Kierkegaard and also (much less excusably) of the 20th-century ethicist and philosopher Emmanuel Levinas, that 'neither of them adequately recognizes that some kinds of human suffering require the concerted effort of public policy change rather than individual response'.[31]

And there is yet something else to be said. May it not be that there is an unsustainable tension built into Kierkegaard's belief that, *coram deo*, there is absolute equality; while *coram homini* all kinds of privilege and hierarchy are apparently acceptable? How shall a person sustain a sense of themselves in both spheres at once? If the charwoman really thinks she has the same dignity as others before God, will she not revolt against gross social injustice? (Presumably the peasants in Germany rose up in 1524 thinking social revolution the logical corollary of Reformation egalitarianism before God.) Or, to put it the other way up, if our charwoman is constantly degraded in worldly matters, how shall she sustain a decent sense of herself as a child of God? Will she not rather come to internalize what Marxists and feminists name a 'false consciousness' as rightly counted inferior? Kierkegaard fails to take on board the false consciousness and feelings of impotence that afflict those who, in patriarchal society, are downtrodden. At the end of the day are we not all of a piece? Indeed, with a

[31] Sylvia Walsh, review of Jamie Ferreira, *Love's Grateful Striving*, *International Journal of Philosophy*, 53/2 (April 2003), 117.

part of himself Kierkegaard may well suspect this to be the case. Which is precisely why a theological concern fuels his opposition to democracy. His insight in this instance suggests that Kierkegaard is otherwise deluding himself when he should know better.

Meanwhile there is every reason to think that Kierkegaard did in fact honour working-class people around him.[32] Furthermore, that he was not past learning. The Kierkegaard who was horrified at the social revolution that broke out the following year would appear to have modified his judgement in the course of the years that followed. At that later stage he turned against the church for its limp, self-serving attitude, manifested through its taking on board a veneer of change that it might maintain its status in the society. It should not be forgotten that those who cheered when, during the final months of his life, Kierkegaard took up his stance against the church were in large part the disadvantaged, on account it would seem of their dislike of the ecclesiastical and social establishment. We should not cast aspersions without thinking through the complexity of Kierkegaard's position. Not least, he had theological beliefs that it is difficult for us to credit. The world (as we have seen) has, for Kierkegaard, the character of a 'meanwhile'. Sceptical thus as to the virtue or necessity of social change, he nevertheless finds this tiny thing, 'the change of eternity', to transform the hierarchies of this world, between rich and poor, master and servant, man and woman when brought into play. The problem arises when the ruler is not benevolent but despotic; when far from exercising Christian charity the husband batters his wife. Thus we may judge it naïve to think admonitions such as Kierkegaard's unsupported by social legislation adequate.

Finally to Kierkegaard's credit it should be said that, blind as he may have been as to the undermining effects of inequality on a person's sense of self, there is no indication that he thought a person should cast him- or herself as a slave to others. There is for example—as we might well have expected to find—no exegesis of *agape*, expounded by Paul in 1 Corinthians 13 as the love which bears and endures all things, as implying that human beings should allow themselves to be trodden

---

[32] Cf. Sibbern's comment of Kierkegaard: 'It was typical of him to want to look after precisely those people whom the public did not value.' (Bruce Kirmmse, ed., *Encounters with Kierkegaard: A life as Seen by His Contemporaries* (Princeton, NJ, 1996), 216.

into the ground. The practice of *agape* builds up and does not destroy the self. Kierkegaard writes: 'But is [the neighbour] also nearer to you than you are to yourself? No, that he is not' (21). Incidentally, we may think that in the work of Levinas there are far fewer safeguards in place against a person taking on board a 'martyr complex' with its attendant self-abnegation. There is in Kierkegaard no hint of a Levinasian 'substitution', whereby I allow myself to be 'held hostage' by the other. Kierkegaard writes: 'There are people of whom it may be said that they have not attained form, that their actuality has not become integrated, because in their innermost beings they are at odds with themselves about what they are and what they will to be' (164). Nothing in his attitude suggests that, in the conduct of their relations with others, people should not be valuing also their own dignity.

The Understanding of God

One of the most creative aspects of Kierkegaard's thought is the way in which, in this text and elsewhere (though I shall consider it in conjunction with this text), he thinks about the understanding of God. Indeed one may judge this a whole lot more productive than his Christology (important as is this latter in enabling us to think through the implications of Christian belief). It is interesting how little attention this aspect of Kierkegaard's thought has commanded. It could potentially have extraordinarily radical repercussions.

In order to gain purchase on Kierkegaard's writing in this respect we should once again consider his Lutheran context. A major theme in that tradition has been the doctrine of ubiquity. Furthermore, God (at least as we apprehend God) is understood as being structured *pro me/nobis*, in relation to me/us. These two taken together affect how God's otherness is conceptualized. Consider in this respect Luther. It is of course well known that the split between Reformation Protestants came over the issue of the presence of Christ in the eucharist. Zwinglian and later Reformed, Swiss, Protestants argued that if the incarnation was to have any real meaning then Christ must have a local presence. Since the ascension, that local presence was at the right hand of God, carrying the corollary that in the eucharist Christ was not present on the altars of the world. To which Luther (with his conception of the ubiquity of God in Christ) exclaimed in incredulity: 'But

Christ is not in heaven like a stork in its nest.'[33] In the part of the world from which Luther came, storks of course build nests precariously perched up there on poles and chimneys.

This doctrine of ubiquity in Lutheran thought has been held in conjunction with a sense of Christ as being *pro me/nobis*. Thus in his Christology lectures, of which we previously had reason to make mention, Bonhoeffer speaks of Christ as present today *pro nobis* as Word (the proclamation of the gospel), sacrament, and church.[34] At the time of penning *Love's Deeds* Kierkegaard was still very little read in Luther. But in a *Journal* entry for 1847, the year of composition, he writes:

Marvellous!...I have never really read anything by Luther. But now I open his *Book of Homilies* and right away in the lesson for the First Sunday in Advent he says 'for you'; that's what is at issue.[35]

If, as has too often been the case, Kierkegaard is read through Barthian (Reformed) eyes, one might expect the qualitative difference between humanity and God to consist for him in God's utter transcendence. But in fact we find something rather different. God is not necessarily to be viewed as a kind of transcendent, numinous, object. His otherness from us would seem to consist rather in difference in kind, in his ubiquity and his being structured as *pro nobis*.

Yet more remarkable is the way in which in *Love's Deeds* Kierkegaard speaks of God as being for us a reflection of what we ourselves are.

The Christian like for like is: God will do unto you exactly as you do unto others. In the Christian sense...this world of inwardness...is actuality.... What you do unto people, God does unto you.... God is actually himself this pure like for like, the pure rendition of how you yourself are. If there is anger in you, then God is anger in you; if there is leniency and mercifulness in you, then God is mercifulness in you.... God's relation to a human being is at every moment to infinitize what is in that human being at every moment (383–84).

<hr />

[33] WA 26.422.27 (1528). (The English translation 'bird' is unfortunate; Luther's German is stork.)
[34] Dietrich Bonhoeffer, *Christology*, trans. John Bowden (London, 1966), Part I 'The Present Christ—The "Pro Me"'.
[35] Hannay, 276 (*Pap.* VIII[1] A 465), n.d., 1847.

What we have here is not some Hammurabic law, an eye for an eye, a tooth for a tooth. The context in which Kierkegaard makes the statement is precisely one in which he is *contrasting* the Christian like-for-like with what (rightly or wrongly) he terms the Jewish like-for-like. It would be an intolerable contradiction were Kierkegaard's meaning that God will do to us as we do to others. In Lutheranism the gospel has always been understood to stand *over against* the law (whether 'law' connotes the Old Testament or, more generally understood, the 'law' we impose on ourselves).

No: Kierkegaard's conception is surely quite other. Namely that as we are to others so will God appear to us, or so will God be in us. Kierkegaard names this a 'redoubling' or 'reduplication'. He writes: 'The only true object of a human being's love is love, which is God, which therefore in a more profound sense is not any object, since he is Love itself' (264–5). This can translate as, that it is only as I myself am loving that I shall be open to that which is love. 'The good', writes Kierkegaard, 'has an infinite connectedness' (255). Again, it is as we are self-denying that we too find ourselves blessed. 'Then the wondrous thing occurs that is heaven's blessing upon self-denying love— in salvation's mysterious understanding all things become his, his who had no *mine* at all' (269). Thus can Kierkegaard say—in what metaphysically is a daring statement: 'God is actually himself this pure like for like' (384). Likewise in the *Postscript* he remarks: 'because God is not something external, but is the infinite itself, is not something external that quarrels with me when I do wrong but the infinite itself that does not need scolding words, but whose vengeance is terrible—the vengeance that God does not exist for me at all, even though I pray' (162–3). One has to do here with a very different conception of God than one might have presupposed.

Kierkegaard in Context

In conclusion we may say that if Kierkegaard is to be understood, let alone justly evaluated, account must needs be taken of his context. One must surely think in concert with Kierkegaard, cognizant of the strengths and insights of the tradition to which he belonged and aware of the limitations in outlook of his surrounding society. It is for lack of these things that much critique seems irrelevant.

The criterion that Kierkegaard brought to his judgement of social and political matters was in the first place biblical. If one's rule of thumb is the New Testament, it could well be said that Kierkegaard conforms quite closely to what is (presumably) his reading of the Pauline gospel. When adjudicating on social matters, Paul's frame of reference is the belief that a new order is inaugurated in Christ, as Kierkegaard's is the eternal destiny of persons. In that new order, the post-lapsarian state of affairs is in Christ, the new Adam, overcome: there is neither Jew nor Greek, bond nor free, no more male and female, for all are one in Christ.[36] In view of the imminently expected eschaton, the present structure of society is not necessarily to be overturned. Thus Paul does not speak out against slavery *per se*; rather, in returning Philemon to his master, does he tell Onesimus to receive Philemon as though receiving he, Paul, himself. In Kierkegaard's case the thought of eternity relativizes the present, which becomes a 'meanwhile'. Thus Kierkegaard's position on male headship does no more than reflect 1 Corinthians 11, which he will have presumed Pauline. But just as does the author of the epistle to the Ephesians, Kierkegaard entreats husbands to love their wives. In the case of Paul as of Kierkegaard, in view of their sense of the dawning of another reality there is a certain indifference to the present order.

Much of the most vehement criticism of *Love's Deeds* has (interestingly) come from Jewish authors: Martin Buber, Adorno, and Levinas join hands in a chorus of condemnation. But these men appear to have little awareness of Kierkegaard's Lutheran context. It would seem that, in Judaism, it is in loving the neighbour that we love God. Only in the third part of *I and Thou* does Buber move from the question of the neighbour to that of God, who is the horizon and context for love of the other person.[37] In Levinas it is as Abraham welcomes strangers into his tent that he finds them to be messengers

[36] Gal. 3.28. Paul's Greek would seem to refer directly to Genesis 1:27: 'male and female created he them'. The words used are not the normal words for 'man and woman' but rather 'male and female', moreover Paul's 'and' interrupts his neither-nor sequence. He may, thus, be saying that in Christ (the Second Adam) the original intention of the creator (equality) is restored. Cf. Krister Stendahl, 'The Bible and the Role of Women' (Philadelphia, PA, 1966), 32f.
[37] Martin Buber, *I and Thou*, trans. Walter Kaufmann (New York, 1970), part III.

sent by God.[38] One would have hoped that something was held in common when Kierkegaard writes that God says: 'If you want to love me, then love the people you see; what you do for them, you do for me'. But no self-respecting Lutheran sees God *through* the world and the neighbour! Rather is it the unexpected agapeistic love shown by God in the revelation in Christ that leads us, in turn, to love the neighbour in a way that *contrasts* with both *eros* and *philia*. The Christian lives *from* God, *towards* the world, in what a later generation of Scandinavian Lutherans would term 'inverted existence'. Kierkegaard modifies this structure in speaking as readily as he does of love also of God. He even says that it is as we love the neighbour that God is what God is for us. But he never forgoes the primacy of revelation, of God's love for us, such that our puny love finds here its well-spring. In this structure it is simply not the case that love of neighbour is a *via* to love of God.

It could of course be argued that his Christianity or reading of the bible imposed a drag on Kierkegaard's recognition of the need for social change. Kierkegaard views this world through the lens of his belief in that beyond. His contemporary Karl Marx was to term the belief in that other world the 'opium' of the people, a hallucination that constituted just such an impediment to progress. Certainly that which Christendom has believed to have been revealed has not been an insubstantial drag on the liberation of women; such that I find Walsh's suggestion that patriarchy is 'structurally incompatible' with Christian love not a little problematic.[39] It is too simplistic to judge Kierkegaard through the lens of socialist ideals (Adorno), or indeed feminist ideals (Walsh). We live today within a whole other value system than did he. Kierkegaard was neither a socialist nor a feminist, but a Lutheran, biblical, Christian, living within a monarchical state. He thinks (as Martin Andric rightly observes) that

[38] Emmanuel Levinas, 'Judaism and Revolution' in *Nine Talmudic Readings*, trans. A. Aronowicz (Bloomington & Indianapolis, 1990), 99. Cf. *Totality and Infinity: An Essay on Exteriority* (Pittsburgh, PA, 1969), 78–9: 'There can be no "knowledge" of God separated from the relationship with men. The Other is ... indispensable for my relation with God.... Precisely by his face ... is the manifestation of the height in which God is revealed. It is our relations with men ... that give to theological concepts the sole signification they admit of.'

[39] Sylvia Walsh, 'The Role of Love in Kierkegaard' in R. H. Bell, ed., *The Grammar of the Heart: New Essays in Moral Philosophy and Theology* (San Francisco, CA, 1988), 239.

Christian love should be free of either pride or resentment, thereby allowing a person to be content with his or her earthly lot.[40] According to Kierkegaard's perception, it is Christianity that is truly revolutionary. The nature of God's love shown for humanity in Christ requires that humans give a certain inflection to human relationships, that they be transformed in the light of God's eternity.

The interesting question which arises for those of us living in the secular modern world we inhabit in Europe today is whether the whole dynamic which informs Kierkegaard's text has been lost. Kierkegaard never suggests that the natural man loves with an agapeistic love. It is the revelation of God's love for us that frees us in like manner to love our neighbour. Martin Matuštík comments that what baffles liberals and existentialists, communitarians and postmodernists alike, is Kierkegaard's sense of what he, Matuštík, names persons' 'radical self-choice' prior to their acts.[41] But it is a self-choice enabled through the knowledge that one has been accepted (thus chosen) by God; the basic thrust of Lutheran faith. Far from finding (as does Irvine Singer) Kierkegaard's discussion of love 'too remote from human experience to be convincing',[42] my judgement is that the book proffers profound insights into the nature of human being. Christianity has had its martyrs who, their self-understanding conferred upon them through their God-relationship, have been ready to lose their lives. The question is whether we who have rejected the Christological myth can find it within us to have sufficiently come into our own that we can be fully present for others. Can the sensed love of God, or perhaps that of other persons, lend us this?

Kierkegaard knows that it is outlandish to be Christian; that the Christian loves with a love that does not conform to the ways of the world. He knows that it may be uncomfortable to put one's relationship to God before one's relation to another if what that other desires of us is a relation incompatible with the nature of *agape*. One offers

---

[40] Martin Andic, 'Is Love of Neighbour the Love of an Individual?' in George Pattison & Steven Shakespeare, eds, *Kierkegaard: The Self in Society* (Basingstoke, 1998), 116.

[41] Martin Matuštík, 'Kierkegaard's Radical Existential Praxis, or Why the Individual Defies Liberal, Communitarian, and Postmodern Categories' in Martin Matuštik & Merold Westphal, eds, *Kierkegaard in Post/Modernity* (Bloomington & Indianapolis, 1995).

[42] Irving Singer, *The Nature of Love*, 3, *The Modern World* (Chicago, IL, 1987), 48.

Christianity, as he says, not as a bunch of flowers, but as a two-edged sword. Kierkegaard was clearly a man of his time, possessed of limitations common to his class and gender. But one could argue that these things are not of the essence of his book; that his core values could well be exercised within a different social and gender politics. Kierkegaard is far from callous or uncaring; he just has other priorities, seeing the person in the first instance in relation to God and in view of their eternal destiny. Seen in his own terms he is radical. Writing in his *Journal* in the year that he writes *Love's Deeds* Kierkegaard comments: 'What is humaneness [*Menneskelighed*]? It is human equality [*Menneske-Lighet*]. Inequality is inhumaneness.'[43] Whereas the friend (or lover) is another 'I', the neighbour is the first '*Du*' (57): you shall love your neighbour as yourself. At the end of the day *Love's Deeds* does not concern politics, social arrangements, nor even (secular) ethics. It elucidates the nature of Christian love. That may be counted both its failing and its strength.

---

[43] *JP* 1:63 (*Pap.* VIII¹ A 268), n.d., 1847.

7

The Sickness Unto Death

Introduction

The Sickness unto Death throws down the gauntlet to Hegel over the nature of the self. Like Hegel, Kierkegaard understands the self as a relation that relates itself to itself. In this both men are progeny of the Lutheran tradition, seeing the self as a dynamic self-relation not as derived substance. In common with Hegel, Kierkegaard will insist as a post-Enlightenment man (in a way not present in Luther) that the self must be said truly to come 'to' itself. But whereas Hegel understands the self to come to itself within its social relations in a purely immanent sphere, *Geist* being mediated into immanence, Kierkegaard will insist that the self can only become itself as that relation that is the self is grounded in what is other than self (which is God.) In this he is at one with Luther, who understands the person to be grounded extrinsically. That God is fundamental to the self being itself is, one must think, a contention to which any religious thinker must subscribe. Kierkegaard has thus a complex notion of the self, both insisting that the self must be said to come 'to' itself, yet also that it is grounded in what is more than self. We shall here think this through.

In the 'Preface' to his *Phenomenology* (1807), a book that Kierkegaard had already read by the time he was writing his doctoral thesis in 1841, Hegel sets out in explicit form a novel (other than that it owes much to the Lutheran background) understanding of the human person. The self is not substance (in an Aristotelian sense) but rather subject; a self that relates to itself. Hegel writes: 'That which has returned into itself is the self and the self is the identity and simplicity that relates itself to itself.'[1] Further, of the self one may say that it is spirit (*Geist*). And finally that it comes to itself not only in being self-reflexive (relating to itself) but also through the relation to what is other than self. Thus:

The spiritual alone is the *actual*; it is essence, or that which has *being in itself*; it is that which *relates itself to itself* and is *determinate*, it is *other-being* and *being-for-self* and in this determinateness, or in its self-externality, abides within itself; in other words, it is *in and for itself* (*an sich und für sich*).[2]

The self we may say is an activity: it relates to other and thereby to itself. It is not simply a given static substance. Kierkegaard will accept this understanding of the self as a dynamic relationship which relates to other in relating to self, but for that 'other' in relating to which the self comes to itself, which for Hegel is other persons in society, he will substitute the relation to God. This also of course changes the nature of the self. Kierkegaard's self has an openness to transcendence which Hegel denies, his proposition overturning Hegel's humanist presuppositions.

Both Hegel and Kierkegaard manifest here that they stand within the tradition of which Luther was the progenitor. It was Luther who crucially broke with the Catholic medieval Aristotelian understanding of the self as substance, derived from God.[3] Though he may not have had a modern, post-Enlightenment understanding of 'the self', the human being is for Luther essentially subject, who comes to himself (or fails to do so) in his relationality. As in Luther's case, but in contradistinction to Hegel, Kierkegaard understands the relation to God to be foundational to the self coming to itself. As we have seen, for Luther there are two possibilities: a resting in God, which is faith, and the attempt to set oneself up in the face of God, which

---

[1] G. W. F. Hegel, 'Preface', *The Phenomenology of Mind*, trans. J. B. Baillie (London, 1949), 84–5.

[2] A. V. Miller, trans., *Hegel's Phenomenology of Spirit*, 'Preface', §25 (Oxford, 1977), 14.

[3] On the significance of Luther's break with Aristotle see Wilfried Joest, *Die Ontologie der Person bei Luther* (Göttingen, 1967), unfortunately untranslated. I briefly discuss Joest's thesis in my *Christian Contradictions: The Structures of Lutheran and Catholic Thought* (Cambridge, 2001), 11–12.

is sin.[4] For Kierkegaard as for Luther faith and sin are alternative stances taken in relation to God. (Sin is not a quality that can be predicated of the self conceived of as substance, nor an unethical act; as would well describe the Catholic Aristotelian understanding.) As in Luther's case the human being must once and again consent to dependence on God (for the temptation is to set oneself up in the face of God), so also for Kierkegaard there is no constant self. Such an understanding relates sin to the conception of original sin, which is disobedience, hubris (pride). By contrast, to have faith is to consent to that relationship of creature to Creator intended in creation.

We should note that what we have here is a phenomenological if also theological depiction of the self (not one derived philosophically from first principles). Hegel's *Phenomenology* depicts the odyssey of the self as it comes to posit itself, to be self-constituting. Kierkegaard's self likewise undergoes an odyssey. There are modes of life in which one fails to be a self, the aesthetic and the ethical stages or spheres. Particularly interesting is it that the ethical, that is to say the attempt to be oneself by oneself, is a dead-end leading only to despair. It is out of despair (as we have already seen in *The Concept Angst*) that for the first time the human being is ready to turn to God. So too for Luther of course the attempt at good works (the attempt to justify oneself) will never satisfy; rather does salvation lie in looking to God. In Kierkegaard the interweaving of the three spheres is complex and by no means a one-way progression. Failing in the ethical, the individual in his despair rather than turning in repentance to God may attempt to drown himself in the aesthetic. Or he may be delivered from his angst through trusting in God.

Subtitled 'A Christian Psychological Exposition for Upbuilding and Awakening', *The Sickness Unto Death* concerns the conditions for healing of the self. It postulates a formula for what it is to be a self, laying out by contrast what it is for a self to fall apart, which is sin. Christ reputedly said to Lazarus (John 11.4) of physical illness: 'this sickness is not unto death'. What then is that sickness which is 'unto death'? It is sin. To be a self is (as we have said) for the self to relate to itself and in relating to itself to rest in God. Now for the Christian—more particularly perhaps for the Lutheran Christian in that Lutheranism is

---

[4] See pp. 21–2.

deeply Christocentric—to relate to God is to relate to Christ. And Christ is the Paradox, fully God and fully human. Consequently, for Kierkegaard it is not simply that faith is to relate to the transcendence that is God, but quite specifically to believe the Paradox. Kierkegaard's book thus falls into two parts. In Part I he advances a general proposition as to what it is to be a self, as the self relating itself to itself, relates to another (which is God). In Part II he superimposes on this understanding the relation to the Paradox. (In this respect the book runs in parallel to the procedure followed in *Postscript*). Kierkegaard in effect imposes an epistemological criterion (belief in the Paradox) on an existential understanding of the self as constituted by its relations.

It would seem no chance that Kierkegaard wrote this book when he did. Within days of completing *Love's Deeds* in the late summer of 1847 he was noting that he was undergoing what he referred to as a metamorphosis, writing: 'I feel now impelled to come to myself in a deeper sense by coming nearer to God in the understanding of myself'.[5] Together with much other work the material was penned amid the fraught atmosphere of the spring of 1848. What was to become *The Sickness Unto Death* was only separated out three weeks prior to its eventual publication in July 1849. An interesting passage relating to the theme of 'the self' was published in *Christian Discourses* sent to the printer in March 1848, a further passage making an advance upon the consideration in *The Sickness Unto Death* finding its way into *Practice in Christianity*. I shall consider these passages in conjunction with *The Sickness Unto Death*. Kierkegaard had earlier thought to publish the collected material under the title *Thoughts which Heal Fundamentally: Christian Therapeutic*.[6] He seems to have hesitated as to whether to employ a pseudonym, eventually choosing that of Anti-Climacus. In contradistinction to the earlier Climacus, who proclaimed himself not a Christian, Anti-Climacus (wrote Kierkegaard) seemed to regard himself a Christian 'on an extraordinarily high level'.[7] Kierkegaard gave his own name as 'editor'.

---

[5] 16.08.1847. Quoted by Walter Lowrie, *Kierkegaard* (London, 1938), 387.
[6] Walter Lowrie, 'Translator's Introduction', *The Sickness Unto Death* (Princeton, NJ, 1941), 135.
[7] *JP* 6:6433 (*Pap*. X^1 A 517), n.d., 1849.

It should not be overlooked, as well it might, that as Kierkegaard wrote this book extraordinary political and social events were unfolding around him. Following the so-called 'February Revolution' in France the world was in turmoil. In Denmark in a matter of months absolute monarchy gave way to the promise of democracy based on a near-universal male franchise, the widest in Europe. In March an uprising in the Danish German-speaking province of Holsten (Holstein) led to the verge of war with Prussia. Kierkegaard's reaction was thus:

[In] 1848, that year which was so significant for me, when I got so much work done, ... in which, additionally, I was supported—dialectically understood— by that frightful political catastrophe [the constitutional revolution] ... in which I had occasion to turn inward in order to study and deepen myself in the religious, supported—dialectically understood—by the political catas- trophe, [I carried out] the most reliable and truest study of the religious which I possess.[8]

One should not fail to note the German proverb with which he prefaces the book: 'Herr! gieb uns blöde Augen für Dinge, die nichts taugen, und Augen voller Klarheit in alle deine Wahrheit.' (Lord! Give us dim eyes for things of no consequence, and eyes full of clarity for all your truth.) Kierkegaard had come to a conclusion as to what actually mattered, and that was to be an individual self who comes to himself in relationship to God, and we might add (as we shall discuss in the next chapter) one who has the courage to stand alone against the crowd.

Finally, a word about vocabulary. One should know that the Danish for 'doubt' is *tvivl*, containing the root for 'two' (as indeed does 'doubt', compare 'double'). While the Danish word here trans- lated 'despair' is *fortvivelse*, that is to say an intensified form of doubt (compare German *Zweifel*, *Verzweiflung*). The Danish *fortvivelse* apparently carries the connotation of a mis-relation to oneself ('a gap between the being that one is and the being that one ought to be'[9]) in a way not immediately evident in the English 'despair'.

[8] *Pap.* X⁵ B 219, Oct 1849. Quoted in Bruce Kirmmse, 'Kierkegaard and 1848', *History of European Ideas*, 20, 169. Cf. *Pap.* X² A 66 quoted by Lowrie, *Kierkegaard*, 392.

[9] Gregory Beabout, 'Kierkegaard on the Self and Despair', *Hermeneutics and the Tradition, Proceedings of the American Catholic Philosophical Association*, LXII (1988), 113.

Exposition

Preface

Everything Christian must be presented as the physician speaks at a sick bedside. 'It is Christian heroism . . . to venture wholly to become oneself, an individual human being, this specific individual human being, alone before God' (xi).

Introduction

Of Lazarus Christ said: 'This sickness is not unto death.' Yet he told the disciples bluntly 'Lazarus is dead' (John 11.4, 11.14). Christ raised him. What then is the sickness unto death? 'Christianity has discovered a miserable condition that man as such does not know exists': the sickness unto death (8).

Part I. The Sickness Unto Death is Despair

A. DESPAIR IS THE SICKNESS UNTO DEATH

(a) Despair is a Sickness of the Spirit, of the Self, and accordingly can take three forms: In Despair not to be conscious of having a self (not despair in the strict sense); in Despair not to Will to be Oneself; in Despair to Will to be Oneself

The book opens with a definition.

A human being [or simply 'Human being,'][10] is spirit. But what is spirit? Spirit is the self. But what is the self? The self is a relation that relates itself to itself, or is the relation's relating itself to itself in the relation; the self is not the relation but is the relation's relating itself to itself (13).

---

[10] Stephen Crites argues *Mennesket* should be translated simply 'human being' (i.e. the human by nature) the individuality implied by the Hongs' translation being mistaken. ('The Sickness unto Death: A Social Interpretation', in G. B. Connell & C. S. Evans, eds, *Foundations of Kierkegaard's Vision of Community: Religion, Ethics and Politics in Kierkegaard* (Atlantic Highlands, NJ, 1992), 149.)

Bracketing for the moment the consideration of spirit, the self is both reflexive (it relates to itself) and dynamic (it is not the relation but the active relating). Kierkegaard names the two components of this relation:

A human being is a synthesis of the infinite and the finite, of the temporal and the eternal, of freedom and necessity; in short a synthesis. A synthesis is a relation between two (13).

'Freedom' here should be equated with 'possibility', its opposite being 'necessity'; early 19th-century terms. It could be remarked that Kierkegaard has moved a good distance from the Cartesian mind/body distinction. He further comments: 'Considered in this way' (as a synthesis between two), 'a human being is still not a self ' (13).

To progress. Kierkegaard writes:

In the relation between two, the relation is the third as a negative unity and the two relate to the relation and in the relation to the relation.... If, however, the relation relates itself to itself, this relation is the positive third, and this is the self (13).

So now the self is a two-ness, which can either fail to relate, or can relate to itself (in which case we can speak of the relation as a positive third). Kierkegaard then proceeds to drop what, in terms of idealism, is a clanger. Such a relation that relates to itself he declares 'must either have established itself ' (the Hegelian and idealist presupposition, other than that of course the relation to others in one's society is crucial) 'or have been established by another' (it is this that is the radical move) (13). There are these two possibilities. Kierkegaard will opt for the second; the relation is established by 'another', a third that enables the self's self-relation. The human self is a derived, a constituted relation. It is 'a relation that relates itself to itself and in relating itself to itself relates itself to another' (13–14). Judith Butler comments that this is 'a mockery of logical transition'.[11]

---

[11] Judith Butler, 'Kierkegaard's Speculative Despair', in R. C. Solomon & K. M. Higgins, eds, The Age of German Idealism [vol. vi of Routledge History of Philosophy], (London & New York, 2003) 367. Samuel Loncar believes that Kierkegaard is specifically countering Fichte, but equally the Hegelian position is denied. The early German idealist J. G. Fichte is in difficulty explaining how the self could posit (establish) itself; Kierkegaard counters that the self is a derived relationship. ('From Jena to Copenhagen: Kierkegaard's relations to German idealism and the critique of autonomy in The Sickness Unto Death', Religious Studies, 47 (2011), 201–16.)

Maybe: Kierkegaard appears to have simply posited the possibility of a wholly different scenario and then to have arbitrarily chosen it.

A digression may however shed some light on this move. In an earlier passage in his *Johannes Climacus*, probably written in the winter of 1842–3, Kierkegaard comments:

Consciousness is mind or spirit, and the remarkable thing is that when in the world of mind or spirit one is divided it always becomes three and never two. Consciousness, therefore, presupposes reflection [i.e. reflexivity]. If this were not so, it would be impossible to explain doubt. True, language seems to contest this, since in most languages, as far as [Climacus] knew, the word 'doubt' is etymologically related to the word 'two'. Yet in his opinion this only indicated the presupposition of doubt, especially because it was clear to him that as soon as I, as spirit, become two, I am *eo ipso* three. If there were nothing but dichotomies, doubt would not exist, for the possibility of doubt lies precisely in that third which places the two in relation to each other. One cannot therefore say that reflection produces doubt, unless one expressed oneself backwards; one must say that doubt *pre*supposes reflection, though not in a temporal sense. Doubt arises through a relation between two, but for this to take place the two must exist, although doubt, as a higher expression, comes before rather than afterwards. Reflection is the possibility of the relation.[12]

In other words there is a third, which one may say is spirit, the lack of which results in doubt (the falling apart of the two). Interestingly here, 'faith' can stand for the relation to the beyond, the lack of which is the falling apart of self which is sin. To be a self one needs faith, possibility.

Moving forward. Given such a definition of the self (that the self relates to itself as it is constituted by another), there are two ways in which the self can fail to be itself. (One could say that there is also a third, to which Kierkegaard alludes in the chapter's title, commenting that it is not in a strict sense despair: the failure even to be conscious of having a self, what Kierkegaard denotes the 'aesthetic' mode of life.) There is, firstly, that despair which consists in a not willing to be oneself; that is to say a failure of the self to relate to itself. But secondly, given that the self is a relation that can only come to itself as it stands in relation to a third, there is that despair which arises from the attempt to be a self by oneself.

Of this second form of despair Kierkegaard comments:

<hr />

[12] *Johannes Climacus*, trans. T. H. Croxhall (London, 1981), 80–1.

If the despairing person is aware of his despair... and does not speak of it as though it was on account of something exterior which had befallen him... and now with all his power seeks to break the despair by himself and by himself alone—he is still in despair and with all his presumed effort only works himself all the deeper into deeper despair (14).

This second form of despair, the attempt to be a self by oneself, is of course a form of 'justification by works', the wager at self-sufficiency. It is only as one sees oneself to fail in this attempt (the failure to be an ethical person) that one is open to God. As Kierkegaard precisely says, in accord with his tradition, the more the person attempts to 'break the despair by himself' he is 'with all his presumed effort', only driving himself yet more deeply into deeper despair. That the self is itself as, relating to itself, this relation relates to another, says Kierkegaard, is the expression for the 'complete dependence' of the relation (it is a constituted relation) (14). The Danish here, *hele Afhaengighed*, is the Danish equivalent of Schleiermacher's *schlechthinnige Abhängigkeit*, the expression used at the outset of his *The Christian Faith* where, famously, he denotes the human relation to God in these terms. Kierkegaard cannot but have known the passage. Schleiermacher differentiates the relationship to God, which is one simply of dependence, from the relationships we have with the world which always involve at least a measure of reciprocity. He too thus (in origin a Reformed theologian) makes the relation to God constitutive of what it is to be a self.

Restating his definition in positive terms Kierkegaard concludes:

The formula that describes the state of the self when despair is completely rooted out [i.e. when the self is indeed itself] is this: in relating itself to itself and in willing to be itself, the self rests transparently in [that] that established it[13] (14).

We should note that neither of these two conditions is given precedence. It is not that there could be a self which then subsequently relates to another (for the self is only itself as the relation which is the self allows itself to be constituted), yet Kierkegaard will also emphasize

---

[13] Kierkegaard simply has the reflexive pronoun, *Det*, that. This was clearly intentional, for he had deleted his original 'in God'; (*Pap.* VIII² B 170, 2, n.d. 1848). Walter Lowrie inserted 'Power'; the Hongs have 'power'; this could be thought misleading.

that the self must self-reflexively relate, in this differentiating his position from a simple resting in another, which would appear to be Schleiermacher's position and closer to an immediacy of relation to God.[14]

(b) The Possibility and the Actuality of Despair

As we have seen (also in The Concept Angst), that we despair derives from the structure of what a human essentially is; despair is the failure of the self to be itself.

The human is constitutively spirit, the eternal.[15] Hence Kierkegaard can comment of despair: 'The possibility of this sickness is man's superiority over the animal and this superiority distinguishes him in quite another way than does his erect walk, for it indicates infinite erectness or sublimity, that he is spirit' (15). Not being in despair is an overcoming of the possibility; did we not have the possibility of being in despair we should be beast not human. Thus healing from despair must involve recognition that one is in despair. Or, as I earlier put it employing Barth's vocabulary, Lutheran thought holds that we are healed (find salvation) out of a situation of despair (a necessary negative Anknüpfungspunkt).[16] As in Luther's case so also for Kierkegaard one must overcome this despair (this falling apart) in each moment. There is no permanent self, a lack of a high doctrine of creation. As Kierkegaard writes: 'Not to be in

---

[14] Kierkegaard scholars can be less than clear here. After discussing what he calls the 'self system' by which the self relates to itself, Mark Taylor comments: 'one further element must be added', as though the relation to God could be subsequent or an addendum. (Kierkegaard's Pseudonymous Authorship: A Study of Time and the Self (Princeton, NJ, 1975), 119). While Merold Westphal writes: 'Only as this relation relates itself to itself does the self as spirit emerge. The self is essentially self-related; its being is to be found in the inwardness of its relation to itself.' This could be misleading, as though the spirit 'emerges', rather than it being that the self fails to be a self unless constituted by the relation to what is more and other than itself. Westphal continues by speaking of Kierkegaard's response to Hegel as 'identifying the other to whom the self primarily relates as God'. But equally we must be clear that there is no prior 'self' which then relates, nor is God in the relevant sense an 'other' but rather that which founds the self. ('Kierkegaard's Psychology and Unconscious Despair', IKC SuD (1987), 41, 45.) On the other hand Butler suggests the relation to God 'temporarily prior', which equally cannot be. ('Speculative Despair', 369.)

[15] See p. 17, 19–20, 25.

[16] See p. 129.

despair must signify the destroyed possibility of being able to be in despair; if a person is truly not to be in despair, he must at every moment destroy the possibility' (15). The achievement of selfhood is a constant activity.

Drawing together what has been said, it follows from the definition of the self that: 'If [the human] were not a synthesis he could not despair, neither could he despair if the synthesis were not originally from God's hand in the right relationship' (Lowrie, 149). Here we have introduced the term 'God' as that which constitutes the self. Kierkegaard adds, in a comment of the greatest significance: 'God, who constituted man a relation, releases it from his hand, as it were—that is, in as much as the relation relates itself to itself' (16). So it is not that the self is simply or immediately derived from God. A post-Enlightenment man, Kierkegaard is advocating a duplex understanding, wishing to hold in tension a sense for the self coming into its own and a necessary relation to God as foundational to the whole. He sums up: despair is a qualification of spirit, the correlation of the fact that there is of the eternal in man. 'But he cannot rid himself of the eternal—no, never in all eternity' (17). Every moment of despair is in effect a rejection of God.

(c) Despair is 'The Sickness Unto Death'

Kierkegaard concludes Part I, 'A' with a preliminary discussion of what will be central to 'B'. A sickness 'unto death' must mean a sickness 'of which the end and the result are death'; we speak of a 'fatal sickness'. From the Christian perspective physical sickness is not such, for death passes into life. A sickness unto death is one 'of which the end is death and death is the end'. But this, says Kierkegaard, is what despair is. It does not lead to physical death; on the contrary, the torment is the inability to die. It is an impotent self-consuming. 'In despairing over *something* [the one despairing] really despaired over *himself*, and now he wants to be rid of himself' (19). As we shall see in 'B', it is this in which all despair consists: an unwillingness to be the self one actually is.

Despair as we have seen takes two forms; in other words there are two forms of wishing to be rid of oneself. Kierkegaard associates these with the two genders. What we have called the 'second' form of despair, the attempt to be oneself by oneself, refusing to be dependent, is aligned with the masculine.

When the ambitious man whose slogan is 'Either Caesar or nothing' does not get to be Caesar, he despairs over it. But this also means something else: precisely because he did not get to be Caesar, he now cannot bear to be himself. Consequently he does not despair because he did not get to be Caesar but despairs over himself because he did not get to be Caesar. This self, which, if it had become Caesar, would have been in seventh heaven, . . . this self is now utterly intolerable to him. . . . If he had become Caesar, he would despairingly get rid of himself, but he did not become Caesar and cannot despairingly get rid of himself. Essentially, he is just as despairing, for he does not have his self, is not himself (19).

The 'first' form of despair, the failure even to will to be oneself, is by contrast aligned with the feminine.

A young girl despairs of love, that is, she despairs over the loss of her beloved, over his death or his unfaithfulness to her. This is not declared despair; no, she despairs over herself. This self of hers, which she would have been rid of or would have lost in the most blissful manner had it become 'his' beloved, this self becomes a torment to her if it has to be a self without 'him'. This self, which would have become her treasure . . . has now become to her an abominable void since 'he' died, or it has become to her a nauseating reminder that she has been deceived. Just try it, say to such a girl, 'You are consuming yourself ', and you will hear her answer, 'O, but the torment is simply that I cannot do that' (20).

Neither individual consents to be that particular self which he or she is from the hand of God.

B. THE UNIVERSALITY OF THIS SICKNESS (DESPAIR)

Just as a physician might say that no one is completely healthy, so could it be said that no one wholly lacks despair. A sense of security and tranquillity can precisely signify despair (the failure even to recognize one is a self; one lives in immediacy). Most human beings fail to recognize that they are destined to be spirit, 'hence all the so-called security, contentment with life, etc.' (26). This is a form of despair. Those who acknowledge despair are those who 'have so deep a nature that they are bound to become conscious as spirit', or those 'whom bitter experiences and dreadful decisions have assisted in becoming conscious as spirit' (26). There are wasted lives. 'Eternity asks you and every individual in these millions and millions about only one thing: whether you have lived in despair', this irrespective of whether you recognized it (27). If you lived in despair 'eternity does not acknowledge you, it never knew you—or still more terrible it knows you as you are known and it binds you to yourself in despair'. Note the Lutheran sense that that which is the opposite of faith, which is sin, is to be bound by oneself apart from God; to sin is to fail to stand in essential relation to God.

C. THE FORMS OF THIS SICKNESS (DESPAIR)

Kierkegaard will analyse the forms of despair: first considered irrespective of whether conscious or not; thereafter consciousness of despair or lack thereof will be the organizing factor.

A. Despair Considered without Regard to its being Conscious or not, Consequently only with regard to the Constitution of the Synthesis

(A) DESPAIR UNDER THE STIPULATION OF A LACK OF FINITUDE, OR OF INFINITUDE

To become oneself is to become concrete.[17] To be concrete is neither to be finite nor infinite; for the self is that synthesis which we have considered. Kierkegaard will consider despair on account of a lack of finitude, and conversely of infinitude; followed by a consideration of despair on account of lack of possibility, or conversely of necessity.

α That despair which, lacking finitude, is an infinitude
Through the imagination (Danish *Phantasie*) the person becomes 'fantastic' (*Phantastiske*), led away from himself in such a manner that he fails to return to himself.

To exist before God may seem unendurable to a man because he cannot come back to himself, become himself. Such a fantasized religious person would say... 'that a sparrow can live is comprehensible; it does not know that it exists before God. But to know that one exists before God and then not instantly go mad or sink into nothingness!' (32).

---

[17] Pointing to the etymology of this word (Latin: to 'grow together') Bruce Kirmmse comments that Kierkegaard intends it also in this sense ('Psychology and Society: The Social Falsification of the Self in *The Sickness unto Death*', in J. H. Smith, ed., *Kierkegaard's Truth: The Disclosure of the Self* [vol. 5 of *Psychiatry and Humanities*], 190).

We have here a depiction of *Anfechtung!*[18] It is this that Kierkegaard will now characterize as a 'fantasized' existence!

β That 'despairing narrowness' of a finitude lacking infinitude

'Every human being is primitively intended to be a self, destined to become himself, and as such every self certainly is angular, but that only means that it is to be ground into shape, not that it is to be ground down smooth' (33). It is for each of us to assume concretion. It is not that a person should abandon himself; such a one 'forgets his name divinely understood, does not dare to believe in himself' (33–4). Such individuals 'mortgage themselves to the world.... They have no self ... for whose sake they could venture everything, no self before God' (35).

(B) THE DICHOTOMY OF POSSIBILITY AND NECESSITY

Insofar as the self is itself it is the necessary; insofar as it has the task of becoming itself it is possibility. Both are essential to the self's task of 'becoming itself in freedom' (35).

α The despair of possibility, lacking necessity

The self 'runs away from itself', having 'no place to which it is to return'; whereas to 'become oneself' is 'a movement in that place' (35–6). A self lost in possibility lacks the power to submit to necessity in a person's life, to one's limitations. (Given his precarious health we may think this something Kierkegaard well understood.)

β The despair of necessity, lacking possibility

With God, everything is possible. This battle is 'the battle of *faith*, battling, madly, if you will, for possibility' (38). Faith is a refusing to believe that circumstances constitute an impossibility (cf. Matt. 19.26). Having lost God and thus also himself, the fatalist is in despair. To pray is to breathe. 'Only he whose being has been so shaken that he has become spirit by understanding that everything is possible, only he has anything to do with God' (40). By contrast the 'philistine–bourgeois mentality' is spiritlessness.

---

[18] See pp. 164–5.

B. Despair as Defined by Consciousness

The greater the degree of awareness, the more intensive the despair. The devil's despair is the most intensive for the devil is 'sheer spirit', hence transparency: there is no obscurity which could allow the devil to find a mitigating excuse. The devil's despair is absolute defiance[19] (42). (That is to say the failure, before God, to look to God: recall that the devil is Lucifer, whose defiance consisted in the attempt to fly higher than God, the ultimate hubris.)

(A) IGNORANT DESPAIR; I.E. THE DESPAIRING IGNORANCE THAT ONE HAS A SELF, AN ETERNAL SELF

It is far from the case that human beings regard being in relation to the truth as the highest good; or that they, as did Socrates, regard being in error the worst misfortune (42–3). Lacking any conception of being spirit, most live in sensate categories of the pleasant and unpleasant. Comparing a human to a house, most people live in the basement.

A thinker [Hegel] erects a huge building, a system, a system embracing the whole of existence, world history, etc. and, if his personal life is considered, to our amazement the appalling and ludicrous discovery is made that he himself does not personally live in this huge, domed palace but in a shed alongside it (43–4).

Were this contradiction to be brought to his notice Hegel would be insulted.

Truth is the index of itself and of the false; *veritas est index sui et falsi*. (It is a theme that has been with us since *Fragments*. In *The Concept Angst* we find that in its spiritlessness paganism, even though it did not know it, from the Christian viewpoint lay in a state of sin (*CA*, 93). While in *Love's Deeds* that which pagans think love is revealed by what is truly love as self-love.)[20] The natural man makes a distinction between despair and not being in despair; i.e. he thinks himself accidentally related to despair. In actuality that which is despair only

---

[19] Cf. Jon Stewart of this section: 'The movement begins with consciousness being unaware of being in despair and moves through stages of greater and greater clarity until it reaches complete self-transparency in defiance.' ('Kierkegaard's Phenomenology of Despair in *The Sickness unto Death*', *Kierkegaard Studies Yearbook* (1997), 128–9.)

[20] See the discussion on p. 21.

becomes clear from the truth of the matter. Since for the pagan spirit does not exist he does not have the criterion for judging what is despair. It would be stupid to deny that pagan people accomplished amazing feats, or that the natural man can live a tasteful life, full of aesthetic enjoyment. Nevertheless: 'Every human existence that is not conscious of itself as spirit or conscious of itself before God as spirit, every human existence that does not rest transparently in God' is one of despair (46). That, says Kierkegaard, is why paganism judged suicide neutrally; it lacked the viewpoint 'before God'.

(B) DESPAIR PROPER: I.E. THE DESPAIR WHICH IS CONSCIOUS OF BEING DESPAIR; WHICH IS CONSCIOUS OF HAVING A SELF AND KNOWS THERE IS SOMETHING ETERNAL; AND WHICH THEN, EITHER IN DESPAIR DOES NOT WILL TO BE ITSELF, OR WHICH DESPAIRINGLY WILLS TO BE ITSELF BY ITSELF

α *The despair that consists in a failure to will to be oneself (i.e. 'feminine' despair)*
Of 'woman' Kierkegaard avers:

She has neither the egotistical concept of the self, nor, in a decisive sense, intellectuality.... The feminine nature is devotedness, givingness.... That is why nature has looked after her: blindfolded, she instinctively sees more clearly than the most clear-sighted reflection.... By nature however woman's devotedness also enters into despair.... In devotion she loses herself and only then is she happy... A man... does [not] gain his self by devotion... he has himself.... Whereas woman with genuine femininity abandons herself, throws her self into that to which she devotes herself. Take this devotion away then her self is also gone (49–50, footnote).

Of this failure to will to be oneself, on the part of both women and men, Kierkegaard comments: 'Immediacy actually has no self, it does not know itself; thus it cannot recognize itself and therefore generally ends in fantasy' (52–3). (Kierkegaard had given an extensive consideration of such failure to be a self in his early aesthetic writing.) A person may be somewhat cognizant of the problem, fooling him- or herself that it arises from an externality. For repentance to arise, there must be radical despair (cf. the Lutheran dynamic); 'so that the life of the spirit can break through from the ground upward' (59). The person moves away, setting up home somewhere else, without tackling the root problem. He fills his time up with not willing to be himself; yet he is self enough to love it. He keeps this matter of his 'self' hidden from all and sundry, making an exception of a single pastor. Enclosed in himself, in his innermost being he confesses his weakness to himself. Such a self must be broken that it may become itself. If he is to be put on the road to faith he must go through an upheaval. Should the despair be intensified, it becomes defiance. (One might think anorexia a perfect example; a defiance arising from lack of self.)

β *The despair of defiance, of willing to be oneself by oneself*
   (*i.e. 'masculine' despair*)
In that the self at least wills to be a self this constitutes a 'higher' form of despair; in one sense close to the truth, it is infinitely far away. (The ethical is headed in the wrong direction.) 'Through the aid of the eternal the self has [to have] the courage to lose itself in order to win itself. Here, however, it is unwilling to begin with losing itself but wills to be itself' (67). (This is of no little interest: having escaped the aesthetic in which it was driven by its latest whim, the ethical self, thinking dependence at all costs to be avoided, wills to be itself. From such a perspective the religious looks like a new form of dependence.) Despairingly willing to be its own master, to create itself, such a self severs itself from any relationship to that which has established it, from the idea that there is such a power. It could be called stoicism. Such despair consists in unwillingness to be comforted, healed by the eternal. An unwillingness to hope that an earthly need, a temporal cross can end constitutes a form of despair. If God and all the angels offered to help him he does not want it. 'Rather than to seek help, he prefers, if necessary, to be himself with all the agonies of hell' (71). As in the case of the despair of weakness consolation would be his undoing.

Part II. Despair is Sin

A. DESPAIR IS SIN

Kierkegaard reformulates his basic definition in further elaborated form. 'Sin is: *before God, or with the conception of God, in despair not to will to be oneself, or in despair to will to be oneself*' (77). The Lutheran

238 KIERKEGAARD: EXPOSITION AND CRITIQUE

understanding is always that sin is *coram deo*, before God, given that to
sin is to fail to stand in right relation to God.

1. The Gradations in the Consciousness of the Self
(The Qualification: 'Before God')

There follows dialogue with Hegel and with a humanist position
more generally. Kierkegaard may well be thinking of his fellow countrymen, nominally Lutheran; but a typically Catholic position could
well be said to fall under his proscription. A master who is a self
before his slaves (Kierkegaard presumably has in mind Hegel's famed
discussion in the *Phenomenology*, which precisely relates to the acquisition of self-consciousness) is actually no self for the criterion (of
being *coram deo*) lacks. (Thus Hegel's conception that a self comes
into its own in relation to society or other persons is mistaken.) The
older dogmatics (? classical arguments for the existence of God),
made God into some kind of externality; but God is not an externality in the sense in which a policeman is. It is not to be thought that on
occasion we commit sins before God (i.e we are not speaking of sin as
though it consisted in sinful acts).[21] 'What really makes human guilt
into sin is that the guilty one has the consciousness of existing before
God' (80) (i.e. sin is a *position*).

From a higher (Christian) point of view, paganism is immersed in
sin; for, though there may be ignorance of this, it is still a despairing
coram deo. One could also hold that pagans did not 'sin', since all sin
is *coram deo*. Kierkegaard remarks sarcastically that it is quite true
that a modern pagan can slip blamelessly through the world, saved by
his superficial Pelagian conception. That is to say, secure in his self-
righteousness he mistakes what is 'sin'; he doesn't commit 'sins',
failing to see that 'sin' is the attempt by himself to be himself *coram
deo*. Scripture always defines sin as disobedience. Such a definition is
considered too 'spiritual'. Why? Because it does not mention murder,
stealing, fornication, etc. (i.e. sins). But, says Kierkegaard, in a most
interesting comment, the definition he has given (the Lutheran
understanding) is *inclusive* of such things (sins), in that in defying
God's commandments they constitute disobedience (81). The definition is 'algebra'; one has but to fill in the particular sin.

---

[21] See pp. 21–2.

That our definition, that despair is sin, is correct, can be tested by posing its opposite: faith.

Very often however it is overlooked that the opposite of sin is by no means virtue. [Which would be the Catholic definition of sin.] In part this is a pagan view which is satisfied with a merely human criterion and simply does not know what sin is, that all sin is before God. No, the opposite of sin is faith, as it says in Romans 14.23 'whatever does not proceed from faith is sin'. And this is one of the most decisive definitions for all Christianity—that the opposite of sin is not virtue but faith (82).

'Faith', says Kierkegaard, is 'that the self in being itself and in willing to be itself rests transparently in God' (82). Thus also (see the biblical quotation) we can see that our definition of sin (the contrary to faith, a resting transparently in God) is correct. Sin is *coram deo* despairingly not willing to be oneself, or defiantly willing to be oneself. As Kierkegaard has said, it is 'a position'.

In an *Appendix* Kierkegaard notes that the definition of sin must include offence, since 'before God' entails 'Christianity's crucial criterion: the absurd, the Paradox, the possibility of offence' (83, my capitalization). The offence is 'Christianity's weapon against all speculation', a reduction of Christianity to concepts native to oneself or the world. A disbelieving Christianity (Hegelianism, or Kierkegaard's contemporaries; but one might also think a Catholic humanism) wants to say that 'sin is sin and that whether it is directly before God or not makes no difference at all'. But this, says Kierkegaard, is paganism. Christianity 'wants to make man into something so extraordinary that he cannot grasp the thought' (83) that he or she is 'before God'. There is no reason to 'defend' Christianity (as does Hegel): like Judas one only succeeds in betraying it with a kiss. The person who *defends* it (who objectifies it) has never *believed* it.

2. The Socratic Definition of Sin

Contrasting Christianity with the Socratic definition (the humanist definition), Kierkegaard will illuminate the former in all its radicality. For Socrates sin is ignorance. But how is ignorance to be understood? Is it the state of someone who has not had the opportunity to know what is the truth, or ignorance subsequent to this opportunity? In the latter case, the 'ignorance' is consequent upon a person's efforts to obscure the knowledge. The sin lies not in the knowing but in his willing. Socrates however 'does not really enter into the whole investigation with which Christianity begins'; the antecedent state, in which sin presupposes itself, which is explained by hereditary sin. (Cf. *The Concept Angst.*) If one thinks sin ignorance (as does Socrates), one is in effect saying it does not exist. Such a definition is in one sense correct! For Christianity assumes that, to know what is sin, there must be revelation. The pagan/Christian distinction lies not in the doctrine of the atonement but far deeper, with the doctrine of sin. 'What a dangerous objection it would be against Christianity if paganism had a definition of sin that Christianity would have to acknowledge as correct' (89–90). (Revelation would change nothing; be inessential.)

What Socrates lacked was the concept of the will, and thereby of defiance. The intellectuality of the Greeks was too naïve to grasp that anyone could knowingly do other than the good. But it is comic to think that when a man says the right thing but does wrong this could be explained by saying he has not understood. The Socratic principle lacks a 'dialectical determinant' befitting the transition from having understood to doing something (93). With its notion of defiance, Christianity speaks to this transition, securing its understanding with the doctrine of hereditary sin. Precisely because he is in sin, no man can by himself declare what is sin. (That is to say the Reformation understanding that the *imago dei* has been lost.) That, says Kierkegaard, is why Christianity commences otherwise; humanity has to learn through revelation what is sin (95). Can Christianity be understood? By no means. It must be believed (faith). It follows that sin has its roots in willing, not in knowing.

Thus, says Kierkegaard, our working definition of sin stands in need of completion: 'Sin is—after being taught by a revelation from God what sin is—before God in despair not to will to be oneself, or in despair to will to be oneself' (96). (We may well say of what has now been added to the definition that there could be no more antihumanist position.)

3. Sin is not a Negation but a Position

Kierkegaard will link the discussion of sin to the paradoxical nature of faith and to the Paradox.

Emphasizing revelation, orthodox (Reformation) dogmatics has on the whole always rejected any definition of sin that made of it something merely negative (weakness, sensuousness, finitude, ignorance, etc.); each fallen person must be taught what is sin and—quite consistently if it is a dogma—it must be believed. Christian teaching is that sin is a position—yet not as though it could be comprehended but as a paradox. Whether or not one will believe must be left to faith. Moreover that sin is a position implies in a quite different sense the possibility of offence, the Paradox. The Paradox is the implicit consequence of the doctrine of atonement (i.e. sin can be taken away if Christ is God). So Christianity first establishes sin as a position—and then undertakes to eliminate this position in a way that the human understanding can never comprehend. (We have the same double procedure as in the *Postscript*; the situation is first paradoxical, then further inflected by the fact that in the case of Christianity we are speaking of the Paradox.)

B. THE CONTINUANCE IN SIN

Being in a 'state' of sin is the new sin, is the sin. (We should not understand 'state' here as in an Aristotelian context, such that sin qualifies the person as an 'accident'; all that is intended is that there is continuity to sin.) The sinner is inclined to take into account only each new sin, giving him impetus on the road to destruction—as though it were not the case that, given the impetus of previous sins, he was already proceeding along that road: sin has become his second nature. It is as though one were to look at the puffs of the steam engine (American, locomotive) when what one should consider is the steady impetus with which it proceeds. The state of sin is worse sin than particular sins; it is what sin is.

(A) The Sin of Despairing over One's Sin

Sin is despair; its intensification the new sin of despairing over one's sin. If sin is severance from the good, then despair over sin is the second severance. Just as a balloonist ascends by throwing off weights, so the person in despair sinks by throwing off all good.

There is 'a new demonic closing up within himself'—the despair over sin (110). He refuses to hear anything about repentance and grace (God's forgiveness). A person who relapses will say: 'I will never forgive myself'; the exact opposite of a broken-hearted contrition that asks God to forgive. The person's distress indicates a movement away from God, a secret selfishness and pride.

(B) The Sin of Despairing of the Forgiveness of Sins (Offence)

The intensification lies in the knowledge that the self is 'before Christ'. Here weakness and defiance are *the opposite* of what they usually connote: the *defiance* of the 'masculine' sin consists in being *unwilling to be weak*—and for that reason wanting to dispense with the forgiveness of sins; while the *defiance* of the sin of weakness (the 'feminine') lies in despairingly *willing to be oneself*—as though there were no forgiveness. God offers reconciliation but in either case the sinner despairs. 'It is almost as if [the person] walked right up to God and said, "No, there is no forgiveness of sins, it is impossible"' (114). To say such a thing a person must become *qualitatively* distanced from God—in order to fight in close combat. 'In order that the "No", which in a way wants to grapple with God, can be heard, a person must get as far away from God as possible' (114). Eventually there comes to be a reluctance to do away with God—as one would have nothing to oppose!

The sin of despairing of the forgiveness of sins is *offence*. The Jews had a perfect right to be offended by Christ on account of his claim to forgive sins: it is offensive to have to believe that a man can forgive sins; i.e. that he is God. Christendom only fails to find this offensive on account of having collapsed the Paradox. Christianity begins with the single individual; it is he who takes offence. By contrast people speak of 'sins' in the plural, among which offence does not feature. Even less do they perceive offence as the intensification of sin.

(C) The Sin of Dismissing Christianity Modo Ponendo [Positively], of Declaring it to be Untruth

This is the sin against the Holy Spirit. (Cf. Matt. 12.31–2 and parallels.) 'Here the self is at the highest intensity of despair; it not only discards Christianity totally but also makes it out to be a lie and untruth' (125). While despair of the forgiveness of sins is a position set against God's offer of mercy, this is offensive war. 'The greatest possible human misery, greater even than sin, is to take offence at Christ and to continue in the offence' (126). In his love Christ cannot make such a stance impossible. The offence takes various forms. The lowest is to decide not to make any decision about Christ. The next up feels it cannot ignore Christ, 'is not capable of leaving Christ in abeyance and then otherwise leading a busy life', honouring Christ in so far as it recognizes that the question 'What think ye of Christ?' (Matt. 22.42) the most crucial of questions. 'A person so offended lives on as a shadow; his life is devastated because deep within himself he is constantly preoccupied with this decision' (130–1). But it is the last form of offence, the positive form, that is here under discussion. It declares Christianity untrue, a lie; either docetically, not acknowledging that Christ was an individual human, or rationalistically, denying he is more than a human being. 'Of course in this denial of Christ as the Paradox lies, in turn, the denial of all that is essentially Christian: sin, the forgiveness of sins, etc.' This offence is 'the highest intensification of sin' (131, my capitalization). (Here stands the present author!)

Christian Discourses, IV
Practice in Christianity, NO. 3, II

I shall here make mention of the passages published in *Christian Discourses* and in *Practice in Christianity* to which I called attention.[22] These passages augment and take further the consideration of the self's relation to God present in *The Sickness Unto Death*. That in *Christian Discourses* was presumably written around the same time as *Sickness Unto Death*; that in *Practice in Christianity* somewhat later. There is furthermore an earlier *Journal* entry from 1846 that bears on the theme.[23] In these passages one gains a strong

---

[22] 'Joyful Notes in the Strife of Suffering', no. 4 in Howard V. Hong & Edna H. Hong, eds & trans., *Christian Discourses* (Princeton, NJ, 1997) (henceforth *CD*); *Practice in Christianity*, no. 3, II, 158–60. I discuss these passages in detail in my *Christian Contradictions*, 261–3 and 276–84 respectively.
[23] Dru, no. 616 (*Pap.* VII A 181), 1846.

sense of the integrity of the self as it comes to itself in relation to God. The passage in *Christian Discourses* speaks of God's omnipotence. On this account God holds himself back, thereby giving the human freedom to be in and of himself; it belongs to the essence of love to make the other free. God is pictured as saying to the human: 'Be... Be something also in apposition me' (Lowrie, 132). It is a very different sense of the human stance in relation to God than that presumed to give rise to *Anfechtung* present in *Postscript*. In the passage in *Practice in Christianity* there is a sense of development as the self becomes itself in and with being drawn to God. Kierkegaard is exegeting the text: 'And I, when I am lifted up from the earth, will draw all to myself' (John 12.32). He asks what it is for something to draw to itself? When it is a case of iron filings being drawn to a magnet they are simply drawn in random and determined fashion. When however it is a case of the self being drawn, to 'truly' draw is to enable it to become itself in and with the drawing. Otherwise what we have is a deception. (A play on words: Danish *drage*, to draw; *bedrage*, to deceive.)

I shall give further consideration to these passages in the final section of the 'Critique'.

Critique

The Debate with Hegel and Humanism

Kierkegaard takes much from Hegel: the self is subject, a self-reflexive relation. But crucially Kierkegaard denies that such a self can come to itself apart from the relation to transcendence; in the second specifically Christian part of the work, God in Christ. The self is a constituted, derived relation. The attempt to be oneself by oneself (the ethical stage) must necessarily fail. It is the ultimate hubris or pride, defiance in the face of God. Indeed the more transparent one is to oneself as to that which one is about, the greater the sin. The devil knows full well he is in denial of God. By contrast Hegel (and more particularly Feuerbach), conceive God to be a human projection. This imagined 'other' is humanity's undoing as, defining themselves negatively in relation to what they have constructed, human beings come to have an 'unhappy consciousness'. It is only through over-coming this projection that humanity can come into its own. As Hegel writes in the 'Preface' to the *Phenomenology*: 'Instead of dwell-ing in this world's presence, men looked beyond it, following this thread to an otherworldly presence, so to speak. The eye of the Spirit had to be forcibly turned and held fast to the things of the world.[24] Marx is of course the child of these perceptions, his 'Theses on Feuerbach' (as this document is known) written in 1845, conjecturing that, that the secular basis 'establishes itself as an independent realm in the clouds' is to be explained by cleavages in that secular basis which must be overcome.[25]

But if Kierkegaard is adamant that the self can only come to itself as it is open to the transcendent, what is notable is that he is equally insistent that the self must come to itself. Thus he does not, with Schleiermacher, depict the self as straightforwardly 'dependent' on God. Together with Hegel the self must be said to relate to itself, must choose to be itself. It is simply that for Kierkegaard it can only truly choose to be itself as it stands in right relation to God. Kierke-gaard is close to Luther in insisting that the natural condition of the human being is to attempt independence from God, even to defy God, which is sin. As we have said, it is not for this tradition that there is any kind of *analogia entis* pertaining between the human and God, such that through creation the human can as it were situate himself on his own ground in relation to God. Justification brings about the re-establishment of what was intended by the Creator as the creature relates to Creator as creature, which is to say stands in a relation of dependence. Yet as we have seen and shall further discuss, in later writing from 1849 Kierkegaard insists that it is *qua* 'self' that the human is drawn to God, for anything else would be a travesty of what it is for a human being to be 'truly drawn'. It should not escape our notice that Kierkegaard was writing this material as in the heat of revolutionary fervour humanity all around him was insisting that the principles enunciated in the French Revolution should be carried to fulfilment. In 1849 the common man in Denmark was to be accorded the dignity of the franchise. Kierkegaard knew in some sense where the future lay.

---

[24] *Hegel's Phenomenology*, Miller, 'Preface', §8, 5.
[25] *Karl Marx: Early Writings* (London 1992), 422.

Kierkegaard's position may thus be read as a rebuff to modernity (certainly a rebuff to Hegel) held together with modernity's recognition of the integrity of the human being. Would that all theologians were as astute as Kierkegaard as to the necessity of this latter. The question surely becomes in what sense one can conceive of 'God', and God as fundamental to the self as it comes to be itself, without this colliding with human autonomy. In this respect the Lutheran tradition would seem to exercise some subtlety. One the one hand God is no entity in relation to which we stand in apposition but constitutive of the self. Luther speaks of the human as living *extra se*, extrinsically, in Christ in God; our lives hid with Christ in God. In the 20th century the Lutheran theologian Paul Tillich will speak of God as the 'ground' of our being. Kierkegaard speaks of the self as 'resting transparently in God'. That God (if God is not to become a superfluous 'other') must be conceived as fundamental to the self would seem to be right. But the question then becomes, if God is fundamental to what it is to be a self, how can one also speak of the self as coming into its own (in relation even to God conceived of as other to self). This latter we have yet to consider.

Kierkegaard depicts the opposite of faith as a closed-up-ness (Danish *indesluttethed*) within oneself. It is in this that the 'spirit-lessness' of the bourgeois man, who in his self-sufficiency and contentedness lives simply in relation to the things of this world, consists. For Kierkegaard, God is to be equated with 'possibility' (as opposed to 'necessity', that we are tied to the limitations of the world and our physicality). That we have 'possibility' is for Kierkegaard an identical thought to that that we are spirit. It follows that by our very nature we stand in relation to that which is God (or Spirit). The dynamic of Kierkegaard's argument thus amounts to saying that we are not ourselves as long as we deny this element of our being: to relate to God is to open up possibility. Furthermore, Kierkegaard clearly believes in eternal life. By contrast, despair is that sickness which is heading in the opposite direction, to the death of the self. To relate to God is a decision, a movement, to be taken once and again, that one will see oneself as having an open future. It is highly existential. Likewise is this true of the Lutheran existentialist theologian of the 20th century Bultmann for whom 'future' and 'God' become synonymous. It is through the act of faith, which is future orientated, that one synthesizes or comes to be oneself. Luther is not other.

It will be clear that Kierkegaard's book is a fundamental challenge to Hegel. The subject of idealism essentially has all he or she needs to become him- or herself, given with the self or present in its relation to the world. Kierkegaard thinks this fundamentally mistaken, a failure to grasp what the self is, for the human in his very being is of the divine, which is to say he is spirit. That the human can despair is but the corollary of man's greatness; that there is of the eternal in man.[26] In saying this Kierkegaard is furthermore countering Hegelian determinism. 'The philosophers', he comments, 'are mistaken when they explain necessity as a unity of possibility and actuality—no, actuality is the unity of possibility and necessity' (35). That is to say Hegel believes that necessarily, in determined fashion, what was always possible comes to be realized as actuality at the appointed time in history. Kierkegaard counters that, on the contrary, actuality, our concrete selves, come to be as in the moment we are able to bring together necessity (what binds us to the world) and possibility (an open future).[27] Now God is that all things are possible: 'For God *is* that all things are possible, and that all things are possible *is* God' (Lowrie, 173–4). As Kierkegaard will contend: 'He who does not have a God does not have a self, either. . . . To pray is also to breathe' (40). In decisive fashion Kierkegaard breaks open Hegelian immanence.

The question which may well occur to us today is whether, though it may be the case that human beings only come 'to' themselves as they relate to a significant other (or others), that 'other' is necessarily God? Again, for many who may not conceive of 'future' in terms of

---

[26] Cf. Judith Butler: 'If Hegel thought that the subject of the *Phenomenology* had taken account of everything along the way which turned out to be outside the terms to be mediated, understanding *what* needed to be synthesized as well as how that synthesis could take place, then the last laugh is on Hegel's subject' ('Speculative Despair', 365).

[27] Cf. Kierkegaard's adoption, in another context, of Plato's famous allegory in *Phaedrus* comparing the two elements in the soul to two horses, one good and one bad, harnessed together, with the third element the charioteer: 'And this', he comments, 'is what existing is like if one is to be conscious of it. Eternity is infinitely quick like that winged steed, temporality is an old nag, and the existing person is the driver' (*CUP*, 311–12).

'eternal life', it may still make sense to say that there is a spiritual dimension to human beings; that it is needful to be open to a higher plane, not simply confining one's life to the acquisition of the goods of this world. What is of significance here is how one conceives of that 'other' to self through which one becomes oneself. Thus what is problematic about Hegel is that his self appears predatory, needing to absorb or subdue otherness. While comparing the early Heidegger adversely with Kierkegaard, Buber remarks:

> Kierkegaard's Single One is an open system, even if open solely to God. Heidegger knows no such relation; and since he does not know any other essential relation his 'to become a self' means something quite different... Kierkegaard's man becomes a Single One for something, namely for the entry into a relation with the absolute; Heidegger's man...cannot breach his barriers.[28]

It is an interesting question whether Buber would have judged the later Heidegger otherwise, but the later Heidegger scarcely makes other people constitutive of self. If others are conceived as persons to whom we can be non-competitively open, can they ever replace God? In quite what does transcendence of self consist?

Does the Book Break its Back?

So far so good. Kierkegaard has simply maintained that the self can only come to itself as it is open to transcendence; that that relationship that is the self is constituted, not self-positing. When giving his preliminary definition for the nature of the self he does not so much as employ the word 'God'. Moreover one may interpret the word God as one will. Given what to this point has been the whole tenor of the book, somewhat startlingly one may think in Part II Kierkegaard tells us that despair is to be equated with 'sin' (not perhaps in itself problematic if that word simply connotes the falling apart of self) but he then proceeds to tell us 'that the definition of sin includes the possibility of offence'. Kierkegaard introduces 'the crucial Christian qualification: before God' which brings in its train 'Christianity's criterion: *the absurd, the Paradox*' (83, my capitalization). In what

---

[28] Martin Buber, 'What is Man?', in *Between Man and Man*, trans. Ronald Gregor Smith (New York, 1965), 171–2 [1938].

has been a phenomenological discourse this arrives as if from nowhere. One is faced with a complete hiatus between the position of those (like myself) who might well say that the human is spirit, that faith alone makes life possible, even that we are only ourselves as we relate to that which is more than ourselves which is God, and those who are able to follow Kierkegaard in his Christology. We shall here consider the tangle that Kierkegaard gets himself into through this move.[29]

For the purposes of this discussion let us call that despair which Kierkegaard has addressed in the first part of the book, the despair which consists in the falling apart of self, 'vulgar' despair. By contrast, let us call the despair of which he speaks in the second part of the book, the failure to acknowledge the Paradox, 'esoteric' despair. Does Kierkegaard's text not break its back over this distinction? The talk of vulgar despair arises from the phenomenological observation that those human beings who know nothing of possibility are only half alive; that human beings cannot live by bread alone. In his attempt to be self-sufficient, the self-enclosed ethical individual fails to be a self, whereupon he despairs. But then, in part II, Kierkegaard takes off from a quite other premise; the necessity of acknowledging a Christological proposition predicated on belief in revelation. If this is the truth of the matter, why commence the book with a discourse on the maladies of humankind? Or, if our interest is indeed in vulgar despair, how can it possibly be suggested that those who deny the Paradox are prone to such an illness? The two disparate starting points makes for confusion, the two halves of the book seemingly discussing different things.

If Kierkegaard is wishing to make a Christological statement as to the necessity of belief in Christ, defining 'sin' as defiance of this proposition, then one has an easy answer to those who like Haim Gordon comment that it is far from evident that the Socrateses of this world are in despair.[30] Gordon's comments are irrelevant, not pertinent to what is here under discussion. Whether conscious of it or not (and Kierkegaard speaks of 'unconscious' despair), through dint of not believing the Paradox such a person is to be defined as in despair. But on any other account such a judgement would appear a misuse of language. For it is far from clear that those who fail to credit the

[29] This is of course the same discussion as that entered upon under 'Methodology' pp. 128–30.
[30] Haim Gordon, 'A Rejection of Kierkegaard's Monism of Despair' in *IKC SuD*.

Paradox are awash with existential angst. In Kierkegaard's day and age perhaps there did lurk some disquiet in the minds of some who, against the conventions of society, had the temerity to proclaim themselves atheists. Might they not on their deathbed confess otherwise? But in today's world there can be few who are so much as troubled by their unbelief. They may speak of some kind of spirituality, even of 'God', but the idea that this man Jesus is in a second nature the second *persona* of a triune God would strike them as farcical. Nor—it may be added—is it clear that Kierkegaard himself considers Christological belief to heal existential (vulgar) despair. He never to my knowledge suggests this. The book thus appears strangely disjointed.

What one should note is Kierkegaard's Lutheran statement that sin is the opposite of faith, not virtue. That this is the case is, as we have said, quite fundamental to that structure, differentiating Lutheranism from Catholicism.[31] Sin is to take up a position of defiance in relation to God, to abjure dependence. It is the refusal of possibility (of God), the refusal to be that particular self that God made one to be. As Kierkegaard remarks elsewhere, 'despair is a kind of bad temper' (*CUP*, 554). In the second part of the book Kierkegaard will cast this in terms of refusal of the Paradox. It should be remembered that the material that became this book was not as he wrote differentiated from the response of offence to the Paradox considered in what became *Practice in Christianity*. Kierkegaard's is one might say the ultimate anti-humanist position, as he himself says pure 'impertinence' against man (Lowrie, 226).[32] The revelation of Christ as 'the truth' casts the non-acknowledgement of Christ into the position that is 'sin'. Presumably it was with this in mind that Kierkegaard

---

[31] This definition of sin comes as news to some. The Catholic Louis Dupré speaks of Kierkegaard's 'original' theology of sin. ('The Sickness Unto Death: Critique of the Modern Age', *IKC SuD*, 85.) Far from original it is intrinsic to Lutheran thought. While John Lippitt comments (*Routledge Philosophy Guidebook to Kierkegaard Fear and Trembling* (London & New York, 2003), 124): 'But righteousness is surely not quite the same thing as sinlessness.' Lippett here appears to read Kierkegaard as though he were a Catholic (or humanist). We are not concerned for the internal constitution of the person. God holds to be righteous (counts as righteous) for Christ's sake the sinner who trusts (i.e. has faith) in Christ in God; the opposite position to which is the attempt to maintain oneself apart from God which is 'sin'. It is precisely around this differentiation between a Lutheran and a Catholic (or humanist) position that Kierkegaard's text revolves; that, as Kierkegaard says, sin is the opposite of faith not of virtue (p. 239). For the Lutheran dialectic see p. 21.

[32] Cf. Kirmmse's 'sheer impudence' (Kirmmse, 'Psychology', 173).

commented of this book that 'crucial categories are directly disclosed there'.[33] It is the Christological casting that is so problematic. In the modern world it would seem daring enough to contend that only in relation to God can an individual come into his or her own; to suggest that this is only possible for those who credit the Christological formula preposterous. But Kierkegaard must perforce say this if he is to be Christian.

The Self before God

The Christological twist not withstanding, Kierkegaard's consideration of the structure of the self in its relation to God may be thought of the greatest interest. As I have elsewhere considered in depth and detail, he is seemingly able to bring together what have been the respective strengths of both Lutheran and Catholic traditions, while letting what may be considered the weaknesses of either tradition fall away.[34] I should like to explore this in brief.

The insight of the Lutheran tradition has surely been that if God is to be God, then the relation to God must be understood as constitutive of the human person. Catholics will be of a mind to respond that Catholicism captures this fundamental nature of the relation to God to the constitution of the self through its doctrine of creation.[35] But this is really rather different than to hold, as does the Lutheran tradition, that there is no self existing in and of itself, but that in each moment the person must 'break open' the self as known to the natural man, basing the self on God. As Luther famously said in that sentence fundamental to his Reformation insight, 'the Christian lives not in himself but in Christ'.[36] The Christian is possessed of a self-understanding that is not an understanding of an isolated self at all, nor is it that of the natural man. Kierkegaard's position is just as dramatic, setting a theistic position (cast in the second part of the book in terms of Christianity) against the world of humanism. In a 'natural' religion (as opposed to Christianity) one might indeed say

---

[33] JP 6:6361 (Pap. X A 147).
[34] Cf. my Christian Contradictions, ch. 4 'Nygren's Detractors' and ch. 7 'Kierkegaard's Odyssey', especially pp. 261–3 and 276–84.
[35] Thus the leading Catholic thinker Herbert McCabe once told the present writer that Catholicism embodies both the things she wished to say.
[36] 'The Freedom of a Christian', in John Dillenberger, ed., Martin Luther: Selections from his Writings (Garden City, NY, 1961), 80.

that one should in each moment base oneself in God, but as Kierke-gaard well knew this would have to be God understood as immanent (what he would have called a Socratic position) or known to humankind apart from particular revelation. One might add that the Lutheran fear has always been that Catholicism is but a form of humanism.

The other side of the coin is that what must appear problematic about some modern Lutheran writers is the lack of a sense that the self indeed comes to itself. Thus the 20th-century Swedish theologian Anders Nygren, holding so much in common with Kierkegaard, quoting Luther (in a sentence plucked from a pre-Enlightenment thinker out of context) will speak of the self as 'merely the tube, the channel, through which God's love flows' to the neighbour.[37] In a post-Enlightenment world this must be inadequate. (Indeed, one senses that Luther in the 16th century has more sense of an integrated self than one would guess from Nygren's statement.) The human being is not a tube or even simply a servant. It is Catholicism which, given its 'high' doctrine of creation and its talk of 'infused grace', has been able to conceive of human beings as able to stand of themselves before God. Thomas Aquinas goes so far as to employ the term *amor amicitiae* (brotherly love, the equivalent of Greek *philia*), as existing between the human person and God, if by a far off analogy.[38] Post-Enlightenment and specifically post-Hegel, Kierkegaard axiomatically grasps that he must speak of the self as truly coming to itself, this also in relation to God.

What is fascinating is that in his later writing Kierkegaard indeed speaks of a self as able to exist before God. Yet he does this without losing the sense that in each moment God is quite fundamental to the self being itself. There is no substantial self and no talk of an *analogia entis*. His is a relational, not a Catholic–Aristotelian conception. One finds such a development already present in the passage to which I have drawn attention in *Christian Discourses*. Kierkegaard had of course remarked in *Love's Deeds* the previous year that we are bidden also to love God. What Kierkegaard here emphasizes is that what he calls the 'reciprocal' relation between God and the human owes entirely to God's love. (It is not that God has made the human to

[37] Cf. Anders Nygren, *Agape and Eros*, trans. Philip S. Watson (New York, 1953), 733–5; quotation 735.
[38] Cf. *Summa Theologica* II ii, qu. 23, art. 1.

possess in himself some kind of substantiality, for example through creation.) Kierkegaard writes:

> Oh, what wonderful omnipotence of love! A human being cannot bear to have his 'creations' be something in relation to himself... But God, who creates from nothing... says 'Become'... [and] lovingly adds 'become something even in relation to me.' What wonderful love; even his omnipotence is in the power of love. From this results the reciprocal relationship (*CD*, 127).

His sense is both of the frailty of the human's utter dependence on God and of what it is that God's love makes possible.

Finally in *Practice in Christianity* Kierkegaard makes an advance beyond anything present in *The Sickness Unto Death* or *Christian Discourses*. The passage is in the third number of that book, thus presumably written in 1849. He speaks of a self that progressively becomes itself as it is drawn in love to God. In this 'drawing' one may well detect echoes of Augustine's Neoplatonism. Yet it is not, as in Augustine's case, a love that should straightforwardly be categorized as a 'higher eros'; a love that loves on account of the fact that it finds in the other its own greatest good. It is not we who are attracted by God's perfection, but God who draws us to himself. Nor is it that the one who loves will be transformed through God's grace into his likeness. The self owes everything to God; were it not for God's love, *coram deo* the human would be nothing. The interesting question is whether this daring Lutheran—for that is surely what Kierkegaard must here be held to be—has said something that confounds Lutheran sensibilities. One may think that such language could never be employed by Luther, nor in the 20th century by Bultmann, Nygren or Bonhoeffer (to name three diverse and eminent Lutheran theologians we have considered). Kierkegaard's language suggests a greater sense of self as the self relates to God as 'other' to the self than a tradition that holds that we are only our selves in the moment as we base ourselves on God can easily allow.

Whether Kierkegaard succeeds in bringing together the strengths of two divergent traditions, or whether there is in his thought a dilemma incapable of resolution is an interesting question. He walks a tightrope. Minimally we are in a very different world than that expounded in the *Postscript*, in which the presence of God arouses in the human the crisis of *Anfechtung*. Of course *Postscript* (as also *Fragments*) are penned under the name of Climacus; while

254 | KIERKEGAARD: EXPOSITION AND CRITIQUE

The Sickness Unto Death and *Practice in Christianity* are the work of his alterity Anti-Climacus. But what I would draw attention to here is what must surely be accounted a change in Kierkegaard's own disposition subsequent to the considerable resolution of his relationship to God during the spring of 1848.[39] In *The Sickness Unto Death* (as we shall yet discuss) Kierkegaard employs passionate language for God.[40] What one should ask is surely the following. How is a rapturous description of love of God to be distinguished from a higher *eros*? It is scarcely *agape*. Ecstasy is not something with which the Lutheran tradition has normally been at ease. It is well known that, given his Neoplatonist context (and on account of his inadequate knowledge of Greek such that he read the scriptures in Latin), Augustine mistakenly thought Paul's *amor dei* to refer to *our* love for *God*, whereas Paul's intent is *God's* love for *us*.[41] The motor of the Lutheran tradition is precisely God's agapeistic love. Has Kierkegaard found a legitimate way to conceptualize a love for God that is something other than that faith which is love?

[39] See p. 302.
[40] See p. 304.
[41] Cf. John Burnaby, *Amor Dei: A Study of the Religion of St Augustine* (London, 1938), 99.

8

Practice in Christianity

Introduction

In the final years of his life Kierkegaard became embroiled in a major controversy with the church. This chapter will consider what was at stake and attempt to form some estimation of the issues involved. Kierkegaard's position is well advanced by his book *Practice in Christianity*, the first two parts of which were largely written in 1848, with some further work being done on it and the third part composed in 1849, the book finally being published in 1850. The lack of response with which the book met may well have caused Kierkegaard to become only the more adamant that he must find a way to bring the issues it tackles into the public domain. This he embarked upon in December 1854, some months subsequent to the death in January of that year of Bishop Mynster. The rumpus he provoked was still in full flow at the time of Kierkegaard's death in November 1855, rumbling on afterwards. Kierkegaard had raised vital questions. As is so often the case, theological issues were we may think intertwined with personal animosities. *Practice in Christianity* takes many a swipe at Mynster. But it was rather Martensen, bishop and primus in succession to Mynster, who called forth Kierkegaard's ire.

Kierkegaard scholars have overwhelmingly viewed this 'church struggle' through a Kierkegaardian lens. But Mynster could be said to have held a perfectly reasonable position. Thus I find myself wanting to challenge received opinion, asking whether Kierkegaard was necessarily right and Mynster necessarily wrong.[1] That many who have commented have been Americans, with no experience of an established church, strikes me as having exacerbated the imbalance in the evaluation.[2] Kierkegaard himself held a complex and ambivalent position, only at the end of the day coming out against the state church. Were we simply concerned with some local squabble that took place in Copenhagen in the 1850s the matter could but be of historic interest (if of considerable interest in that it was Kierkegaard who stirred it up). One must however think that the issues concerned have been present ever since, with the 4th-century Constantinian settlement, the church became established. They are not easy of adjudication. Interestingly it would seem that Dietrich Bonhoeffer took note of this 'church struggle' as he participated in that which took place in the Third Reich. Nor have the issues found resolution in our secular age today.

It will be necessary in this Introduction to fill in some background. I shall in particular attempt to say something of Mynster; crucial if we are to understand both sides of the argument. After the Exposition of *Practice in Christianity*, there will follow an additional section, 'Aftermath', before we turn to the Critique.

Together with the other Scandinavian countries, Denmark emerged from the Reformation with a Lutheran state church, to which the overwhelming majority of the population belonged. As was the case in the German states, the clergy were supported through a church tax; in Denmark they were in effect civil servants. The Danes have an expression 'broad church' and there has been a sense that the church is there for all the people. From 1834 the primus of this church was

[1] The kind of material to which I am alluding would be exemplified by words placed under the picture of Mynster in Joakim Garff's biography of Kierkegaard (*Søren Kierkegaard, A Biography*, trans. Bruce Kirmmse, Princeton, NJ, 2005). Having cited Kierkegaard's words to the effect that Mynster is a poisonous plant, the script continues: 'And he does not look entirely harmless as he sits here in the powerful ecclesiastical uniform; paradoxically his missing teeth lend him a greedy, shark-like air.' It would not have occurred to me that Mynster's quiet reply to Kierkegaard—after he had received a book such as he had—deserved the epithet 'shark-like' (see p. 279).

[2] Even in the case of Bruce Kirmmse's erudite writing, there is a presupposition that there is *per se* something wrong with established churches, for what reason is unclear. See for example his 'Call Me Ishmael—Call Everybody Ishmael: Kierkegaard on the Coming-of-Age Crisis of Modern Times', in George Connell & Stephen Evans, eds, *Foundations of Kierkegaard's Vision of Community: Religion, Ethics and Politics in Kierkegaard* (Atlantic Highlands, NJ, 1992).

Jacob Peter Mynster, a revered figure held in awe for his polish and presence. Of a Sunday the Copenhagen élite, including the Kierkegaard family, would gather to hear Mynster preach in the Cathedral church, Vor Frue Kirke, the Church of the Virgin, which stands in the centre of Copenhagen. Mynster had confirmed Kierkegaard and had been a seminal figure in his life. 'I was brought up on Mynster's sermons—by my Father' Kierkegaard was to record.[3] He had counted Mynster a friend of the family. Kierkegaard's senior by 38 years, after Kiekegaard's father's death, Mynster became in some sense a 'father figure'. *The Corsair* had noted with some sarcasm that Mynster was the only person about whose opinion Kierkegaard cared.

Born in 1775 and losing both his parents by the age of four, Mynster and an older brother were brought up by an austere stepfather, who would subject the family to evening devotions consisting largely in long ruminations on his sin. Shy of disposition and lacking toys (other than a collection of conch shells in which the boys delighted) the boy took to reading. It was the stepfather who determined that Mynster should study theology. Exceptionally, he completed his degree with honours aged but 19. The next years were spent as private tutor to the son of a wealthy aristocrat. Living on the family estate in considerable isolation, Mynster availed himself of the library; reading Aeschylus and Homer, Kant and Rousseau, taking an interest in economics and making an extended study of Adam Smith, and he was of course widely apprised of German literature. Tutoring the talented boy in English, German, and French texts, Mynster could himself also read Dante in Italian. He opined that 'almost every sort of reading is grist for a cleric's mill'.[4] Desiring to write, he reviewed in verse the well-known Danish Romantic poet Adam Oehlenschläger, won an essay competition, and started publishing his sermons. It is thought not improbable that Mynster's writing style influenced Kierkegaard's in the latter's edifying discourses.

These years were followed by a decade as a country parson, during which again Mynster read. Lacking the companionship of his social and intellectual equals he suffered considerably from depression, the Napoleonic wars and British occupation only serving to increase his isolation. Concerned that Napoleon might force Denmark to close

---

[3] *JP* 5:6073 (*Pap.* VIII A 397).
[4] Garff, *Kierkegaard*, 612.

the Baltic Sea to British shipping, thereby depriving Britain of the supply of timber needed to build warships, the British determined to pre-emptively seize the Danish fleet. In their bombardment of Copenhagen in 1807 they used Congreve rockets designed to cause fire; 2,000 civilians were killed and 30 per cent of buildings destroyed. Mynster recalled a dark and drizzly night when, climbing a thatching ladder and seeing an ominous glow in the sky in the direction of Copenhagen, he realized that the city, 'the site of everything dearest to me',[5] was on fire. Mynster heartily disliked the insufferable British officers billeted on him, but he bore no love for Napoleon, writing of the 'hypocritical phrases with which—in the midst of the most horrifying bloodshed and the most heartless extortion—it was continually asserted that all this was being done for the sake of the well-being and salvation of the human race'.[6]

Mynster's chance came aged 36, in 1811, when this 'cultivated, diligent and mature man' (as Kierkegaard's biographer depicts him[7]) gained a position at the Cathedral church. Four years later he finally married, most happily. Once discovered, Mynster's rise was meteoric: he became court chaplain; was given further promotions; until in 1834, appointed Bishop of Zealand and Primus. Mynster was very much a society figure. But he also undertook extensive pastoral tours through Denmark. Of his preaching he wrote:

I have always had the pleasure of having a large audience, drawn from various social classes. If I have often been dissatisfied with myself for having spoken edifyingly to the lower social classes perhaps less frequently than I should have, I have also seen consoling evidence to the effect that this was not entirely the case: I had many plain citizens and manual labourers among my regular listeners.[8]

Collections of his sermons, published every year from 1846 to 1853, became model sermons for training pastors, while Mynster's 1833 work *Betragtninger over de christelige Troeslaerdomme* (*Observations concerning Christian doctrine/teaching*) was one of the most popular devotional books of a generation, running to a fourth edition in 1855 after his death. Never could it have occurred to this powerful man

---

[5] Garff, *Kierkegaard*, 615.
[6] Garff, *Kierkegaard*, 614.
[7] Garff, *Kierkegaard*, 617.
[8] Garff, *Kierkegaard*, 618.

that it would be Kierkegaard who would carry him into history, nor that posterity would judge him harshly through the latter's eyes.

The setting of the Vor Frue Kirke strikes one as theatrical. The previous building having burnt down in the 1807 conflagration, the Cathedral was rebuilt in the fashionable neoclassical (Biedermeier) style. The famed Danish sculptor Bertel Thorvaldsen, resident in Rome, was commissioned to make sculptures for the church; which he executed just too large to fit into the arches designed for them and which, consequently placed in front of those arches, dominate the space. Each figure of an apostle stands holding the instrument of his torture, while Peter and Paul, at the head of the two columns of sculptures on either side of the nave, look to Christ. Situated above and behind the Communion table, a more than life-size Christ, clad in toga, his arms spread wide, displays in his open palms (as I have only recently realized, able to approach the sculpture more closely) the wounds of crucifixion. In the statue's pedestal are carved the words 'Kommer til Mig' ('Come Unto Me'). It was in the space of Vor Frue Kirke that Kierkegaard would give his discourses at the communion on Fridays and on a Sunday Mynster preach.

A pastor to his flock, Mynster thought words of comfort fundamental to the Christian gospel. His *Observations* asks in the opening chapter, 'Where shall my weary soul find rest?' Treating, under the title 'The Comprehensibility of Christianity for Everyone', the text of Matthew 11.25–30 which contains the verse 'Come unto me', Mynster says that the invited are everyone who has experienced 'anxiety and sorrow' and anyone with a 'righteous and God-fearing mind'. Rest consists in 'certainty for the doubter, strength for the struggling, comfort for the sorrowful'. The honest person, opines Mynster, has the ability to comprehend the 'highest as well as the most comforting truths'; namely that 'God so loved the world that he gave his only Son, so that everyone who believes in him may not perish but have eternal life' (John 3.16). Lacking in paradox or dialectic and posing no essential difficulty, he claims that God provides the one who is upright with 'happiness and blessing'.[9] Mynster was wont to speak of those 'quiet hours' in which the Christian turns apart from the

<hr>

[9] Quoted by Christian Fink Tolstrup, '"Playing a Profane Game with Holy Things": Understanding Kierkegaard's Critical Encounter with Bishop Mynster' in *IKC PF*, 264.

world. In 1848, by which date he had come to view Mynster askance, Kierkegaard was to write: 'He has always been very fond of "these quiet hours in holy places" because...he distributes the religious as an ingredient in life, not as the absolute.'[10]

If Mynster's lifestyle was somewhat excessive (Kierkegaard wrote a piece lampooning a dinner party at which the guests dined on turtle soup), Kierkegaard's was likewise lavish. Having agreed to vacate by Easter Day 1848 the flat that he still occupied in the family house, Kierkegaard moved into a splendid new apartment building on a corner with views through no less than ten windows in two directions; soon moving together with his servants into a yet more spacious apartment in the same building. The first to admit the profligacy of his life-style, while contending that it was the necessary condition for his productivity, Kierkegaard went through a small fortune in these years. The accounts show payments to hat makers, drapers, and silk merchants, while he spent no small sum on carriage drives into the countryside, and his table fare was the cause of astonishment.[11] Across the street from these apartments was one of Copenhagen's notorious poorhouses, ropes stretched across the rooms so that the inhabitants could attempt to gain some sleep while standing. The description of the over-populated town, confined within its ancient fortifications, is truly mind-boggling. Kierkegaard was disturbed by the stench from tanneries close by, the effluence from their trade running through open sewers. Average life expectancy for men was 34, for women 38 years; considerably lower than in the surrounding countryside.

For all that Mynster and Kierkegaard held in common, in class, disposition, and outlook (both had opposed the reigning Hegelianism, both heartily disliked the popularism of Grundtvig, and both were monarchical conservatives), the two men reacted differently to the revolution of 1848. Mynster's aim (it must have seemed axiomatic to him) was that the political turmoil should not cause the church's position in Danish society to become dislodged. That it might accord with the new political doctrines, it was in future to be known as a *Folkekirche* (people's church). When the question as to its freedom of action in its own sphere was left unclear by the new constitution,

---

[10] *JP* 6:6150 (*Pap.* IX A 39), n.d., 1848.
[11] For a description see Garff, *Kierkegaard*, 533.

Mynster chaired a commission, through the work of which its status was assured. Thus while other icons of the *ancien régime* fell, Mynster remained standing; a point not lost on the cartoonists.[12] Equally horrified by the turn of events (to the end of his days he referred to 1848 as 'the great catastrophe'), Kierkegaard responded otherwise; writing to his friend the elderly professor J. L. A. Kolderup-Rosenvinge, who awaited a dictatorial leader to put the world to rights: 'You are expecting a tyrant, while I am expecting a martyr.'[13] Short of martyrdom, Kierkegaard did not know what could bring this bourgeois church back to Christianity. Toying with the idea of martyrdom himself, he judged that he did not have the strength for it, 'nor perhaps that sort of courage'.[14] In Kierkegaard's eyes Mynster had become an opportunist, selling his soul to keep his position. 'Yet I love Bishop Mynster', he confided to his *Journal*, such was his ambivalence.[15]

Exposition

The text consists in three 'numbers', each based on a biblical quotation. It is built around the classic Lutheran doctrine of the 'two states' of Christ, his humiliation and his exaltation.

NO. 1. 'COME UNTO ME ALL YOU WHO LABOUR AND ARE HEAVY-LADEN, AND I WILL GIVE YOU REST'

The Invitation

The starting point is the conclusion reached in *Fragments*. Christ's presence can never become a thing of the past; the believer's situation always one of contemporaneity. Contemporaneity necessitates faith. Christ, says Kierkegaard, is the sign of offence and the object of faith.

---

[12] Bruce Kirmmse, 'Kierkegaard and 1848', *History of European Ideas*, 20, 168, referring to a comment of Kierkegaard's, JP 6:6854 (*Pap.* XI B 15), 15 March 1854.
[13] Kirmmse, '1848', 172; quoted from Niels Thulstrup, *Breve og Aktstykker*, I (Copenhagen, 1953–4), 206–7.
[14] JP 6:236 (*Pap.* IX A 225), n.d., 1848.
[15] JP 6:6173 (*Pap.* IX A 85), n.d., 1848.

He poses no conditions: 'The invitation to all throws open the Inviter's arms and there He stands, an everlasting picture [*evigt Billede*]' (Lowrie, 14).[16] Furthermore, when it is a question of a sinner 'he does not merely stand still, open his arms and say "Come unto Me"', but waits as did the father of the prodigal son. He has walked infinitely far, from being God to becoming man, that he might seek sinners (20).[17] Knowing that it is of the essence of suffering to go off alone, Christ actively seeks out the sufferer.

The Halt

Just when we should expect to see a crowd approaching, in fact they recoil. For the inviter insists on being the definite historical person he was 1,800 years ago, living under the conditions in which he spoke the words of invitation. Who is the inviter? Jesus Christ who sits in glory at the Father's right hand? From glory he has not spoken one word. To be a believer one must come to him in his humiliation. His coming in glory can but be believed; by the person who has adhered to him as he existed.

We have reached a major theme. There is no way that from the results of his life in world history one could prove that Christ is God. 'One cannot *know* anything at all about Christ; he is the Paradox, the object of faith ... But all historical communication is the communication of *knowledge*' (25, my capitalization). People say: 'has not history adequately ... established who he was, that he was—God?' (26). But the most that history could demonstrate is that he was a great man, perhaps the greatest of all. 'That he was—God—no, stop; with the help of God that conclusion will surely miscarry' (27). By *definition* one cannot demonstrate that which is infinitely qualitatively different. The 'demonstrations for the divinity of Christ that Scripture sets forth' (as people think them to be), his miracles, resurrection, and ascension, are not 'demonstrations' at all! (26). Far from showing that faith is in harmony with reason they demonstrate that it *conflicts* with it.

[16] Walter Lowrie, ed. & trans., *Training in Christianity* (Princeton, NJ, 1944), 14 (henceforth Lowrie, 14 etc.).
[17] Howard V. Hong & Edna H. Hong, eds & trans., *Practice in Christianity* (previously translated as *Training in Christianity*), (Princeton, NJ, 1991), 20 (henceforth 20 etc.).

Furthermore, his words become 'untrue' if I make the person who said them other than he was. If it is made to appear *that it was God* who said these words they are untrue, for it is *untrue* that one who appeared to be God said them.

To judge Christ according to the results of his life is blasphemy: that is what one would do in the case of one who was but a human being. It is to fail to acknowledge that Christ was God. By contrast, if we begin with the assumption that he was God, the 1,800 years are irrelevant. Says Kierkegaard, we have to start in one of these ways; from 'below', attempting to prove he was God, or from 'above' with the assumption. Consider the first. At some point we shall be guilty of a *metabasis eis allo genos* (a term in Aristotle, a change in genus or kind); 'suddenly by way of a conclusion obtaining the new quality, God' (27). The question would arise as to what the results must be—how great the effects, or how many centuries pass—in order to demonstrate that he was God! Thus does Kierkegaard critique the nascent 'quest of the historical Jesus': 'These brilliant results in world history, which almost convince even a professor of history that he was God' (30).

Some of the statements that Kierkegaard makes in conjunction with this discussion are significant.[18] 'If it perhaps is so that even in the year 300 Christ was not completely demonstrated to be God, there would be something to it'; it would follow that 'the people who lived in the year 300 did not regard Christ as God, even less those who lived in the first century' (27–8). That is to say Kierkegaard assumes that the disciples who lived contemporaneously with Christ believed him 'God'. Indeed he adds rhetorically: 'has not Christ himself claimed to be God?' (28).[19]

In the case of the God, the idea that the results of his life are more important than that he lived is blasphemy. That God has lived on earth as an individual human being is 'infinitely extraordinary'. Had it been devoid of results that would make no difference. 'What extraordinariness would there be in the fact that God's life has had extraordinary results? To talk in this manner is nonsense' (31–2). Christ's abasement is not something that *happened* to him; Christ himself *willed* to be the lowly one. What mockery of God were one to

---

[18] See pp. 88–9.   [19] Cf. p. 273.

presume to say that the persecution Christ suffered was accidental (34). (That Christ, and the Christian, necessarily suffer will be a major theme.)

The problem is that Christ has been made into neither one nor the other: neither the person he was on earth, nor the one who will come in glory, but into someone of whom one has learned from history that he was 'some kind of great somebody' (35). One becomes a Christian without even noticing it. 'Everything became as simple as pulling on one's socks'; that is to say it is a linear movement, one is not brought up against the offence of a paradox. Christianity has become paganism.[20] Comments Kierkegaard: Christianity has been abolished without this being recognized.

There must be what Kierkegaard would call 'reduplication': the inviter must be commensurate with the invitation. Had Christ in glory issued the invitation there would be no paradox. To *believe*, we must be confronted with abasement. But to let oneself be helped by the actual human being who was Christ meant risking one's honour, life, and goods; minimally 'exclusion from the synagogue' (37).

'Come here, come here, all, all you who labour and are burdened, come here, see, he is inviting you, he is opening his arms!' When an elegant man dressed in silk says this in such a pleasant, melodious voice that it gives a lovely echo in the beautiful vaulted ceiling, a silken man who spreads honour and esteem upon listening to him [i.e. Mynster preaching in Vor Frue Kirke];...—well, then there is some sense to it, isn't there? But whatever sense it has for you, this much is certain—it is not Christianity; it is the very opposite, as diametrically opposite to Christianity as possible— remember the inviter!' (38).

One cannot accept the invitation but not the inviter.
Was this easy for contemporaries? Do miracles help?

In the situation of contemporaneity...signs and wonders...are something exasperatingly annoying, something that in a very embarrassing way almost forces one to have an opinion, something that, if one does not happen to feel like believing, can be a burdensome thing to be contemporary with, especially since it makes existence far too strenuous, especially the more intelligent, developed, and cultured one is (41).

[20] See p. 264.

The contemporary will ask 'Does he have a permanent job?', and so forth (43). Or he will say 'I certainly do perceive that there is something very profound in what he says'—but the problem is who it is that he is (44). Thus does Kierkegaard deride modernity's lauding the ethics while bracketing the question of Christ's identity, thinking the result Christianity.

Kierkegaard proceeds to mock various positions taken up; spoofs that would apparently have been attributable to known persons in his society. Thus, the clergyman might say:

The authentic expected one will look entirely different, will come as the most glorious flowering and the highest unfolding of the established order. That is how the authentic expected one will come, and he will conduct himself quite differently; he will recognize the established order as the authority, will summon all the clergy to a convention, present to it his achievements, together with his credentials—and then if in balloting he has the majority he will be accepted and hailed as the extraordinary that he is: the expected one (47).

While the philosopher: 'He has no doctrine, no system; basically he knows nothing' (48). And the solid citizen: 'I have earnestly taken my son to task, warned and impressed upon him that he should not go and mess up his life by joining this man. . . . As Pastor Grønwald said last evening at the club: "That life will have a horrible ending"' (51).

So to the second period in the inviter's life. People turn against him. 'The powerful sprung the trap—and now the people, who now see themselves completely deceived, turn their hate, their indignation, against him' (56). Not least is this a comment on mob behaviour as Kierkegaard believed he witnessed in 1848 or perhaps the *Corsair* affair.

The Invitation and the Inviter

This desertion would presumably not have come about had the Inviter held a merely human conception of compassion for a merely human conception of misery.

Humanly speaking, there is actually something shocking, something at which one might become so embittered that [one] would have an inclination to kill the man—at the thought of bidding the poor, and sick, and suffering to come to him, and then to be able to do nothing for them but only to promise them forgiveness of sins (Lowrie, 64).

The person might say: 'Now let us be human. A human being is no spirit. And when a human being is almost starving to death, then to say to him: I promise you the gracious forgiveness of your sins—this is outrageous' (61). If your problem is toothache or your house has burned down 'but it has escaped you that you are a sinner', then it is cunning of the inviter to say he heals all sicknesses but when one comes to him to acknowledge only one sickness—sin.

Christianity as the Absolute; Contemporaneity with Christ

Christianity did not come into the world 'as a showpiece of gentle comfort as the preacher [Mynster presumed] blubberingly and falsely introduces it—but as the *absolute*' (62). He does not wish to be transformed into a cosy human God, but to transform, and he wills this out of love. 'Be quiet, it is the absolute' (62). (The quotation with which Bonhoeffer opens his Christology lectures.)[21] The gospel speaks of Christian suffering. There pertains an infinite difference between God and humanity. Christ's life on earth, a 'sacred history, stands alone by itself, outside history' (64).

NO. 2. 'BLESSED IS HE WHOSOEVER IS NOT OFFENDED IN ME'

We should fear that which can kill faith, the offence. 'Faith conquers the world by conquering at every moment the enemy within one's own inner being, the possibility of offence' (76). Whether you will be offended Christ leaves up to you; whether you will inherit eternal happiness or bring about your eternal unhappiness.

With the Father he knows from eternity that only in this way can the human race be saved: he knows that no human being can comprehend him, that the gnat that flies into the candlelight is not more certain of destruction than the person who wants to try to comprehend him or what is united in him: God and man. And yet he is the Saviour and for no human being is there salvation except through him (77).

Kierkegaard attacks a (Hegelian) demolition of Christianity: the God-man is not a symbol for a union of God and man understood

---

[21] Dietrich Bonhoeffer, *Christology*, trans. J. Bowden (London, 1966), 27.

in general terms. That the human race is supposed to have a kinship with God is ancient paganism. Rather is the God-man the unity of God with an individual human being (particularity). Thus it is 'certain that the understanding must come to a standstill on it' (82). Other than out of the possibility of offence one never comes to faith.

The Exposition

Kierkegaard will consider three types of offence.

(A) The possibility of offence that is not related to Christ as Christ (the God-man) but simply as an individual human being who comes into collision with an established order.

Compare Matt. 15.1–12. Christ is asked by the scribes and Pharisees, 'Why do your disciples transgress the tradition of the elders and not wash their hands when they eat?' To which, quoting Isaiah he replies: 'This people keeps close to me with their mouths and honours me with their lips, but their hearts are far from me.' The disciples say to him: 'Do you know that the Pharisees *were offended* when they heard this saying?' (85–6). In contrast to a shallow outwardness, Christ emphasizes inwardness, this inducing collision. The established order always insists on being 'objective' and thus above an individual. (An anti-Hegelian comment.) 'Every time a witness to the truth transforms truth into inwardness... every time a genius internalizes the true in an original way—then the established order will in fact be offended at him' (87).

Kierkegaard takes on Hegel in *The Philosophy of Right.*

How come Hegel has made conscience and the state of conscience in the single individual 'a form of evil'?[22] On what account? Because he deified the established order. But the more one deifies the established order, the more natural is the conclusion: ergo, the one who disapproves of or rebels against this divine established order—ergo, he must be rather close to imagining that he is God (87 adapted).

---

[22] Cf. *Hegel's Philosophy of Right*, trans. T. M. Knox, and with notes (Oxford, 1942), Second Part (iii), 86–104.

But the person is not blaspheming; that it so appears is an acoustic illusion reflected back from the fact that the established order has deified itself. 'This deification of the established order is the perpetual revolt, the continual mutiny against God'; it 'is the smug invention of the lazy, secular human mentality that wants to settle down and fancy that now there is total peace and security' (88). The individual may well be the gadfly (a reference to Socrates)[23] needed to stop the established order from falling asleep or into self-deification.

But today is there not congruity? In the past godliness suffered, today the more devout the more esteemed. 'If Christ came to the world now he would first become a professor and would steadily advance' (89). But this was the outlook of the scribes and Pharisees! Hidden inwardness is held in suspicion: the established order wants to 'browbeat the single individual into a mouse-hole' (90). Whereas God uses the single individual to prod the established order out of self-complacency. To live in the established order is to exempt oneself from anything that causes pain: if you are a student, the professor is the criterion of truth, if a clergyman, the bishop is the way and the life, if a clerk, the justice minister. Making a quip at the expense of Hegelianism, Kierkegaard comments: 'The established order is the rational, and you are fortunate if you take the relativity assigned to you—and, for the rest, let the ministries, the council, or whatever take care of it' (90). When, in the face of the established order, an individual appeals to his relationship to God could this not be held self-deification? No; for every human being has this same relationship with God. Even though he only behaves as should every human being people take offence at Christ.

(B) The possibility of essential offence in relation to loftiness, that an individual human being speaks or acts as if he were God.

We come to 'essential' offence, pertaining to the Paradox. Kierkegaard will first consider the offence relating to the fact that this human being gives himself out to be God. (In view of our consideration, it is interesting that Kierkegaard does indeed think that Christ did this.) He takes two biblical texts.

[23] See p. 295.

Compare Matt. 11.6. In prison, John the Baptist sends a messenger to Christ to ask whether he is the one who should come or they should look for another. Christ does not answer directly: Kierkegaard's theme, that he cannot do so but requires faith. Christ responds that the blind see, the lame walk, lepers are cleansed, the dead raised up, and the good news preached to the poor, adding 'Blessed is he who is *not offended* at me' (95). Suppose he had said: 'Look at me; then you will certainly see that I am God.' 'But try it!' says Kierkegaard. 'No, the simplest means to put an end to all this sentimental paganism that in Christendom is called Christianity is quite simply to place it in the situation of contemporaneity' (95). The contemporary sees miracles: this individual human being is making himself something close to God. And he sees an individual human being. Now he is in tension. It depends upon you whether you choose offence or faith; it is your heart that is disclosed. But Christendom has 'a fantasy picture of Christ, a fantasy God-figure, directly related to performing miracles' (97).

Compare again John 6.51–2, 61, 66–7. Christ says he is the 'living bread; . . . If anyone eats of this bread he will live forever', adding 'does this offend you?'; and thereafter many of his followers draw back. These words 'living bread' are placed in the eucharistic liturgy. A doctrine of the ubiquity of Christ's body has been advanced[24] and, given one has in Christendom a fantastic Christ-figure, the whole thing becomes comprehensible, not beginning to contain the possibility of offence. Christ says to the twelve 'Do you also wish to go away?' Further:

[Christ] says that he will raise on the last day only the person who eats his body and drinks his blood—certainly defining himself as God in the most decisive terms. He says he is the bread that comes down from heaven— another striking expression in the direction of the divine. And since he knew that his followers grumbled about this and found it a hard saying, he says, 'Does this offend you?' And then he adds something even stronger, 'What if you were to see the Son of man ascending where he was before?' Thus, far from yielding or compromising, he directly makes himself totally different from what it is to be a human being, makes himself the divine—he, an individual human being (100).

---

[24] See pp. 214–15.

Since this man is in fact God the possibility of offence is constantly present. 'To forgive sinners is in the most decisive sense a qualification suggestive of God' (Lowrie, 103).

(C) The possibility of essential offence in relation to lowliness, that the one who passes himself off as God proves to be the lowly, poor, suffering, and finally powerless human being.

And secondly we have the contrary offence: that one who is God is a lowly man.

Compare Matt. 13.55–7; Mark 6.3. The people say: 'Is this not the carpenter's son? Is his mother not called Mary? And his brothers James and Joseph and Simon and Judas?...Whence, then, did that man get all this? And they *were offended* at him.'

Compare again Matt. 26.31, 33; Mark 14.27, 29. Peter tells Christ he shall not suffer. Christ responds: 'This night you will all *be offended* at me.' The passage, says Kierkegaard, is discussed as though to be God is 'a direct superlative of what it is to be a human being' (104); the speaker supposing that, even had Jesus only been a man, Peter should not have denied him and, given who he was, this is extraordinary. But had Christ simply been a man Peter would not have denied him: 'What causes Peter to be quite beside himself... is that he had believed that Christ was the Father's only begotten Son.' That a human being falls into the hands of his enemies is human; 'but that the one whose almighty hand had done signs and wonders... stands there powerless...—precisely this is what brings Peter to deny him' (104).

There follows a discussion of discipleship. In the Lutheran tradition the theme would seem to be prevalent that discipleship will bring with it suffering: cf. John 15.20: 'if they persecuted me, they will persecute you'. The Danish *Christi Efterfølgelse* (German *Nachfolge*), literally 'following after' (the disciple being one who 'follows after') differs in emphasis from a Catholic *imitatio* tradition. It is not for the disciple to become *like* Christ (in himself a little Christ);[25] rather is it that looking to another he shares his fate. To translate this Lutheran theme by 'imitation' can therefore be misleading. Nevertheless, it is

---

[25] See p. 169.

true that the connotations of 'imitation' may also be strongly present in Kierkegaard's use of the term. He had for some time possessed a copy of the *De imitatione Christi* of Thomas à Kempis (1380–1471) and a full Danish translation, under the title *Om Christi Efterfølgelse*, appeared in the year *Practice in Christianity* was written.[26] Kierkegaard differentiated himself from Luther in this matter. The Epistle of James (which Luther had derided as an 'epistle of straw' on account of the fact that it made no mention of justification by faith) was a favourite text on account of its stress on being doers of the word (Jas. 1.22–7). As Kierkegaard commented, he lived in a different age from Luther and a different emphasis was needed.[27] Discipleship becomes a major theme in Kierkegaard's last years. Neither is speaking of Christ as a 'pattern' very satisfactory. The Danish *Forbilledet*, example, and *Forbillede* (prototype/pattern), have in common as component the word for picture/example (cf. German *Vorbild*); an example is a picture held before one. The double entendre is intentional as Kierkegaard has the statue of Christ in Vor Frue Kirke in mind.

The follower says Kierkegaard (cf. Matt. 10.24; Luke 6.40) is not above his master but like him.

For truly to be a Christian certainly does not mean to be Christ (what blasphemy!) but means to be his imitator, yet not a kind of prinked-up, nice-looking successor who makes use of the firm and leaves Christ's having suffered many centuries in the past; no, to be an imitator means that your life has as much similarity to his as is possible for a human life to have (106).

In Christendom, common human suffering has been substituted for Christian suffering. Christian suffering is voluntary and associated with offence. So: someone is unfortunate enough as to lose everything. The pastor 'bravely meditates on words of consolation' (Mynster presumed), but His Reverence has become all mixed up (109). To lose everything is not the same as voluntarily giving everything up. If I do the latter, choosing danger and difficulties, it is impossible to

---

[26] Alastair Hannay, *Kierkegaard: A Biography* (Cambridge, 2001), 395.

[27] It would however be a gross misunderstanding to think that Luther does not lay a considerable stress on works (arising from faith); indeed Kierkegaard would appear to know this. While Kierkegaard never casts in doubt that justification is by faith alone. For a consideration of Kierkegaard's judgement of Luther see my *Christian Contradictions*, 264–8.

avoid *Anfechtung*,[28] while unavoidable human suffering must be endured just as in paganism. It is only when the self-contradiction of the suffering appears that the offence becomes evident, hence Matt. 18.8–9: 'If your hand or foot offends you, cut if off'. Christ speaks of *offence*. Better to enter into life lame than to be cast into eternal fire. Christianity makes eternal happiness the absolute good. From the point of view of the natural man such a remedy is madness!

Kierkegaard has made a complete *diastases* (or separation) between Christianity and worldly matters. He remarks: 'That a man, fully and firmly convinced, therefore in fear and trembling that only in faith in Christ is there eternal happiness, outside it only eternal perdition, and that offence is the danger—that he could get it into his head to venture everything—in that there is meaning' (112). Turning to Christianity for help must cause tribulation. To be sent out by the Father's only begotten Son will involve being persecuted (cf. Matt. 10.23), cast out from society, and finally put to death; moreover in such a way that everyone who so persecutes will think he does God a service. But say to a person: 'Go out into the world, this is what is going to happen to you'—the understanding will say what's the use of that? Well, there is none: it expresses that there is some absolute. This occasions an offence to the understanding.

Kierkegaard concludes: 'Christianity resembles a hatred of what it is to be a human being, the greatest curse and torment upon what it is to be human' (117). Peter says: 'Lord, spare yourself; this shall never happen to you!' Christ answers: 'Get behind me Satan! You are an offence to me for you do not perceive what is of God but what is of man' (118–19). The possibility of offence lies in this, that the world sees in the believer a criminal. 'The infinite loftiness of living for the absolute is expressed by becoming scum in the world, an object of mockery and disdain' (120).

The Categories of *Offence*, That is, of Essential Offence

The God-man has been made into a speculative unity of God and man (Hegelianism). In Scripture the God-man is called a 'sign of contradiction'. What contradiction could there be in a speculative

---

[28] See p. 157.

unity of God and man? Or else Christ has been thrown out, his teaching alone retained. People think Christianity is direct communication, the teaching more important than the teacher. But that can be true only of a human being. Or Christendom has 'made him fantastical and has fantastically imputed to him direct communication' (128), such that people are under the illusion that, had they been contemporary with Christ, they would immediately have recognized him. Christ becomes a man who was himself aware of being extraordinary but of whom contemporaries failed to take notice.

And now the God-man! He is God but chooses to become this individual human being. But this is the most profound incognito. People say that Christ has said directly that he is God; 'they maintain that Christ has given us a direct answer to a direct question' (135). But such pastors know not what they are saying; they abolish Christianity. Christ was an offence to the Jews and foolishness to the Greeks. Yes, Christ did indeed say very directly that he was the Father's only begotten Son. That is to say the *sign of contradiction*— has *very directly* said it. People take the direct statement and fantastically form a character corresponding to it (preferably sentimental, with the gentle look, the friendly eye, or whatever else such a foolish pastor can hit upon), and then it is *directly* certain that Christ is God.

The true God cannot be directly recognizable. If he does not become the object of faith he is not true God. And, if he is not true God, nor can he save people. Thus through his incarnation he plunges a person, indeed mankind, into the most horrible decision. Yet he does this out of love; to save people. If they are to belong to him, saved through faith, he must keep people at a distance. He suffers death for them. The possibility of offence confirms in every moment, 'the chasmic abyss between the single individual and the God-man over which faith and faith alone reaches' (139). But modern philosophy has deluded us into thinking that faith is immediate. (Here Kierkegaard would be at one with Hegel in criticizing such a 'romantic' view.)[29] In this way Christianity becomes a teaching, and the next stage is to have 'comprehended' it.

[29] See pp. 16, 41.

NO. 3. 'AND I IF I BE LIFTED UP WILL DRAW ALL UNTO ME.' (JOHN 12.32)

No. 3 consists in seven discourses on this text. It was largely written later than the rest, in 1849, and there is a difference in tone. I shall simply draw attention to certain passages.

DISCOURSE III

The discourse, *inter alia*, attacks Mynster. 'The abased one' (Christ) wanted on any terms to save humankind, sacrificed his life for it. Does this sight not move you?

> Surely you will not let yourself be deceived if one or another of the silver-tongued speakers (who do a bad job or at least do not know what they are doing) wants to deceive you with his eloquence by talking fascinatingly about Christ's sufferings or even by fascinatingly wanting to place himself [before] the cross—as an observer [cf. the title of Mynster's well-known book, in which he characterizes preaching as making 'observations']... You will bear in mind that if there is to be any earnestness in... standing near his cross, then it has to be in the situation of contemporaneity, where it would therefore mean *actually* to suffer with him, not to make observations at the foot of the cross, but perhaps oneself nailed to the cross beside him—to make observations (171).

DISCOURSE IV

As do a number of discourses, the discourse pursues the theme of imagination and suffering; such passages often appear autobiographical. Every human being possesses to some degree the power of imagination, 'the first condition for what becomes of a person' (186). The youth has an image of perfection, of the ideal. Then he discovers actuality: it is as though he has been deceived. Governance (Kierkegaard's word for God) leads him 'further and further out into suffering'.

> He understands now that suffering cannot be avoided... Now existence has turned the screw as tight as it can tighten the screw on a human being; to live under or to endure life under this pressure... Now he is probably able to bear it—yes, he must be able to, since Governance does it with him—Governance, who is indeed love.... Let us assume that he perseveres until he dies: then he passed his test. He himself became the image of perfection he loved (191).

In this world 'the truth is victorious only by suffering' (193). 'The cruelty', says Kierkegaard, comes from the Christian's having to express what it is to be a Christian while living in the environment of the world. That truth is persecuted is a frightful discovery. Accused of every evil, the Christian is 'forced back into concern about himself; whether the fault might not lie in himself' (197).

And if he is living in Christendom, this takes place amidst a general mumbling and muttering by fantastic characters belonging to that part of the clergy who must be called the so-called pastors who, in pursuance of their livelihoods, assure us that the loving person is loved by God and people and that this is Christianity, this—not that the loving person becomes the sacrifice (197).

The person's suffering is only intensified by people making him anxious, telling him that 'his life is an un-Christian exaggeration, because, unlike other Christians, he refuses to let Christianity be something one supposedly should only have hidden in one's innermost being—perhaps so well concealed that it is not there at all' (197). (From other remarks it would seem that Kierkegaard suspected this latter of Mynster.)

DISCOURSE V

In the matter of 'truth', each generation must begin anew. (This has of course been a constant theme of the authorship: 'history' is neither here nor there; nor can an institution—the church—embody the truth.) Only as it becomes a life in one can one know the truth. Truth is conceived as cognition, whereas in primitive Christianity it was understood as existing, as being. 'When the truth is the way, being the truth is a life': Christ says of himself: 'I am the Truth and the Way and the Life' (John 14.6) (207).

'Established Christendom' thinks itself the church triumphant. Christ said 'My kingdom is not of this world'. As soon as Christ's kingdom compromises with the world, Christianity is abolished. In the present situation the degree to which my being a Christian has more 'truth' will be recognizable by the 'quite extraordinary esteem I enjoy in this world' (a dig not least at Mynster); if one lived in a true Church militant suffering would ensue (213). Someone will say that to think that the church should be militant today is unreasonable, since we are all Christians! We are supposed to keep our being Christian hidden, since it is a given that all are Christians. Consider the one who takes it upon himself to confess Christ today. He does not judge others; he simply expresses that he is a member of the militant church. Established Christendom will come to his aid through persecution and the like.

Kierkegaard furthermore attacks the Grundtvigians, among whom his elder brother Peter Christian had found a home. Followers of the charismatic Grundtvig, they were a populist movement which campaigned among other things for the dissolution of parish bonds (obliging people to attend their own parish church) in favour of free congregations. The Danish for 'congregation' (cf. also the German *Gemeinde* and indeed the English Latin root) of course connotes 'gathering'. Struggling in a Christian manner, says Kierkegaard, is always undertaken by individuals, since before God each is an individual, 'fellowship' being a lower category than 'the single individual'. (One doubts, incidentally, that Luther, who had the highest regard for the *Gemeinde*, the gathered congregation, would have expressed himself thus.) The 'congregation', avers Kierkegaard, belongs to eternity, where all single individuals who endured the struggle in time will be gathered.

Suppose a person were to say: 'Despite everything you say... it is... an impossibility that all of us become martyrs.' A suitable reply is: Is it impossible for you to become one? What have you to do with 'all'? (224). The beginning of the test is to be 'so turned inward that it seems as if all the others do not exist;... one is quite literally alone... before God, alone with Holy Scripture as a guide, alone with the prototype before one's eyes' (225). Further, suppose the interrogator were to ask, have you the strength to become a martyr? 'Were you always so strong that you never felt the need for gentle and reassuring words to be spoken to you?' Kierkegaard by no means fails to appreciate the significance of the question he says, indeed he feels the need for gentleness and has 'never enjoyed "alarming"' (226). But gentleness lies the other side of the consequences of being Christian; this does not compare to (Mynster's) confusion of gentleness with ordinary human comfort.

Christianity is the 'unconditioned'. If anything other pertains then Christianity has been abolished. 'We have heard long enough and loudly enough this brazen talk that one must go further' (Martensen). Believing on the basis of 'reasons' (i.e. Martensen's Hegelianism) has been substituted for obedience. 'Without authority, Christianity creeps around in Christendom . . . and we do not know whether we should take our hats off to it or whether it should bow to us' (227). In a barbed comment directed at the fact that, to keep abreast of the times, the state church had transmuted into a 'People's Church' Kierkegaard comments: 'It was almost as if a vote would be taken. All right, let it pass; on these conditions we accept Christianity' (231). The church triumphant and established Christendom are untruth; the worst tragedy that can befall the church.

DISCOURSE VI

In reading Discourse VI we should hold in mind those 19th-century images of Christ that portray him looking all-but-divine, not least the Christus in Vor Frue Kirke. 'If we have dozed off into . . . infatuation' (the prayer that heads the discourse reads) 'wake us up, rescue us from this error of wanting to admire or adoringly admire you instead of wanting to follow you and be like you.' Christ asked for disciples (*Efterfølgere*) not admirers.

'Observing' one may come close to something, but it also signifies keeping a distance, lacking what is decisively Christian about the sermon, the *You and I*, such that the speaker should continually come back to himself helping the listener to do likewise. 'It is Christian truth which is observing me.' God, the invisible listener, 'looks to see whether my life expresses what I am saying' (reduplication). Speaking of the preacher who 'proclaims so enthusiastically, movingly, and with tears in his eyes that of which his life expresses the very opposite!' (Mynster), Kierkegaard comments that when the 'I' has dropped out, so too the 'you' is abolished: what the preacher says ceases to be of concern (233–5).

Christians have become admirers rather than disciples. 'Divine loftiness and adoring admirer, correspond perfectly to each other' (237). Christ asks for imitators of a life: his life was designed to make 'admirers' impossible. The one who admires has a 'wonderful hiding place: . . . I acknowledge and confess that I admiringly adore Christ as the truth'. The difference lies in this: an after-follower (disciple) *is* or strives *to be* what he admires: an admirer remains detached (241). Admiration is the appropriate stance towards what it is beyond my control to resemble; beauty, extraordinary talents, etc. In relation to 'that which is in everyone's power, the universally human, that is, the

ethical, that which every human being shall and therefore also presumably can do' (the Kantian presupposition) admiration is inappropriate (242). I am not to admire but to commence immediately in my
effort to resemble that person. Nicodemus was an admirer: he came
to Christ by night. 'The danger of actuality' was too much for him; he
wished to keep himself detached (247). Kierkegaard has Nicodemus
say to Christ: 'I confess it, I myself feel how humiliating this is for me
and how disgraceful, indeed also how very insulting it is toward you)',
commenting 'see in what a web of untruth an admirer entangles
himself' (248). We know Kierkegaard to have read a sermon by
Mynster on Nicodemus before writing this.

Finally of interest are Kierkegaard's comments on the concept of
Christian art, 'a new paganism' (254). Making clear reference to
Thorvaldsen Kierkegaard remarks: 'I do not comprehend this artistic
indifference...that the picture of the goddess of sensuality [Venus]
found in his studio occupied him just as much, so that not until he
finished it did he start to portray the crucified one' (255). Could he,
Kierkegaard, have carved the Christ? It would be such an impossibility 'that it is incomprehensible to me how it has been possible for
anyone' he says, commenting on 'the calmness with which a murderer can sit and sharpen the knife with which he is going to kill
another person' (254). Such a 'figure', an 'idealized portrait', corresponds to a world of admirers. Would the artist not notice Christ's
displeasure? 'This is not a proposal to assail the artist or any particular work of art' comments Kierkegaard disingenuously (256).

Aftermath

We may think it hardly surprising that Kierkegaard had entertained
severe doubts about publishing such work. As was his practice, he
delivered a copy to Mynster (!). A month later he received a visit from
Mynster's son-in-law, Pastor Paulli. We learn from Kierkegard's *Journal* what Paulli had to say. Mynster was indignant; the book played
'a profane game with holy things'.[30] When Paulli had enquired whether

---

[30] *JP* 6:6691 (*Pap.* X³ A 563).

he should report Mynster's views to Kierkegaard, Mynster responded that no doubt Kierkegaard would come to see him and he would tell him himself. Kierkegaard made haste. Mynster commented that he had no right to reprimand him (not a pastor, Kierkegaard could not be defrocked, nor dismissed from a teaching position for he held none); that 'each bird must sing with its own beak' (a Danish saying); and that people might say of him what they would. Kierkegaard responded that, had he distressed him, Mynster should say so, for this had not been his intention. Of the book Mynster commented: 'Well I certainly do not believe that it will prove beneficial.' Kierkegaard said he was a young man (he was 37, Mynster 75) and that this was how the matter seemed to him at present. Essentially, Mynster refused to be drawn. Kierkegaard was relieved. Mynster had observed that half the book was directed against Martensen, the other half against himself. But little of the work would appear to be directed against Martensen and there is no evidence from the latter's autobiography that he thought so.

What realistically did Kierkegaard think the book could achieve? That Mynster might be induced to make some declaration to the effect that the present church in no way resembled that of the apostles? In a *Journal* entry written three and half years later, subsequent to Mynster's death, Kierkegaard remarked:

If he could have been moved to end his life with a confession to Christianity that what he had represented was not really Christianity but leniency it would have been much to be desired, for he sustained a whole age.[31]

But if this was his intent, Kierkegaard was wildly mistaken in his reading of the situation. It would seem likely that Niels Tolstrup is correct in his estimate of Mynster: 'His conscience was clean...and thus he could not take the attack from Kierkegaard seriously. He felt insulted, but not chastened.'[32] The book made little impact. Kierkegaard was neither denounced by the church authorities nor rebuked in the religious press, writing in his *Journal*: 'Nothing has happened yet, all are silent—and Mynster talked this [mild] way.'[33]

---

[31] *JP* 6:6853 (*Pap.* XI^1 A 1), 1 March 1854.
[32] Tolstrup, 'Profane Game', 267.
[33] Hannay, 508–10 (*Pap.* X^3 A 563).

This allowed breathing space. The book sold reasonably well and Kierkegaard lay low.

On 30 January 1854 Mynster died. In a memorial sermon Martensen referred to the deceased as one in a line of 'witnesses to the truth, stretching across the ages from the days of the Apostles up to our own times'.[34] This was too much for Kierkegaard who immediately put pen to paper. It is questionable whether in what unfolded the bone of contention for Kierkegaard was Mynster or rather Martensen. Kierkegaard had over many years been envious of Martensen. He had had to watch as Mynster groomed him to be his successor. In the eyes of the world Martensen was a success story: he himself noted of his 1849 *Christian Dogmatics* that it had been translated into many languages and was discussed throughout Christendom.[35] Particularly difficult for Kierkegaard was an occurrence in 1854. Sorting through his father's papers, Mynster's son came upon memoirs, which were immediately published. Kierkegaard had to see that whereas Martensen was warmly praised, those memoirs contained not a single mention of his father, elder brother, or himself. That was how little impact the Kierkegaard family had made upon Mynster's life. Kierkegaard, however, laid his writing aside. A campaign was afoot to raise money by public subscription for a monument to Mynster and it was as yet unsettled whether Martensen should succeed him. Furthermore a conservative administration was in power and Kierkegaard risked being sued for libel.

Upon the advent of the succeeding liberal administration Kierkegaard fired his opening salvo, publishing an article in the periodical *Faedrelandet* (*The Fatherland*) (18 December 1854): 'Was Bishop Mynster a "Witness to the Truth": One of the "Authentic Witnesses to the Truth"—Is This the Truth?' Not only, said Kierkegaard, had Mynster suppressed the fact that 'witnessing to the truth' brings suffering in its train, but Mynster's life lacked congruity with Christianity. Of a 'witness to the truth', Kierkegaard commented that finally he is crucified or beheaded or burned or broiled on a grill, his lifeless body thrown

---

[34] Garff, *Kierkegaard*, 729; another translation in Bruce Kirmmse, *Kierkegaard in Golden Age Denmark* (Bloomington & Indianapolis, 1990), 449–50.

[35] From Martensen's side we have a record of one reasonably decent conversation between the two men. He thought he had missed the opportunity to build on it. See Michael Plekon, 'Kierkegaard, the Church and Theology of Golden-Age Denmark', *Journal of Ecclesiastical History*, 34, no. 2 (1983), 262.

in some out-of-the-way place by the executioner's assistant. (That the words for 'witness' and 'martyr' are closely related in Greek as in German can scarcely have escaped Kierkegaard.) By contrast, Mynster had been weak and pleasure-loving, great only as an orator.[36] Responding to this attack on his sermon, Martensen—not always a pleasant character—was as below the belt and wounding as he could be.[37] While Kierkegaard noted of Martensen that he was a 'glob of snot'.[38] During the nine months that were to be left to Kierkegaard before, in September 1855, he was taken into hospital to die, he carried on a relentless campaign against the church, first in *Faedrelandet*, subsequently founding his own broadsheet *Øjeblikket* (eye-blink; i.e. moment/instant; as German *Augenblick*).

What is fascinating is the alacrity with which Kierkegaard, the erstwhile staunch conservative who in 1848/9 had fulminated against 'the mob' and democracy, took up the possibilities which the political change offered. Power now lay with the ballot box, the majority of those enfranchised being labourers or peasants. Though for a short while, under the Ørsted administration, it looked as though (as was to be the fate of every other country in Continental Europe) the forces of reaction would take over, with its defeat the Danish revolution was assured. His experience with *The Corsair* having served to alienate him from his own class, none of whom (Mynster included) had lifted a little finger to help him, Kierkegaard would employ freedom of the press as a stick with which to beat them. As David Law remarks, Kierkegaard's writing changed 'register'; he produced what Robert Perkins names 'instant' writing for the street.[39] Having lost none of his penchant for striking metaphors nor his acid wit, rhetoric poured from his pen. Thus Kierkegaard complains that the church has simply baptized the world: 'Brothels have remained the

---

[36] 'Was Bishop Mynster a "Truth-Witness", One of "the Authentic Truth-Witnesses"—Is *This the Truth?*', in Howard V. Hong & E. H. Hong, eds & trans., *The Moment and Late Writings* (Princeton, NJ, 1998), 6, 8 (henceforth *TM* 6, 8, etc.).
[37] See the summary given in Garff, *Kierkegaard*, 736–8.
[38] Quoted by Garff, *Kierkegaard*, 741; no reference.
[39] David Law, 'The Contested Notion of "Christianity" in Mid-Nineteenth-Century Denmark: Mynster, Martensen, and Kierkegaard's Antiecclesiastical, "Christian" Invective in "*The Moment*" and Late Writings', in *IKC TM*, 54f; Robert Perkins, 'Kierkegaard's "Instant Writing" on the Triumph of Aestheticism in Christendom', in *IKC TM*, 284–318.

same as in paganism, dissoluteness proportionately the same, but they have become "Christian" brothels. The brothel keeper a "Christian" brothel keeper' (*TM*, 185). As Jørgen Bukdahl remarks, Kierkegaard had turned into a 'scandal journalist'.[40]

Kierkegaard's outburst was greeted with astonishment, the more so as people had thought him an admirer who had counted himself Mynster's friend. Kierkegaard had tried out his ideas on his relatives. Henrik Lund had married Kierkegaard's sister and, subsequent to her death, remarried; by his second marriage having a son Frederik Troels-Lund who was to recall his parents' amazement that the deceased was spoken of in this way.[41] As the campaign continued, Danish society was divided. We have a mass of material.[42] Particularly interesting is the response of Kierkegaard's former teacher, the philosopher F. C. Sibbern. Writing to a female correspondent who had asked after his opinion, Sibbern opined:

As for the phrase 'witness to the truth', I think it is very incorrect to wish to emphasize that it involves undergoing martyrdom.... Part of being a witness to the truth is that [a person's] preaching must contain *truth*. And how can it best be recognized? By its *fruits*...If I see that a person's preaching has a beneficial effect on the souls of many people, so that they are ennobled by it, warmed and edified by it, and if I see that they then praise and thank him for it, then I may be most likely to see this as a proof of the fact that he is a witness to the truth....

I see an awful proof of the arrogance and ingratitude that rules the world if a man who has exercised such a great and beneficial effect upon so many people by his preaching...is now to be attacked because someone else has got another notion of Christianity into his head.... In its type and spirit, Mynster's Christianity was closest to that of Melanchthon [presumably eirenic and scholarly intended] even though he could also be quite outspoken. No one can deny that he worked zealously in the vineyard of the Lord. Kierkegaard has done so in another fashion, but with a certain one-sidedness. *Now* his one-sidedness is to be everything!...I would...view the anger he has stirred up against himself as a good testimony to the Danish people's sense of truth, justice and gratitude.[43]

[40] Jørgen Bukdahl, *Søren Kierkegaard and the Common Man*, trans. Bruce Kirmmse (Grand Rapids, MI, 2001), 120.
[41] Bruce Kirmmse, ed., *Encounters with Kierkegaard: A life as Seen by His Contemporaries* (Princeton, NJ, 1996), 184.
[42] See the material collected in Kirmmse *Encounters*, 99ff.
[43] Kirmmse, *Encounters*, 104.

One can see how such a judgement could be reached.

Those of Kierkegaard's class and those in the church were for the most part appalled. Kierkegaard had touched a raw nerve. Wife to the literary critic and herself a leading actress, Johanne Luise Heiberg, who had always been a supporter of Kierkegaard, commented that he was an 'unfaithful beast'.[44] It seems she considered him a traitor to their class. It was all manner of sectarians, freethinkers, and the poor who lent Kierkegaard their support; they loved to see the church attacked. There was abroad much bitterness, not least on account of the fact that when a cholera epidemic had broken out in Copenhagen in 1853, 4,000 dying, a large number of clergy had found it convenient to take their holiday. Again, it was younger people who were supportive and it was they who were to accompany Kierkegaard's funeral cortège from church to graveside. Martensen noted with disgust that Kierkegaard had found a following among women.[45] He himself attacked Kierkegaard with atrocious vindictiveness, descending to comments on his appearance.[46] One man wrote to Martensen that he thought Kierkegaard:

Fully deserves [a 'thrashing' (a phrase which Martensen had cited)] ... if it were not for the fact that such well-deserved punishment would make him into a martyr and *eo ipso* into a 'witness to the truth' in his own imagination. . . . The most painful punishment for him would have been to have taken no notice of it.[47]

Brøchner, however, reported to Kierkegaard that he had 'found many people to be in profound sympathy with him'.[48]

Was Kierkegaard misunderstood in his intention? In an article published in *Faedrelandet* on 31 March 1855 under the title 'What do I want?' Kierkegaard responded to his question: 'Very simply—I want honesty' (*TM*, 46). He may well have thought that he himself should be included among those whose lifestyle might be deemed incommensurate with Christianity. But it was hard for others to draw such a distinction. Chancing upon Kierkegaard in one of the fine restaurants in town a pastor, Vilhelm Birkedal, recorded:

[44] 9 July 1855, quoted by Kirmmse, *Golden Age*, 483.
[45] Kirmmse, 'Epilogue', *Golden Age*, 484, note 14.
[46] See a summary in Garff, *Kierkegaard*, 737–8.
[47] Kirmmse, *Encounters*, 102.
[48] Kirmmse, *Encounters*, 248.

He sat in front of no small portion of food fit for a king and a very large goblet of sparkling wine.... Then I saw for myself that he did not apply to himself this 'dying away from the world' or this (at any rate bloodless) martyrdom...because what he had prepared for himself here was a quite generous enjoyment of the world.

The incident, Birkedal wrote, 'occasioned no small amount of struggle in my soul', for he had previously counted Kierkegaard a spiritual mentor.[49] Given that Kierkegaard was taking issue with the disparity between Mynster's mode of living and his preaching, it could well be thought problematic should there be a perceived dissonance in Kierkegaard's case.[50]

Of significance is Grundtvig's response, given the Grundtvigians were the leading movement pressing for church reform. Now installed as the new primus, Martensen feared that Grundtvig would come out in Kierkegaard's favour. He need not have worried. Responding to Kierkegaard's 'What Christ Judges of Official Christianity' (*TM*, 127–37), Grundtvig told his congregation that they should not fear Christ's judgement for he would be mild and understanding, castigating moreover as false prophets those critics who called the clergy 'deliberate misleaders' and 'wolves in sheep's clothing'. Speaking of the permissibility of having many of one's Christian joys and sorrows in common with the world, Grundtvig spoke of gradual spiritual growth. Kierkegaard responded in kind, claiming that all Grundtvig desired, other than disestablishment of the church, was a tranquil life, lived among those who were essentially at home in this world (*TM*, 207–8).[51]

Having expended the last ounce of his strength and exhausted his finances in the struggle, Kierkegaard was increasingly unwell. On 2 October he collapsed in the street. Initially taken by carriage to his apartment, Kierkegaard insisted that he go to the public hospital. The young medic who admitted him noted:

He considers the sickness fatal. His death is necessary for the cause which he has devoted all his intellectual strength to resolving, for which he has worked alone, and for which he believes that he alone was intended...If he is to go

---

[49] Kirmmse, *Encounters*, 107.
[50] Cf. George Pattison's consideration of Kierkegaard's stress on 'ethical communication': *The Philosophy of Kierkegaard* (Chesham, 2005), 128–9.
[51] *The Moment*, no. 6, 23 August 1855.

on living, he must continue his religious battle; but in that case it will peter out, while, on the contrary, by his death it will maintain its strength and, he believes, its victory.[52]

Kierkegaard understood his predicament as that of a martyr. In an account of a conversation with him in hospital, Kierkegaard's friend Emil Boesen noted that he had said:

[Mynster] was a colossus; strong forces were needed to topple it, and the one who did it had to pay. When they hunt wild boar, the hunters have a specially selected hound and they know quite well what is going to happen: the wild boar is felled but the hound pays the price. I will die gladly.[53]

No one got to the bottom of Kierkegaard's illness. There has been speculation that he had some form of epilepsy; Kierkegaard himself had been wont to refer to his 'thorn in the flesh'.[54] He lingered on for six weeks before death followed. There was a sense in which, his life's work complete, Kierkegaard had lost the will to live. In January 1855 Regine had emigrated with her husband who had been appointed Governor of the Danish possessions in the West Indies. On the very day of her departure she had succeeded in encountering Kierkegaard in the street, saying under her breath 'God bless you: may it go well with you'. Caught off guard—for they never spoke in these 'chance' encounters—he greeted her.[55] He was to be thankful that she was spared the final months of his notoriety. More significantly, his money had run out.

We have pictures of considerable serenity on Kierkegaard's part during his final months. Encountering him at the Athenaeum reading room (where Kierkegaard ostentatiously spent Sunday mornings that he might be seen not to be attending church), Kristian Arentzen noted that 'his powers were visibly waning, but his eyes glowed with a quiet glow of love'.[56] A few weeks subsequent to Kierkegaard's death, Brøchner commented: 'He retained a loving concern for others, even for life's smallest details; ... gentleness, friendliness even

[52] Hannay, *Kierkegaard*, 411–12.
[53] Kirmmse, *Encounters*, 125.
[54] Garff, *Kierkegaard*, 715. See an account of other earlier attacks in Kirmmse, *Encounters*, 112.
[55] Hannay, *Kierkegaard*, 408.
[56] Kirmmse, *Encounters*, 115.

playfulness.'[57] Writing at a later date, the by then avowed atheist Troels-Lund left us a remarkable account of his last encounter with Kierkegaard in hospital, which he said had marked him for life.[58] While Henrietta Lund (Kierkegaard's niece and Troels-Lund's half-sister) wrote:

When I entered the little room and was received by the glow that practically shone from his face, I got the impression that a feeling of victory was mixed in with the pain and sadness. Never have I seen the spirit break out of its mortal frame and impart its brilliance in that way, as if it were the very transfigured body on the Day of Resurrection.[59]

The invective against Mynster however continued to the end, Kierkegaard telling Boesen: 'You have no idea what sort of a poisonous plant Mynster was.'[60]

As Kierkegaard had predicted, in the short term the controversy in no way died down. He had raked up questions not easy of dismissal. Writing to Hans Christian Andersen, the Swedish literary critic Frederikke Bremer remarked that the Kierkegaard affair had awakened a great deal of interest there: 'Most people—myself included—know that he was *right in much and wrong in much*. He is no pure manifestation of the truth and his sickly bitterness has certainly stood in the way of clarity and reasonableness in the judgements reached about him.'[61] Kierkegaard's reputation was to take some years to recover. His grave, today a site of pilgrimage, lay untended and without headstone for some twenty years. But by the 1870s the Danish critic and man of letters Georg Brandes was working on his biography of Kierkegaard; while Henrik Ibsen's drama *Brand* is certainly modelled on Kierkegaard's fiery attack on the church.[62] This, however, was in Scandinavia, where alone Kierkegaard could be read.

[57] H. Brøchner to C. K. F. Molbech, 17 Feb. 1856, Kirmmse, *Encounters*, 252.
[58] Kirmmse, *Encounters*, 190.
[59] Garff, *Kierkegaard*, 786; cf. Kirmmse, *Encounters*, 172.
[60] Cf. Boesen's account of his hospital conversations with Kierkegaard, Kirmmse, *Encounters*, 121f, quotation 125.
[61] 14 December 1855, Kirmmse, *Encounters*, 136.
[62] Kirmmse, *Golden Age*, 485.

Critique

Kierkegaard's attack on the church and his society is far from easy to evaluate. The fact that what we see here is only too familiar—disputes, misunderstandings, and small-town chatter played out before our eyes—should not however blind us to the importance of the issues raised. The people of Copenhagen were struggling with pertinent questions that, with the dawn of modern times, confronted them. Genuinely different views of the nature of the church and what its relation to society should be had emerged. Nor have these questions by any means been resolved.

The Nature of the Church

The kernel of what was at stake between Kierkegaard and Mynster was surely this. Should there be a broad state church, a spiritual home for the Danish people, which could provide a focus for the nation in times of crisis or rejoicing, able also to offer guidance and comfort to individuals whether or not they normally attended Christian services, a place where they might negotiate life's transitions. Or by contrast should there be what Kierkegaard looked for, which might reasonably be called a 'confessing church', standing for defined and stringent Christian beliefs, based on a certain reading of the New Testament, its members apparently ready (in the 19th century) for 'martyrdom'? Ever since Augustine's squabble with the Donatists in the early 5th century the catholic (universal) church had opted for the first of these, though the second tendency had not infrequently also been present in an uneasy juxtaposition. Augustine had been adamant that the church must embrace all manner of persons, the validity of baptism universally recognized, knowing full well that the consequence of this would be that (as he put it) tares would grow together with the wheat.[63] By contrast 'confessing' churches, often having arisen through the need of their members to defend themselves against a hostile world (as indeed in the case of the Donatists), and

---

[63] Augustine 'On Baptism, Against the Donatists', Book IV.

given that not all can lend them their allegiance, tend to veer towards sectarianism. It is apparent that this was what some feared about Kierkegaard's campaign; we have seen Sibbern's remarks.

Nor should it be thought that, on account of its being established, a church has necessarily thereby lost its soul. For all that he may have been self-serving, Mynster too had credible ideals. In his *Betragtninger* Mynster considers this question as to the nature of the church. Noting that there are those who consider the degradation of the church to have gone so far that the only solution is to found new communities, he however questions that what we truly want is that the entrance to the church should be narrow, or whether we should not rather give as many as possible the opportunity to share in the goodness on offer. Such openness, Mynster notes, makes it unavoidable that the unworthy will also be included. But, he asks, do we really wish to erect a judgement seat at the church door? Judging, Mynster opines, should be left to the Lord when he comes, for he alone knows human beings and can judge with justice.[64] In arguing thus Mynster, as he no doubt recognized, stood in line to a long tradition. Calvin, no less, remarks that it is for God alone to judge who belongs to the smaller and invisible church within the wider body of the visible church, in turn quoting Augustine, who comments that 'many sheep are without and many wolves are within'.[65] Both Mynster and Martensen thought in terms of the classical distinction between the visible and invisible church.

Together with being of such a theological conviction, Mynster also held (together with many in the early 19th century, no less a man than Schleiermacher thought in these terms) certain sensibilities as to the importance of 'people' or *folk* (German *Volk*). One should consider the context. Politically divided, were they ever to throw out the French invader German-speaking peoples had needed to foster an identity. The Danish, likewise, had been threatened by Napoleonic hegemony and in their case overrun by the British. Mynster was no fanatic nationalist. It had taken considerable pressure to elicit from him the response he finally wrote to Oehlenschläger's

---

[64] J. P. Mynster, *Betragtungen über die christlichen Glaubenslehren*, trans. Theodor Schorn (Hamburg, 1840), 558–9. Thanks owe to David Law for this reference.

[65] John Calvin, *Institutes of the Christian Religion*, book IV, ch. I, § 7–9.

poem. Nevertheless, he understood the Danish state church to encompass the Danish people. Perhaps the most difficult episode of his career had been the row over his insistence that there could be no sects, such that contrary to the will of their parents, the children of Baptists should be baptized and confirmed. Interestingly, against his better judgement, Kierkegaard had out of loyalty supported Mynster in this matter. In the event Mynster lost out when the king changed sides, becoming somewhat embittered by the loss of face he suffered. To such a man, at the helm of such a church at the time of the emergency that 1848 represented, it must have seemed self-evident that it was his duty to steer the church to accommodation with the new state, safeguarding its status and privileges.

The question becomes that as to at what point a church, in accommodating itself to the state, has overstepped the mark. One should here be cognizant of the fact that in every Danish village the pastor was in effect the state's administrative official, exemplified by the fact that baptism conferred citizenship. As late as 1852, after the time at which, with the new constitution, there had been some recognition that not all belonged to the state church, Mynster was preaching in the following terms.

There are other countries in which the different religious confessions are all at large . . . so that no one can say which is the general religion of the people. But with us—thank God!—we can still tell which it is. . . . Let us hold fast to the beautiful, living term 'People's Church'; it signifies that this is the Church to which the people cling, the Church whose confession is rooted in the people . . . Praise and thank God that we still have such a People's Church that holds together the vast preponderance of the people, so that those who deviate from it can quickly be added up. There are indeed people living among us who confess another faith . . . but everyone feels that they are in many respects guests and foreigners and that in essential ways they are not a part of our people.[66]

From our present perspective this must surely be judged unacceptable.

It is in the light of such a context that one must read Kierkegaard's position. Since his early opposition to Hegelianism, Kierkegaard had opposed the conflation of Christianity with the mores of bourgeois

[66] Quoted by Bruce Kirmmse, 'The Thunderstorm: Kierkegaard's Ecclesiology', *Faith and Philosophy*, 17/1 (2000), 88.

society. Taking as his benchmark the church of the New Testament and the early years of conflict and martyrdom preceding the Constantinian settlement, Kierkegaard in the years following 1848 became increasingly uneasy as the church made what he knew was a compromise of convenience with the new state. Already by 1849 he is writing:

How did the illusion of a Church triumphant ever arise?...There is yet another fallacy that has contributed to [this] illusion.... This fallacy is the pretence...that we as such are all Christians.... [To] introduce...triumph into temporality...means to abolish Christianity.... What Christ said, 'My kingdom is not of this world'...is eternally valid.[67]

The question for Kierkegaard was that as to how one might reintroduce Christianity into Christendom. But what should perhaps be noted is his reluctance to break with the idea of a state church, a position not reached until 1851.[68] Quite remarkably considering its content, Kierkegaard saw *Practice in Christianity* as *defending* the establishment, thinking the only possibility of the church's survival lay in its reformation. It is in this context that it becomes comprehensible that, that Mynster should at least give a sign that he knew that this church was not that of New Testament, became in Kierkegaard's eyes paramount.

The crisis of 1848 found Mynster and Kierkegaard in different situations, understanding otherwise what were their respective responsibilities. The church's primus, Mynster did not doubt where his duty lay. And indeed it must be said that had he not been there to negotiate a settlement (which, incidentally, has endured to this day), the outcome for the church might have been considerably less favourable. Kierkegaard, meanwhile, was a footloose thinker lacking any immediate responsibility for church or state.

But there were also differences of background and churchmanship. Kierkegaard's upbringing had been heterogeneous. If as a boy he had sat at Mynster's feet, he had also of an evening been taken to meetings of the Moravian Brethren (Herrnhuter), a much less 'official' form of

---

[67] *PC* Part III, no V, 209, 211.
[68] So the historian Bruce Kirmmse reckons. (Bruce Kirmmse, '"But I am almost never understood..." Or, Who Killed Søren Kierkegaard?', in George Pattison & Steven Shakespeare, eds, *Kierkegaard: The Self in Society* (Basingstoke, 1998), 183.)

religion.[69] Some of their hymns find their way into *Practice in Christianity*.[70] Thus there were class differences. Kierkegaard was but one generation away from the poverty of peasant existence on the Jutland heath. There were also evidently differences in temperament. As primus, Mynster had struggled to hold the church together, steering a mid-path between rationalists and Grundtvigians. The young man had written his doctorate on Lessing's eirenic parable *Nathan der Weise* (*Nathan the Wise*). By contrast, the young Kierkegaard had written his on irony. Despite these tensions, Kierkegaard's loyalty was such that as late as 1851 he could write: 'I can only collide with the Establishment if Mynster makes a blunder.'[71] In the event it was Martensen who committed the blunder. Meanwhile Kierkegaard's outlook had morphed into advocating disestablishment.

Kierkegaard's Stance

As is so often the case with human affairs, what lay behind Kierkegaard's attack on the church would seem to have been multilayered; the personal being inextricably intertwined with political and theological convictions. That the church of his day was in need of reform is beyond dispute. On becoming primus in 1854, Martensen was dismayed at what he found.[72] During his latter years Mynster had let things slip. The clergy had indeed become civil servants and doubtless many were preoccupied with their standing. (There was even a hierarchy as to the kind of cloth of which vestments could be made.) Kierkegaard knew the situation a farce. It is unsurprising that his invective cut home with so many. That, at significant cost to himself, Kierkegaard sought to rectify what was amiss is certainly the case. But it is far from evident what he could reasonably have hoped for. Less pious pretentiousness, greater humility and conformity to Christian ideals to be sure. But honesty as to the gap which had

---

[69] Cf. Kirmmse's comments on Kierkegaard's closeness to the peasant pietist tradition, *Golden Age*, 485.

[70] Cf. A. J. Burgess, 'Kierkegaard, Brorson, and Moravian Music' in *IKC PC*, 211–43.

[71] *Pap.* X⁴ A 228 n.d., 1851, quoted by Fr.-Eb. Wilde 'Established Order', in George Arbaugh, Niels Thulstrup, & Marie Mikulová Thulstrup, *Kierkegaard and Human Values* [vol. 7, *Bibliotheca Kierkegaardiana*], 12.

[72] Cf. Garff, *Kierkegaard*, 746.

opened up between the present day and the New Testament? When Kierkegaard remarked rhetorically that St Paul had no paid position, the Jew Goldschmidt responded somewhat facetiously that he was a tentmaker! Goldschmidt had earlier expressed himself on the 'barrel' of gold that Kierkegaard had inherited, such that unlike his fellow citizens he did not need a paid position.[73] Moreover, it was surely unrealistic to imagine that the pre-Constantinian church could serve as a model for the present. Nor was Kierkegaard himself living in conformity with its ideals.

It must further be remarked that the conflict was not wholly to Kierkegaard's detriment, giving him a notoriety he appears to have relished. He had not always been a success, his books frequently not sold. Now he had created a stir, he was in the public eye as he had not been since his early success with *Either/Or*. Encountering him in the street, people reported that he appeared to be thriving on it.[74] Within a few weeks of its first publication, Kierkegaard could pride himself that the circulation of *Øjeblikket* roughly matched that of the established *Faedrelandet*; he had to ask for an additional 500 copies to be printed.[75] Not least was the campaign a good way of getting back at Martensen, now uneasily occupying the bishop's chair (and sending his wife and son-in-law to spy out what Grundtvig might say in his sermon that he might ascertain whether he was likely to join Kierkegaard's cause).[76] Persons are made up of complex motifs, differences of churchmanship and theology not always quite what they seem. When J. F. Giødwad, the editor of *Faedrelandet*, sought out Kierkegaard's advice as to whether he should be publishing 'reconciliatory' pieces, Kierkegaard responded that, on the contrary, he should publish direct attack that the distinctiveness of his position might be evident.[77]

But more fundamentally, underlying Kierkegaard's campaign lay the fact that he himself had changed. He was not unaffected by the *Zeitgeist* of 1848, writing:

[73] Article written in April and published in September 1855 in *Nord og Syd*, quoted by Kirmmse, *Encounters*, 108–9.
[74] Cf. Garff, *Kierkegaard*, 771.
[75] Garff, *Kierkegaard*, 753.
[76] Garff, *Kierkegaard*, 767.
[77] Garff, *Kierkegaard*, 742.

Then came 1848. That helped. There came a moment when, overcome with blessedness, I dared to say to myself: I have understood the highest.... But almost at the same time something new rushed upon me: the highest of all is not to understand the highest but to act upon it.[78]

Kierkegaard translated the call for action into his own terms. The thought that one must live out a theological stance in practice was surely not foreign to one who had penned the *Postscript*. Nevertheless it was for Kierkegaard a departure. The issue of contemporaneity, always crucial for him, came to take the form of recognition that discipleship demanded a life of imitation. And in Kierkegaard's eyes witnessing to the truth inevitably brought in its train suffering at the hands of the world. With his failing health he must have known that his time was limited; were he to make his point it could not be delayed. In the final months of his life he went onto the offensive. Death could equal 'martyrdom for the truth'. Yet Kierkegaard was as ever perspicacious, writing: 'With respect to Christ's death, I cannot will this in the same way, because Christ's death is not a task for imitation, but is the atonement... Thus the situation is not a simple and straightforward one in which Christ is the Exemplar and I ought only to will to be like him.'[79]

Thus we should turn once more to Kierkegaard's Christological stance. Imitation of Christ was predicated upon a belief in incarnation. It was a conviction existentially underpinned by Kierkegaard's prayer life. He writes in his *Journal*:

How silly to be upset if one gospel writer said one thing and a second another; [the Christian] can turn to Christ in prayer and say: This disturbs me, but is it not true that you still are and remain with me? It is nonsense that the significance of historical details should be decisive with respect to faith in Him who is present with one and with whom one speaks daily and to whom one turns.... Believe that Christ is God—then call upon him, pray to him, and the rest comes by itself. When the fact that he is present is more intimately and inwardly certain than all historical information—then you will come out all right with the details of His historical existence.[80]

---

[78] *Pap.* X⁴ A 626, quoted by Liselotte Richter, 'Kierkegaard's Position in his Religio-Sociological Situation', in Howard A. Johnson & Niels Thulstrup, eds, *A Kierkegaard Critique* (Chicago, 1962), 66.

[79] *JP* 1:693 (*Pap.* X¹ A 132).

[80] *JP* 1:318 (*Pap.* VIII¹ A 565), n.d., 1848.

How quite one could know that one's awareness of God in prayer was of Christ, of the one who in the form of a human being lived on earth, is unclear. But for Kierkegaard this trumped the considerations which others, among them his friend Brøchner, were beginning to ask.[81] In consequence, notwithstanding the extraordinary difference in the historical circumstances pertaining, Kierkegaard draws direct lines of association between past and present. Therefore he can write: 'But I am not at all afraid of creating scandal. The Christianity of the New Testament is simply sheer scandal; and the word itself is of course the Greek *skandalon*, which in the New Testament is continually used about Christianity.'[82]

Meanwhile, in a post-Enlightenment world others were trying to find a rather different yet equally tenuous relationship to the past. For Schleiermacher, who influenced a generation, this was to be found in the consciousness of God handed down over the centuries in that community which is the church. Mynster and Martensen find in the church and its sacraments a communion with the divine. While these men struggle, each in their own way, to find a bridge between modernity and faith, Kierkegaard sees with perhaps the greater clarity that Christianity can only be believed in stark contradiction to the epistemology or ethics of the modern world. The differences in ecclesiology go hand in hand with divergent theologies. While Mynster and Martensen belong to the 19th century, it is Kierkegaard's sense of scandal, of the givenness of a revelation that does not fit the ways of the world, which will be rediscovered in the nemesis dealt to theology by the crisis of the First World War. But Barthian theology, taking its inspiration not least from Kierkegaard, notwithstanding the prestige lent to it mid-century by the example of the Confessing Church in Germany, might be said to have had even less foundation in the wider culture of the times than had Kierkegaard's.

The truth of the matter was that by the mid-19th century Christianity was losing its hold on European culture and neither stance could save the day. It was not that the underclass that supported Kierkegaard held to his Christology; the point was that he had attacked the privilege and power of a church that they also disliked. Indeed it is an interesting question whether, as some have surmised, Kierkegaard's

---

[81] See pp. 86–7.   [82] *TM* 587 (*Pap.* XI^3 B 155), n.d., 1855.

attack may have weakened the church and its hold over the people. Meanwhile, as critics at the time noted, Kierkegaard seemed to singularly lack concrete proposals for reform. Those for example who tried to enlist his aid for the cause of civil marriages met with no response. As Kierkegaard himself commented:

> I have not fought for the emancipation of 'the Church' any more than I have fought for the emancipation of Greenland commerce [Greenland was a Danish dependency], of women, of the Jews, or anyone else. With my sights upon 'the single individual'. . . I have . . . consistently fought . . . to alert him against letting himself be deceived. . . . Just as I regard it as an illusion for someone to imagine that it is external conditions and forms that hinder him in becoming a Christian, so is it also the same illusion if someone imagines that external conditions and forms will help him to become a Christian (*COR*, 54).[83]

Kierkegaard remained true to himself. In the last issue of *The Moment*, found on his writing desk after his death, he returns again to Socrates: 'My task is a Socratic task, to audit the definition of what it is to be a Christian.' Kierkegaard sought like Socrates to be a 'gadfly', his favourite term for his hero, recalling the term Plato employs in the *Apology* to describe Socrates' relation to the Athenian state. And so in some of the last words we have from his pen, addressing Socrates directly he sighs, 'How I long to be able to speak with you for only a half hour' (*TM*, 341).

Practice in Christianity rounded out the authorship, clarifying the implications of Kierkegaard's Christology for the sphere of praxis. It cannot have made comfortable reading. Much of what he has to say is relevant for persons of any persuasion. Imitation is something other than admiration; appropriation for one's daily living other than academic concerns. Whether Kierkegaard's invective did much to serve his cause must be difficult to judge. His struggle with Mynster is not the story of two men one of whom was a saint while the other to be vilified. It pertains, more interestingly, to the question of whether and how Christianity is able to be adapted to the modern world. Many years later Brandes commented of *Practice in Christianity*:

---

[83] Howard V. Hong & Edna H. Hong, eds & trans., *The Corsair Affair* (Princeton, NJ, 1982), 54.

I consider this book one of his most admirable writings, and it is a work above all distinguished for acuteness of thinking and love of the truth. He who cannot find time to read many of the works of Kierkegaard's last period must at least read this book thoroughly. In it he will find Kierkegaard's whole train of thought and his most profound feeling.[84]

But such a commendation was written by one who, a Jewish free-thinker, had been persuaded to desert his faith not least through reading Kierkegaard. One may appreciate much about Kierkegaard's stance without necessarily adhering to his theology.

---

[84] Quoted by Walter Lowrie, 'Preface', Søren Kierkegaard, *Training in Christianity* (Princeton, NJ, 1941), vi.

9

The Point of View for Kierkegaard's Work as an Author

It is unsurprising that it should have been in 1848 that Kierkegaard composed his major autobiographical piece. That tumultuous year proved significant also for him. At odds both with the clamour for political reform and the preposterous reaction of his own class, Kierkegaard was stimulated to pen a prodigious amount. The question was in quite what form and when to publish this mass of material. As we have seen, in the event he brought out *The Sickness Unto Death* in 1849 and *Practice in Christianity* the following year. In November 1848 Kierkegaard had noted in his *Journal* that *The Point of View for My Work as an Author*, subtitled *A Report to History*, was as good as finished.[1] As it lay unpublished a year later he found it to read 'like a dying man's confession'.[2] Appearing in part in 1851, the work did not see the light of day as a whole until published posthumously by Kierkegaard's brother Peter Christian in 1859.

Kierkegaard's concern in this text is twofold. In the first place as elsewhere in writing from this period he wants to draw attention to the category he conceives to be 'his category': the individual. It has become both theologically and politically critical to him. In a note contemporary with the book, making reference to Thermopylae (the

---

[1] *JP* 6:6258 (*Pap.* IX A 293).
[2] Hannay, 366 (*Pap.* X[1] A 117).

narrow pass where, in 480 BC, intending to thwart the invading Persians the Greek army took a stand), Kierkegaard writes:

'The Individual' is the category through which, in a religious respect, this age, all history, the human race as a whole, must pass. And he who stood at Thermopylae was not so secure in his position as I who have stood in defence of this narrow defile, 'the individual', with the intent at least of making people take notice of it.[3]

In 1848 Kierkegaard was horrified by the phenomenon of 'the mob', more particularly by the patriotic hysteria whipped up in the conflict over Schleswig-Holstein. Theologically, he knows that a person must take the step of faith alone. Politics and theology alike demand an authenticity and a courage acquired through coming to one's self in relation to God.

In the second place, Kierkegaard is 'politically' motivated: he intends to determine how 'posterity' shall read the authorship—for he surmised that it would. His line is that this disparate body of work had from the start solely a religious *telos* in view. We possess the following vignette. Kierkegaard had sent Mynster an autobiographical piece and some discourses, noting of their subsequent conversation that Mynster had commented: 'Yes, there is a thread to the whole but spun later; but after all you do not say any more yourself'. To which he had responded that what was to be noted was 'my having been so possessed by one thing over many years and amid so much productivity that my pen had not made one single detour'.[4] This judgement notwithstanding, in the short piece published in 1851 Kierkegaard remarks: 'So it is that I understand everything *now*. From the beginning I could not thus survey what has been in fact my own development.'[5] These appraisals are not necessarily inconsistent. Kierkegaard had felt his way forward, completing one book, pausing, going off on a seemingly different tack; yet in retrospect to one end, so that he now saw the inner consistency.

---

[3] Walter Lowrie, trans., No. 2 of 'Two Notes Concerning the Individual' in *The Point of View for My Work as an Author: A Report to History* (New York, 1962), 128 [henceforth *Point of View*]; (*PV*, 118). In the case of *The Point of View for My Work as an Author* and related short autobiographical pieces published with it I have in preference used Lowrie's translation while giving the Hongs' *PV* reference in brackets.

[4] *Pap.* X[4] A 373, quoted by Gregor Malantschuk, *Kierkegaard's Thought* (Princeton, NJ, 1971), 6.

[5] 'My Activity as A Writer' appended to *Point of View*, 150; (*PV*, 12).

Certainly the authorship develops. Some of the earliest writing we have from Kierkegaard's pen shows him struggling with his Christian inheritance. In June 1835 the 22-year-old notes:

There are such great contradictions in Christianity itself that an open view is hindered, to say the least. . . . I grew up so to speak in orthodoxy, but as soon as I began to think for myself the huge colossus gradually began to totter. I call it a huge colossus advisedly, for taken as a whole it actually possesses great consistency and through many centuries the separate parts have fused together so tightly that it is difficult to pick a quarrel with it. . . . The main foundation I was obliged to leave *in dubio* for a time.[6]

During these years while his father lived, evading theology, Kierke-gaard immersed himself in philosophy, the classics, and literature. There were personal as well as intellectual reasons for pursuing this escape. *Journal* entries from 1834 on 'the idea of a master-thief' suggest that Kierkegaard was attempting to wrest some secret from the father. The following year he stumbled on the information he sought—and was devastated. He noted: 'Then it was that the great earthquake occurred, the frightful upheaval which suddenly drove me to a new infallible principle for interpreting all the phenomena.'[7] In the autumn of that year, taking distance from his father, Søren moved out of the family home, only to achieve reconciliation shortly before the father's death. Some (pointing also to passages in *Fear and Trembling*) have suggested that the 'earthquake' could have been the discovery of child incest on the part of the father. In any case Kierkegaard took on board his father's conviction that he would outlive all his children. He had a profound need to convince himself that sin was not inherited. Subsequent to his father's death he was to write: 'After my death no one will find among my papers a single explanation as to what really filled my life (that is my consolation).'[8]

Kierkegaard presented his master's (i.e. doctoral) thesis, which became his first book, *The Concept Irony*, in the philosophy faculty. Socrates is his hero. Early work, culminating in the voluminous *Either/Or*, explores 'aesthetic' versus 'ethical' modes of life. The unsatisfactory nature of both appears to foreshadow a third possibility, the religious.

---

[6] Hannay, 30 (*Pap.* I A 72), 1 June 1835.
[7] *JP* 5:5430 (*Pap.* II A 805).
[8] Dru, no. 431 (*Pap.* IV A 85), 1842.

In 1837 Kierkegaard had averred: 'I think that if ever I do become an earnest Christian my deepest shame will be that I did not become one before, that I had to try everything else first.'[9] We may be thankful that he did try everything else first or his authorship would not be half so engaging. Kierkegaard characterizes his inner debate thus.

If I did not know that I was a true Dane I might almost be tempted to suppose I was an Irishman in order to explain the contradictions at work within me. For the Irish have not the heart to baptize their children completely, they want to preserve just a little paganism, and whereas the child is normally completely immersed they keep his right arm out of the water so that in after life he can grasp a sword and hold a girl in his arm.[10]

Early autobiographical remarks reflect a young man wrestling with different life possibilities. Opting for Christianity, the fact that in the midst of modernity Kierkegaard (in the words of St Paul) had been forced to 'work out his own salvation' was to leave its mark on the authorship.

Thus it may well be said of the early authorship of 1842–4 that it possesses the stature and has the intriguing nature that it does on account of the fact that Kierkegaard could envisage standing outside Christianity. His writing differs markedly in tone from that of other major theological thinkers. In his texts Kierkegaard will give a place to the stance of the ancient pagan world or that of humanists, frequently showing its integrity, even though from a Christian perspective he must find it mistaken—leading in turn to a comprehension of the uncomfortable place which Christian claims must occupy in the modern world. It is far from clear that this inner debate is not still in process within him as he writes. Kierkegaard is not yet bitter or scathing as he was later to become. He finds no mileage in denigrating a Socrates, a Lessing, or a Kant (heroes, or in the case of Kant one he reveres). Meanwhile, developing what he has gleaned from his native Lutheranism as articulated by Hamann, he grasps that the 'truth' of Christianity must cast humanism into a place designated 'sin'. Mustering all the ire he can find, Kierkegaard proceeds to throw his dialectical abilities into the fight against the dishonesty of a Hegelian 'mediation' between the world and faith. Far better

---

[9] Hannay, 95 (*Pap.* II A 202), 8 Dec 37.
[10] *JP* 5:5556 (*Pap.* III A 223), n.d., 1840–2?

humanism than a bungled attempt to interpret Christian truth in innocuous terms, then covering one's tracks.

Kierkegaard understands only too well what the Enlightenment represents; with part of himself he had lived it. Modernity must influence how Christianity is cast, most notably in the insistence that the self is not a nothing but must be held to come into its own. In the early authorship he will think through the challenge that these developments pose to inherited belief in the spheres of ethics, epistemology and biological–scientific discovery, and thus also how Christian claims should be positioned. Kierkegaard is after all a highly educated intellectual, one who takes Kant, Hegel, Schleiermacher, Feuerbach, indeed early biblical scholarship (though he doesn't want to be bothered with it) so seriously that he must mount a radical (and thus in some sense novel) response. Christianity can no longer find the 'fit' with culture it had previously enjoyed. Very well then it must return to its pristine roots, proclaiming its Truth in the face of the truths of the world. But to do this within the modern age slants Christianity differently. Kierkegaard's theology acquires an edge. The Christian can only relate to Christian claims through faith; reason is unavailable. Kierkegaard sets out options in all their stark contrast, inviting his reader to 'choose'. It is precisely this that makes the debate with him so invigorating. One cannot in this manner enter into dialogue with a Karl Barth, taking up a position within his own thought system, for Barth's (totalitarian) theology allows of none.

It is in the *Postscript* that the existential scenario as to what it means to be a human being who lives *coram deo* and more specifically who is Christian, is played out in all its excruciating convolutions. On one level the book is bizarre, for no one could live as does our individual. It could be reckoned an anti-Hegelian farce. Of Kierkegaard's major works the *Postscript* is perhaps the most humorous. But it is also deadly serious, calculated to alert and provoke. The stringent demands of the God-relationship are in danger of becoming lost. If the book concerns 'becoming' a Christian, this is not to be confused with the Catholic understanding of life as a *via* consisting in sanctification. The 'becoming' is a coming to recognize what is involved in being Christian; and, in the book's last fifty pages, the leap is portrayed. Faith is pitted against reason. The way is so 'inward' that our individual whose horizon is the idea of eternal life goes about his business as does every other. The finite is strictly incommensurate for the infinite. Yet this lodestone from beyond the world qualifies the things of the world as a mere meanwhile. Kierkegaard's position represents a ratcheting up of Lutheran faith to a kind of absurdity in the fight against Hegelianism. One wonders if it may not also reflect conflict or uncertainty within he himself. But it was above all this book that became a resource for a new genre of philosophical writing, predicated upon an acute awareness of the turmoil of human dispositions called forth by the task of living: existentialism. Kierkegaard's discussion of human subjectivity was to prove seminal.

Subsequent to the *Postscript* the authorship changes in character. Kierkegaard appears to close down on the questions he has posed. The quest has led to a hair-raising predicament in which one cannot realistically survive as a Christian and human being. As the fashion for Hegelianism recedes, the debate with Hegel seems less urgent. Kierkegaard's circumstances become more difficult: he senses he may not have long to live and (through his mistaken purchase of government bonds during the conflict over Schleswig-Holstein) his finances are seriously depleted. Kierkegaard has a profound need to 'find' himself, to come into his own in relation to his God. Going through various 'conversion' experiences, *de rigueur* in his society, he finds some peace. Thus the strengths of the later authorship are quite other. In *Love's Deeds* Kierkegaard writes a stunningly wise upbuilding discourse. *Sickness Unto Death* envisages what it would mean to be all of a piece—in the second half with its inherent radicality in view of Christological presuppositions. A passage in *Practice in Christianity* brings to a new level Kierkegaard's conception of what it is to stand in the light of God's love as one is drawn to God. That book rounds out the major authorship, seamlessly interweaving Kierkegaard's Christological position with the demands of discipleship. In the final months, in the face of a church and society that have lost all sense of the cost of that discipleship, conceiving of himself as a martyr/ witness Kierkegaard in a final fling of energy mounts a frontal attack.

Our estimate of Kierkegaard must be that, even judged by the standards of his day, he was in many respects conservative. Yet his conservatism had a radical edge, making it interesting rather than complacent. Such a position was fuelled by his reading of scripture and his uncomplicated conviction that earthly matters should be subordinated to that of the individual's relation to God. This conservatism can be traced through differing fields: his lack of interest in biblical scholarship, his political opinions, his estimation of the march of 'science', and his view of the relationship that should pertain between the sexes.

It will be good to commence with the last of these, for it is not incidentally related to Kierkegaard's theology. The axis of his thought, personally and theologically, is the father–son relationship. This is taken for granted in theological thought to an extent that it tends to pass unnoticed. In Kierkegaard's case it determines the whole tenor of the authorship. Kierkegaard's God is a transcendent if (ultimately) loving father. God is the beyond, the other. As may be the case in Lutheran Protestantism more widely (it is notably so of Luther himself), that which men count 'motherly' is built into the image of the Father God (unlike in Catholicism where it finds instantiation in a lesser and female figure).[11] This dominance of the male correlates with Kierkegaard's home background. What we know of his parents' relationship is that, within months of his first wife's death, the father had seduced a distant relative working as a servant-girl in the household and, upon her becoming pregnant, taken her to wife. The wedding contract was unusual, the limited rights that she was granted betraying that he held her a social inferior. She was to be the mother of his seven children, the youngest of whom, Søren Aabye, was the apple of his father's eye. Kierkegaard was apparently cut up by his mother's death. We know this—interestingly—through the report of Martensen's mother, whom Kierkegaard would visit during her son's long sojourn abroad, doubtless to ask after his former tutor and to keep her company.[12] Nevertheless it must be a cause for astonishment that, throughout thousands of pages, including *Journals* to which Kierkegaard confides his thoughts, there is not a single mention of the mother. How come? The relationship can hardly have been incidental.

Furthermore Kierkegaard's portrayal of his relation to Regine is significant here. With considerable insight he was to write: 'My engagement to her and the breaking of it is really my relationship

[11] For my further thoughts on this see my 'The Sacred, The Feminine and French Feminist Theory', in Griselda Pollock & Victoria Turvey Sauron, eds, *The Sacred and the Feminine: Imagination and Sexual Difference* (London, 2007), 61–74.

[12] Cf. Jørgen Bukdahl, *Søren Kierkegaard and the Common Man* (1961), trans. Bruce Kirmmse (Grand Rapids, MI, 2001), 47.

to God, if I may dare say so.'[13] And again: 'That I was cruel is true; that I, thinking myself committed to a higher relationship...had to be so...is a certainty.'[14] Late in the authorship, in *The Sickness Unto Death*, Kierkegaard will employ what for a Protestant writer is markedly erotic language to convey the human relation to God: 'A believer...is a lover;...as a matter of fact, when it comes to enthusiasm, the most rapturous lover of all lovers is but a stripling compared with a believer' (*SuD*, 103). The passage is provocative as to the intensity of Kierkegaard's love affair with his God. It may well be that (however lonely he at times found himself) Kierkegaard believed himself to have a vocation to celibacy; in effect he tells us as much. But it was also a question of the demands of his work, which in itself constituted a calling. That he loved Regine is not in doubt; that he made her into his muse may well be the case.

In his designation of the 'place' of women Kierkegaard was conservative. The first writing of his we possess is a speech at a student debate lampooning the idea of women's suffrage.[15] Yet there are few theologians who grasp as does he that, whether on account of nature or nurture, women and men think and react differently; have different 'sins'. In Kierkegaard's world there are two sexes, not one. His depiction of woman can be horrific (though in this he stands in a well-worn philosophical tradition, stretching from Aristotle to Sartre, which has judged woman 'incomplete'). At other times one may think his comments exactly *apropos*. At an early date, in *Either/Or*, Kierkegaard has Judge William say, in a remark both observant and bombastic: 'A woman comprehends the finite; she understands it from the ground up...She is in harmony with existence as no man can or ought to be....Woman explains the finite; man pursues the infinite...She is nature's mistress' (*E/O* II, 311, 313). As he became older and more infirm, or more isolated, Kierkegaard became in this regard more extreme; there are passages that are frankly a perverse misogyny. Yet it is no simple story, for in his personal relations with

---

[13] Walter Lowrie, *A Short Life of Kierkegaard* (Princeton, NJ, 1970), 147.

[14] H. Rosenmeier, ed. & trans., *Kierkegaard: Letters and Documents* [vol. xxv, *Kierkegaard's Writings*] (Princeton, NJ, 2009), no. 239, p. 334.

[15] See his supercilious comments 'Another Defence of Woman's Great Abilities', in Julia Watkin, ed. & trans., *Early Polemical Writings* (Princeton, NJ, 1990), 3–5.

women Kierkegaard seems to have treated them of whatever class with respect.

Politically too Kierkegaard was conservative. Again, however, it is a complex picture. He had no time for the widespread yearning that came to the fore in 1848 that, acting collectively, humanity might better its lot. He is fearful of the plank being pulled out from under a monarchical constitution, judging that all hell will be let loose. He can be dismissive of the populace. Kierkegaard writes:

Even the art of printing is an almost satirical discovery, for since when, oh God, have there been so many people with something to say. The result of that tremendous discovery has simply been to disseminate all the twaddle which would otherwise have died at birth.[16]

There is always the thought that, were the concept of equality to take root, what would become of the (unequal) relation to God, to whom one must submit in obedience. Yet theoretically and also in practice Kierkegaard knew that one must care for the poor as individuals. The son of a *nouveau riche* family, it is possible that Kierkegaard saw himself as an outsider, an interloper, into educated society. This would explain his ready critique of the pretentiousness of his social equals. If pilloried in the popular press and sensing himself misunderstood, it is also true that Kierkegaard was not always open to modernity. Fascinated by trains and the new steam omnibuses, there was a level at which he didn't much like the march of history. The quest for 'progress', social and scientific, was diverting humanity from what should concern persons, their relationship to God.

In his response to the scientific advances of his day Kierkegaard was a Luddite. But here again it is not that he holds arcane views for the sake of obtuseness; rather he fears that, through a mistaken obsession, men will be distracted from cultivating their higher destiny. Given that the study of the natural world does not lead to God in Christ, its investigation must be sheer dilettantism. Kierkegaard writes:

Almost everything that flourishes nowadays under the name of science (particularly natural science) is not science at all but curiosity. —*In the end all corruption will come from the natural sciences...*

[16] Dru, no. 617 (1846).

That a man should simply and profoundly say that he cannot understand how consciousness comes into existence—is perfectly natural. But that a man should glue his eye to a microscope and stare and stare and stare—and still not be able to see how it happens—is ridiculous. . . . Looked upon as an amusement, as a way of killing time, the discovery of the microscope is reasonable enough, but to take it seriously is utterly stupid. . . .

If God were to go about with a stick in his hand things would go particularly hard with all those solemn people who make discoveries with the help of the microscope.[17]

For Kierkegaard: 'The confusion lies in the fact that it is never dialectically clear what is what, how philosophy is to make use of natural science'.[18] Kierkegaard could not envisage that scientific developments might lead to paradigm shifts that would threaten the theological world he knew. Or perhaps, with part of himself, he suspected that they could—and this fuelled his contempt.

Kierkegaard was of course apprised of the dawning biblical textual criticism and historical contextualization of the sacred documents, attempting through his writing to immunize faith to its implications. It seems he was agitated by and dismissive of such work, wishing not to look into it too closely; one suspects because it might pull the rug out from under his fixed convictions, entered into through faith. Expounding on his investigative work into the historical origins of biblical documents on the walks they took together, Brøchner found it well nigh impossible to engage Kierkegaard's interest. Kierkegaard had reached an a priori conviction that such questions were beside the point. However we should note that, in the case of the creation story, following Kant, Hegel, Schleiermacher, and others, Kierkegaard is fully prepared, while keeping a historical dimension, to treat it as an insightful myth; besides which such a stance fitted his sense of the existential individuality of each as responsible for his or her own conduct. What Kierkegaard actually believed of 'Adam' is unclear. Was he evading thoughts to which it would have been too dangerous to allow entrance?

I wish then to turn to a large subject that I have often pondered as I considered the disparity between my own outlook and that of

---

[17] Dru, no. 617 (*Pap.* VII A 186, 1846).
[18] Dru, no. 619 (*Pap.* VII¹ A 200).

Kierkegaard. What is it that has changed, what tectonic plates shifted, so that I should come to such radically different conclusions than he? For in terms of the elapse of time, as compared with the long evolution of human society it is but the blink of an eye. My own father's life overlapped with that of Regine by some six years. The consideration is the more interesting for the fact that Kierkegaard lived this side of the watershed that the Enlightenment and Romanticism represent. The major challenges to Christianity that affect my own thinking—the work of Kant, Hegel, Schleiermacher, and Feuerbach—were already on the scene and Kierkegaard was well apprised of this body of thought. Indeed, his authorship can be read as a response to the crisis that modernity represented for Christianity. Is it simply a case of further quantitative changes leading to a qualitative shift in outlook, not only in my case but in that of the majority of Europeans living today? I shall consider in brief the worlds of biblical criticism, scientific advance, and social and cultural change.

Shortly after Kierkegaard's time, in late 19th-century Germany, rapid advances were made in gaining a sense for the historicity of the biblical documents. One would have hoped that Kierkegaard, an otherwise intelligent man, would not have remained unaffected by what transpired (though this aspiration may be naïve in view of Barth's magnificent endeavour to enable theology to pull the ladder up after it). As we have discussed, Kierkegaard writes as though the reported speech of Jesus came from the lips of one who self-consciously knew himself God. His measure of Christianity is the Chalcedonian formula; a statement conceived by men who axiomatically took this to be the case. It must make some difference if one cannot think the historical Jesus to have proclaimed himself the Son of God. Overwhelmingly today scholars do not think the picture of Christ we find in John's gospel, the basis for Kierkegaard's account of him as the Teacher of *Philosophical Fragments*, could have been written by the beloved disciple or be of an early date. Jesus did not stand there and challenge his contemporaries to believe that here was God incarnate; that is a later handling of the material. The dawning recognition of this during the 19th century, culminating in Bultmann's famous statement in his *Jesus* of 1926 that, of the mind of Jesus, we could know nothing, must kick away the presuppositions on which Kierkegaard's Paradox rests.

Consider by way of comparison with Kierkegaard the life and work of Albert Schweitzer, living as he did after this advance in German critical scholarship. Like Kierkegaard, Schweitzer strove to be a faithful disciple of Christ (however different in temperament the two men might be). Schweitzer published in 1906 a book in which he attempted to estimate the import of biblical scholarship: *Von Reimarus zu Wrede: Geschichte der Leben-Jesu-Forschung* (*From Reimarus to Wrede: the history of Life-of-Jesus-Research*—the book translated into English as *The Quest of the Historical Jesus*). Reputedly, Schweitzer made heaps of books on his floor tracing the course of this quest, fearful lest in her cleaning his landlady should disturb them, as Archimedes for his circles. In pursuing the train of research, Schweitzer could not induce it to come out at a point such as he might have wished. What does he do? Bringing the book to a conclusion on a note of resignation, he appends in the final lines the thought that those who are prepared to work, struggle, and suffer will, 'as an unspeakable secret, come to experience who he is...'[19] The dots in the original German are removed in the English translation, substituting an apparently triumphal ending for one full of mystery. The academic endeavour failing to deliver the goods, Schweitzer exits for Lambarene to live in practice the life of discipleship. One might say that this was also Kierkegaard's stance in his final years. But in his case the kernel of the matter, that for which he contends, is the Chalcedonian formula.

The question as to the import of scientific advance is extraordinarily complex. If Kierkegaard failed to take on board the implications of the shift of paradigm that was coming, it must be said that so too have the overwhelming majority of theologians, who still today speak as though little has changed. In Kierkegaard's day Hegel had presented a system in which reality was all of a piece; which did not allow of a disjuncture between this world and a more ultimate 'reality' set over against it. Kierkegaard thought Hegel determinist (though a monistic system need not be) and undermining of individual responsibility (though again, such a world-view need imply nothing of the sort). But, crucially, he knew that this was not Christianity, neither in its Jewish background nor its Greek formulation. Here one must

[19] Albert Schweitzer, *Von Reimarus zu Wrede: Eine Geschichte der Leben-Jesu-Forschung* (Tübingen, 1906), 401.

express oneself carefully, for Kierkegaard was a deal more sophisti-
cated than many a conservative Christian scholar: his God (I have
tried to suggest) is by no means simply an anthropomorphically
conceived 'Other' set on high. What he knows is that we have no
language for God: his God is, one might say, radically other. Kierkegaard's position is diametrically opposed to belief in any *analogia
entis* between God and humanity, in this at one with his Lutheran
heritage. Yet for all the riders one may wish to make, Kierkegaard has
to posit as a corollary of revelation that 'that which is God' is not of
this world but set in apposition to it. This is a presupposition of the
Judaeo-Christian tradition.

Given what we have now come to recognize this whole paradigm is
cast in doubt. We have advanced beyond the microscopes Kierkegaard suspected to a new mathematical model in which space and
time are inter-changeable; indeed, in which there is no one point
from which one could 'measure' all else, such that the universe could
be held to have an 'edge' or time a 'beginning'. The theological
understanding inherited from ancient times in which 'God' is somehow 'outside' or 'before' no longer makes sense; the world of the
Creeds in which Christ is 'begotten not made', through whom all
things are made, in which eternity is juxtaposed with time and Christ
in consequence a Paradox. If we are to pursue the theological endeavour we must needs undergo a quite fundamental revolution of which
Kierkegaard could have had no inkling. It is from this perspective that
one has to say (though one may reject his particular formulation)
that it was Hegel who stood on the side of the future and Kierkegaard
who belonged to the past. Of course such a recognition is not
dependent on scientific advance. Long before our current knowledge
Friedrich Nietzsche wrote his history of the demise of Platonism:
'How the "Real World" At Last Became a Myth'.[20] While Kierkegaard's understanding of 'God the Father' was sophisticatedly
nuanced, it is still the case that on account of his crediting of the
possibility of particular revelation, he was perforce on the wrong side.

The ethical and cultural changes that have occurred place a different kind of question mark against what Kierkegaard would say. We
have already raised the question of the difficulty for the Abrahamic

---

[20] 'How the "Real World" At Last Became a Myth: History of an Error', *Twilight
of the Idols*, trans. R. J. Hollingdale (London, 1990) [1889], 50–1.

religions of accommodating the moral imperative of women's equality. But this is part of a wider scenario in which the normativity of male, white, Eurocentric thought is coming to be relativized. Of course it could be said that, in taking on the form of a semitic male in the 1st century AD, God in Christ took on what it is to be human, which includes us all. I have suggested that, in that it believed particular instances exemplifications of a universal, the ancient world had at its disposal a thought-form which allowed of a more inclusive Christology than has been possible since the rise of Nominalism. But there are problems here. In formulating his Christology, Kierkegaard fails to take advantage of the possibilities of real universals. Why so? We may presume that neither he nor his contemporaries would have been able get their minds around such thinking. Further, even given the possibilities of real universals, there is a sense in which one race and more particularly one gender (for *sex* is the great *division* of humanity, the Latin 'se' root connoting to divide or cut) can never include or represent the other. If in our age we have come to honour eclecticism as the new moral imperative, this must minimally place a question mark against Christology. After all, the consequences of the fact that metaphorically God has been seen in terms of one sex to the exclusion of the other have scarcely been insignificant.

Furthermore, since the Enlightenment it has become an ethical question as to whether one should stand in a heteronomous relation to anyone else (or to God). This was an issue that notably Kant raised as pertaining to human maturity. Wholly logically Kant's 'Christ' is the 'new man' (one's new self), who (symbolically) takes full responsibility for one's conduct.[21] It would for him be less than edifying that an (external) saviour should atone for one. It is a conundrum of which Kierkegaard is fully aware; confronting in his *Fear and Trembling* Kant's ruling out of a heteronomous relation to any supposed revelation as unethical. Subsequent to the Enlightenment it has for many become just such an ethical a priori that one's own moral judgement should take precedence. If there is an undecidability about *Fear and Trembling*, Kierkegaard's emphasis on obedience to God, as he conceives of God, must make that conception profoundly problematic for many today. One assumes that his response would be that, warped as is the human

[21] Immanuel Kant, *Religion Within the Limits of Reason Alone*, trans. Theodore M. Greene & Hoyt H. Hudson (New York, 1960), 68–9. See p. 51.

will, human beings of their own accord are unable to make ultimate choices.[22] But this in itself implies an attack on and disparagement of human integrity that many would find unacceptable.

Kierkegaard had evidently taken cognisance of Feuerbach's position; indeed there is reason to think it may have triggered his writing of *Philosophical Fragments* as a counter-statement. He could not however foresee how the projection thesis would develop, or what might allow it to accrue plausibility. It was to take varying forms in the work of Marx, Nietzsche, and Sigmund Freud. Most recently feminist analysis has given it another twist, charging that the Judaeo-Christian myth is a projection of the male subconscious, calculated to justify male hegemony.[23] What has undergirded the rise of the suspicion as to projection is social change; something of which Kierkegaard was perspicacious enough to be wary. At least within the Continent to which both he and I belong, the demise of a hierarchical society has brought in its train a mind-set in which the concept of a transcendent God strikes the majority of people as neither plausible nor desirable. Quite apart from the onset of secularity, the fact that this God has been cast in male terms has served to make many women judge this 'God' not for them. Kierkegaard suspected that this belief in transcendence was not where woman was—and he despised her for it. Did it—one wonders—ever occur to him that she might cast her spirituality in quite other terms? It is such questioning that one should bring to the authorship, not the essentially inconsequential matter as to whether Kierkegaard was personally nice to women.

There is then much that one might embark upon in an imagined conversation with Kierkegaard; matters that for the most part Kierkegaard scholars have been unwilling to concede or which appear not to register on their radar.

In what respects, by contrast, has Kierkegaard made a lasting contribution, undimmed by time? I believe that what above all remain prescient today are his theological paradigm for the structure

---

[22] This is of course a complex matter. Luther never suggests that in regard to earthly matters (an occupation or spouse) a human being lacks freewill, remarking 'God did not make heaven for geese' (*WA* 18.636.21–2).

[23] See for example the work of Luce Irigaray, which is deeply Feuerbachian.

of the self, his astute pastoral insights, and not least (though least recognized) his conceptualization of the nature of God.

In his conception of the self, Kierkegaard comes straight out of the Lutheran tradition, but he significantly modifies his heritage that his understanding may accord with a requirement not present in a pre-Enlightenment world. In casting aside Aristotelian ways of thinking in favour of a self understood as an acting agent, constituted by its relations, Luther had indeed been innovative.[24] It is no chance that it was out of this tradition that in Hegel there arose a conception of a reflexive self that relates to itself in response to the other. What is significant about Luther's thinking is that there is no constant self; rather must one in the moment once and again take that step of trust which is faith, for it is in God who is other than the self that the self is grounded. Kierkegaard builds on this legacy. Holding in common with Luther that the self can only be itself as (to employ his vocabulary) it 'rests transparently in God', he knows he must also speak of the self as coming into its own. This must (presumably) stand in tension with the willingness to give way on one's autonomy that we have just discussed. In the passage in *Practice in Christianity* that, in respect to his understanding of the self forms the climax of his author-ship, Kierkegaard advances a model whereby the self progressively comes 'to' itself as it is drawn to God, on whom it is yet dependent.

Of Kierkegaard's pastoral acumen little more need be said. *Love's Deeds* (among works that we have here considered) speaks for itself. There is a wealth of pastoral wisdom present in Kierkegaard's edifying discourses, as also scattered throughout the pseudonymous author-ship. Whatever judgement one may form of his theology, in this body of work the man's sheer humanity shines through. One may assume it is on this account that Kierkegaard's opus is received with gratitude by many who do not subscribe to his theology. One may also com-ment that (with the notable exception of Martensen, a vein of hatred for whom runs through the authorship, marring it) Kierkegaard did not allow his theoretical, theological position to colour his relations to others. In an autobiographical piece penned in 1850, 'My Position as a Religious Writer in "Christendom" and my Tactics', he com-ments: 'I have never fought in such a way as to say: I am the true

---

[24] Cf. p. 222.

Christian, others are not Christians.... I have attacked no one as not being a Christian, I have condemned no one.' And he continues by remarking that Johannes Climacus (the pseudonymous author of *Fragments* and *Postscript*), denying that he is a Christian concedes this claim to others, 'the remotest possible remove, surely, from condemning others!'[25]

Theologically, though primarily thinking in terms of God's transcendence, Kierkegaard is far from simply holding God to be some anthropomorphic, numinous being, set over-against humanity. God is for him 'other' in a sense that we cannot quite conceive. As a Lutheran and post-Kantian, Kierkegaard never speaks as though, extrapolating from ourselves, we could somehow divine the nature of God. In what are tantalizing remarks, in *Love's Deeds* as we have considered he goes so far as to suggest that God becomes for us what we are for others. To have been able to engage Kierkegaard as to how he conceived of God must then be one of the more interesting conversations one could have had. For despite these considerations he did in his prayer-life turn to one, 'God', whom by analogy he considered a 'father'. Indeed he could write: 'My father died—and I got another in his stead: God in Heaven—and then I found out that, essentially, my first father had been my stepfather and only unessentially my first father.'[26] Perhaps this greater literalism belongs to the life of prayer, a different exercise than theological consideration as to what God may be. But how, we may ask, if one is to hold a conception of God commensurate with the shifts in understanding that have taken place—so necessary if one is to be all of a piece—could one today persist with such vocabulary?

What is creative about Kierkegaard's concept of God owes to his Lutheran heritage. Unlike either Reformed or Catholic Christianity, which in this respect may be more akin to one another than to Lutheran thought, this latter is disinclined to consider God in abstraction from the human self. This is true not simply of Luther

[25] Walter Lowrie, trans., 'My Position as a Religious Writer in "Christendom" and my Strategy', Nov 1850, 153 (*PV*, 15), Supplement to 'My Activity', *Point of View*.
[26] Peter Rohde, ed., *The Diary of Søren Kierkegaard* (New York, 1960), 45 (1845). (No further reference given.)

but of diverse figures; including, in the 20th century, those not uninfluenced by neo-Orthodoxy, as Bultmann (who commences from the human condition), or Bonhoeffer (who speaks of Christ as ontologically in his very form *pro nobis*).[27] In this has always lain the danger for this tradition, for could it not be that God is but a projection of the human imagination? It was Lutheranism that spawned Feuerbach, son of a Lutheran manse; as before him it was also Kant's and Hegel's context. Nietzsche likewise was the son of a Lutheran pastor, his mother a pastor's daughter. Of course the counter to this is that Lutherans have ever believed in the revelation of a transcendent God; it is the proclamation of the unexpected message of the gospel on which the whole turns. Kierkegaard attempts to hold together a phenomenological starting point and a revelation grasped in faith which will secure Christian belief against the reductionist charge of subjectivity.

However, when all is said and done the overwhelming significance of Kierkegaard's work must surely lie in the clarity with which he articulated what it is in which Christian claims consist; furthermore, what it must mean for a human life to relate to such a 'truth'. Kierkegaard himself judged that it was in this that his life's work essentially consisted, his mission to make evident—in the midst of modernity—what it was that Christianity claimed: no more and no less. As he writes: 'The only analogy I have before me is Socrates. My task is a Socratic task, to revise the definition of what it is to be a Christian.'[28] And again:

No, my contention has been this: I know what Christianity is, my imperfection as a Christian I myself fully recognize—but I know what Christianity is. And to get this properly recognized must be, I should think, to every man's interest, whether he be a Christian or not, whether his intention is to accept Christianity or to reject it.[29]

---

[27] See p. 215.

[28] *Kierkegaard's Attack upon Christendom*, ed. & trans. W. Lowrie (Princeton, NJ, 1968), 283. Cf. John Heywood Thomas: 'The only analogy I have for myself is Socrates; my task is a Socratic task, to reach the concept of what it is to be a Christian.' ('Kierkegaard's Alternative Metaphysical Theology', *History of European Ideas*, 12 (1990), 57).

[29] Lowrie, 'My Position', 153; (*PV*, 15).

And yet again: 'I depict what Christianity is; I am unusually well qualified to do that and quite literally understand it to be my calling.'[30] In respect to his stated intent Kierkegaard's success, in the opinion of the present author, may be judged to be without parallel. It is in this that his seminal importance lies.

In view of this an interesting question arises pertaining to whether any distinction is to be made between Kierkegaard's 'experiments in thought' and what may have been his own sentiments. Holding in the pseudonymous works to the logical conclusion that those who willingly deny the Paradox cannot enter into eternal life, there is some indication that speaking personally his attitude was other. Shortly after Mynster's death in 1854 Kierkegaard writes in his *Journal*:

What the old bishop once said to me is not true—namely, that I spoke as if the others were going to hell. No, if I can be said to speak at all of going to hell then I say something like this: If the others are going to hell, then I am going along with them. But I do not believe that; on the contrary, I believe that we will all be saved and this awakens my deepest wonder.[31]

If this is what Kierkegaard most truly thought one may be thankful. Nevertheless, given what had been a constant theme of the authorship, Mynster may surely be exonerated from blame for having come to the conclusion that he had. Kierkegaard's comment must seem like a volte-face in view of his Christological writings. If the necessity of adherence to the truth of the Paradox is not their *telos*, then what do these books concern? Kierkegaard did not appear to be making a merely theoretical point. Or, if the thoughts committed to his *Journal* were really his opinion, why conduct (and with such ferocity) the campaign that he had?

How one might reconcile this disparity is an interesting question. Of accepting Christianity, Kierkegaard writes in *Practice in Christianity* (though one senses that this thought could have found expression at any stage of the authorship) that 'only the consciousness of sin can force one, if I dare put it that way... into this horror' (*PC*, 67–8). Was it that Kierkegaard's sense of guilt seemed to him to necessitate

[30] Quoted by Marie Mikulová Thulstrup, 'His Self-Understanding as a Christian', in Marie Mikulová Thulstrup & Nils Thulstrup, eds, *Kierkegaard as a Person* [vol 12, *Bibliotheca Kierkegaardiana*] (Copenhagen, 1983), 166. (She gives: *JP* 6:649 (*Pap.* X² A 45) but this is incorrect.)
[31] *JP* 6:6947 (*Pap.* XI³ B 57), n.d., 1854.

Christian belief, while on other counts he was disturbed by its implications? Faith becomes a desperate remedy for a desperate illness: sin. Kierkegaard appears unable to live without an utter conviction as to his deliverance. It is remarkable then that he so clearly admired Lessing, it would seem for his balance, sagacity, and ability to live without answers. Kierkegaard writes in 1841 'My doubt is terrible. —Nothing can withstand it—it is a cursed hunger and I can swallow up every argument, every consolation and sedative—I rush at 10,000 miles a second through every obstacle.'[32] And later in 1846: '*Ethics and religion are the only certainties.* They say: Thou shalt believe.'[33] These comments are thought-provoking. For those living in the age of early Dickens life was precarious, with a lack of any kind of social security or decent medical knowledge. Yet today most of us live without religious certainty or any belief at all in eternal life. Perhaps humankind can only deal with so much insecurity?

Kierkegaard shows with startling clarity in the spheres of both epistemology and ethics that Christian claims are not to be assimilated to reason, humanistic ethics, or modernity. As he rightly said, either the moment in history is of significance; in which case all that we thought we knew from modern science, or which derives from the conscience of the natural man, is to be overturned. Or else the moment doesn't exist; in which case there is no reason to depart from what we should otherwise have reason to think. Nature and history are each and together a (presumably non-determinative) causal nexus, while we may have an ethic which (as Kant believed) is grounded in an inextirpable conscience or (as Hegel suggested) brought about through human socialization. As my erstwhile teacher Arthur McGill was wont to put it: 'Either Christ is everything or nothing.' Where Kierkegaard is perfectly correct is in grasping that if Christ be anything, he is everything. To deify a mere mortal, who becomes immediately knowable as 'God', is paganism. Though the context within which Kierkegaard struggled with the way in which an assimilation of Christian claims to human thought had been attempted was that of Hegelianism, what he has to say is of much wider application. Would that the church in our day, as also in Kierkegaard's,

---

[32] Dru, no. 354 (*Pap.* III A 103), 1841.
[33] Dru, no. 617, p. 184 (*Pap.* VII A 186), 1846. Cf. p. 171.

would recognize what it is that it must proclaim if is it is to remain Christian; if indeed there be anything to proclaim.

To embark on a project of thought. Suppose Kierkegaard is correct that, in one particular human, the eternal entered time. What are the implications? That there has in history occurred an unthinkable particularity. Kierkegaard knew Christianity to be predicated on this particularity; it forms the basis of his authorship. What makes dialogue difficult is that he did not quite see this for the impossibility that it is. His concern centres on the issue as to how the eternal could enter time, such that a contingent historical event could be the absolute (a problem he had inherited, mediated through 18th-century philosophy, from the ancient world). This obscured for him the problematic claim to particularity *per se*. Moreover, lacking a sense for the predictability of nature, his understanding of causation is medieval rather than modern: he discerns God as directly behind all events, such that just about anything is possible. Of course one of Kierkegaard's disposition may respond that God is 'other than' and 'enters into' our reality. But today such talk, as though there were an 'outside', may not make sense even metaphorically. To avoid the scandal of particularity one could take a universalist route, such that it is through 'the cosmic Christ' that creation takes place and in whom all will find salvation; a line of defence of which Kierkegaard with his stress on incarnation would not have wanted to avail himself. But in this case there is no end to the realms of speculation in which we are caught up. And indeed, we are returned both to the question as to what sense it could make to say of Christ that he somehow exists 'outside' space and time and also that as to the unity of Christ's person. Given the choices, what can it mean to have faith in Christological propositions?

It is a dialogue on this scale that one must undertake with Kierkegaard, involving nothing less than the question as to whether Christianity is epistemologically valid and morally acceptable. Standing at the tipping point of the scales when the myth that for 2,000 years had encompassed humanity was found wanting, Kierkegaard saw the issues with a perspicacity which was unmatched. Perforce a man of his time, if also in some respects behind his time, he struggled with the issues within the framework that they presented themselves to him. It is however not difficult to cast the dilemmas that he saw in somewhat other and indeed heightened terms. On that account his thought remains pertinent to questions as to the truth and efficacy of Christianity today. Kierkegaard regretted that there was, as he put it, not a single mother's soul with whom he could converse on the matters with which he wrestled. The present book represents, not least, an attempt across the decades to enter into such a conversation. If at this point in history we are to desert our Christian past, while it is to be hoped retain some form of spirituality, there is much to consider as to what that can mean. I would suggest that, perhaps surprisingly, in some of Kierkegaard's thinking as to what it is that we might understand by God he can contribute here. But the primary gift of the authorship is the way in which it allows one to think through the contentions and implications of Christianity, and according to our lights to choose.

Kierkegaard's own estimate of his authorship is striking. Cutting himself free from the world's chatter and meeting with scant response from his contemporaries, he had stood toiling at his desk. He was thought eccentric, his publications frequently remaindered. As he remarked:

This is how I actually am treated in Copenhagen. I am regarded as a kind of Englishman, a half-mad eccentric...My literary activity, that enormous productivity, so intense it seems it must move stones....: that literary activity is regarded as a sort of hobby [like] fishing and such...I do not receive the support of a single word from reviews and the like.[34]

Few, he felt, grasped the import of his authorship, yet rightly judging its importance he persisted. To the *Point of View* he confided:

Should it prove that the present age will not understand me—very well then, I belong to history, knowing assuredly that I shall find a place there and what place it will be. Humble as I am before God, I also know this...that (in respect to genius) extraordinary gifts were bestowed upon me...What may betide me in the immediate future I know not; how it will be in the following age when I have passed into history, that I know.... Suppose that, if I should live longer, time will deprive me of all, and suppose that the following age will make the fullest reparation—how can that really harm me, or how can it profit? The former does not harm me if I merely take care to be absent, and

[34] JP 6254 (*Pap.* IX A 288).

the latter will not profit me, since then I shall have become in the solemn sense of the word an 'absent one'.[35]

And again (in none too modest a judgement): 'As for what importance I have as an author, I feel history will testify that it is a turning-point in the world, and moreover that something exceptional has been achieved: this I know, truly without bombast.' Adding however in despair: 'But my contemporaries would not accept my achievement. My writings were not read—on the contrary the market-town took delight in depicting and mocking me.'[36]

If not a turning-point in the world, one must think Kierkegaard's influence has been more far-reaching than he could ever have imagined. What is striking is the diversity of the movements of thought that would claim him as their own. Yet this stems from the eclectic nature of this extraordinary authorship. In the 20th century Kierkegaard was to be seen as the progenitor alike of Barthian neo-orthodoxy (dialectical theology) and of atheistic existentialism; more recently he has been adopted by post-modernists. Influential in the world of Christianity as befits such an authorship, his work has met with a resonance in much wider circles. What such people have admired is Kierkegaard's plumbing of the depths of the human spirit. In the 20th century as I have mentioned such widely disparate figures as Karl Barth, Martin Heidegger, Jean-Paul Sartre, and Reinhold Niebuhr acknowledged their debt. Ludwig Wittgenstein apparently simply remarked: 'Kierkegaard was by far the most profound thinker of the last century. Kierkegaard was a saint.'[37]

Saintly or not, Kierkegaard continues to delight and fascinate his readers. In the 1980s the present writer was seriously told by the philosophy and religion editor of a major publisher that there was no call for an introductory book on Kierkegaard. But of recent years there has been a renaissance in Kierkegaard studies. As may be the case with every great thinker, each generation finds its concerns mirrored in his. No one can truly open up Kierkegaard for others, for each brings her or his own questions to the authorship. As one

---

[35] 'Epilogue', 'Point of View', 99 (PV, 94–5).
[36] Hannay, 487–8 (Pap. X^2 A 623).
[37] In conversation with M. O'C. Drury. M. O'C. Drury, 'Some Notes on Conversations with Wittgenstein', Acta Philosophica Fennica, 28, nos 1–3 (Amsterdam, 1976).

whose journey Kierkegaard has accompanied now for over four decades, I must hope that this book will enable some to gain purchase on his writing. The nicest comment I have received on the book came from a Kierkegaard scholar who remarked: 'I think Kierkegaard would have liked it, if I may say so'. Personally I think he would have been amazed and horrified in equal measure! But be that as it may. What alone is of consequence is that my portrayal of Kierkegaard's work is such that he would have recognized it. Furthermore, that as we celebrate the bicentenary of his birth, I have succeeded in articulating the questions we should be posing to the authorship today. For Kierkegaard should be read not out of reverence to a memory but as a living presence, enabling us each to consider where we stand. It was precisely for such a reader that he wrote.

Further Reading

The emphasis here is on articles or shorter pieces which can usefully follow on from reading the present work. The siglum (sigla) *for the Kierkegaard book (or books) or the topic considered in this present work for which the item cited would be particularly relevant has (or have) been placed in parentheses after the item.*

Agacinski, Sylviane, 'We are Not Sublime: Love and Sacrifice, Abraham and Ourselves', in Jane Chamberlain & Jonathan Rée, eds, *Kierkegaard: A Critical Reader* (Oxford, 1998, 129–50) (*FT, LD*).

Andic, Martin, 'Is Love of Neighbour the Love of an Individual', in George Pattison & Steven Shakespeare, eds, *Kierkegaard: The Self in Society* (Basingstoke, 1998), 112–24; alternatively 'Love's Redoubling and the Eternal Like for Like', in *IKC LD* (Macon, GA, 1999), 9–38 (*LD*).

Butler, Judith, 'Kierkegaard's Speculative Despair', in R. C. Solomon & K. M. Higgins, eds, *The Age of German Idealism* [vol. 6 of *Routledge History of Philosophy*] (London, 1993), 363–95 (*FT, CUP, SuD*).

Bukdahl, Jørgen, *Søren Kierkegaard and the Common Man*, trans. Bruce Kirmmse (Grand Rapids, MI, 2001) [1961] (*PC*).

Carr, Karen, 'The Offense of Reason and the Passion of Faith: Kierkegaard and Anti-Rationalism', *Faith and Philosophy*, 13/2 (1996), 236–51 (*CUP*).

Crites, Stephen, *In the Twilight of Christendom: Hegel vs. Kierkegaard on Faith and History* (Chambersburg, PA, 1972).

Dalrymple, Timothy, 'Adam and Eve: Human Being and Nothingness', in Lee Barrett & Jon Stewart, eds, *Kierkegaard and the Bible, Kierkegaard Research: Sources, Reception and Resources*, 1, 1: *The Old Testament* (Farnham, 2010), 3–42 (*CA*).

Dooley, Mark, 'Murder on Moriah: A Paradoxical Representation', *Philosophy Today*, 39 (1995), 67–81 (*FT*).

Dooley, Mark, 'The Politics of Exodus: Derrida, Kierkegaard, and Levinas on "Hospitality"', *IKC LD* (Macon, GA, 1999), 167–92 (*LD*); alternatively 'Kierkegaard and Derrida: Between Totality and Infinity', in E. Jegstrup, ed., *The New Kierkegaard* (Bloomington, IN, 2004) (Advanced).

Emmet, Dorothy, 'Kierkegaard and the "Existential" Philosophy', *Journal of the Royal Institute of Philosophy*, 16 (1941), 257–71 (*CUP*, political philosophy).

Fackenheim, Emil, 'Schelling's Philosophy of Religion', *University of Toronto Quarterly*, xxii/1 (1952), 1–17 (*CA*).

Furtak, Rick Anthony, 'The Kierkegaardian ideal of "essential knowing" and the scandal of modern philosophy', in *Kierkegaard's Concluding Unscientific Postscript: A Critical Guide* (Cambridge, 210), 87–110 (*CUP*).

Hampson, Daphne, Ch. 1 'Luther's Revolution', Ch. 7 'Kierkegaard's Odyssey', *Christian Contradictions: The Structures of Lutheran and Catholic Thought* (Cambridge, 2001) (*SuD*, SK *qua* Lutheran).

Kirmmse, Bruce, 'Psychology and Society: The social Falsification of the Self in The Sickness unto Death', in Joseph H. Smith, ed., *Kierkegaard's Truth: The Disclosure of the Self* (New Haven, CT, 1981), 167–92; alternatively 'The Sickness Unto Death', ch. 23, *Kierkegaard in Golden Age Denmark* (Bloomington & Indianapolis, 1990) (*SuD*, the self).

Kirmmse, Bruce, 'Kierkegaard and 1848', in *History of European Ideas*, 20 (1995), 167–75 (*PC*, politics); alternatively, ch. 24, 'Training in Christianity', ch. 27, 'The Attack on Christendom', in *Kierkegaard in Golden Age Denmark* (Bloomington & Indianapolis, 1990) (*PC*, historical).

Kirmmse, Bruce, 'Call Me Ishmael—Call Everybody Ishmael: Kierkegaard on the Coming-of-Age Crisis of Modern Times', in George Connell & Stephen Evans, eds, *Foundations of Kierkegaard's Vision of Community: Religion, Ethics and Politics in Kierkegaard* (Atlantic Highlands, NJ, 1992), 161–82 (*PC*, political philosophy).

Kirmmse, Bruce, 'Kierkegaard and MacIntyre: Possibilities for Dialogue', in John Davenport & Anthony Rudd, eds, *Kierkegaard After MacIntyre: Essays on Freedom, Narrative and Virtue* (Chicago & La Salle, IL, 2001), 191–210 (Kierkegaard's thought forms).

Law, David, 'The Contested Notion of "Christianity" in Mid-Nineteenth-Century Denmark: Mynster, Martensen, and Kierkegaard's Antiecclesiastical, "Christian" Invective in "*The Moment*" and Late Writings', IKC '*The Moment*' and Late Writings (Macon, GA, 2009), 43–70 (*PC*, historical).

Matuštík, Martin J., 'Kierkegaard's Radical Existential Praxis, or: Why the Individual Defies Liberal, Communitarian, and Postmodern Categories', in Martin J. Matuštík & Merold Westphal, eds, *Kierkegaard in Post/Modernity* (Bloomington & Indianapolis, 1995), 239–64 (The individual, Advanced).

Milbank, John, 'The Sublime in Kierkegaard', in Phillip Blond, ed., *Post-Secular Philosophy* (London & New York, 1998), 131–56 (Kierkegaard's thought forms, Advanced).

Pattison, George & Steven Shakespeare, 'Introduction: Kierkegaard, the Individual and Society', in George Pattison & Steven Shakespeare, eds., *Kierkegaard: the self in society* (Basingstoke, 1998), 1–23 (Schools of Kierkegaard scholarship).

Perkins, Robert, 'The Constitution of the Self in Hegel's *Phenomenology of Spirit* and in Kierkegaard's *Sickness Unto Death*', in Merold Westphal, ed., *Method and Speculation in Hegel's Phenomenology* (Brighton, 1982), 95–115 (*SuD*).

Perkins, Robert, 'Abraham's Silence Aesthetically Considered', *IKC FT* (Macon, GA, 1993), 155–76 (*FT*).

Perkins, Robert, 'Kierkegaard's "Instant Writing" on the Triumph of Aestheticism in Christendom', in *IKC 'The Moment' and Late Writings* (Macon, GA, 2009), 283–318 (*PC*).

Plekon, Michael, 'Towards Apocalypse: Kierkegaard's *Two Ages* in Golden Age Denmark', *IKC Two Ages* (Macon, GA, 1984), 245–66 (*PC*, historical).

Ricoeur, Paul, 'Two Encounters with Kierkegaard: Kierkegaard and Evil; Doing Philosophy after Kierkegaard', in Joseph H. Smith, ed., *Kierkegaard's Truth: The Disclosure of the Self* (see under Kirmmse), reproduced as 'Philosophy after Kierkegaard', in Chamberlain & Rée, eds, *Kierkegaard* (see under Agacinski), 9–25 (*CA, SuD*).

Roberts, David, *Kierkegaard's Analysis of Radical Evil* (New York & London, 2006) (*SuD*).

Roberts, Julian, 'Kierkegaard', *German Philosophy: An Introduction* (Cambridge, 1988) (*PF*).

Saxbee, John, 'The Golden Age in an Earthen Vessel: The Life and Times of Bishop J. P. Mynster', in Jon Stewart, ed., *Kierkegaard and his Contemporaries: the culture of golden age Denmark* (Berlin, 2003), 149–63 (*PC*).

Sheil, Patrick, *Starting with Kierkegaard* (London, 2011) (Introductory).

Solomon, Robert C, 'The Secret of Hegel (Kierkegaard's Complaint): A Study of Hegel's Philosophy of Religion' & 'Kierkegaard and Subjective Truth', *From Hegel to Existentialism* (New York & Oxford, 1987), 56–86 (*CUP*).

Stack, George, 'Kierkegaard: The Self as Ethical Possibility', *The Southwestern Journal of Philosophy*, 3 (1972), 35–61 (The self, existential).

Steiner, George, 'Introduction', in *Fear and Trembling; The Book on Adler* (London, 1994); reproduced as 'The Wound of Negativity: Two Kierkegaard Texts', in Chamberlain & Rée, eds (see under Agacinski), 103–13 (*FT*).

Stewart, Jon, 'Kierkegaard and Hegelianism in Golden Age Denmark', in Jon Stewart, ed., *Kierkegaard and his Contemporaries* (Berlin, 2003), 106–45.

Stewart, Jon, 'Kierkegaard's Recurring Criticism of Hegel's "The Good and Conscience"', in *Idealism and Existentialism: Hegel and Nineteenth- and Twentieth-Century European Philosophy* (London & New York, 2010); alternatively 'Hegel's View of Moral Conscience and Kierkegaard's Interpretation of Abraham', *Kierkegaardiana*, 19 (1998), 58–81; also forms ch. 7 of Jon Stewart, *Kierkegaard's Relations to Hegel Reconsidered* (Cambridge, 2003), 305–35 (*FT*, Hegel).

Taylor, Mark C., 'Journeys to Moriah: Hegel vs. Kierkegaard', *Harvard Theological Review*, 70 (1977), 305–26 (*FT*).

Taylor, Mark C., 'Kierkegaard on the Structure of Selfhood', *Kierkegaardiana*, 9 (1974), 84–101; alternatively *Journeys to Selfhood: Hegel and Kierkegaard* (Berkeley & London, 1980), ch. 3 (*SuD*, the self).

Taylor, Mark C., 'Christology', in Niels Thulstrup & Marie Miklová Thulstrup, eds, *Theological Concepts in Kierkegaard* [vol. 3 *Bibliotheca Kierkegaardiana*] (Copenhagen, 1982), 167–206 (*PF*, *CUP*, Hegel).

Thulstrup, Niels, 'Commentator's Introduction', in D. Swenson, trans., *Søren Kierkegaard, Philosophical Fragments* (Princeton, NJ, 1967) [1955], xlv–xcvii (*PF*).

Thulstrup, Niels, 'Mynster', in Niels & Marie Miklová Thulstrup, eds, *Kierkegaard's Teachers* [vol. 10, *Bibliotheca Kierkegaardiana*] (Copenhagen, 1982), 15–69 (*PC*).

Tolstrup, Christian Fink, 'Jakob Peter Mynster: A Guiding Thread in Kierkegaard's Authorship?', in Jon Stewart, ed., *Kierkegaard and His Danish Contemporaries*, II: *Theology* [vol. 7, *Kierkegaard Research: Sources, Reception and Resources*] (Farnham, 2011), 267–87 (*PC*).

Verheyden, Jack, 'The Ethical and the Religious as Law and Gospel', in D. Z. Phillips & Timothy Tessin, eds, *Kant and Kierkegaard on Religion*, Claremont Studies in the Philosophy of Religion (London & New York, 2000), 153–77 (*FT*, SK qua Lutheran).

Walsh, Sylvia, *Thinking Christianly in an Existential Mode* (Oxford, 2009) (Introductory).

Westphal, Merold, 'Kierkegaard and Hegel', in Alastair Hanney & Gordon D. Marino, eds, *The Cambridge Companion to Kierkegaard* (Cambridge, 1998), 101–24 (*FT*, *CUP*, Hegel).

Index of Persons

Index of Subjects

world
outward expression in, false
wish for 155–6, 158, 169
regaining of the 25, 43–5, 55,
56 n. 27, 169, 180; see also
Kierkegaard's theological
structure, 'inverted'
existence
relativity of the 141, 143, 156–7,
165, 193, 213, 217, 272
see also Kierkegaard's theological
structure
see also Lutheran thought

**Kierkegaard's theological
position on**
biblical criticism, lack of 17,
85–90, 131–2, 144–5, 263,
269, 293–4, 306, 307; see
also historical Jesus, quest
of; see also theological
issues & traditions; biblical
criticism; see also
Kierkegaard as systematic
theologian, Christology
Catholicism, implied criticism
of 81, 124, 134–5, 155–6,
158–9, 169, 196, 207, 238–9,
250; see also theological
issues & traditions;
Catholic thought;
compared with Lutheran
Christendom 18–19, 63, 141,
143, 238, 264–5, 268–9,
271–3, 275–7, 291–2;
see also Index of Persons;
Kierkegaard, Søren
Aabye; SK's view of
contemporaries
Christianity
Christian art 278; see also
Denmark; Vor Frue Kirke

claims of/SK's recognition of
nature of 2, 11–12, 19–20,
41, 56–7, 62–9, 96, 151–3,
154–5, 159–63, 177–8, 239,
314–16;
see also Kierkegaard as
systematic theologian;
eternal in time/
incarnation and also
Paradox, the and also
revelation
God
arguments for existence
of 70–3, 98, 150, 238
Kant on 12
of Christ as God 71,
126, 262
see also historical Jesus,
quest of
classical view of as changeless/
perfect 63, 71–2, 77–8,
97–8, 152
critique of 59, 97
see also thought forms major;
eighteenth-century
philosophy of religion;
absolute/contingent
see also Kierkegaard as
systematic theologian;
assurance; false objective
attempt at
historical Jesus, quest of
false nature of 17, 85, 144–5, 161,
262–3
Schweitzer's response
compared with 308
miracles 28–9, 88–9, 91–4,
262, 264, 269; see also
thought forms major;
eighteenth-century
philosophy of religion;
miracles